Global Careers

With so much of our ever increasing interest in the global environment in the management of 'talent', understanding the issue of global careers is crucial for students and managers alike. From an individual career perspective, becoming an effective expatriate global manager is an important aim that an executive needs to 'have under their belt' at the height of their career.

This exciting new addition to the Routledge Global Human Resource Management series captures broad research extending to a large set of diverse motivations, experiences and outcomes of international work in global 'for profit' and 'not for profit' organizations, and delivers nuanced insights into the management of international employees for firms and governmental/non-governmental organizations.

This text covers global career issues in depth, working at the intersection of career and international human resource management and using a multitude of perspectives, most prominently organizational and individual ones. Chapters include theories, frameworks and concepts, supporting research/data where relevant, managerial implications, summaries, learning points, figures and tables. The theory is illustrated with up-to-the-minute case studies from organizations such as HSBC, PricewaterhouseCoopers or the United Nations.

Global Careers will be essential reading for all those studying or concerned with career management, human resource management and international business.

Dr Michael Dickmann is a Senior Lecturer of Human Resource Management at Cranfield University, School of Management.

Dr Yehuda Baruch is a Professor of Management at Rouen Business School, France and formerly Professor of Management at UEA, Norwich UK, a Visiting Professor at the University of Texas at Arlington, USA and a Visiting Research Fellow at London Business School.

Routledge Global Human Resource Management Series

Edited by Randall S. Schuler, Susan E. Jackson, Paul Sparrow, and Michael Poole

Routledge Global Human Resource Management is an important new series that examines human resources in its global context. The series is organized into three strands: content and issues in global human resource management (HRM); specific HR functions in a global context; and comparative HRM. Authored by some of the world's leading authorities on HRM, each book in the series aims to give readers comprehensive, in-depth, and accessible texts that combine essential theory and best practice. Topics covered include cross-border alliances, global leadership, global legal systems, HRM in Asia, Africa and the Americas, industrial relations, and global staffing.

Managing Human Resources in Cross Border Alliances
Randall S. Schuler, Susan E. Jackson and Yadong Luo

Managing Human Resources in the Middle East
Edited by Pawan S. Budhwar and Kamel Mellahi

Managing Human Resources in Africa
Edited by Ken N. Kamoche, Yaw A. Debrah, Frank M. Horwitz and Gary Nkombo Muuka

Globalizing Human Resource Management
Paul Sparrow, Chris Brewster, and Hilary Harris

Managing Human Resources in Asia-Pacific
Edited by Pawan S. Budhwar

Managing Human Resources in Latin America
An agenda for international leaders

Edited by Marta M. Elvira and Anabella Davila

Global Staffing
Edited by Hugh Scullion and David G. Collings

Managing Human Resources in Europe
A thematic approach
Edited by Henrik Holt Larsen and Wolfgang Mayrhofer

Managing Global Legal Systems
International employment regulation and competitive advantage
Gary W. Florkowski

Global Industrial Relations
Edited by Michael J. Morley, Patrick Gunnigle and David G. Collings

Managing Human Resources in North America
Current issues and perspectives
Edited by Steve Werner

Global Leadership: Research, Practice and Development
Mark E. Mendenhall, Joyce S. Osland, Allan Bird, Gary R. Oddou and Martha L. Maznevski

Performance Management Systems
A global perspective
Edited by Arup Varma, Pawan S. Budhwar and Angela DeNi

International Human Resource Management
Policy and practice for multinational enterprises (Third edition)
Dennis R. Briscoe, Randall S. Schuler and Lisbeth Claus

Global Careers
Michael Dickmann and Yehuda Baruch

Global Careers

Michael Dickmann and Yehuda Baruch

Routledge
Taylor & Francis Group

LONDON AND NEW YORK

First published 2011
by Routledge
270 Madison Avenue, New York, NY 10016

Simultaneously published in the UK
by Routledge
2 Park Square, Milton Park, Abingdon, Oxon OX14 4RN

Routledge is an imprint of the Taylor & Francis Group, an informa business

Typeset in Times New Roman and Franklin Gothic by
Swales & Willis Ltd, Exeter, Devon
Printed and bound by TJ International Ltd, Padstow, Cornwall

Library of Congress Cataloging in Publication Data
A catalog record has been requested for this book

ISBN13: 978–0–415–44627–3 (hbk)
ISBN13: 978–0–415–44628–0 (pbk)
ISBN13: 978–0–203–84275–1 (ebk)

Dedication

To my wife and my children:

Liliana, whose support and inspiration made this book a reality

Anna, whose creativity and inspiration never fail to astonish

Nicolás, whose energy and determination are wonderful

Sophia, whose artistic expression and personal understanding run deep

Oliver, whose joy and 'picardía' warm hearts.

(Michael Dickmann)

To my wife, who follows me all over the globe; to my global children, born in Israel, bred in the UK; and to the memory of their ancestors from Romania, Hungary, Spain, Greece, Russia and Poland.

(Yehuda Baruch)

Contents

Illustrations

Figures

Tables

Boxes

Cases

Author biographies

Michael Dickmann is a Senior Lecturer at Cranfield School of Management, UK. He lectures in the areas of international and strategic HRM and is currently the director of the Cranfield MSc in International Human Resource Management. Much of his research focuses on human resource strategies, structures and processes of multinational organizations, global careers and mobility.

Michael has published widely in academic journals and for practitioners. He has worked as an HR Director and has undertaken consulting projects for governments, the UN, other supranational organizations, International NGOs and in the private sector. He has worked in his native Germany, Australia, the USA, Colombia, Spain and Britain.

Yehuda Baruch (DSc Technion, Israel) is Professor of Management at Rouen Business School, France. He has published extensively in the areas of Global and Strategic HRM, careers, and general management, including some 100 refereed papers and over 30 books and book chapters. He is editor of *Group & Organization Management*, former editor of *Career Development International* and former chair, Careers Division, Academy of Management.

Chris Debner is a Senior Manager in Ernst & Young's Human Capital Practice. He leads the EMEIA centre of excellence for Global Mobility Advisory.

Joost Smits studied employment and social security science and also has a Master's degree in European Social Policy Analyses. He has worked at Ernst & Young, Human Capital, Eindhoven, Netherlands for over 12 years. He advises multinational companies on their cross-border employment both from a tax and security perspective.

Foreword

Global Human Resource Management is a series of books edited and authored by some of the best and most well-known researchers in the field of human resource management (HRM). This series is aimed at offering students and practitioners accessible, coordinated and comprehensive books in global HRM. To be used individually or together, these books cover the main bases of comparative and international HRM. Taking an expert look at an increasingly important and complex area of global business, this is a groundbreaking new series that answers a real need for serious textbooks on global HRM.

Several books in this series are devoted to HRM policies and practices in multinational enterprises. For example, some books focus on specific activities of global HRM policies and practices, such as global compensation, global staffing, global performance management, global talent management, and global labour relations. Other books address special topics that arise in multinational enterprises across the globe, such as managing human resources in cross-border alliances, global legal regulations, and developing the HR function in multinational enterprises. In addition to books on various HRM activities and topics in multinational enterprises, several other books in the series adopt a comparative, and within region, approach to understanding global HRM. These books on comparative HRM can adopt two major approaches. One approach is to describe the HRM policies and practices found at the local level in selected countries in several regions of the world. The second approach is to describe the HRM issues and topics that are most relevant to the companies in the countries of the region.

This book, *Global Careers*, co-authored by Michael Dickmann and Yehuda Baruch, utilizes the multinational enterprise perspective. That is, it addresses all facets of career management in multinational enterprises, including cross-cultural working, sourcing workers globally, pre-departure and post-arrival considerations, support during and after global assignments, outcomes of global work, and security, risk and remuneration issues in global career management. In covering many of these issues, the authors consider organizational, individual and societal perspectives. This book is extremely well conceptualised and well written. It is divided into three sections and includes 12 chapters, all written by the authors, complete with the most recent and thorough references, tables and figures. Throughout there are numerous examples of what multinational enterprises are doing in global career management. No doubt it is a highly valuable book for any global human resource student and scholar or any global human resource professional.

This Routledge series, **Global Human Resource Management**, is intended to serve the growing market of global scholars and professionals who are seeking a deeper and broader understanding of the role and importance of HRM in companies as they operate throughout the world. With this in mind, all books in the series provide a thorough review of existing research and numerous examples of companies around the world.

Because a significant number of scholars and professionals throughout the world are involved in researching and practising the topics examined in this series of books, the authorship of the books and the experiences of companies cited in them reflect a vast global representation. The authors in the series bring with them exceptional knowledge of the HRM topics they address, and in many cases the authors have been the pioneers for their topics. So we feel fortunate to have the involvement of such a distinguished group of academics in this series.

The publisher and editor also have played a major role in making this series possible. Routledge has provided its global production, marketing and reputation to make this series feasible and affordable to academics and practitioners throughout the world. In addition, Routledge has provided its own highly qualified professionals to make this series a reality. In particular we want to indicate our deep appreciation for the work of our series editor, John Szilagyi. He has been very supportive of the series from the very beginning and has been invaluable in providing the needed support and encouragement to us and to the many authors in the series. Together with Routledge staff including Simon Whitmore, Russell George, Victoria Lincoln, Jacqueline Curthoys, Lindsie Court and Sara Werden, he has helped make the process of completing this series an enjoyable one. For everything they have done, we thank them all.

Randall S. Schuler, *Rutgers University and Lorange Institute of Business Zurich*

Paul Sparrow, *Lancaster University*

Susan E. Jackson, *Rutgers University and Lorange Institute of Business Zurich*

Michael Poole, *Cardiff University*

Preface

Global careers are certainly not a new phenomenon, as traders, missionaries, occupying armed forces, or some administrators (such as those running foreign parts of empires as varied as the Greek, Roman, Spanish, Portuguese or British) have worked for centuries abroad. However, the advances in travel, information access and worldwide competitive pressures have meant that global career paths have become more commonplace. Yet the career paths also display much variation, including migrants, self-initiated foreign workers, traditional expatriates, globetrotters, diplomats, or permanently mobile international workers.

The work expatriates perform overseas obviously impacts the local operation. Moreover, in many cases it will have effects on their fellow workers at home, and their home societies, even if it is through remittances of expatriate workers for their families in poor countries. Overall, the increase in globalization has meant that many economies have benefited from global manufacturing, service, trade and consumption. Although expatriates clearly perform an activity that is crucial to the creation and development of wealth, there is insufficient understanding about the processes involved.

The above trends have meant that labour markets are global more than they have ever been, even though restrictions apply. While citizens of the European Union (EU) have the right to work in other EU countries, there are work permit restrictions in virtually all countries of the earth. However, due to the increasing spread of multinational companies (MNCs) and other international organizations and the substantial influence they may wield, as well as due to most work permit regulations that facilitate individuals to move across borders within their organizations, the regulatory hurdles for company-sponsored specialists have become increasingly surmountable. This situation can be dramatically different for individuals who want to migrate to a foreign country due to a variety of non-company reasons, such as insecure home country situations or a personal quest for a better life.

Global careers have many interesting facets and require positive characteristics for those individuals – for need or wish – who have embarked on a journey into different cultures, societies and environments. However, there is also a high potential for negative experiences due to different legal and social contexts in their host countries. Especially those persons who are not sponsored and supported by their employers to work abroad face high risks, often also to their career progression, their work identity and their social networks at home when they muster the courage to cross national borders for work.

There is a rich and fascinating debate in the professional and academic literature regarding modern careers, expatriation, migration and international human resource management (HRM). While the avid reader can gain many insights from the diverse schools of thought, there is still much under-explored in this emerging topic. Moreover, there exists, to our knowledge, no authoritative book that strives to provide an integrated approach using a variety of perspectives. This is the first book dedicated entirely to the specific topic of global careers. Throughout, we use an individual perspective and/or an organizational viewpoint and embed these in a wider context of society. This book provides a timely overview of existing knowledge of global careers and develops frameworks, cases, strategies, policies and practice insights from which scholars and practitioners can benefit.

Readers of this volume will find that we, the authors, have freely assembled knowledge that crosses the boundaries of disciplines (e.g. international HRM, psychology, economics, sociology, organizational behaviour, strategy) and level of analysis (e.g. micro vs. macro). Because this is the case, scholars disagree upon the importance and applicability of some of the insights. Rather than finding this dysfunctional, we believe that this highlights the diversity of opinions and willingness to engage in scholarly debate in our academic community.

Our book is divided into three sections. The first looks at global careers in the competitive context, exploring social spaces and the multifaceted career (re-)actions and diverse international career paths of actors. The second section uses a temporal perspective and concentrates on the interaction of individuals and their organizations in their distinct, national environments. In this section we explicate the reasons and driving forces for global careers, look at pre-departure preparations, the multitude of individual and organizational behaviours during working abroad, repatriation issues and analyse outcomes from a variety of perspectives. The third section concentrates on practical global career insights, limitations and structural considerations. Moreover, it discusses social security, risk and remuneration considerations. The last chapter provides a reflective summary of the book and offers our vision of the future of global careers. Overall, the reader will find 12 chapters in this volume, the majority being co-written by the two authors. Chapters 10 and 11 were written by one of the authors, Michael Dickmann, in collaboration with experts from Ernst and Young, a professional service firm.

In conclusion, this book seeks to demystify the often less understood and under-examined processes, policies and practices, attitudes and behaviours relating to global careers. This text should prove to be a valuable resource for those engaging in the manifold aspects of the management of global careers. Further, we hope that it is a source of understanding and inspiration for all students of careers, international mobility and international HRM – may these be persons in formal education or educators whose professional research interests are covered. And finally, we expect this book will inspire future generations of executives and young careerists to embark on the global adventure for both their own personal development and to enhance their organizations.

Acknowledgements

This book would not have been possible without the guidance and support of many of our colleagues in diverse universities and professional organizations around the world. We benefited especially from the insights and encouragement of the editors of this series of Routledge international HRM books.

As with many extensive texts, this book has taken on a life of its own and, due to its importance, has claimed a space in our lives which was in competition with that of our families. We thank wholeheartedly our partners and our children for their support, tolerance and understanding.

We are also grateful to Randall Schuler and Paul Sparrow who shared their expertise by serving as our panel of external reviewers. We would like to express our sincere appreciation to our many colleagues in the Academy of Management who encouraged and supported our efforts to produce this book. Lastly, we reserve special thanks to Carole White and her husband Alan for supporting the genesis of this book through all its stages.

Part I

Global careers in context: competitive configurations, multifaceted career patterns and their social spaces

1 Global careers: an introduction

Objectives

This chapter:

- defines the major constructs in relation to global careers;
- outlines key theories relating to global careers;
- depicts major migration trends;
- gives a first introduction to expatriation and its challenges;
- outlines the book's structure and flow;
- provides an introduction to a global career framework which will guide the reader throughout this book.

Introduction

Some 50 years have passed since the world was first depicted as a 'global village' (MacLuhan 1960). A formal definition by Reilly and Campbell (1990) suggests that globalization is 'the integration of business activities across geographical and organizational boundaries . . . it is the freedom to conceive, design, buy, produce, distribute and sell products and services'. The meaning of 'global' has evolved, and the trend is for more people and organizations to become 'global'. A new global infrastructure has emerged that enables people and communities to cross national borders (less so cultural borders), and further enables people to work outside their national home with the option to return to it. The changes cover wide-ranging areas including technological, sociocultural, political, legal and economic issues.

It has been an axiom of management that business is becoming, or has become, global in scope. For business, a major effect of globalization is the existence of greater threats, but at the same time, greater opportunities. The threats are caused by a more variable environment and increased competition whereas the opportunities are generated by increased growth of the markets and the business. Industries and companies operate not so much in local or national spheres, but in a worldwide market for goods and services. This view has become highly pervasive. Yet, as we will explicate below, we would not fully endorse this globalization perspective for all parts of the world's population.

At the individual level, working globally has become a reality for many people, in particular the privileged – people from affluent countries and individuals who hold desired skills and qualifications. The international opportunities associated with globalization are less pronounced for rank-and-file workers as these might not possess scarce capabilities that are demanded by organizations. Moreover, legal regulations and lesser personal funds, as well as less extensive networks or information access can also inhibit cross-border worker mobility.

The issues surrounding global careers correspond greatly with the impetus for firms to go global. These vary, but basically stem from the need and will to expand and to be efficient, innovative and locally responsive. Global markets are larger than local ones. Workforces in different countries exhibit different skill sets, knowledge bases and labour costs. Global expansion may take different routes, with diverse implications for the flow of people across borders. Opening a subsidiary in another country normally requires a number of expatriates. However, the size of expatriation will depend on strategic choices (Bartlett and Ghoshal 1992; Baruch and Altman 2002) as well as practical implications. Conversely, a franchising strategy would not require substantial individual moves, if any, from the home country. Whatever the strategic choices, they will have implications for global HRM and organizational career systems as well as individual career actors.

There is a vast increase in global flows of capital, goods and services. Further, there are a growing number of individuals, especially highly educated people, who have experienced living, studying, operating, or just travelling in multiple countries. Firms do not limit themselves to national borders, and advances in technologies help to accelerate the process.

The increase in cross-border flows of money and the products of work is testimony to the idea that markets really are becoming more global. Future competition will simultaneously take place at a local, national and cross-national level if there are the means available to deliver products and services to customers at a distance. Certain products are limited to local delivery (e.g. hairdressing services and, for now but possibly not in the future, bus driving), but a wider range of products and services are not anchored to a single local place. Many knowledge-based products are developed and delivered via the internet. Several individual careers, built on providing services to a local set of customers, and in particular to large organizations, may not be sustainable in the longer term. The exception may be when there are practical and significant barriers to external competition (e.g. local regulations). New standards are developed, which are internationally binding (e.g. ISO 9000), and increasingly firms have to perform to global standards in order to compete and survive.

The implications for careers are vast. A growing number of individuals are seeking and finding opportunities to work abroad, either of their own choice or due to external pressures. Some of these undertake the strenuous journey to move abroad unsupported by their employers. For instance, there are millions of migrants in today's world. Others might only seek to work for a limited time abroad or even strive for a job that allows them foreign travel while still living in their country of origin. Some individuals go abroad – and others simply stay abroad – and open their own businesses. Others move overseas to study, and find it too tempting to stay rather than return to their home country. Still others might work for their firms as expatriates and are, therefore, normally sponsored by their employers. This array of individuals with international experience indicates that there are a large number of managers with international experience and/or global potential.

For businesses that require a worldwide presence, such people are mostly an asset, either as employees or as service providers. Some of these people will work for a limited time period (e.g. typical expatriation times are two to three years). Others might become 'permanent' expatriates, for their firm, or self-designated global citizens, and will spent their entire careers in a variety of countries. The reasons may be due to the individual or the employer. Sometimes, permanent work abroad is necessary due to the organization's mission. For example, the UN's World Food Programme needs permanent expatriates willing to go to many, often unsafe, hardship locations. The traditional one company, one country model of employment is slowly crumbling. Moreover, those who try to stick to the traditional model find they cannot compete with the new breed of younger managers, whose reference groups might be essentially global. Opportunities will accrue to those whose careers reflect the global nature of business.

There is a major divide between the so-called developed countries and the developing ones. People move fairly frequently and with no major difficulties within Europe or between Canada and the USA. It is more difficult to move across continents, e.g. from Europe or Japan to the USA and vice versa. A 'Green Card' is not easily attainable for people aspiring to work in the USA and neither are work permits in Europe. However, the difficulty level substantially increases for moves from developing countries.

Firms needing to send employees to work across borders face a multitude of obstacles to overcome, for instance if a person wishes to immigrate to an oil-rich emirate or for a Third World country citizen who aims to work in a Western country. This is particularly true for third country nationals (TCNs). A TCN is an employee working for a company in a country which is neither their country of origin nor the country where the company's headquarters resides. An example is a person from Portugal working for Nissan (headquarters in Japan) in a factory located in the UK. While many TCNs work in the Gulf (for example, from India, Egypt, Palestine, and a significant number from Europe and Australia), they can gain a temporary work permit and employment rights, but not citizenship. More lenient, but still serious obstacles are put in the way of a person immigrating to most European countries. These individuals might only have access to citizenship after some four to five years of working with a formal work permit. The opposite flow is less pronounced. Unless we talk of someone who wishes, for example, to retire in an exotic south-Asian country, people do not tend to emigrate en masse to the 'Third World'. Many persons expatriate for a limited time period due to commitment to their employers, the expectations of their employers, or in exchange for financial benefits (See Baruch and Altman (2002) as described in Chapter 3).

Yet, neither immigration nor expatriation are without variations, nor are they the only forms of global work. Below, we embark on a first discussion of the diverse nature and terminology of global careers.

What is a global career?

The dilemma starts here. There is no clear definition about what a global career is, and it is unclear what is meant by 'global firm' or global organization. At the organizational level, some claim that there are no truly global organizations – Hu (1992) has argued that the 'global company' is a myth, or as he titled his paper: 'Global or Stateless Corporations are National Firms with International Operations'.

Box 1.1 Nestlé – a global firm?

Nestlé is one of the very few firms that seem to be truly global. Less than 5 per cent of their personnel and less than 5 per cent of their production remain within the national borders of Switzerland, where their HQ is located. Yet, Nestlé sets its pride in being 'Swiss'. The culture and ethos of the firm is based on its Swiss roots.

It is typical for almost all MNCs to have their HQ, much of their operations, and in particular, their cultural roots, based in a certain country. To complicate the issue, there are other organizations that are, or may be considered, 'global', which are not merely business firms. Supranational organizations such as the European Union (EU), the United Nations (UN) or the North Atlantic Treaty Organization (NATO), international non-governmental organizations (INGOs), churches, diplomatic services, and even many national armed forces operate across national borders. Their HQ can be located at a 'global city' such as Brussels or Geneva, but the operation is not limited to specific countries. INGOs such as Water Aid or Greenpeace operating all over the world, send their employees and volunteers to manage operations and work for them in many locations. In terms of 'talent war' and 'talent management', they compete for global human talent, and face similar issues to those that business organizations face when looking for expatriates to manage overseas operations. The scope of INGOs' activities is expanding continuously, as new challenges emerge. In certain cases, established business organizations might well learn from INGOs about key elements of expatriation. One example could be security, an issue that requires great attention in many less-stable destinations.

Box 1.2 Coca-Cola – a global firm?

Coca-Cola is another firm that many consider to be truly global. It operates across the globe. Popular myth claims that Coca-Cola is among the best-known expressions around the world (second only to 'OK'). Yet, Coca-Cola sells 'America' (USA) across the world. Like McDonald's, they market and sell American products, the US-American culture, and the 'American Dream' in more than 100 countries around the world. Yet, the core strategy and operation is set and diffused from the HQ in the USA.

At the individual level, Baruch (2002) identified an ambiguity in the definition of global careers: is it an expatriate or someone who was an expatriate in the past (cf. Black and Gregersen 1999)? Alternatively, is it an individual who works across nation states (cf. Bartlett and Ghoshal 1992) or an international commuter who travels across borders to his or her place of work (Harris et al. 2003)? What is the role of time and cross-cultural understanding for having a global career? Is it really enough to work for six months abroad for an individual to claim to have a global career? We will explore these issues in more depth in Chapters 4–7.

If we adopt the definition of 'career' as 'an evolving sequence of a person's work experience over time' (Arthur et al. 1989), then a 'global career' might be thought of as 'an evolving sequence of a person's work experience over time when part of the sequence takes place in more than one country'. Similarly, based on Baruch and Rosenstein's (1992) definition of career as 'a process of development by [an] employee along a path of experience and roles in one or more organizations', a global career is when this process takes place in more than one country.[1]

A more simplified definition suggesting that a global manager is a manager who works for a company, or owns a business, which operates across national borders, would cover almost any manager in mid-sized or large firms. In this book we focus on global careers that progress and evolve outside of a single country. There are many ways to envisage global careers, and in Chapter 4 we offer a 'glossary' of the wide options to articulate a variety of modes for global careers. A typical case is expatriation, but immigration, globetrotting and other international experiences form many ways of having global careers.

Global careers in context

Global careers take place in a specific cultural context, with several levels of culture-related constituencies involved. Schein posits:

> Societal, occupational, and organizational cultures influence the structure of the external career, prestige associated with given careers, the legitimacy of certain

---

1 While we are sensitive to the different notions of 'career' in different countries and cultures (see below and Chapter 12), we are attracted to the generic quality of these definitions.

motives underlying careers, success criteria, the clarity of the career concept itself, and the importance attached to career versus family and self development. How career occupants view their careers and the degree of variation in such views within given societies, occupations, and organizations is also culturally patterned.

(1984: 71)

Indeed, career research is inevitably culture-bounded (Schein 1984: 71), due to the following reasons:

• culture influences the concept of career itself;
• culture influences the importance of career relative to other facets of life, like personal and family issues; and
• specifically for managerial roles, culture influences the bases of legitimacy of managerial careers.

Regarding the first reason, cultural influences on the concept of career, countries and organizations differ in the degree to which they explicitly specify the external career paths (Schein 1984). Such paths are supposed to serve as the common denominator for certain people in certain occupations, and are followed by members of a given occupation, explicitly or implicitly, as well as being observed by organizational career systems (Baruch and Peiperl 2000). The motives and ambitions that are considered legitimate for the pursuit of global careers are subject to society's approach about global careers, and the nature of the psychological contract individuals hold with their employers (Guzzo et al. 1994). Different degrees of prestige will be attached to different paths, where in some places going global is a clear sign of success, but might also be a 'refuge' for those who cannot make it at home. These differences will strongly influence the way people feel about their careers, the kind of motivation that is considered to be appropriate for a career and how successful people will feel (Dickmann and Doherty 2010).

Similarly, the role of work for the individual person, coupled with the perception of the meaning of work within the culture will determine relevance and investment of energy and emotion in other facets of life, in particular the family. The family, certainly the spouse, is a crucial factor determining the success or otherwise of a global assignment, and while the impact may be direct or indirect, it is often very strong.

Lastly, the importance of culture to the nature of managerial careers, which characterizes most international assignments, is a factor influencing the way people progress their careers, and their inclination to opt for a global career. Other contextual factors apart from cultural are mostly economic and political. These are dealt with elsewhere in the book.

Career implications of globalization

The nature of globalization created a realm of work where people have international careers. Most of them are 'partially global', or not directly associated with a functional or industry-related career. Such is the 'overseas experience' (Inkson et al. 1997) where young people spent some time abroad, typically about a year, either before or after their university/college studies. Others opt to study abroad (sometimes leading to them settling abroad – Baruch et al. 2007), which might or might not lead to a permanent stay in the country where they studied. Nevertheless, these are different from simple tourism, as persons having such global experience gain more than just seeing new places and mingling with different people. They overcome a process of exposure to different national culture(s), ways of life and work, and sometimes the immersion in different language(s). This experience will stay with them throughout their working life and enrich their ability to work in a world different from the one they grew up in.

There are many forms of working abroad which will be explicated in Chapter 4. The most common types of global careers are: (1) career moves resulting from migration; and (2) career moves intended for a limited period of time, often expatriation. The second type is typically induced by the employing organization.

Work-/career-related migration: Under this type, people leave their home country to seek employment in a different geographic location outside the borders of their country of origin and/or country of nationality. Often the time of stay in the host country is not precisely defined or planned and might depend on a range of external circumstances and internal thoughts and emotions. The host country can become their new homeland. Alternatively, this can be temporary work, with no intention or even practical ability to gain naturalization in the new country (like that of people working in the oil industry in the Persian Gulf). This work-related migration is associated with socioeconomic and political issues. It can lead to 'brain gain', 'brain drain' or 'brain circulation', concepts that are explored in more depth in Chapters 2 and 9.

Global careers induced by organizations often take the shape of expatriation. Expatriation is a period of time spent in an overseas operating unit of the organization. The employee will typically work there for two to three years and then return to their country of origin. There may be a number of variations to this basic mode. This can be a one-off expatriation, where the person gains this global experience and returns to their 'normal' work/position routine. It can be the first in a string of expatriation assignments in different countries. It may be extended to a considerably longer time in the host country. Sometimes expatriation is prompted by both the organization and the individual (Dickmann and Harris 2005). Also the person might leave the parent firm and work for others who operate in that country, becoming a 'professional expatriate'.

Globetrotter career: This is where a person, while staying the majority of his or her life in the home country, experiences continuous consecutive global missions, tasks and roles, necessitating constant overseas visits. Some authors describe people with this work pattern as 'frequent flyers' (Sparrow et al. 2004) or global managers (Cappellen and Janssens 2005). The specific population that sometimes enjoy, sometimes suffer from, such a continuous stream of working around the globe can comprise a variety of professions. It can be the technology-savvy engineer or IT professional, needed for their technical expert knowledge. It can be the company's lawyer; it might be the executive representing the firm. Subject to their seniority and urgency of the trip, they might fly in business class or even in the firm's private jet, will stay a day, two days or a week, and move back, or to another location, to deal with another major issue.

The types presented above cannot have a clear-cut distinction, as plans can change. People planning to immigrate might find after a short time that they cannot adjust to the local country, or that it is not possible to gain a working visa, and might decide to return to their country of origin or home base. Some expatriates might fall in love with their host country and stay there for longer, even permanently. They could stay as employees of their original firm, but they might start working for local firms, or for other MNCs operating in that country (the professional expatriate – see Baruch and Altman 2002).

Migration today

Living abroad is a widespread phenomenon. The UN estimated that there were 191 million migrants in 2005 (UN 2006), representing 3 per cent of the global population. Migration to developed countries is high with 9.5 per cent of the population in these countries being migrants. In turn, the migrant stock in developing countries is equivalent to 1.4 per cent of the population. Overall, 60 per cent of migrants (115.4 million) live in developed countries which, in turn, have 1.2 billion inhabitants.

Migration patterns are driven by a range of reasons. Due to political instability, persecution, high levels of insecurity (including environmental factors) there were 13.5 million refugees in 2005 (UN 2006). Climate changes and other environmental developments are seen as a key driver for migration with some commentators estimating that 200 million people might be forced to move due to environmental factors by 2050 (Norman Myers, quoted by IOM 2009). While migration has always been an integral part of human–environment interaction, climate change is seen to increase the pressures for displacement (IOM 2009). Other important reasons for migration include conflict, public health situations, gender policies and their implications, the openness of borders and diverse levels of economic development.

We will concentrate on work-related issues in relation to migration as many of the other issues will go beyond the scope of this book. While we cover societal impacts – such as brain drain, brain gain or brain circulation – we will focus on organizational or individual effects such as those pertaining to the identity, selection, development, careers and career outcomes of individuals in a global context.

Working abroad

The EU is a fascinating area to look at given that inhabitants of any of the 27 member states have the right to legally live and work in other member countries. Within the EU, approximately 2 per cent of the workforce was born in a different member state to that where they currently work (European Labour Force Survey 2005) and about 4 per cent of the EU population has lived in a different EU country at some time (MIE 2006). The highest cross-border mobility within the EU is demonstrated by some of the 'new' EU member states such as the Baltic countries and Poland and is linked to economic factors (PwC 2006).

The low internal EU migration numbers are lower than the international migration to developed countries would indicate. This is surprising given that some of the EU states (Germany, France, the UK and Spain in descending order) are home to some of the world's largest migration stock (UN 2006). The key barriers to internal EU moves are identified as losing one's social network, language issues and the expectations of worse housing conditions (PwC 2006: 11).

Much migration is driven by individuals who cannot rely on the support of employers or other organizations. While we will discuss self-initiated foreign workers in more depth in Chapter 5, we will now provide an overview of company-sponsored international assignees and trends in other forms of organization-supported work abroad.

Trends in organization-supported foreign work

One of the longest-established surveys on trends in international work is that conducted by GMAC Global Relocation Services since 1993. The 2008 survey gathered data from 154 companies primarily located in the Americas and Europe, Middle East and Africa (EMEA). In the last few years (since 2004) the survey has seen the number of expatriates increasing, with two-thirds of companies believing that their international assignee population had increased in comparison to the preceding year and that this trend is likely to continue (GMAC 2008). The authors quote the steady expansion of the EU and the strengths of emerging economies (especially China) as key reasons for the growth in expatriation numbers. Noting a stronger increase of global mobility among companies that are headquartered outside the USA, the writers speculate that this might be a response to the Sarbanes-Oxley Act of 2002 which increased the compliance costs of US firms. The USA, China and Great Britain were the most popular assignment destinations. China, India and Russia were, as in the surveys in preceding years, the primary emerging locations for expatriates with international assignee numbers increasing strongly.

Another trend is that of the increased use of TCNs. The differences are striking. Whereas in the decade from 1993 three-quarters of all assignments were to or from the organization's parent country, in the period after 2002 only 59 per cent involved the country in which the head office is located (GMAC 2008). While one likely effect (and driving force) is the reduction of labour costs for the employer, there are manifold career implications for individuals which will be discussed in Chapters 8 and 9.

The high competitive pressures in the global economy and the unfolding economic crisis after 2007 have meant that organizations are searching for cost-saving solutions with vigour. More than half of organizations in the survey (58 per cent) were reducing expenses for international assignments (IAs) with the second most popular cost-saving initiative becoming localization (GMAC 2008). Another survey indicates that localization can be driven by the individual – the desire to remain in the host country was the most popular reason – and the organization, with skills required long term and cost control being particularly important (ORC 2007). Different forms of localization are discussed in Chapter 11.

In the last few years, the GMAC survey showed that the percentage of female expatriates was about 19–20 per cent. This is an increase compared to the pre-2005 survey levels when it ranged between 10 and 18 per cent. The reasons for the relative underrepresentation of female expatriates are manifold and are discussed in Chapters 4 and 6. While a majority of expatriates are married – 60 per cent in 2007 (GMAC 2008) – this percentage is declining over time. Of those who have a spouse or partner, 83 per cent were accompanied on their foreign sojourn. There seem to be less international assignees who are accompanied by their children over time with the average being 52 per cent since 2002. The family challenges included schooling, housing and health issues and general concerns about security or cost of living.

Other concerns which often led to the rejection of the organization's offer to work abroad were related to dual career issues. GMAC (2008) found that 54 per cent of partners were employed before but not during the assignment while only 20 per cent were employed both before and during the assignment (with 12 per cent being employed during but not before the foreign sojourn). While some companies offer language training (almost three-quarters), education assistance (one third), sponsored work permits (almost a third) and networking assistance (almost a fifth), dual careers remain a significant barrier to international mobility.

The data above confirms trends that were identified at the turn of the millennium. The number of expatriate assignments and other types of international work is increasing (CReME 2000). The average assignment duration is declining (Dickmann et al. 2006) and expatriation flows from one developing country to another are increasing. Partly for cost reasons, individuals are increasingly chosen to work abroad at an early stage in their career or when they are more seasoned professionals and their children are likely to have left home (Harris et al. 2003). Overall, however, most international assignees are in their mid-careers when they work abroad (CReME 2000).

Global career theory – brief summary of individual perspective

Global career theory integrates theories of career and their relevance and applicability within global operations. In Chapter 3 we elaborate and expand on the nature and notion of career theory and its relevance for the global context.

The career theories and concepts we will cover are career choice, social learning, career stages theories, the boundaryless career, the intelligent career, the protean career, the post-corporate career, the Kaleidoscope career, and related issues such as gender and diversity. Much of the writing on career issues was led by psychology scholars (Khapova et al. 2007), but the field benefited from a wide area of research contribution from various fields (Arthur et al. 1989). Recent reviews of career scholarly work manifest this richness of theoretical contribution to careers, and in particular the global career area (Sullivan and Baruch 2010; Baruch and Bozionelos 2010). The types of IAs take a variety of shapes (Baruch et al. 2009), and different factors can influence the success or otherwise of global careers (Cerdin and Le Pargneux 2009).

We will deal with career choice, career stages, and the way current career models are applied within a global context. In particular, we focus on the boundaryless career, taken as the leading career theory, which reflects on the changing nature of careers. The boundaryless career actor starts within an organization, moves across to other organizations, and further on to cross national borders and various cultures.

Global career theory – brief summary of organizational perspective

Global career management confronts HRM with two major challenges. First is the need to manage careers in MNCs, where diverse operations in different countries require variation in the HR system. This means a need to understand many constituencies with a variety of needs, and to make adjustments, while keeping to an overall (general) career strategy. One issue is whether it is a singular versus segregated HRM system, and is concerned with the operation of coherent and systematic HRM in various locations and operations. In a singular system, an MNC would strive for an integrated organizational culture, identity, a coherent overall strategy as well as standardized policies and regulations. This means that the firm will have one HR system to deal with HR issues across the board (and borders), including all career issues. While there are likely to be variations within the actual policies and practices across borders, underlying principles would be integrated (Dickmann et al. 2009). On the other hand, different countries imply and impose different HRM considerations. These are related to the cultural, economic, sociological and legal context, to name a few aspects of substantial impact. This global–local dilemma and the different forms in which organizations draw up their international strategies, structures, policies and practices will be further explicated in Chapter 2.

The second challenge is concerned with global assignments. Most typical is the management of expatriation and repatriation, but there are other less extensive global assignments too. In addition, employees may need to work in teams that span many different countries and cultures.

The challenges do not end with the physical movement from country to country – this is merely the first surface stage. The psychological aspects of working and adjusting to persons from other cultures are far more challenging. Managing global careers requires a balance between treating everyone in a similar way (equal opportunities for all) and recognizing that different people will have different expectations, aspirations, and prospects of achieving successful international work. Much of the discussion focuses on expatriation and repatriation and concentrates on personal qualities that would support successful expatriation (Guzzo et al. 1994). However, expatriation and repatriation may need different adjustment processes (Harvey 1997).

Among the changes that have shaped contemporary career systems are developments in the social and economic realms, as well as in individual identities. Global macro-economic and social forces have provided impetus for a growing number of global careers (Baruch 2006). Consumerism is global, and subsequently marketing, with the internet as a major force in shaping life and work for most of the global workforce.

It used to be the role of the organization to plan and manage the careers of its employees at all levels (Schein 1978; Hall 1986; Gutteridge et al. 1993; Baruch 1999). Much of the responsibility for such planning and management has now moved to the individual employee (Baruch and Bozionelos 2010). However, organizations should not abandon their responsibility, but try to achieve a balance between delegating parts of the responsibility and action to the employees, and managing the required input for offering career trajectories that will fit their employees (Baruch 2006; Lips-Wiersma and Hall 2007). The change in career systems does not mean that organizations need to abandon their role in managing careers completely (Baruch 2006). Instead, the organization has a new significant role – being a supporter, enabler, developer of its human assets, both internally and globally. The organization is the enabler of successful careers, not the commander who moves the chess pieces across the board. Organizations can arrange their system to fit the changing needs of the employees and the environment, by strategically aiming to gain both internal and external integration of their career practices (Baruch 1999).

Working globally has a number of implications for career planning and management. The boundaries that are being crossed are multiple: geographic, cultural, mental and linguistic, to name but a few. Individuals cross these boundaries, and so, too, do organizations. MNCs have to develop HRM frameworks that will ensure global positions are filled and that people are trained and prepared for their new assignments, both technically and emotionally (e.g. taking care of family issues). Further, certain adjustments of HRM systems are required for operation in different countries and cultures. Self-initiated global career moves are an emerging trend (Dickmann and Harris 2005; Altman and Baruch 2008). Lastly, the HRM system needs to make sure that the talent and the learning are diffused and used upon the return of their global managers (Mir and Mir 2009; Bonache and Dickmann 2008).

In Chapter 3 we review three theoretical contributions concerning the management of overseas operations, in particular in terms of expatriation/repatriation. First we will focus on Heenan and Perlmutter's (1979) distinction between *ethnocentric* (home country oriented); *polycentric* (host country oriented); *geocentric* (worldwide oriented); and *regiocentric* (region oriented) management. This taxonomy has inspired many subsequent authors.

The second theoretical contribution we explore is Bartlett and Ghoshal's (1989) categorization of MNC strategic models. Using three dimensions – those of global integration, local responsiveness and worldwide innovation – they offer a four-quadrant matrix with the categories: international, global, multinational and transnational. This is a stages based model, where firms may progress until reaching the final transnational stage, which is a 'best practice' desired model of operation.

Lastly, we examine Baruch and Altman's (2002) theoretical framing that focuses on the management of expatriation and repatriation at the strategic level of career management. The five-option taxonomy expresses a variety of strategic approaches that organizations may hold in managing expatriation careers. This framework will be applied to general expatriation, as well as to repatriation.

In addition, in Chapter 3 we cover the process of expatriation from initiation, preparation, induction, performance, preparation for return, and repatriation. We note the various modes according to which repatriation can end. A separate discussion will deal with the issue of success and failure of expatriation.

Global career theory – societal perspective

Careers do not take place in a vacuum. Society is the general context (together with the economic context) where global careers emerge, progress and mature. Society and the economy enable and shape global careers, and reward them (or otherwise). In particular, issues such as cultural intelligence (Earley and Ang 2003) as an individual property, and openness to other cultures, as both individual and national properties, feed into the system of acceptance or rejection of globalization in different parts of the world.

Societies benefit from 'talent' and successful careers. However, they vary with respect to how careers are viewed and what career patterns are encouraged. The institutional literature distinguishes between coordinated market economies as well as liberal market economies (Parry et al. 2008). Some of the institutions favour strong general vocational training systems and in-depth functional or occupational knowledge (see Dickmann 2003 for the case of Germany). Other countries have a relative lack of deep vocational training and are prone to value generalist insights and skills. This is reflected in the relative career patterns in different countries which will influence global careers, e.g. through the selection criteria for IAs.

MNC career systems

Organizations employ a mix of strategy and practice for effective management of their resources, including their human resources. Part of this dual mix focuses on career systems. Sonnenfeld and Peiperl (1988) suggested the examination of career systems according to two dimensions. Firstly, supply flow, which refers to the labour markets wherein organizations look for managerial potential (i.e. internal versus external labour markets). Secondly, assignment flow, which reflects the base for development and promotion, and indicates the degree to which assignment and promotion decisions are based on individual performance on the one hand, versus overall contribution to the group or organization on the other. This framework can be useful for explicating the global element of career management. Typically, candidates for expatriation will come from within the organization. Yet, under certain circumstances and strategies (such as the professional strategy of Baruch and Altman 2002), the supply of expatriates could be external. As for the assignment flow, often an expatriate will be the single representative, or one of few, for the firm in their overseas location, and will work individually. On other occasions an expatriate might be more integrated into a group.

To develop and maintain effective strategic HRM, organizations should develop a strategic alignment between the HRM and the general operation of the organization (Holbeche 1999; Boxall and Purcell 2008). This principle is valid for the management of careers. It is the interest of the firm to operate in global markets. Thus it has to employ a global HRM system to take care of its people within this global operation.

From strategy to practice

Strategy, as inspiring and directing as it may be, will not have an impact unless reflected and reinforced by the policies and, in particular, via the practices that take place in the field to manage careers. The importance and prominence of organizational career planning and management (CPM) as part of HRM has been recognized by many scholars (Van Mannen and Schein 1977; Gutteridge 1986; Mayo 1991). Career systems and practices have been described in a number of works (London and Stumpf 1982; Gutteridge et al. 1993; Baruch and Peiperl 2000). In Chapter 3 we offer a wide overview of the full spectrum of career planning and management practices with its implications for global career planning and managing.

It becomes increasingly clear that future leaders are often seen to have had to manage globally. Thus they need global skill sets (see Harris and Dickmann 2005) which we will discuss in more depth in Chapters 3 and 7. Examples of firms which have a policy stating that for top positions people are encouraged to have foreign experience include many well-known MNCs such as LMVH, Henkel, General Electric, Shell and McKinsey. The most common forms of acquiring these cross-national capabilities include being a manager with international responsibilities and working abroad.

Expatriation process and its cyclical nature

Global careers come in different shapes, and many of them offer a cyclical progress (see Table 1.1). A single expatriation is a certain 'mini-career cycle', in a similar way to the general development of career stages (see Baruch 2004). First, a person (and his/her family) plunges into a new situation, after certain preparation and anticipation (parallel to the 'foundation' stage). The first period, the 'honeymoon' stage is like a career entry, learning about the new place, its rules, rites, culture and regulations. At this point the 'performance' stage emerges, where the person advances in performance, learning and benefiting from the experience. This leads to re-evaluation. In the case of expatriation, the outcomes will lead either to early return, reinforcement, or a decision to stay (naturalize, or become a perpetual expatriate). For the immigrant it will be the decision to finally make the new country his or her new home. The 'decline' and 'retirement' stages can represent a case of lower level of performance towards the end of the assignment, when the mind is already on the next career role at the home operation – or a decision to leave the organization upon return.

Such cycles may characterize further periods of expatriation or other types of global career options (see Chapter 4). When people flourish in their global career, each cycle can represent a spiral progress, where the lessons learned in each 'round' are built upon and used to make a fast positive progress in consecutive assignments.

Table 1.1 Baruch's integrated model of general career stages

Stage	Description
(a) Foundation	Childhood and adolescence experience and education help in planting the seeds of career aspiration.
(b) Career entry	Usually through attainment of profession. Can be done via being an apprentice, training on the job, attending college, university or other professional training. Usually even for qualified people, the first stage of work will include further professional establishment.
(c) Advancement	Both professional and hierarchical development within organization(s) or expanding own business. This stage can be characterized with either continuous advancement or reaching a plateau. In today's career environment and concepts, this stage will typically be associated with several changes of employer.
(d) Re-evaluation	Checking match between aspiration and fulfillment; re-thinking job/role/career. Can emerge from internal feeling or need (e.g. bored due to lack of challenge, life-crisis), or external force (redundancy, obsolescence of the profession). May end with decision to keep in the same path or to change career direction, returning to stage (b).
(e) Reinforcement	After making the decision a reinforcement of present career or returning to the learning stage (b) for re-establishment of new career.
(f) Decline	Most but the few (who have full life of advancement till the latest moment) will start at a certain stage to envisage withdrawal from working life, which can be swift or long term, spreading over few years.
(g) Retirement	Leaving the labor market (not necessarily at age of 65).

Source: Baruch (2004: 54)

Organizational view

The use of expatriation imposes substantial costs on any MNC, and the costs associated with such assignments are much higher than for 'conventional' employees (Dickmann et al. 2006). This message is reinforced by the cost of failure which, again, can far exceed the cost of failure within a traditional managerial role within the home country boundaries. Finding the right person for the right assignment, and at the right time, then, becomes increasingly important for HRM. MNCs should develop and implement strategies to position and then leverage expatriate resources to help their foreign subsidiaries gain a competitive advantage. They need to have a systematic expatriate staffing strategy and policies, backed up by practices, so that the human resource management will be aligned with such a wider strategy (Gong 2003).

MNCs must generate clear metrics for evaluation of the expatriation (and repatriation) processes (see Chapters 8 and 9). In selecting expatriates, MNCs' evaluation of candidates should be based not only on their technical skills, such as management or technological knowledge, but also on their motivation, global frame of mind, and adaptability for knowledge transfer, both explicit and tacit (Zaidman and Brock 2009). One of the roles of expatriates is to enable and facilitate knowledge transfer and knowledge sharing (Wang et al. 2009). Employing the resource-based view of the firm, Wang et al. argue that making a learned choice of particular expatriates to work in a certain subsidiary will enhance the subsidiary's performance due to the value of knowledge transfer.

The success or otherwise of expatriation should be evaluated by multi-factor measurement. It includes the preparation for expatriation, the induction process (and how long it took before the expatriate was able to operate effectively, if ever). Then the 'standard' evaluation of the performance through the expatriation applies, until it is time for preparation to repatriate. The process does not end here, as it is crucial to follow the repatriation and its outcomes. The diverse outcomes include highly positive scenarios and added value to the firm in the subsequent roles, as a best case scenario. However, the results can also be negative.

Success of the process would encourage future generations of prospective candidates for expatriation to select this option. This can generate a virtuous cycle of success, with strong competition for future expatriation, whereas a vicious cycle would mean that failures will be costly to start with, and will be followed by the refusal of future candidates to consider IAs; a nightmare for any global HR manager.

Repatriation and its challenges

The academic literature up to the 2000s tended to neglect the study of repatriation for two major reasons. Firstly, with the rapid growth of expatriation in the 1990s, the focus on the repatriation that followed came in this century. Secondly, originally there was no expectation of taking repatriation as a challenging process. It was conceived as a simple 'returning to normal' mode. Both HR managers and academic scholars assumed that there was no place like home and that people would just happily return. Such views were proven wrong. Some of the challenges stem from managerial and career-related issues. Others are concerned with the reverse culture shock (RCS), which came as a surprise. HR managers were sensitized to the issue and expected a culture shock, which occurs when people become shocked from meeting a new culture upon expatriation, as it is new and different from their original culture (Ward et al. 2001). Yet, what was less anticipated was that when expatriates returned home to the apparently known territory, they experienced a 'reverse' culture shock (Rodrigues 1996).

Overview of the book and its dual perspective

In each of the chapters of the book we explore different perspectives of global careers. While we concentrate on expatriation processes, this is not the only form of global careers. Further, we will present the dual nature of global careers as reflected from both individual and organizational perspectives, due to the mutual dependency of assignees on their employers and organizations on their internationally working talent.

Chapter 2 outlines the historical development of international organizations and depicts key organizational considerations of global management. We explicate strategies, structures, policies and practices of MNCs and their relevance to global careers. There are a number of International Human Resource Management frameworks, and we discuss them in the context of cross-border HRM. We then move to the individual level to illuminate global career implications for individuals.

Chapter 3 delves into career theories, moving from individual to organizational perspectives, and discusses career diversity. In terms of organizational practices, we explore the portfolio which HRM can employ to manage global careers. We end the chapter with a discussion of the meaning of cross-cultural working – global/multicultural teams, self-initiated global careers, national business systems and cultures.

In *Chapter 4* we present a comprehensive view of the wide range of options for global careers, moving from expatriation to a variety of types of international work and offer an integrative framework to cover these options. We then discuss the issue of diversity as well as national variations of the contexts in which careers are embedded. Earley and Gibson's (2008) model of culture intelligence seals the chapter, adding a unique view of our understanding of the global environment from a career standpoint.

Chapter 5 distinguishes between organizational and individual perspectives in international resourcing, and explores individual motivations and barriers (push and pull forces) to working abroad. These motivations and barriers are discussed in the light of the diverse backgrounds for self-initiated and company-sent assignments. We also cover organizational considerations and HR strategies, policies and practices for the management of global careers.

Figure 1.1 A framework of global careers[2]

The issue of pre-departure is covered in *Chapter 6*. Both individual and organizational considerations associated with pre-departure for international work are the focal points of this chapter. We cover the activities and actions that should be undertaken by the person, the family, and the organization before the assignment. The organizational side comprises a set of policies and practices to be applied before international work. These are subjected to a variety of national and societal issues relating to work-related cross-border moves. All these are discussed bearing in mind the prospect of their anticipated impact on performance and careers during and after the assignment.

Using a chronological sequence, *Chapter 7* focuses on the career during the assignment. We assess the underlying philosophies, patterns and approaches organizations hold for their international assignees. Global assignments can influence leadership development and performance. They can have an impact on the future retention and career progress of individuals involved. Knowledge management is another issue of relevance during and after the assignment. From an HRM point of view, the psychological adjustments for the host country culture and family challenges are of paramount importance. Global assignments can deliver positive or negative career capital – and the actual outcomes depend greatly on the way the individual and the organization form their psychological contracts.

2 The framework presented in this figure will accompany the book, and in each chapter we will present the figure and indicate which parts of the framework are covered in the specific chapter.

Chapter 8 depicts the 'after the assignment' phase and explores what happens upon moving back home or on to a different country after an international work assignment. We discuss organizational repatriation support practices and their anticipated effects, knowledge transfer and other implications of returning from international work. In particular we identify key effects in repatriation. Finally, we discuss individual, organizational and societal global career implications in the short term.

The focus of *Chapter 9* are the longer-term outcomes of global careers and international work. We discuss ways to evaluate international work experiences. We explore the impact of international work on individuals, organizations and nation states on issues such as acquisition and use of career capital, career satisfaction and subsequent employment.

Chapters 10 and 11 take a different point of view, written in collaboration with specialized consultants, and discuss the practicalities of financial and economical considerations for individuals and firms engaged with global employment arrangements. The focus of *Chapter 10* is the range of strategic and operational approaches to social security and other regulatory issues for the provision and maintenance of social security. It deals with regulation, mostly within the EU, and how organizations are to cope with these. *Chapter 11* explores wider remuneration, compensation and risk issues and factors influencing them. It illuminates compensation criteria and presents steps to design a global mobility policy.

We end the book with a reflective discussion of earlier chapters, where *Chapter 12* provides an integrative summary. We distinguish global career strategies and practices and offer a glimpse of things to come – the trends and likely implications of global careers for the future – lessons and challenges for the twenty-first-century management of global careers.

Summary and learning points

In this opening chapter we outlined the overall framework that we will follow along the book. We covered the issue of globalization in general, and the implications of globalization to people management and, in particular, for career planning and management. We defined global career and positioned it within the context of current career systems and global business. We explored the trends of global movements and their relevance to global work.

Key learning points include:

- The nature of business is becoming more global and, as a result, there are a growing number of global careers and need for their management.
- There are a number of theories concerning global careers, dealing with careers from different perspectives and levels of analysis – individual, organizational and national levels in particular.
- A global career might involve immigration; but could also be restricted, within the organizational boundaries, to expatriation and repatriation management.

- Individualization of careers poses new challenges to organizational career management, and global careers are no exception, with more self-initiated global moves persisting.
- Expatriation and repatriation still form the major issues for global careers and their management in terms of HRM.

References

Altman, Y. and Baruch, Y. (2008) 'Global protean careers: a new era in expatriation and repatriation', paper presented at the *European Academy of Management* conference, Ljubljana, May 2008.

Arthur, M.B., Hall, D.T. and Lawrence, B.S. (1989) 'Generating new directions in career theory: the case for a transdisciplinary approach', in M.B. Arthur, D.T. Hall and B.S. Lawrence (eds) *Handbook of Career Theory*, Cambridge: Cambridge University Press.

Bartlett, C. and Ghoshal, S. (1989) *Managing across Borders*, London: Hutchinson Business Books.

Bartlett, C. and Ghoshal, S. (1992) 'What is a global manager?', *Harvard Business Review*, 70(5): 124–132.

Baruch, Y. (1999) 'Integrated career systems for the 2000s', *International Journal of Manpower,* 20(7): 432–457.

Baruch, Y. (2002) 'No such thing as a global manager', *Business Horizons*, 45(1): 36–42.

Baruch, Y. (2004) *Managing Careers: Theory and Practice*, Harlow: FT-Prentice Hall/Pearson.

Baruch, Y. (2006) 'Career development in organizations and beyond: balancing traditional and contemporary viewpoints', *Human Resource Management Review*, 16: 125–138.

Baruch, Y. and Altman, Y. (2002) 'Expatriation and repatriation in MNCs: a taxonomy', *Human Resource Management*, 41(2): 239–259.

Baruch, Y. and Bozionelos, N. (2010) 'Career issues', in S. Zedeck (ed.) *Industrial and Organizational Psychology Handbook*, APA publication, forthcoming.

Baruch, Y. and Peiperl, M.A. (2000) 'Career management practices: an empirical survey and theoretical implications', *Human Resource Management*, 39(4): 347–366.

Baruch, Y. and Rosenstein, E. (1992) 'Career planning and managing in high tech organizations', *International Journal of Human Resource Management*, 3(3): 477–496.

Baruch, Y., Altman, Y. and Adler, N. (2009) 'Topic: global careers and international assignments: the current discourse', *Human Resource Management*, 48(1): 1–4.

Baruch, Y., Budhwar, P. and Khatri, N. (2007) 'Brain drain: inclination to stay abroad after studies', *Journal of World Business*, 42(1): 99–112.

Baruch, Y., Steele, D. and Quantrill, J. (2002) 'Management of expatriation and repatriation for novice global player', *International Journal of Manpower*, 23(7): 659–671.

Black, J.S. and Gregersen, H.B. (1999) 'The right way to manage expats', *Harvard Business Review*, 77(2): 52–63.

Bonache, J. and Dickmann, M. (2008) 'The transfer of strategic HR know-how in MNCs: mechanisms, barriers and initiatives', in M. Dickmann, C. Brewster and P. Sparrow (eds) *International Human Resource Management – The European Perspective*, London: Routledge.

Boxall, P. and Purcell, J. (2008) *Strategy and Human Resource Management*, Palgrave: Basingstoke.

Cappellen, T. and Janssens, M. (2005) 'Career paths of global managers: towards future research', *Journal of World Business*, 40(4): 348–360.

Cerdin, J.-L. and Le Pargneux, M. (2009) 'Career and international assignment fit: toward an integrative model of success', *Human Resource Management*, 48(1): 5–25.

CReME (2000) *New forms of international working*, report by the Centre for Research into the Management of Expatriation, Cranfield University: Cranfield.

Dickmann, M. (2003) 'Implementing German HRM abroad: desired, feasible, successful?', *International Journal of Human Resource Management*, 14(2): 265–284.

Dickmann, M. and Doherty, N. (2010) 'Exploring organisational and individual career goals, interactions and outcomes of international assignments', *Thunderbird International Review*, 52(4): 313–324.

Dickmann, M. and Harris, H. (2005) 'Developing career capital for global careers: the role of international assignments', *Journal of World Business*, 40: 399–408.

Dickmann, M., Johnson, A. and Doherty, N. (2006) *Measuring the Value of International Assignments*, London: PricewaterhouseCoopers and Cranfield School of Management.

Dickmann, M., Müller-Camen, M. and Kelliher, C. (2009) 'Striving for transnational human resource management – principles and practice', *Personnel Review*, 38(1): 5–25.

Earley, P.C. and Ang, S. (2003) *Cultural Intelligence: An Analysis of Individual Interactions across Cultures*, Palo Alto, CA: Stanford University Press.

Earley, P.C. and Gibson, C.B. (2008) *Multinational Work Teams: A New Perspective*, New York: Routledge.

European Labour Force Survey (2005) Data quoted in L. de Vries and J. Goeman, *Managing Mobility Matters 2006*, report for the European Union, Amsterdam: PricewaterhouseCoopers.

GMAC (2008) *Global Relocation Trends: 2008 Survey Report*, Woodridge, IL: GMAC Global Relocation Services.

Gong, Y. (2003) 'Toward a dynamic process model of staffing composition and subsidiary outcomes in multinational enterprises', *Journal of Management*, 29: 259–280.

Gutteridge, T.G. (1986) 'Organizational career development systems: the state of the practice', in D.T. Hall *Career Development in Organizations*, San Francisco, CA: Jossey-Bass.

Gutteridge, T.G., Leibowitz, Z.B. and Shore, J.E. (1993) *Organizational Career Development*, San Francisco, CA: Jossey-Bass.

Guzzo, R.A., Nooman, K.A. and Elron, E. (1994) 'Expatriate managers and the psychological contract', *Journal of Applied Psychology*, 79(4): 617–626.

Hall, D.T. (1986) *Career Development in Organizations*, San Francisco, CA: Jossey-Bass.

Harris, H. and Dickmann, M. (2005) *The CIPD Guide on International Management Development*, London: The Chartered Institute of Personnel and Development.

Harris, H., Brewster, C. and Sparrow, P. (2003) *International Human Resource Management*, London: Chartered Institute of Personnel and Development.

Harvey, M. (1997) 'Dual-career expatriates: expectations, adjustment and satisfaction with international relocation', *Journal of International Business Studies*, 28(3): 627–658.

Heenan, D.A. and Perlmutter, H.V. (1979) *Multinational Organizational Development: A Social Architecture Perspective*, Reading, MA: Addison-Wesley.

Holbeche, L. (1999) *Aligning Human Resources and Business Strategy*, Oxford: Butterworth Heinemann.

Hu, Y.-S. (1992) 'Global or stateless corporations are national firms with international operations', *California Management Review*, 34: 107–126.

Inkson, K., Arthur, M.B., Pringle, J. and Barry, S. (1997) 'Expatriate assignment versus overseas experience: contrasting models of international human resource development', *Journal of World Business*, 32(4): 351–368.

IOM (2009) 'Migration, climate change and the environment', International Organization for Migration, online, http://www.iom.int/jahia/jsp/index.jsp (accessed 09.07.2009).

Khapova, S.N., Arthur, M.B. and Wilderom, C.P.M. (2007) 'The subjective career in the knowledge economy', in H. Gunz and M.A. Peiperl (eds) *Handbook of Career Studies*, Los Angeles, CA: Sage.

Lips-Wiersma, M. and Hall, D.T. (2007) 'Organizational career development is not dead: a case study on managing the new career during organizational change', *Journal of Organizational Behavior*, 28: 771–792.

London, M. and Stumpf, S.A. (1982) *Managing Careers*, Reading, MA: Addison-Wesley.

MacLuhan, M. (1960) *Explorations in Communication*, Boston, MA: Beacon Press.

Mayo, A. (1991) *Managing Careers*, London: IPM.

MIE (2006) 'Mobility in Europe: Analysis of the 2005 Eurobarometer survey on geographical and labour market mobility. A report of the European Foundation for the Improvement of Living and Working Conditions' http://www.eurofound.europa.eu/pubdocs/2006/59/en/1/ef0659en.pdf.

Mir, R. and Mir, A. (2009) 'From the colony to the corporation: studying knowledge transfer across international boundaries', *Group and Organization Management*, 34: 90–113.

ORC (2007) *Survey of International Localization Policies and Practices*, Organization Resource Counselors Worldwide: New York.

Parry, E., Dickmann, M. and Morley, M. (2008) 'North American MNCs and their HR policies in liberal and coordinated market economies', *International Journal of Human Resource Management*, 19(11): 2024–2040.

PricewaterhouseCoopers (2006) *Managing Mobility Matters 2006*, report by L. de Vries and J. Goeman for the European Union, Amsterdam: PricewaterhouseCoopers.

Reilly, R.R. and Campbell, B. (1990) 'How corporate performance measurement systems inhibit globalization', *Human Resource Management*, 29(1): 63–68.

Rodrigues, C. (1996) *International Management*, Minneapolis/St Paul: West Publication.

Ronen, S. and Shenkar, O. (1985) 'Clustering countries on attitudinal dimensions: a review and synthesis', *Academy of Management Review*, 10: 435–454.

Schein, E.H. (1978) *Career Dynamics: Matching Individual and Organizational Needs*, Reading, MA: Addison-Wesley.

Schein, E.H. (1984) 'Culture as an environmental context for careers', *Journal of Occupational Behaviour*, 5(1): 71–81.

Sonnenfeld, J.A. and Peiperl, M.A. (1988) 'Staffing policy as a strategic response: a typology of career systems', *Academy of Management Review*, 13(4): 568–600.

Sparrow, P., Brewster, C. and Harris, H. (2004) *Globalizing Human Resource Management*, London: Routledge.

Sullivan, S.N. and Baruch, Y. (2010) Advances in career theory and research: critical review and agenda for future exploration, *Journal of Management*, forthcoming.

United Nations (2006) *Migration 2006*, United Nations: Department of Economic and Social Affairs, Population Division, online, http://www.iom.int/jahia/jsp/index.jsp (accessed 09.07.2009).

Van Mannen, J. and Schein, E.H. (1977) 'Career development', in J.R. Hackman and J.L. Suttle (eds) *Improving Life at Work: Behavioral Science Approaches to Organizational Change*, Santa Monica, CA: Goodyear.

Wang, S., Tong, T.W., Chen, G. and Kim, H. (2009) 'Expatriate utilization and foreign direct investment performance: the mediating role of knowledge transfer', *Journal of Management*, 35: 1181–1206.

Ward, C., Bochner, S. and Furnham, A. (2001) *The Psychology of Culture Shock*, London: Routledge.

Zaidman, N. and Brock, D.M. (2009) 'Knowledge transfer within multinationals and their foreign subsidiaries: a culture-context approach', *Group and Organization Management*, 34: 297–329.

2 The organizational context: exploring strategic international HRM

Objectives

This chapter:

- outlines the historical development of international organizations amid their competitive environment;
- depicts the key organizational considerations with respect to international management options – it will introduce the concept of configurations and describe international strategies, structures, policies and practices of MNCs;
- explores a range of frameworks of International Human Resource Management (IHRM) in order to deepen insights into scope, processes and outcomes of cross-border HRM;
- identifies the organizational career management options and approaches that each of the IHRM configurations entails;
- illuminates some of the global career implications for individuals;
- presents a case of IHRM configuration in a major German multinational in order to discuss the advantages and drawbacks of a chosen cross-border HR approach.

Introduction

International careers are linked to a range of individual, organizational and societal factors – planned as well as through serendipity. This chapter will focus predominantly on organizational factors that will set the context for individuals' global careers. It will chart the historical development of multinationally operating entities and explore some of the strategic, structural and operational

Figure 2.1 A framework of global careers: SIHRM in the global competitive context

considerations in doing so. It will investigate the global–local dilemma and other tensions that arise from organizations operating across borders. Based on these pressures, it will present a range of possible strategies, structures, policies and practices – sometimes called organizational configurations – that multinational firms might adopt.

We will then examine the implications for IHRM and global careers. Thus, in our framework (see Figure 2.1) we concentrate on the organizational strategies, structures and operational activities serving as the base for individual careerists seeking a global career. While work-related, multifaceted behaviour (WMB) of individuals is obviously very important for the study of careers, this chapter will commence by focusing on organizational strategies, structures, policies and practices before exploring global career aspects.

Historical development of international organizations

Going back 4,000 years in history, Assyrian 'commercial organizations' had head offices and subsidiaries, foreign workers, defined hierarchies, activities in several geographical regions and a strategy to search for new markets and resources (Moore and Lewis 1999). These characteristics are similar to those of many modern MNCs.

Overseas operations in Africa and the Mediterranean were one of the signs of King Salomon's wealth. Akin to some of today's very biggest MNCs, Roman organizations were truly global – in the sense of having activities in all of the then known world – in that they operated in Europe, Asia and Africa. The Roman organizations followed their army which was building a global empire. The international expansion of some current MNCs, especially that of professional service corporations and manufacturing suppliers, is often driven by following their customers and providing a worldwide service.

While religion (e.g. Crusaders) and wealth (e.g. Vikings) combined with power (e.g. Conquistadores in Latin America) were incentives for some international work, the real precursors of modern MNCs are often seen to be the great trading companies such as the Hudson's Bay Company, the Royal African Company, the Muscovy Company and, of course, the English and Dutch East India companies (Carlos and Nicolas 1988). These not only had a wide geographical presence, they also faced some of modern MNCs' challenges and employed early versions of management techniques to cope with these.

These trading companies had a network of operating stations across different continents; they chartered ships for transport, signed on professionals (such as captains, but also experts with skills in foreign languages, negotiations, logistics and goods handling etc.). Because of the wide spread of their warehouses and operating units, the trading companies faced the agency problem of having to delegate much responsibility and authority to their local representatives. How could they ensure that these individuals would act in their best interests rather than in their own?

With very slow transport and communication, distance created a control challenge. In one sense, the trading companies attempted to send their trusted personnel (akin to a modern day expatriate) with the goal to establish social coordination through personal behaviour as well as moral and professional standards. These would ideally be family members. But there were also more explicit, harder control measures implemented. These included accounts, written explanation and other records of decisions, and the need to report back the compliance to home-country directives. Performance measures were established – such as ships sailing on time, loading quality and loss, the ratio of capital to tonnage and other capital measures – and local representatives could be dismissed if their performance was deemed to be insufficient. In turn, financial incentives were developed for compliance and good performance, with bonuses being paid. Harder control approaches included the searching of ships, the use of pursers on naval vessels and even the reading of private correspondence. This meant that a bureaucracy of salaried employees had to be created in the head offices, with the English and Dutch East India companies having more than 350 administrators in their heyday (Evans et al. 2002). While within these bureaucracies a 'career' could be made, the head office had the power to send out individuals to far-flung countries to control foreign operations, a practice that is common to this day. Historically, the colonization of regions – first through the conquest of land and then the administration of the colonies – meant a bureaucratic organization of far-flung operations. Moreover, missionary activities undertaken by churches included a range of international coordination of activities and resulted in early forms of international careers. Overall, these management approaches have similarities with those of international organizations after the industrial revolution.

Jones (1996) outlines a big geographical spread of large multinational manufacturers in 1914. The likes of Singer, J&P Coats, Nestlé, Lever Brothers, Bayer, St Gobain, L.M. Ericsson and Siemens had managed to set up manufacturing operations abroad, often transplanting superior technology across borders. These organizations had often begun to expand abroad in the nineteenth century and, where possible, had a tendency to also use trusted home-country individuals to run foreign operations. For instance, Siemens in Russia and Great Britain was run by two brothers of the founder (Dickmann 1999). Communication by then had, of course, been separated from physical transport with the arrival of telegraph and telephone which facilitated control somewhat. Banking and other financial services expanded internationally to aid the increasing trade flows and other needs of organizations that either expanded internationally or traded across borders.

The first cross-border mergers happened, with that between Shell (UK) and Royal Dutch (Netherlands) being a prime example. Rapid colonization and the lure of raw materials and other resources aided the international expansion of industry and finance. It looked as if a golden age of international business was approaching, a process that was severely slowed by two world wars, economic depressions and protectionism. Only after the Second World War and especially towards the end of the twentieth and the beginning of the twenty-first centuries did globalization unfold its full velocity. Much of this book will concentrate on recent and current phenomena associated with international work.

The MNC in the global economy

Perlmutter's four types of international management

Despite thousands of articles about globalization, a definition of the concept and the precise capturing of the effects of the underlying strategies, structures and policies on performance remain elusive (Coriat 1997: 242; Evans et al. 2002). Below, are some key ideas with respect to the competitive responses of organizations and their adopted configurations (strategies, structures, policies and practices) outlined. A good place to start is the 'classic' contribution made in the 1960s by Howard Perlmutter who distinguishes between polycentric, ethnocentric and geocentric management (Perlmutter 1969). A decade later a fourth concept, intimately linked to geocentrism but on a regional scale, was developed which was called regiocentrism (Heenan and Perlmutter 1979).

Polycentrism

A polycentric organization may pursue resource-seeking or market-seeking goals in its expansion abroad. It attempts to be as locally responsive as possible and top management is persuaded that international integration of policies and practices is not beneficial. Possible reasons might be that the other country's circumstances are seen as too different, or the assumption that local management knows best. In contrast, a company that pursues ethnocentric management will attempt to internationally integrate its policies and practices since it believes its ownership advantages, superior experience and scale effects increase its competitiveness. A geocentric enterprise coordinates policies where it is beneficial and leaves local autonomy to adapt where it is necessary. While the geocentric entity develops approaches on a worldwide scale, a regiocentric organization strives for a similar balance of locally responsive and cross-border integrated principles, policies and practices within regions. This raises the question of whether the business strategy, policies and practices of an MNC's subsidiaries are predominantly determined in their home country, in their various host countries or on a global, supra-country level. Perlmutter used a managerial perspective to analyse the patterns of MNCs – his ideas have been taken up and extended by a variety of authors. The organizational types are described in more detail below.

MNCs have a breadth of linkages with their home countries. They are embedded in their home culture and institutions, follow national laws and regulations and recruit on the local labour market. Porter's (1990) argument about the competitive advantages of nations implies that MNCs depend upon the positive characteristics of their nation states that enable them to have high productivity in their industries.

MNCs' policies and practices are shaped by specific regional or national characteristics. Generally, the national culture and institutional environment are seen to influence to a significant extent the way a company operates (Lane 1989; Whitley 1992). The existence of cooperative relations in the industry or region can aid research and development (R&D), the public education system influences the human resource capital accumulated (Lane 1992) and regulations such as environmental protection laws impact on production processes or technology use (Räsanen and Whipp 1992). Possible effects might include that transfers of home practices are likely to encounter barriers (Dickmann 2003). Therefore, home-country practices are likely to be less effective outside the country of origin. It is implied that companies should pursue polycentrism and adapt to their local environments.

The above described societal effect is challenged by the globalization argument. According to some authors, national institutional barriers are losing importance as it becomes ever easier to cross linguistic, structural or trade barriers (Ohmae 1990). Spurred on by increasingly 'footloose' capital, highly educated, mobile workers and new information technology, a global diffusion of technology and knowledge is taking place. This raises the issue of how important national institutions are in reality for the policies, practices and outcomes of global MNCs (Parry et al. 2008).

Ethnocentrism

Corporate structures, strategies, control mechanisms and innovations are often determined or generated in the country of origin (Hu 1992). The upper echelons of corporations are filled to an extremely high percentage with home nationals and R&D is disproportionately located in the country of origin. Further, strategic decisions are taken at the centre of the firm which almost always remains in its home nation. Thus, many companies pursue an ethnocentric approach to internationalization in that they are seen to transfer policies and practices abroad. Examples of the transfer of 'Japanese', 'US-American' or 'German' practices have been quoted widely (Lawler et al. 1989; Wilkinson and Oliver 1992; Yang 1992; Dedoussis 1995; Dickmann 2003). Ethnocentrism is seen to have advantages with respect to the diffusion and exploitation of home-country innovation (Dickmann et al. 2009), encourages economies of scale and it has implications in terms of control and coordination (Ferner 2000). In terms of IHRM the degree of standardization around country-of-origin ideas depends in part on the desirability and feasibility of international transfer (Dickmann 2003).

Regiocentrism and geocentrism

Some advocates of globalization have detected a trend towards MNCs becoming supra-country enterprises in an attempt to access markets and achieve cross-border efficiency. Rugman presents a table of the 'world's leading multinational enterprises' in which ten MNCs have a value higher than 85 per cent for 'transnationality' – taken to be the mean of the ratio of foreign to total activities for three indices: sales, assets and employees (Rugman 1998). Interestingly, the country of origin of these companies tends to provide a relatively small home market – four are from Switzerland, two from Canada while none is from the US or Japan – so that one prime reason for internationalization might be a market seeking push.

Beyond Perlmutter

Other writers have also moved away from the home–host country distinction to focus on a supra-national level. It is argued that with the internationalization of competition the management tasks have changed – the identification of global solutions amid competing pressures (or dualities) has become the focus of attention rather than the effective transfer of head office policies (Evans et al. 2002). Issues of international integration, innovation and international control have become more prominent (Hedlund 1994). To improve global competitiveness, international coordination between all parts of the MNC is seen as important (Prahalad and Doz 1987). These universalist approaches hold in their extreme form that some rules or mechanisms are universally applicable irrespective of local cultural, institutional or other factors (such as history). Globally standardized corporate strategies, structures and processes are seen as an expression of the business logic. If this is the case, the nationality of a multinational company is (becoming) increasingly irrelevant.

But the 'societal effect' school cautions us that national influences are important in the functioning of any corporate policy or practice (Ferner and Quintanilla 1998). Another school advocates globally applicable management approaches that involve either integration around home-country practices or coordination that approximates neither home nor host approaches (Dickmann and Müller-Camen 2006). It is implicitly assumed by the proponents of international standardization that once an MNC has determined its ideal policies, it is powerful enough to implement them globally. Examples of global sourcing and production (automotive industry, textiles) are abundant. Examples of global marketing and branding (Coca-Cola's beverages, Intel's micro-processors, Apple's iPods, Procter &

Gamble's Pantene) and global quality standards (McDonald's, Xerox) can also be identified.

The global context: searching for competitive advantage

What are the key success factors in the process of internationalization? Dickmann and Müller-Camen (2006) argue that while an ethnocentric MNC achieves scale economies it lacks the flexibility to respond to local market pressures. This flexibility, on the other hand, is a hallmark of the polycentric organization. However, its fragmentation of resources is likely to carry efficiency penalties since its production facilities are split and in areas such as R&D, marketing or HRM a duplication of effort may occur. There is a need to strike a balance between conflicting requirements of efficiency and sociocultural responsiveness to solve the 'global–local dilemma' (Evans and Lorange 1989).

Prahalad and Doz (1987) argue that organizational culture can provide a 'corporate glue' that counteracts the centrifugal forces – for example, the 'not invented here' syndrome, a tendency to disregard 'foreign' product or process innovations – associated with local responsiveness. Thus, while simultaneously achieving global integration the drawbacks of inefficiencies are seen to be avoided and organizational culture can overcome the global–local dilemma. Martinez and Jarillo (1991) explored the interrelationship of integration and local responsiveness in a study of subsidiaries in Spain and were able to empirically identify subsidiaries that used a multifocal strategy combining high responsiveness and high integration.

Even if it is possible to solve the global–local dilemma, this does not on its own make a multinational successful. Instead, many authors have identified knowledge creation, transfer and exploitation as a key to corporation success in international markets (Porter 1985; Pucik 1992, Bonache and Zárraga-Oberty 2008). Increasingly authors move away from the dominant strategy and structure focus to include corporate processes that might help to create competitive advantage.

An MNC needs efficiency to achieve global competitiveness. Moreover, it requires flexibility to be able to respond to national preferences and changing customer demands. Lastly, the firm would facilitate knowledge creation and transfer in order to be able to create differentiated products and services. However, none of the above theories explain how to become simultaneously nationally responsive, globally effective and innovative. Buckley (1995: 64) and Dickmann et al. (2009) maintain that the work of Bartlett and Ghoshal does exactly this.

Bartlett and Ghoshal (1989) suggest that there are four international configurations among which one is an 'ideal': the 'transnational' which integrates global efficiency, local responsiveness and worldwide innovative capability. Bartlett and Ghoshal argued that:

- The ideal firm should be organized so that foreign subsidiaries have considerable managerial autonomy and have a differentiated role within the organization (responsiveness within a network). The relatively equal power distribution relies more on informal – a shared organizational culture – rather than formal control mechanisms.

- It should capture global economies of scale by integrating activities where possible across borders in order to minimize costs.
- It should create specialized units that have R&D capabilities. Their ideas, services and products should be diffused globally throughout the firm. Lateral and vertical international communication flows are designed to develop knowledge jointly and to share ideas across borders.

One of the appeals of Bartlett and Ghoshal's theory is that they outline how to change MNCs' international structures and processes. The next section outlines what an MNC can do to successfully become a transnational.

Becoming a transnational: the role of organizational culture and HRM

The importance of corporate culture for success has often been stressed (Denison 1990; Schein 1992) – in fact, some authors talk about the 1980s being the decade of organizational culture (Evans et al. 2002: 12, 38). Prahalad and Doz (1987: 255ff.) have argued that organizational culture can be a means to overcome the global–local dilemma. They claim that a meta-culture can provide the corporate 'glue' that holds the organization with its global interest and the individual local business together. A shared international vision and goals, as well as the same management principles, and a homogeneous culture are seen to provide a common orientation.

Bartlett and Ghoshal (1989: 199–207) outlined in more detail how to overcome the global–local dilemma. Any move towards the transnational has to work on three levels. It needs to change formal structures and responsibilities, interpersonal relations and processes, and individual attitudes and mentalities. The transnational is characterized by a systematic differentiation of roles and responsibilities in its different parts. This facilitates the evolution of centrifugal powers where managers are likely to put local above global loyalties (Bartlett and Ghoshal 1989: 70). The transnational has a cohesion challenge.

Bartlett and Ghoshal (1989: 206) advocate mechanisms to build corporate cohesion not just at the level of culture but, rather, at the level of international HRM and individual leadership. They suggest levers, such as personal assignments or increased networking, which were used by Philips and Unilever. This is in broad agreement with Schein (1992) who isolates five 'primary mechanisms' leaders can use to embed and reinforce cultural values. These include: (1) teaching and (2) coaching, (3) criteria used for allocation of rewards and sanctions, (4) deliberate role modelling, as well as (5) criteria used for choosing followers which are often systematized and HRM-centred in large MNCs. At another point, Bartlett and Ghoshal emphasize the key role of HRM in overcoming the global–local dilemma and in building a cohesive transnational. They assert that 'a fundamental prerequisite for the normative integration a transnational seeks is a sophisticated HRM system. The transnational uses systems of recruitment, training and development, and career path management to help individuals to cope with its diversity and complexity' (p. 71).

Thus, the role of IHRM and, among other activities, careers, their underlying strategic elements and careerists' approaches to their work experiences (Sonnenfeld and Peiperl 1988), become crucial for competitive success. This raises the question of how sophisticated IHRM can be created. A first step is to understand the scope, the various influences and interdependencies of cross-border HRM. This leads us to explore frameworks of IHRM.

Frameworks of IHRM

Early frameworks of HRM moved beyond traditional notions of personnel management, stressed the need for internal consistency (Beer et al. 1985) and outlined the interrelationship of HR strategy with business strategy (Fombrun et al. 1984). For decades, organizational career management had been attributed an important role in the people management literature. With globalization seemingly accelerating, the international aspects of HRM became more prominent in academic and professional writing. Increasingly, models of strategic international HRM (SIHRM) emerged.

One of the earliest and among the most famous models of SIHRM is based on an article by Schuler, Dowling and De Cieri (1993). The authors depict exogenous

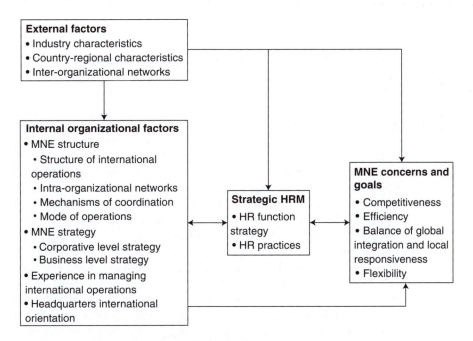

Figure 2.2 A model of strategic HRM in multinational enterprises

Source: Adapted from De Cieri, H. and Dowling, P. (1999) 'Strategic human resource management in multinational enterprises: theoretical and empirical developments', in P.M. Wright, L.D. Dyer and J.W. Boudreau (eds) *Research in Personnel and Human Resource Management: strategic human resources in the twenty-first century, 4th Supplement*, Stamford, CT: JAI Press.

and endogenous factors as well as strategic MNC components that have an impact on SIHRM issues, functions, policies and practices. These, in turn, impact on key MNC goals such as effectiveness, efficiency, responsiveness, learning and transfer as well as flexibility. Their framework gave a good overview of the manifold influences and relationships within SIHRM and stressed the need for internal and external alignment. De Cieri and Dowling (1999) built on their ideas and drew up an SIHRM model (Figure 2.2) that depicts the dynamic feedback effects more clearly.

Driven by the need for extra-organizational fit, SIHRM design has to take account of external factors. One way to analyse the external context of an organization would be to conduct a PESTEL (political, economic, sociocultural, technological, ecological and legal) analysis. The model in Figure 2.2 points to the strong impact of country-regional and industry characteristics. Industry characteristics and the nature of the demand for an organization's products or services have, for instance, an impact on how locally responsive a firm needs to be and how internationally integrated it can be. Certain sectors – such as the computer, oil or car industries – seem to be highly globalized while others are still more local. Peter Brabeck, the former CEO of Nestlé describes some of the organizational choices well:

'One way to accelerate growth in other industries would be greater centralization to cut costs and release resources for marketing. That is a strategy Nestlé adopts in products where tastes vary little across borders – its pet food business for example.' But Mr Brabeck believes many of the group's competitors have

---

Box 2.1 Understanding IHRM: external pressures and internal factors

Tasks:

1 *External factors*. Take your organization or an international organization that you are familiar with. Conduct a PESTEL analysis (PESTEL: Political, Economic, Sociocultural, Technological, Ecological, Legal). Describe the most important exogenous factors and analyse their influence on the HRM in the organization. How much choice does the organization have in terms of its HRM strategies and policies? What are the effects in different countries? What impact does this have on the ability to integrate HR approaches across borders?

2 *Internal factors*. Analyse your organization's HR strategy (or a sub-unit of your organization). Is the structure clearly suited to achieve the strategy? What implications do strategy and structure have for HRM? What implications do they have for standardization across borders? What is the impact on how and where ideas and approaches are developed? What is the impact on the diffusion of knowledge, on innovation and learning? What effects does the 'gestalt' of HR strategies, policies and practices have on the national and international careers of individuals in the organization?

failed to match Nestlé's performance because they have tried to adopt such strategies in human foodstuffs, where tastes vary enormously from country. US groups, in particular, tend to see Europe as a homogenous market.

'The emotional link to the local customer is extremely important in our business. That is why it remains a fragmented industry and that is why we try to stay as close as possible to local consumers.'

(The Financial Times, 13 March 2000)

We have seen above that these strategic choices have an impact on the structure of the organization and, thus, on HRM and also on careers. Moreover, the inter-organizational networks and alliances will determine some of the responsiveness, flexibility and competitiveness of the organization and will have an impact on the SIHRM strategy as well as associated practices (e.g. learning, knowledge transfer, international moves).

The institutional literature points out the importance of the local environment in many areas, including the educational standards – which will impact on the training, development and career approaches of organizations. Knowledge is embedded in a host country's local context and 'system' (Birkinshaw et al. 2002). Thus, some knowledge is specific to a host country with respect to its economy, language or other sociocultural factors (Edwards and Ferner 2004). The legal and regulatory environment might determine the rights and powers of works councils and trade union organizations and has strong impacts on staffing and development decisions and investment levels. The comparative HRM literature is full of detailed analyses between countries such as the UK, USA, Germany, France, Spain, China and Japan (see Müller 1998; Ferner and Quintanilla 1998; Edwards et al. 2004; Ferner et al. 2005). Important policy changes – such as the subsequent steps in the expansion of the EU and the growth of European directives in the last four decades – have an enormous impact on external context and internal organizational factors. Therefore, these three sets of external factors partly determine the SIHRM and IHRM policies and practices of firms.

Alfred Chandler posed the dictum 'structure follows strategy' (1962). Therefore, the corporate- and business-level strategies, even the product- and/or country-level strategies have an impact not only on SIHRM but also on the structure of the organization. Therefore, if the strategy is geared to be innovative, we would expect many mechanisms that foster the creation of new ideas or approaches, the diffusion of these across borders and the exploitation of innovation in different countries. This would have an effect on the structure of international operations, the creation of intensive intra-organizational networks, formal and informal mechanisms of coordination (Ferner 2000) and operational modes. We already saw above that the international orientation of the head office has an impact on the likely organizational structures and policies (Heenan and Perlmutter 1979) and that the administrative heritage or, as it is called in the model, the experience in managing international operations, will have resulted in learning effects (Adler and Ghadar 1990). Moreover, differences in subsidiary roles influence international knowledge flows. For example, 'receptive' subsidiaries make a heavier use of communication mechanisms than 'autonomous' local operating units (Martinez and Jarillo 1991). Bartlett and Ghoshal's four organizational configurations

(1989) capture the choices that firms can make and their associated advantages and disadvantages well. They link strongly to the MNC concerns and goals listed in the SIHRM model.

Based on external and internal determinants, one of the key goals of the MNC is competitiveness. Porter (1985) outlined some of the main factors as efficiency, quality and innovation. Translated into the realm of global management, Bartlett and Ghoshal clarify that this competitiveness is linked to innovation, efficiency and responsiveness – the balance of global integration and local responsiveness in the SIHRM model. Lastly, the flexibility concern of MNCs is related to the dynamic and highly complex context that these organizations face. In essence, it is related to learning and the creative process of determining how and what to standardize across the MNC and at what level. Given the high importance that various authors have attributed to HRM, organizational culture and leadership in creating and delivering an adequate enterprise configuration, the 'middle' box of strategic HRM is crucial in the fulfilment of MNC concerns and goals. The next section will explore IHRM strategies, structures and operational policies and processes in more depth.

Exploring IHRM further: strategies, structures, policies and practices

The motives for standardization

Harzing (2000: 103) proposes that MNCs' policies and practices are located on a continuum that runs from high degrees of integration/coordination/globalization to high degrees of differentiation/responsiveness/localization. On this continuum, each position can be captured by a measure of 'standardization' (Dickmann and Müller-Camen 2006). Transferring HR insights and approaches has a range of advantages connected to the standardization of HR philosophies and practices (Dickmann et al. 2009). First, it allows an efficiency gain in that the development of HR approaches, their communication and maintenance is more efficient and avoids the duplication of effort. Second, a prominent reason is to establish or maintain internal equity and consistent HR approaches across national borders (Rosenzweig and Nohria 1994). As Bonache and Brewster (2001) and Bonache and Zárraga-Oberty (2008) have argued this is important in firms with large numbers of expatriates. Standardizing HR policies and practices, for instance with respect to talent identification, development and career processes, is likely to add to perceived equity and avoids a local perception of a 'glass ceiling'.

Third, and more strategically, the quality of the standardized HR approach might add to the competitive advantage of the organization. A firm that believes that the way it has organized its HRM generates competitive advantage and believes in the feasibility of transfer is likely to be willing to standardize across borders (Dickmann 2003). For instance, Beechler and Yang (1994) found that Japanese MNCs transferred many of their HR approaches to their US subsidiaries, such as teamwork, cooperative labour relations, job flexibility and intensive training. They did so as they believed that it was a good way to manufacture high-quality products with zero defects – one of their perceived competitive advantages.

A fourth reason to have a high degree of standardization depends on the interdependence levels of head office and local operating unit(s). The more the country-of-origin unit depends on local operating units – e.g. for their raw materials – the higher the need for control (Rosenzweig and Nohria 1994; Rosenzweig 2006). In turn, the more the local operating unit is dependent on other parts of the organization (for instance, for production supplies or technology), the more likely it is that the head office will attempt to standardize strategies, policies and practices. One reason is that control and coordination becomes easier with higher levels of standardization (Edström and Galbraith 1977), another is that the higher familiarity of the approaches might make them more appealing to head office managers (Perlmutter 1969).

Finally, a fifth motive for standardization is the perceived need to facilitate flows of information and knowledge among MNCs' different units. One of the positive effects is that this gives a clearer orientation across borders. Further, Bonache and Dickmann (2008) describe how all parts of a globally operating corporation can be the prime location and origin of innovations and expertise. If the different parts of an MNC are managed in a similar vein and according to the same principles and processes, the cross-border diffusion and application of ideas and capabilities is easier.

Using the terminology employed by Bartlett and Ghoshal, Dickmann and Müller-Camen (2006) maintain that high HR standardization refers to 'global' HRM characterized by highly integrated IHRM strategies, policies and practices. In turn, 'multidomestic' HRM is characterized by locally developed and implemented HR strategies, principles and practices. Overall, these result in low cross-border standardization and often a 'not invented here' syndrome.

Knowledge networking and four configurations of SIHRM

The authors go on to suggest a second dimension which they call knowledge networking. Knowledge networking captures a large range of internal communication and coordination mechanisms aimed at creating approaches with common principles on a meta-level and HR policies and practices that are operationally integrated (Dickmann et al. 2009). Overall, a high degree of knowledge networking aims at creating an innovative HR organization that has its strengths in the exploration, transfer and exploitation of people management ideas and that facilitates cross-border exchanges of learning and experiences.

Dickmann and Müller-Camen (2006) have identified four key international configurations along the two dimensions of standardization and knowledge networking. These are the multidomestic, global, cognofederate and the transnational firms.

The *multidomestic* firm has low standardization and low knowledge flows. Country managers would be the most important managers in the system of relatively autonomously operating local affiliates. Knowledge management would be predominantly local so that local responsiveness and innovation happens but is unlikely to be rolled out internationally. In essence, management might have a polycentric mindset, believing that learning cannot be transferred nor is it valuable to transfer across national borders (Perlmutter 1969).

The *global* company has high standardization with moderate knowledge flows. Most of the knowledge flows originate in the head office and unidirectional communication is being used. While the standards and processes are being set in the corporate centre, reporting of data (but few new ideas) is being expected from the local subsidiary. Business managers have a key role in this configuration and are aiming for increased worldwide efficiency. In Perlmutter's terms this is an ethnocentric approach that assumes that one size fits all, i.e. that the business model of the country of origin/head office can be implemented worldwide. This configuration is often seen as especially efficient and geared to the diffusion and exploitation of head office innovation, knowledge and capabilities (Bartlett and Ghoshal 1989; Dickmann and Müller-Camen 2006).

Some companies work hard to optimize their approaches to the many dualities and tensions that cross-border operations entail. They strive to be simultaneously integrated and differentiated. Sophisticated communication and coordination is necessary to identify the internal and external circumstances in which IHRM standardization is desirable and possible. Conversely, they need to create a flexible approach in circumstances in which responsiveness to the local context is necessary. Beyond the two types of IHRM outlined above, which have a decidedly strong approach to either local responsiveness or global integration, there exist two other configurations. These are distinguished by their higher degrees of knowledge networking.

The *cognofederate* organization has moderate levels of standardization with high knowledge flows. While new ideas originate from all parts of the loosely connected corporate network, there is no strong power centre and the assumption is not that standardization for efficiency gains is an overriding goal. Dickmann (1999) quotes one board member of Adhesives who pointed out that 'we are not the Vatican'. Country managers, and to a reasonable extent functional managers, are key executives in this configuration.

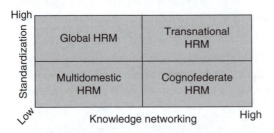

Figure 2.3 Four IHRM configurations
Source: Adapted from Dickmann and Müller-Camen (2006)

The *transnational* enterprise has high levels of standardization and knowledge networking in its quest to be simultaneously responsive, efficient and innovative on a worldwide scale. Knowledge creation and exploitation originates from all parts of this highly interactive network of organizational units. There is no overwhelming centre of power but cohesion is facilitated through strong and shared cultural norms and values. The dispersed operating (e.g. in centres of excellence) corporate managers have the key role in sustaining this flexible organization and to foster, coach and support talented individuals who can manage the dynamic tensions associated with the transnational.

Case study 2.1 Standardization and knowledge networking in Adhesives

History

Adhesives was founded in 1876. The first important products were detergents. From 1923, adhesives were produced followed by fat-chemical products in 1945 and three years later by cosmetics and body care products. Currently it has several thousand products sold around the world with a particular focus on European markets.

In 1913, its first foreign subsidiary was established near Basel in Switzerland. The firm's early international expansion continued in the 1930s, in that branches in seven European countries were opened in order to support exports. In the 1950s, production plants were founded in Austria, Italy, France, Turkey, Brazil and South Africa, while a branch was established in Japan. In 1960, the firm had 20,000 employees (3,300 abroad) and in 1970, 30,000 (7,500 abroad). During the 1970s and 1980s, the expansion continued and production was increasingly located abroad. Thus, in 1989, the concern employed 38,000 staff, out of which the majority (21,000) was located outside Germany. At the beginning of the twenty-first century the group had two-thirds of foreign staff.

Given a history of many international acquisitions, the company uses a pragmatic balance of global integration and local responsiveness in production. While the size of local operations may present an incentive to standardize HR policies and practices internationally, the growth pattern by acquisition may present a substantial barrier due to existing local patterns and cultural norms. This diverse administrative heritage, however, may increase the benefits of international knowledge networking and can, therefore, be beneficial for innovation.

Standardization and knowledge networking within IHRM

The employee structure at Adhesives is highly international. Adhesives' personnel management combines a pragmatic use of local advantages and a German approach. In an interview with one of the authors, the then board member for HR, summarized the general intent of strategic standardization of Adhesives' IHRM as 'we want to harmonize the philosophy but the method is determined locally' (interview notes). Thus, international leadership guidelines were developed in an international forum involving all European HR heads. Beyond international coordination of principles and objectives, however, Adhesives selected only a few specific operational areas for intensive international cooperation (see Table 2.1). Overall, standardization depended on the perceived importance of the area, its contribution to the company's success and the determination of the head office in Düsseldorf to integrate policies (interview notes). Local exceptions and idiosyncratic approaches, however, were possible.

Table 2.1 IHRM configuration in Adhesives

	Meta level	**Operational level**
Standardization		
General HRM	*Leadership*: international principles and guidelines *Security*: guidelines related to healthy work environment; job security through standard work contracts *Other – innovation*: principle of international cooperation to elicit best ideas and learning	Competency framework
Recruitment & selection	Search for global best talent	R&S essentially local, using diverse criteria
Training & development	Commitment to the development of staff, preference for dual vocational training to be used in local operations	Some cross-cultural seminars and top management development integrated, dual vocational training not implemented everywhere
Career management	International equality of career prospects; International Assignment policy	Integrated approach for upper/middle management (highest four levels); database of high potentials (some local units opted out)

Performance management	International principles and guidelines	Standard processes and forms for top four management levels (management review and target dialogue) *developed in Germany*
Remuneration	Comparability of task and performance-related compensation	Integration around Hay for upper five levels, lower management local; some local variation possible

Knowledge networking

General HRM	Development and review: concurrent international development of HR principles, multinational development of HR strategy, feedback on implementation from local units Control and coordination: little international coordination budgets; no local HR budgets set or reviewed in headquarters; only basic local reporting of results (e.g. headcounts); 1 global meeting, bi-national monthly regional meetings, frequent visits	Explicit feedback in European HR director committee on overarching systems and instruments every two months. Global competency framework designed in international (European) cooperation. High frequency of international HR meetings and visits
Recruitment & selection	International discussion of long-term international resourcing needs; no global committee (other than for board members)	International discussion of diverse selection instruments
Training & development	Cross-nationally coordinated long-range aims for future leaders developed; cultural cornerstones defined	Head office design and international review of some international management seminars; a few have explicit cultural aims
Career management	Top career deciders drawn from headquarters; career principles	Some cross-border exchange of data

	sometimes formally discussed in European Head of HR Group	on high potentials; coordinated through more than 1% of staff abroad on IAs
Performance management	General international performance management principles discussed cross-border	No international review of performance carried out
Remuneration	Headquarters HR management set guidelines	Central remuneration committee reviews rewards, formal cross-border discussion of experiences

Sources: reworked, based on Dickmann (1999); Dickmann and Müller-Camen (2006); Dickmann et al. (2009)

Knowledge networking

Adhesives' international knowledge networking could be characterized by tight consultation and cooperation between HQ and subsidiaries. In addition to a yearly 'Summit' meeting of general management, all top European HR executives met six times a year in the Personnel Advisory Group Europe (PAGE). These meetings were predominantly used to exchange ideas internationally and to discuss processes in areas that might be coordinated. The direction of knowledge exchange was often multilateral and ideas were derived from many parts of the network. On the downside, we may expect that high costs of information exchange with little standardized organizational or HRM operational approaches could be ineffective.

The intensive international communication meant that it might become ever harder to press the head office view against joint resistance. Meanwhile, a senior HR executive in Germany claimed that there was no intention to be the 'Vatican' and to determine policies despite resistance of subsidiaries. Therefore, higher knowledge networking did not mean that internal corporate control became easier or more efficient. The high autonomy of subsidiaries may have meant that only very global formal controls could be used – this created the need to introduce more informal, sophisticated integration mechanisms.

Overall, intensive knowledge networking with flexible standardization theoretically combines innovativeness, efficiency and local responsiveness so that few HR dysfunctionalities may be expected.

Case questions

1 Why do you think Adhesives used the specific standardization and knowledge networking approach in IHRM?
2 Considering a multinational company that you are familiar with: how does its IHRM differ?
3 What other possibilities did Adhesives or your example have? What are the advantages and disadvantages associated with these?
4 What are the possible effects on global careers for an HR professional? How could one balance the possible dysfunctional career effects?

Career implications of the IHRM configurations

The career implications associated with each of the four IHRM configurations are relatively neglected in the literature. Below, we develop a schematic overview of careers in the context of specific SIHRM configurations. Later chapters in this book will add significant detail to the overview descriptions.

Global careers in multidomestic firms are infrequent due to the importance of the understanding and management of the local context. The low degree of standardization and knowledge networking means that people who do work abroad for a multidomestic organization not only have to learn to adapt to national cultures and environments, but are also confronted with radically different organizational patterns. While certain meta-level visions, missions, strategies or understanding of quality and professionalism might be integrated across borders to some extent, the way these are 'lived' locally will vary. Whereas it is difficult to find totally multidomestic organizations, some moderately multidomestic firms are within the professional service sector (some accounting companies, law firms). These might have a core of high potentials which might be working abroad – often on international projects for large clients – but many managerial careers are typically national.

In extrema, working in a multidomestic organization means that the highest local positions are often 'reserved' for local professionals (sometimes these have been inpatriates to the head office for some time to create networks and trust). Almost all training and development is locally developed and delivered, recruitment, selection, compensation, employee communication and performance management will be highly local. In effect, a national 'glass ceiling' for careers exists and the strength of an organization lies in its responsiveness to the domestic context and local innovation. Potential disadvantages are associated with not using scale effects, such as the duplication of effort (e.g. in the design and maintenance of managerial approaches) and the diffusion and exploitation of ideas across borders. Because many companies learn over time from their international experiences, it often seems the case that firms become more moderately multidomestic over time (Dickmann and Müller-Camen 2006). This development also results in more cross-border careers for successful managers and other

Table 2.2 Characteristics of global careers in four configurations

	Multidomestic	Cognofederate	Global	Transnational
Cross-border careers are . . .	Infrequent	Moderately frequent	Frequent	Frequent
Typical Managerial career paths are	National	National	International (Mostly country-of-origin staff)	International (all managerial staff)
Key barriers are . . .	Highest local position for HCNs: 'glass ceiling' for non-country of origin managers to progress beyond national posts; predominantly local rather than international training, development or networks	Mixture of best position for HCNs and 'Best Persons': no significant barriers but due to high local power tendency to select local managers	Highest positions for PCNs: 'glass ceiling' for most non-country of origin managers to progress to high position locally or globally, high standardization might mean tensions and locally inadequate policies, processes and behaviour prescribed	Best Person for highest positions: no significant barriers
Key enablers are . . .	Knowledge of local business and culture, locally adequate business and communication skills, local networks	Knowledge of local business skills and capability, flexibility, tolerance for ambiguity and listening skills, diplomacy, local and international networks	Parent-country and global business understanding, business, communication and influencing skills, parent-country networks	Knowledge and understanding of global and local business, highly developed cultural sensitivity, learning orientation, interpersonal skills, flexibility and openness, diplomacy and influencing skills, parent, diverse local and global networks

specialists. Table 2.2 outlines the characteristics of global careers in the four organizational types.

The cognofederate enterprise combines low standardization with high knowledge networking. The Adhesives case displays many of these attributes. Cross-border careers are moderately frequent. Key reasons for these might be related to individual development and the exploration of new ideas. While this type of organization aims to facilitate learning, it might feel that innovation would be stifled if the head office exercises too much power and influence in local matters. Essentially, it is a fairly democratic form of international management in which only key issues – either defined by the head office or supra-national decision committees – are likely to be standardized. Because much power resides locally, the foreign operating units often have the right to veto or reject ideas for international integration with the argument that these approaches might not work in their domestic market context. Popular arguments for non-standardization relate to local culture, national regulations, broader societal patterns, the domestic educational context or the specific sub-culture of the operating unit.

In essence, typical managerial career paths are national in a cognofederate enterprise. However, in comparison to multidomestic firms, the chances of non-home country nationals (HCNs) gaining positions abroad are higher. This would often be due to a perception of superior knowledge and skills in those areas where these are also applicable in their host country. Some of the attributes that would further an international career in a cognofederate organization relate to having knowledge of local business and demanded capabilities, a high degree of individual flexibility, tolerance for ambiguity, well-developed listening skills, diplomacy and social capital that is both international and local. Nevertheless, because power is highly local, there is a tendency for local managers with their superior understanding of the context, their existing social networks and their proven ability to operate successfully in the local environment to be selected and promoted to high-ranking posts.

The next two organizational configurations have a higher degree of standardization. Many companies – often US firms such as Procter & Gamble, Hewlett Packard or General Electric – have adopted a global style of management and IHRM. The high standardization means that many of the ideas and approaches developed in the country of origin will be deployed around the world. Cross-border careers are frequent, especially from home-country nationals who know the firm's strategies and operations well and are highly regarded and trusted in the head office. While the worldwide standardization allows the use of scale and scope efficiencies and the transfer and exploitation of centrally developed ideas, it runs the risk of being locally unresponsive and not being sensitive enough to pick up some of the useful ideas that might emerge in local operations.

While international careers in global organizations are frequent, they tend to be primarily the domain of parent-country nationals who often have worked in corporate head offices. Because these individuals are familiar with the operational necessities and are trusted to not simply control foreign operations but also to teach the parent-country approach and to instil/create and manage a local culture that is akin to that of the head office these expatriates have a strong coordination function. Useful attributes for these global careerists include global business understanding, communication and influencing skills and good parent-country networks. In extreme cases a 'glass ceiling' for local managers means that many of the key functions are being staffed by parent-country expatriates. The resulting high standardization might mean that locally inadequate policies, processes and behaviours are fostered. Mistrust and tensions between locals and foreigners might result (Hailey and Harry 2008).

The last configuration is that of a transnational. Cross-border careers in the transnational organization are frequent (compare Baruch and Altman (2002)). Typical managerial career paths are international – be that through expatriation, the participation in cross-national project groups, being a global manager who travels extensively abroad etc. – due to the high need for international communication, sense-making and knowledge exchange. The network of interdependent organizational units which is seen to have similar powers is characterized by high innovation and many, dispersed centres of excellence. One potential drawback in the search for common approaches is that the communication efforts – incurring costs in terms of time, investment in technology and other opportunity costs – are highly resource-intensive. Thus, this configuration is especially useful in industries with high needs for frequent or substantial innovative leaps. Knowledge- and network-intensive sectors such as management consulting or investment banking as well as R&D departments within large corporations – e.g. in the pharma, IT or engineering sectors – might benefit substantially from adopting relatively high degrees of standardization and knowledge networking simultaneously.

In this 'ideal' form (Bartlett and Ghoshal 1998) there are no significant company barriers to international careers other than those that might be located in the personal attributes, social capital or motivational and effort patterns of individuals. The best person is meant to be selected for vacant positions irrespective of country of origin, gender, race, age or other diversity issues. Attributes that would further an international career include the knowledge and understanding of global and diverse local businesses (inside the own company and externally), a strong learning orientation, highly developed cultural sensitivity, flexibility and openness, diplomacy and influencing skills and a large range of networks spanning local and global operating units. The list could go on: the core of the capabilities relate to success factors that make individuals innovative and effective in diverse and dynamic environments.

Summary and learning points

This chapter has explored SIHRM considerations. It has charted the historical development of international organizations and outlined the global competitive context. Thus, issues of the global–local dilemma and how to overcome the resulting tensions were discussed. We presented ideas about how to be successful in a globalized world and outlined the need to be worldwide innovative, locally responsive and internationally efficient. Illustrating and further developing these ideas, the chapter explored frameworks of SIHRM, presented an in-depth case study of IHRM in Adhesives and outlined some theoretical implications for global careers.

Key learning points include:

- The historical roots of organizing for international operations and the attempts to manage some of the challenges of cross-border activities go back far in time. While the Assyrian commercial organizations had foreign workers, defined hierarchies, activities in many geographical regions and goals to search for new markets and resources, the great trading companies of the pre-industrial age had developed some management policies and practices similar to those that are still employed today.
- Problems of communication and learning, international integration, control and coordination have been seen as challenges for many years and managerial attempts to deal with these have evolved over recent centuries.
- A range of corporate choices to overcome these challenges has been proposed by several authors. Heenan and Perlmutter suggest a concept that is based on management mindsets, market conditions and regions. Bartlett and Ghoshal suggest that firms strive to achieve either a mixture of local responsiveness, global efficiency or worldwide innovativeness, or all of these simultaneously, to compete successfully in diverse markets around the world.
- To become Bartlett and Ghoshal's ideal configuration, transnational companies need to create highly flexible, interlinked organizational units that are shaped by many centres of excellence and a highly equal – but not completely equal – distribution of power. To avoid some of the dysfunctional effects of not having a strong corporate centre, the role of organizational culture becomes crucial. Stringent control and coordination mechanisms as well as sophisticated HRM are important to create a transnational organization.
- Depictions of SIHRM show the links to the organizational context, business strategy, HRM consistency of principles, policies and practices and a range of other factors. De Cieri and Dowling's framework outlines clearly the external and internal factors that have an impact on SIHRM and demonstrate the complexity of global manpower management. Universalist, institutionalist, cultural and other influences are important in shaping an organization's IHRM.
- Dickmann and Müller-Camen apply Bartlett and Ghoshal's ideas to the realm of IHRM and develop a framework. Depending on the degree of standardization and knowledge networking, global, multidomestic, cognofederate and transnational HRM configurations exist. Each of these is associated with a set of advantages and potential drawbacks. A case study of a cognofederate organization is presented to illustrate some of the considerations and design approaches that are being used in industry.
- Broad career implications of each of these configurations are outlined and discussed. These include the set of capabilities that are most valuable in each of these international types and the existence of potential barriers.

References

Adler, N.J. and Ghadar, F. (1990) 'Strategic human resource management: a global perspective', in R. Pieper *Human Resource Management: An International Comparison*, New York: de Gruyter.

Baruch, Y. and Altman, Y. (2002) 'Expatriation and repatriation in MNCs: a taxonomy', *Human Resource Management*, 42(2): 239–259.

Bartlett, C. and Ghoshal, S. (1989, 2nd edn 1998) *Managing across Borders*, London: Hutchinson Business.

Beechler, S. and Yang, J.Z. (1994) 'The transfer of Japanese-style management to American subsidiaries: contingencies, constraints, and competencies', *Journal of International Business Studies*, 25(3): 467–491.

Beer, M., Spector, B., Lawrence, P., Mills, D. and Walton, R. (1985) *Human Resource Management: A General Manager's Perspective*, New York: Free Press.

Birkinshaw, J., Nobel, R. and Ridderstråle, J. (2002) 'Knowledge as a contingency variable: do the characteristics of knowledge predict organization structure?', *Organization Science*, 13(3): 274–289.

Bonache, J. and Brewster, C. (2001) 'Knowledge transfer and the management of expatriation', *Thunderbird International Business Review*, 43(1): 145–168.

Bonache, J. and Dickmann, M. (2008) 'Transfer of strategic HR know-how in MNCs: mechanisms, barriers and initiatives', in M. Dickmann, C. Brewster and P. Sparrow (eds) *International Human Resource Management: A European Perspective*, London: Routledge.

Bonache, J. and Zárraga-Oberty, C. (2008) 'Determinants of the success of international assignees as knowledge transferors: a theoretical framework', *International Journal of Human Resource Management*, 19(1): 1–18.

Buckley, P.J. (1995) *Foreign Direct Investment and Multinational Enterprises*, Ipswich: Ipswich Book Company.

Carlos, A. and Nicholas, S. (1988) 'Giants of an earlier capitalism: the chartered trading companies as modern multinationals', *Business History Review*, 62: 398–419.

Chandler, A. (1962) *Strategy and Structure: Chapters in the History of American Industrial Enterprise*, Cambridge, MA: MIT Press.

Coriat, B. (1997) 'Globalisation, variety and mass production: the metamorphosis of mass production in the new competitive age', in J. Rogers Hollingsworth and R. Boyer (eds) *Contemporary Capitalism: The Embeddedness of Institutions*, Cambridge: Cambridge University Press.

De Cieri, H. and Dowling, P. (1999) 'Strategic human resource management in multinational enterprises: theoretical and empirical developments', in P.M. Wright, L.D. Dyer and J.W. Boudreau (eds) *Research in Personnel and Human Resource Management: Strategic Human Resources in the Twenty-First Century, 4th Supplement*, Stamford, CT: JAI Press.

Dedoussis, V. (1995) 'Simply a question of cultural barriers? The search for new perspectives in the transfer of Japanese management practices', *Journal of Management Studies*, 32(6): 731–745.

Denison, D.R. (1990) *Corporate Culture and Organizational Effectiveness*, New York: Wiley.

Dickmann, M. (1999) 'Balancing global, parent and local influences: international human resource management of German multinational companies', unpublished thesis, University of London, Birkbeck College.

Dickmann, M. (2003) 'Implementing German HRM abroad: desired, feasible, successful?', *International Journal of Human Resource Management*, 14(2): 265–284.

Dickmann, M. and Müller-Camen, M. (2006) 'A typology of international human resource management strategies and processes', *International Journal of Human Resource Management*, 17(4): 580–601.

Dickmann, M., Müller-Camen, M. and Kelliher, C. (2009) 'Striving for transnational human resource management – principles and practice', *Personnel Review*, 38(1): 5–25.

Edström, A. and Galbraith, J. (1977) 'Transfer of managers as a coordination and control strategy in multinational organizations', *Administrative Science Quarterly*, 22: 248–263.

Edwards, T. and Ferner, A. (2004) 'Multinationals, reverse diffusion and national business systems', *Management International Review*, 44(1): 49–79.

Edwards, T., Colling, T. and Ferner, A. (2004)'Comparative institutional analysis and the diffusion of employment practices in multinational companies', paper presented at *Multinationals and the International Diffusion of Organizational Forms and Practices* Conference, Barcelona, Spain, 2004.

Evans, P. and Lorange, P. (1989) 'The two logics behind human resource management', in P. Evans, Y. Doz and A. Laurent (eds) *Human Resource Management in International Firms: Change, Globalization, Innovation*, Basingstoke: Macmillan.

Evans, P., Lank, E. and Farquhar, A. (1989) 'Managing human resources in the international firm: lessons from practice', in P. Evans, Y. Doz and A. Laurent (eds) *Human Resource Management in International Firms: Change, Globalization, Innovation*, Basingstoke: Macmillan.

Evans, P., Pucik, V. and Barsoux, J.-L. (2002) *The Global Challenge: Frameworks for International Human Resource Management*, New York: McGraw-Hill.

Ferner, A. (2000) 'The underpinnings of "bureaucratic" control systems', *Journal of Management Studies*, 37(4): 521–539.

Ferner, A. and Quintanilla, J. (1998) 'Multinationals, national business systems and HRM: the enduring influence of national identity or a process of "Anglo-Saxonization"', *International Journal of Human Resource Management*, 9(4): 710–731.

Ferner, A., Almond, P. and Colling, T. (2005) 'Institutional theory and the cross-national transfer of employment policy: the case of "workforce diversity" in US multinationals', *Journal of International Business Studies*, 36: 304–321.

Fombrun, C., Tichy, N. and Devanna, M. (1984) *Strategic Human Resource Management*, New York: Wiley.

Jones, G. (1996) *The Evolution of International Business*, London: Routledge.

Hailey, J. and Harry, W. (2008) 'Localization: a strategic response to globalization', in M. Dickmann, C. Brewster and P. Sparrow (eds) *International Human Resource Management: A European Perspective*, London: Routledge.

Harzing, A.-W. (2000) 'An empirical analysis and extension of the Bartlett and Ghoshal typology of multinational companies', *Journal of International Business Studies*, 31(1): 101–120.

Hedlund, G. (1994) 'A model of knowledge management and the n-form corporation', *Strategic Management Journal*, 15(S2): 73–90.

Heenan, D.A. and Perlmutter, H.V. (1979) *Multinational Organizational Development*, Reading, MA: Addison-Wesley.

Hu, Y.-S. (1992) 'Global or stateless corporations are national firms with international operations', *California Management Review*, 34: 107–126.

Inkpen, A. and Beamish, P. (1997) 'Knowledge, bargaining power, and the instability of international joint ventures', *Academy of Management Review*, 22(1): 177–202.

Lane, C. (1989) *Management and Labour in Europe: The Industrial Enterprise in Germany, Britain and France*, Worcester: Billings and Sons.

Lane, C. (1992) 'European business systems: Britain and Germany compared', in R. Whitley (ed.) *European Business Systems: Firms and Markets in their National Contexts*, London: Sage.

Lawler, J., Zaidi, M. and Atmiyanandana, V. (1989) 'Human resource strategies in southeast Asia: the case of Thailand', in B.B. Shaw, A. Nedd, G.R. Ferris and K.M. Rowland (eds) *Research in Personnel and Human Resources Management* Suppl. 1, Greenwich, CT: JAI Press.

Martinez, J. and Jarillo, J.C. (1991) 'Co-ordination demands of international strategies', *Journal of International Business Studies*, 22(3): 429–444.

Moore, K. and Lewis, D. (1999) *Birth of the Multinational*, Copenhagen: Copenhagen Business Press.

Müller, M. (1998) 'Human resource and industrial relations practices of UK and US multinationals in Germany', *International Journal of Human Resource Management*, 9(4): 732–749.

Ohmae, K. (1990) *The Borderless World: Power and Strategy in the Interlinked Economy*, London: Collins.

Parry, E., Dickmann, M. and Morley, M. (2008) 'North American MNCs and their HR policies in liberal and coordinated market economies', *International Journal of Human Resource Management*, 19(11): 2024–2040.

Perlmutter, H. (1969) 'The tortuous evolution of the multinational corporation', *Columbia Journal of World Business*, 4(1): 9–18.

Porter, M.E. (1985) *Competitive Advantage*, New York: Free Press.

Porter, M.E. (1990) *The Competitive Advantage of Nations*, London: Macmillan.

Prahalad, C. and Doz, Y. (1987) *The Multinational Mission*, New York: The Free Press.

Pucik, V. (1992) 'Globalization and human resource management', in V. Pucik, N.M. Tichy and C.K. Barnett (eds) *Globalizing Management: Creating and Leading the Competitive Organization*, New York: John Wiley and Sons.

Räsanen, K. and Whipp, R. (1992) 'National business recipes: a sector perspective', in R. Whitley (ed.) *European Business Systems: Firms and Markets in their National Contexts*, London: Sage.

Rosenzweig, S. (2006) 'The dual logics behind international human resource management: pressures for global integration and local responsiveness', in G. Stahl and I. Björkman (eds) *Handbook of Research in International Human Resource Management*, Cheltenham: Edward Elgar.

Rosenzweig, P.M. and Nohria, N. (1994) 'Influences on human resource management practices in multinational corporations', *Journal of International Business Studies*, 25(2): 229–251.

Rugman, A. (1998) *Multinationals as regional flagships*, Financial Times: Mastering Global Business: London.

Schein, E.H. (1992) *Organizational Culture and Leadership*, San Francisco, CA: Jossey-Bass.

Schuler, R., Dowling, P. and De Cieri, H. (1993) 'An integrative framework of strategic international human resource management', *International Journal of Human Resource Management*, 4(4): 717–764.

Sonnenfeld, J.A. and Peiperl, M.A. (1988) 'Staffing policy as a strategic response: a typology of career systems', *Academy of Management Review*, 13(4): 588–600.

Yang, J.Z. (1992) 'Americanization or Japanization of human resource management policies', *Advances in International Comparative Management*, 7: 77–115.

Whitley, R. (1992) 'Societies, firms and markets: the social structuring of business systems', in R. Whitley (ed.) *European Business Systems: Firms and Markets in Their National Contexts*, London: Sage.

Wilkinson, B. and Oliver, N. (1992) 'Human resource management in Japanese manufacturing companies in the UK and USA', in B. Towers (ed.) *The Handbook of Human Resource Management (Human Resource Management in Action)*, London: Routledge.

Managing careers: individual and organizational perspectives

Objectives

This chapter:

- provides an overview of individual career theories;
- covers theories at the organizational level;
- explores societal level implications of global careers;
- identifies career practices and their relevance for the management of a global workforce;
- presents an integrative framework for the career practices.

Introduction

There is nothing more practical than a good theory – so said the eminent thinker, Kurt Lewin, and we fully endorse this notion. We begin the global careers journey with a presentation of career theories. In particular we aim to focus on their relevance to careers that are not locally bounded.

The framework bears in mind the connection between individual inputs, the workplace and work environment, and the wider society. Among the career theories we cover are theories of career choice and contemporary career views.

We then present an organizational perspective, mostly related to the need to expatriate and repatriate employees in order to manage different operations in various locations. Different strategies can be employed by different firms, and these HR strategies might be related to the overall business strategy.

The following and largest section of the chapter is devoted specifically to a variety of career practices and we will point out their relevance to global career

Figure 3.1 A framework of global careers: organizational and individual perspectives

management. We end with an integrative perspective of the way career practices may be operationalized by organizations.

Career theories

One of the advantages of the field of career studies is its wide scope, building on a variety of theoretical perspectives. In a twisted way, this wide perspective and multiplicity of theories is also the root for an apparent weakness of the field, due to a possible lack of coherence. In this section we cover the major career theories within a global context.

In their *Handbook of Career Theory*, Arthur et al. (1989) have pointed out that the theory of a career is not under the cover of any one theoretical or disciplinary view. They presented eight viewpoints of theoretical career concepts: psychology, social psychology, sociology, anthropology, economics, political science, history and geography. Most of these fields are within the boundaries of behavioural and social sciences. Other attempts have been made to enrich career studies by employing alternative theoretical perspectives, such as the utilization of new science (Bird et al. 2002; Parker and Arthur 2002). Chaos theory (Glieck 1988) has also been proven to serve well in this direction, for both general HRM (Bailyn 1993) and specifically for careers (Pryor and Bright 2003). Yet, the two leading theoretical perspectives lenses for studying careers are psychology and sociology.

Origin of career theories and the global aspect

Careers develop within the interplay that takes place between the three major 'participants' – individual, work institutions and the whole society.

Career theories build on the interaction between the individual and nature of the world of work and organizations within the society. As such, management and behavioural sciences theorists paved the way to career theories by delineating the nature of work and organization in the era that followed the Industrial Revolution and beyond. This makes it strong ground for Moore et al. (2008) to posit that early career theories indirectly build on the theories and ideas of Durkheim (1933) and Weber (1965). Durkheim focused on the nature of the relationship between the individual and societal structure. The industrialization of society had implications for the role of work in people's life. For Weber, bureaucracy developed alongside the process of industrialization, creating occupational groups and organizational structures, which served as the anchors for career development and progress, though career paths were articulated only later. These theories were universalistic, and did not distinguish between local or global careers.

In his pioneering work on careers, Hughes (1928, 1937), perhaps the first career theorist, focused on structural factors and forces that constrained and shaped human behaviour within the labour market, at the time, mostly within a single organization. Institutions provide the framework, the regulatory, even the moral ground for work, hence careers. Studying careers from the sociological perspective is later to be found implicitly in the work of Giddens (e.g. Giddens 1971, 1997). Organizations are institutional inventions, using multiple resources, but of these, the human resource is at the centre of career studies. According to Hughes, the division of labour has strong implications to the make-up of society and the individual psychological being. This way, for example, people develop an identity that relates to and reflects both their occupation and institution affiliation.

Hughes also pointed out the distinction between an objective and a subjective career, later described in a number of studies and works (Barley 1989; Baruch 2004a: 76–78). Mitchell et al. (1979), in their Social Learning theory have explicated the differences between the two. Social learning, by its nature, takes into

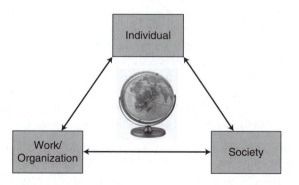

Figure 3.2 Career theory: the participants in the system

account global impacts on careers. The nature of learning varies across cultures, in association with cultural variation across nations (Hofstede 1980).

Hughes' Chicago School of Sociology studied the life histories of local communities, aiming to understand how people construed their lives, in particular for our context, their working lives. Using the term career, these studies refer to a heuristic concept, applicable to a wider range of situations than contemporary usage in management circles would imply. Later, the concept of careers was restricted to the organizational domain, but contemporary contributions return to the original wider framework of life scope, not just organizational and professional life (Hall and Mirvis 1995; Baruch 2004b).

Khapova et al. (2007: 119) summarized the way major career theories originated in psychology, social-psychology and sociology and correspond with the duality of objective vs. subjective careers, time perspective, and the multidimensionality of careers. These issues were all crucial elements in career theories, whatever the theoretical underpinning from which they emerged.

Most of the theories were developed in the USA, without significant attention to their global compatibility or making the assumption that they fit across cultures. A number of studies have focused on testing similarities and differences across cultures for these concepts, and evaluating the validity of career theories beyond national boundaries.

Career theory – individual perspective within global context

Naturally, this theoretical stream of individual career perspective builds mostly on psychology, and is led by psychology scholars. Two major streams are career choice and career stages. For the most part, the prominence and relevance of these theories remain in place for both the local and global context.

Career choice

Some careers are prone to being global, or at least to have a global dimension, either as a mainstream or as an optional path. The extreme case of a full or total global career is probably that of a diplomat. People who aim to work for the Foreign Office, e.g. to be future diplomats are aware that this choice, if successful, will generate a career that spans across a number of borders. Similarly, when opting to work for an MNC, employees are aware of, and may aspire to, a global career trajectory, which could involve one or more expatriation periods. In many others, often smaller, organizations this is a more remote option. In many local organizations – e.g. small shops, local law firms, local government centres – a global career in the traditional sense of working abroad is just not relevant.

The global aspect adds a new dimension to most career theories. For example, Holland's RIASEC model (1958, 1959) identifies people's vocational or occupational preferences, and helps also in determining a fit between a person choice and organizational characteristics (sometimes even team characteristics) that can be expressed in similar terms. RIASEC stands for *Realistic, Investigative, Artistic, Social, Enterprising* and *Conventional*. These types refer to six categories of people and six models of occupational environments. Yet, none of these relates to a global option. This might mean that occupational inclinations are separated from the question of global or local. Nevertheless, congruence of person–environment has been the subject of much research, and proven to be of essence for success. Person–environment fit is a fundamental issue in the behavioural sciences, though its prescription cannot be accurate. At the individual person level, some people would be more inclined to have a global mindset (Baruch 2002).

The choice of occupation would determine the propensity for a future global career. Some jobs are transferable across cultures, others less so. Even occupations that are fairly global might require people to overcome a number of regulatory hurdles before they can consider a global move (e.g. practising medicine or law would require such a procedure).

The boundaryless career

Ashkenas et al. (1995) wrote about the diminishing traditional boundaries within organizations. They argued that organizations go through fast changes and become boundaryless. They suggested the following four aspects to demonstrate the breaking of the chains of organizational structure: vertical, horizontal, external and geographical.

Geographical boundarylessness means that, for many organizations, operations take place in many locations, even to the point that sometimes one cannot spot a specific location. The virtual organization is an extreme case, where the location has no impact (apart from the time of day or night which for some can be morning and for others can be evening). Many other types of operation are not restricted to a specific place.

The migration of talented youth from developing to advanced countries has traditionally been seen as a brain drain (see Tung and Lazarova 2006, who contrast brain drain with brain gain), which exacerbates international inequality by enriching already wealthy economies at the expense of their poor counterparts. The phenomenon of brain drain has gained much attention in recent decades. The increased interest in the topic can be due to rapid globalization, and a host of political, economical, sociological, and technological factors (Baruch et al. 2007). Its scope is growing steadily (e.g. Carrington and Detragiache 1999; Mahroum 2000). Most of the national-level brain drain occurs when highly educated or skilled people move from developing countries to developed countries, and the typical case is moving from Asia or Africa to North America and Europe (Creehan 2001; van Rooyen 2001; Crush 2002; Altbach and Bassett 2004).

The intelligent career framework

Career communities are member-defined communities from which people draw career support (Parker and Arthur 2000: 105). They are different from configurations of personal networks, as they are self-defined, self-organized, informal entities for engagement in certain practices, creating a sense of belonging and identity. Taking the case of expatriates, the community can be of the local group of expatriates living in the 'enclave' in a Gulf state, which may be from several firms; or a collection of families from a certain country, living in a similar quarter of London or Paris. The connection to such communities is largely about generating the social career capital (part of the three components of the intelligent career (or 'career capital') of Arthur et al. (1995), the knowing-why, knowing-how, and knowing-whom). The knowing-why, in terms of career progress and generating new future opportunity can be self-evident in the case of a global career move, yet such a move contains a high level of risk. The knowing-how should be there, as it is difficult to go to a new environment without basic knowledge of how to perform. The knowing-whom is challenging, as existing networks often cease to be relevant, and much needs to be re-established in the new environment.

Brain gain, brain drain

Many developed countries benefit immensely from the influx of a talented, motivated workforce. The high-tech industry in countries such as the USA and the EU requires human capital input, and thus has greatly benefited from foreign incoming competence, including talented immigrants from developing countries. Some came to wealthy Western countries with the initial plan of tertiary education, but then opted to stay put (Baruch et al. 2007). More than half of Silicon Valley's scientists and engineers are foreign-born, primarily in Asia, and only a small proportion planned to return home (Saxenian 2006). One change which Saxenian envisaged was that highly skilled emigrants can transform the brain drain into brain circulation by returning home to generate new start-ups, collaborate with existing businesses and, at the same time, maintain their social and professional networks in the developed countries where they studied and started to establish themselves (e.g. USA, UK). In addition to gaining professional and scientific knowledge, they have also acquired the understanding of capital markets and business models and transformed them to their home countries. Along the same line, Carr et al. (2005) suggested the term 'talent flow' to manifest that the concept of brain drain is too uni-dimensional and limited in reflecting the true scope of global knowledge transfer.

Changes in the world economy have undermined the core–periphery model. The increasing mobility of high-skilled workers and information, combined with the fragmentation of production in the information and communication technology sectors, provide unprecedented opportunities for formerly peripheral economies to benefit from decentralized growth based on entrepreneurship and experimentation (Saxenian 2006).

New psychological contracts

One of the theories that connect the individual and the organization is the 'new psychological contract'. In one way, it can be taken as a natural evolution of the employment relationships but, at another level, it is a totally new way to examine the relationship between people, their employers and their careers.

In layman's terms, the psychological contract is 'the unspoken promise, not present in the small print of the employment contract, of what the employer gives, and what employees give in return'. Such a contract is fundamentally different from the formal, legal employment contracts in their context and expected impact (Spindler 1994; Conway and Briner 2005). The idea of the psychological contract was originally suggested by Levinson and his colleagues in the early 1960s (Levinson et al. 1962). It was re-introduced to organizational studies and developed later by Kotter (1973) and followed by others (Nicholson and Johns 1985; Robinson and Morrison 1995; Rousseau 1995; 1996). The beginning of the 1990s saw a significant change in the nature and notion of the psychological contract (e.g. Hiltrop 1995), as these contracts are based on an interactive process of an exchange relationship. Contemporary organizational structures and hence, career systems, are characterized by perpetual changes. To keep the right people, organizations and employees need to develop new psychological contracts in line with their business culture (Baruch and Hind 1999). Breaching the contract might not have the clear legal consequences of breaching a legal contract, but the impact is nevertheless substantial (Robinson et al. 1994).

The Kaleidoscope Career Model within a global context

The Kaleidoscope Career Model (KCM) is one of the next generation career concepts (Sullivan and Baruch 2009). Based on empirical investigation and insights of its originators (Mainiero and Sullivan 2006) the KCM reflects career realities, mostly of professional workers. Like a kaleidoscope that produces changing patterns when the tube is rotated and its glass chips fall into new arrangements, the KCM describes how individuals change the pattern of their careers by rotating the varied aspects of their lives in order to arrange their relationships and roles in new ways. While originally tested within the US boundaries, the model can be expanded to cross-border boundaries. These changes reflected by the metaphorical kaleidoscope might occur in response to internal changes, such as those due to maturation, or environmental changes such as being laid off. With specific relevance to a global career, such change might occur when an employer decides to widen the operation to an overseas destination, or to offer a local employee an option for expatriation. Another similar case is when a person or a family makes an immigration decision. Individuals evaluate the choices and options available to determine the best fit among work demands, constraints and opportunities as well as relationships and personal values and interests.

In a similar way to a kaleidoscope that uses three mirrors to create infinite patterns, the KCM makes use of three career parameters. These parameters or motivators are: (1) *authenticity*, in which the individual makes choices that permit him/her to be true to him/herself; (2) *balance*, whereby the individual strives to reach an equilibrium between work and non-work (e.g. family, friends, elderly relatives, personal interests) demands; and (3) *challenge*, which is an individual's need for stimulating work (e.g. responsibility, autonomy) as well as career advancement. These three parameters are simultaneously active over a lifespan, and are highly relevant when a cross-border career decision or transition is involved. Over the course of the lifespan, as a person searches for the best fit that matches the character and context of his/her life, the kaleidoscope's parameters shift in response, with one parameter moving to the foreground and intensifying as that parameter takes priority at that time. The other two parameters lessen in intensity and recede to the background, but are still present and active, as all aspects are necessary to create the current pattern of an individual's life/career.

Research on the KCM has found gender differences in career enactment. Sullivan and Mainiero (2007) found most men focus on challenge from early to mid-career, then on authenticity and then on balance later in their career, while most women followed a pattern of challenge early in the career, then balance and finally authenticity. Indeed, organizations should bear in mind gender differences in perspective when cross-border career decisions are necessary. Besides gender, age is another factor, as generational differences exist in the need for authenticity, balance and challenge. Members of Generation X (born 1965–1983) had significantly higher needs for authenticity and balance than Baby Boomers (born 1946–1964), with no significant difference in the need for challenge between the two generations (Sullivan et al. 2009). The variance in age input was further reinforced in the phenomenon of self-initiated expatriation (Altman and Baruch 2008; Doherty et al. 2011).

Career theory – organizational perspective in global context

One major challenge for MNCs is how to run a coherent and systematic HRM operation when the organization is spread over different locations, with different perspectives of the nature and notion of 'career'. Such diversity means that the HRM system should accommodate a set of different, sometimes contradictory financial, economical, legal and cultural environments. Yet, the system is expected to be that of a single organization, with its unique culture and 'way of doing things'. The specific element of management of expatriation and repatriation processes is a challenge to the HRM system. Expatriation is, indeed, one of the ways through which MNCs aim to develop and maintain such a single culture worldwide.

Box 3.1 Cross-border performance-related payment

An example to manifest the challenge of variance across borders for coherent operation is the prospect of introducing performance-related payment (PRP) across the board. PRP is a system where remuneration takes into account the performance of the individual employee or of specific teams as a factor in calculating their salaries and bonuses. Some firms have such a system in place for all or for some of their employees. Individual-based PRP can be a very effective management and motivation system in a competitive culture, and in roles where individual contribution can be distinct from each other. Yet, introducing individual-based PRP could backfire if imposed on an operation within a collectivist culture, or when the performance is highly related to teamwork. In the latter case, team-based PRP can be put in place. But, then, there will be less consistency within the firm as a whole.

The challenge is finding the right balance between a uniformity of HRM rules and the need to motivate across diverse cultures.

One major consideration for the management of expatriation and repatriation is the strategic approach of the firm. In Chapter 2 we discussed both Perlmutter's (1969) and Bartlett and Ghoshal's (1989) frameworks. The two are very useful for general global strategy development, yet, they offer an 'ideal' type, which could realistically be achieved by few firms. A more recent model, which focuses specifically on the strategic management of expatriation/repatriation was offered by Baruch and Altman (2002). Unlike the above models, it reflects on practice and actual operation rather than offering an ideal model to follow.

Baruch and Altman's (2002) theoretical framing focuses on the HR management of expatriation and repatriation as part of organizational career systems. Their five-option taxonomy expresses a variety of approaches organizations might hold in managing expatriation careers, and deviates from the traditional tendency to build models that fit mostly or solely for the typical US MNC. The options are based on several dimensions – values, time, global vs. local focus, individual vs. company criteria, and nature of the psychological contract. Each option implies a different organizational approach to the management of careers and the meaning of IAs. The following description of the five options is adapted from Baruch and Altman (2002):

- *The Global (or Empire):* This is the 'archetype' large global MNC, with an established reputation in global operation, including HRM, where expatriation management is an integral part. The Empire corporate philosophy views expatriation as fundamental to the organization and to careers within the organization. Period(s) of expatriation are an inevitable part of career paths for any executive. Deviation from the norm will exclude managers from following the mainstream career path. For the Empire, globalization is an inherent property and part of the organizational ethos. The company will have a comprehensive set of procedures and practices in place. Moreover, people in the company as well as those joining would expect expatriation to be at the core of their professional and managerial career.
- *The Emissary (or Colonial):* The Colonial company has established overseas markets with a long-term view as to its international aspirations; however, it is firmly rooted in a particular culture and this serves as its repository ideology, power base and expatriate source. The organizational culture is typically indoctrinated with an ingrained obligation – a sense of duty backed with high commitment and loyalty. Employees might be asked to accept an expatriate role and, in line with the ethos 'for God, King and Country', are not expected to refuse.

- *Peripheral:* This model fits companies operating in peripheral geographies, where expatriation experience is most desirable for individuals who wish to experience the big world. Expatriation would be a means to benefit employees. Globalization is an expansion strategy, as local markets are insufficient to offer growth, and the company might have, by design, targeted itself as export oriented. What is different in the Peripheral option is that people will be queuing up to get the chance of expatriation. It will be perceived as a perk by both the individuals and the employer.
- *Professional:* The Professional strategic option is based on buying in knowledge and expertise. Its goal is to concentrate on home country strengths and keep people within specified geographical borders. Hence the strategy prefers outsourcing of people for cross-border activities, having delivery through people external to the company. These may be local people, or TNC specialists. The company relies on external people, in effect outsourcing the expatriation process.
- *Expedient:* The emergent approach for newcomers to the global scene, which characterizes most firms in the process of developing policies and practices. An ad-hoc and pragmatic approach, the Expedient option is more of a 'mixed bag' in which can be found a wide range of companies entering globalized markets or wishing to become global players. Eventually they could end with any of the above options, or a hybrid one.

To these five options we need to add that a 'hybrid' mode is a typical way to operate when in a certain location one of these options fits best, whereas in another, a different option will do better. Much is subject to the condition and the attractiveness of the host country to prospective expatriates.

Mutual dependency in international careers

Modern global career implies not only an interaction between an organization and an individual but also – and increasingly – a mutual dependency between the two parties (Larsen 2004). Within the traditional career system, employees had to adhere to the conditions and opportunities provided by the organization. While this notion still exists (Baruch 2006), organizations need to accept and match the expectations and demands of the employee, in particular within a global context (Dickmann and Harris 2005). Larsen (2004) highlights the relevance of the knowing-how ingredient of the intelligent career (Arthur et al. 1995) in terms of complex problem solving, consultancy service, etc. for the success of a global assignment. Larsen points out the emerging dual dependency in global careers and discusses this interdependency from the viewpoints of both individual and organization.

At another level of interdependency, nations depend very much on the investment and employment offered by global MNCs when these enter new markets and new labour markets in their search for advanced 'brain-power' (Tzafrir et al. 2007). Employees in these overseas operations may move later as TNC or impatriates (see Chapter 4) and develop global careers, which previously was not a likely option.

Career practice

Career practice: what needs to be done?

Career practices – needed for managing globally

Early works covered a wide range of career practices that organizations might employ to plan and manage careers. Based mainly on Baruch (1999, 2004a), and Baruch and Peiperl (2000), we offer the following comprehensive review of the variety of career practices and their specific relevance to global career management.

Posting (advertising) internal job openings

Whenever a position needs to be manned, the organization can look to fill the vacancy with either internal or external people. The choice depends on the organizational strategy and structure (see Chapter 2), the level and type of position and the organizational career norms. When a global operation needs to fill a position, one basic consideration would be whether to opt for locals or make it open globally. If the local option is chosen, the position will neither be posted in the home country – avoiding the expatriation option – nor in the other operations globally – avoiding TCN expatriation. This can be an easy choice, but some might feel that they were blocked from having global opportunities. Alternatively, the firm might decide that they wish to have an expatriate, an executive from the home country where the main operation and headquarters is located, to fill the position. Then they will only post it in the parent country. Again, local employees in the host country may feel deprived of the option to fill a managerial position. As a result, these considerations need to bear in mind the wider career perspective within the firm (as well as the associated costs for each option). In some cases, in particular when there is no adequate talent or competence within the firm, they can publish outside like any conventional job advertisement.

Many organizations will have a policy that requires internal job posting before any external search is conducted. The use of job posting manifests to the employees that the organization prefers internal promotion to recruiting from outside (focus on internal labour market). In the past, job posting was offered either on notice boards or in the company newsletter. Current practice utilizes intranet or e-notice boards.

Formal education as part of career development

Under this practice, the organization selects people of managerial or technical potential and sends them on a training programme of formal study as part of their development path. Once the organization has identified a gap between needs in a global position and the existing competencies, such training can be put in place, either internally or externally. For global assignments such as expatriation, a language course could be essential and so, too, is preparation for the local culture and customs. Organizations might wish to avoid such long-term investment in people, but without it the prospects of success would decline significantly. As a consequence, short-term specific training might be sponsored by organizations to prepare future expatriates before departure.

Training for preparing an expatriate (and other international managers) for the role and to manage their expectations is a crucial ingredient for avoiding failure (Cavusgil et al. 1992; Sullivan and Tu 1993; Caligiuri 2000). The training should be wide in terms of cover, and include cultural preparation. The cultural orientation can be run by former expatriates from the intended host country, or by external firms which specialize in such preparations.

Lateral moves to create cross-functional experience

These are on the increase, and it seems they will continue (Baruch 1999). These can be seen as elementary career planning and management practices which most organizations with HRM systems need to apply. The flattening of organizational structures has become a reality for many, which has increased the barriers to traditional hierarchical careers. One way for individuals to become noticed is to acquire unique knowledge and experience through expatriation. This IA might be at the same managerial level as their former position, but yet will be taken as progress and increases promotion potential. Organizations need to clearly indicate that such a route reflects career success rather than failure (i.e. being sent overseas is not an indication of 'deadwood' but of being a high-flyer) or at least that it is a standard expectation.

Retirement preparation programmes

Expatriation will not be typically associated with preparation for retirement. Yet, if an executive is serving in an expatriate position and is approaching retirement, HRM should bear in mind the physical distance, and the option that the retiree might wish to retire in the host country rather than return home.

Booklets and/or pamphlets on career issues

Booklets, pamphlets or leaflets on career issues form a formal presentation by the organization of all kinds of career-related information. They introduce what is on offer by the organization in terms of career opportunities and provide an introduction to all available career planning and management practices. Some of this can be a presentation of career paths, the competencies required for each position on the path, the timescales needed for career developments (e.g. minimal time in a certain position before promotion) and conditions set for certain developments. The aim of such booklets is to provide everyone in the organization with relevant information, releasing the direct manager from the job of presenting that information to subordinates. Booklets may be turned into electronic versions as part of the company website. Such information should be available regarding global position and expatriation processes and procedures, including the anticipated remuneration (which will be different according to the destination country) due to variance in the cost of living.

Dual ladder

The Dual ladder is a parallel scheme of hierarchy, created for non-managerial staff, such as professional or technical employees. This CPM is less relevant for expatriation/repatriation.

Induction

The process of introducing people to their new organization is the first career practice new employees experience (titled induction or socialization). This is a process whereby all newcomers learn the behaviours and attitudes necessary for assuming roles in an organization (Van Mannen 1976). For moving to a different operation in a foreign country, it remains essential to introduce newcomers to the varied aspects of their local organizational life culture. These can be related to ideology or philosophy, culture, policies, rules and regulations, norms, expected behaviours and performance, and any other information, including social, that will help them to master their jobs and become integrated into the local workplace.

Unlike typical induction programmes for young newcomers to the organization, in preparing for expatriation there is a much wider age, and sometimes seniority, span of expatriates. An induction process for the experienced professional or manager is very different from that directed at young school leavers or new graduates. In an ideal world, the person formerly holding the post would be a good person to lead the induction (unless it is a new post).

Assessment and development centres

Assessment centres have gained a lot of interest in academia and among organizational practitioners. They have often been found to be a reliable and valid tool for career development. Assessment centres can be used as a selection tool for global recruitment, and as an indicator of global managerial potential. Large organizations can have their own centres whereas small firms generally use external institutions.

One example of a tool that looks at both national culture and individual personality is the Spony Profiling Model (SPM). The SPM is built on the research of Hofstede and Schwartz and depicts personality traits in relation to national cultures. Individuals (and their organizations) can understand in what dimensions and how much they have to adapt in order to be similar to predominant norms in the country of expatriation. Of course, while this might allow understanding of the intellectual and emotional adjustment needed, it does not give an indication whether the individual is willing and capable of making these adjustments nor whether it is desirable to conform to the specific local cultural expectations and norms.

Mentoring and coaching

The principal aim of mentoring is to bring together a person with managerial potential and an experienced manager, who is not necessarily the direct manager. Such a senior manager can provide advice, tutoring and support to newcomers.

This practice has gained much attention and proved positive within organizations (e.g. Baugh et al. 1996). Both mentors and protégés benefit from this practice (Kram 1985), and the organization can shape the kind of mentoring relationships. Such a win-win situation can be replicated in mentoring for expatriates as, for the expatriate, the move resembles entering a position as a newcomer. In fact, dual mentoring might be needed – one mentor in the home operation, and one local person to help and support in organizational and non-organizational issues of settling down in an environment with different culture and code of conduct.

Mentoring also manifests possible pitfalls (Scandura 1998) and can become dysfunctional, but the reasons for this in a global context can go beyond the typical issues of collision of interests between the direct manager and the mentor or cross-gender mentoring problems. Yet, other challenges exist, such as the availability of appropriate mentors, with fewer prospective candidates with relevant experience who can serve as mentors.

The idea of career coaching has emerged as a major growth area and as a key element of organizational career management (Feldman 2001). It supports executives' strategies for career advancement. Among the main purposes of career coaching, Feldman counts its use as grooming middle- and upper-level managers for advancement, as well as helping executives and upper-level managers adjust to major changes in the workplace – both cases highly applicable for expatriation situations. One advantage to using external coaching is that the firm might be able to identify consultants with the right global experience to provide worthy coaching. In times of transition, such as expatriation (and, indeed, repatriation too), coaching can be an effective way to support global executives in entering their roles and with coping with issues that emerge, both managerial and personal.

Career workshops

Career workshops are short-term workshops focusing on specific aspects of career management and which aim to provide managers with relevant knowledge, skills and experience. Participating in career workshops can contribute to the effectiveness of the employee (Sweeney et al. 1989). Career workshops usually focus on specific aspects such as identifying future opportunities, and can be specifically directed towards preparing executives for expatriation assignments. The impetus for sending people to these workshops can come from their manager, mentor or the HR counselling system. With the increasing number of organizations going global, future global career workshops could be provided by MNCs for their managers.

Performance appraisal in global context

There is a close connection between the performance appraisal (PA) system and career development. Valid and reliable PA would provide answers to issues such as promotions, appointments, redundancy, and in identifying training and development needs. For our discussion here, the PA system faces two challenges in a global context – convergence versus divergence within the system, and its fit to expatriate positions.

MNCs that operate in different countries might realize that while they prefer to have a single system across all the divisions and locations, the PA system might have to undergo adaptation phases to fit operation and culture in different countries. Different dimensions of evaluation, different scales, and different importance of certain qualities might be required in various geo-locations. Increasingly used methods of PA include 360-degree feedback (which can take the form of peer appraisal, upward appraisal, or other sources in addition to that given by the direct manager) (Baruch and Harel 1993; Bernardin et al. 1995). These can serve as valuable PA sources, increasing reliability and validity of the process, and are useful in particular as a feedback tool and for development purposes. Yet, in some non-Western countries, the use of 360-degree feedback will not be well received by executives – such as in authoritarian cultures. Also, this practice is time consuming to conduct and the analysis of the results is complex.

The other challenge is the use of PA for choosing people for future development, e.g. selection of high-potential employees for expatriation assignments. Once an appropriate and valid process is utilized to identify the future expatriate, they will move to the new place and operate there. Then they will be subjected to the PA system that is in use in the destination, host country. It might or might not be similar to that at the home operation. The performance evaluation for the expatriate manager will be subject to the question of which system will be used – the one at home (the Headquarter system), or the one in place at the local, host country PA system. For example, should a 360-degree feedback or performance-related pay be used if it is only conducted at the home operation and not in the host operation?

Career counselling

Career counselling is a two-way communication with the employee. Two main sources are available for conducting this practice – the in-house counselling offered by the HR department of the direct manager, or it can also be provided by external consultants (Baruch 1999). It will not be easy to run it for expatriates, but with improved technology, video-conferencing and other contact means, even personal issues can be discussed properly. Further, it is typical to bring the expatriate for annual visits, and some of that time can be used for career counselling services. Like coaching, some such services can be purchased from external consulting organizations.

For career counselling to be fruitful, managers need to have a good grasp of the career options available, and the direction of future organizational developments.

Succession planning

Succession planning is a framework of organizational planning in which the organization determines the possible replacement of managers within the organization, and evaluates the potential for promotion of managers. Succession planning (also labelled management inventory) can be valuable for both global positioning in general, and especially for expatriation assignments, under long-term planning. Inputs for the creation and updating of succession planning will come from several sources – primarily from the PA system, mentors' perceptions, assessment centre results and career counselling. Special attention is needed in responding to equal employment opportunities when unique populations might require explicit attention. Such is the case in allocating women to cultures where locals might resent being managed by female managers. Being politically correct might not help the cause of the organization in delivering high performance.

Special programmes for ethnic minorities, women, disabled employees, dual-career couples etc.

Organizations should develop special programmes to tackle all possible kinds of discrimination, such as the 'glass ceiling' effect for women, i.e. not being pro-moted above a certain managerial level (Morrison et al. 1987). Many programmes are meant to support the population discriminated against, sometimes even to create 'positive discrimination'. It is important, though, that such 'positive discrimination' will not imply desertion of selection according to skills, competencies and fit for the job. Problems of discrimination exist for many groups, not just for women. Ethnic background, disability, age and religious discrimination can prevent appropriate people from utilizing their contribution.

In general, global positions should not be influenced by personal background that is not relevant for job performance. Yet, in some instances it might be useful for organizations to employ sensitivity in global appointments, bearing in mind the attitudes of locals towards such differences. Organizations grapple with questions such as whether it would be wise to send a black manager to a subsidiary in a country that is renowned for its lack of tolerance to racial equality. As mentioned above, it might be politically correct, and even educative, but on the other hand it might backfire. In some countries with religious rules and regulations, local women might not even be legally allowed to occupy managerial roles. Often the dilemma pitches ethical considerations against local custom.

Special programmes are not necessarily concerned with discrimination. The case of dual career couples directs us into another matter, i.e. how to enable two people to develop side by side when both have a career (in their working life). HR systems must recognize this, especially where international relocations become necessary as part of career progress (Punnett et al. 1992; Baruch 1995; Harvey 1997).

Special programmes for high-flyers

All employees, as the prime asset of the organization, deserve investment in their career by their organization. However, the so-called high-flyers or those with high potential are perceived as a special asset, able to make a unique contribution to the future of the organization, and thus worth having more attention and resources dedicated specifically to them. Derr et al. (1988) looked at high-flyers as a scarce resource, and because of the demographic reduction in workforce numbers, including managerial layers, suggest that organizations will look for more ways of developing future leaders. In contrast with the variety of distinct practices dis-cussed in this paper, 'Special programmes for high-flyers' could form a group of practices and activities of those mentioned in the list, applied extensively for the high-flyers. For high-flyers in MNCs, expatriation might be considered an essential part of their career path if they are aiming at top executive positions later in their career.

Building psychological contracts

The psychological contract between the employee and the workplace is acknowledged as a crucial element of the employment relationships and beyond (cf. Rousseau 1995, 1996; Morrison and Robinson 1997). The beginning of the 1990s saw a significant change in the nature and notion of the psychological contract and in the future employers will have to clarify this concept – as a set of mutual expectations which need to be agreed upon, explicitly or implicitly – with their employees (see also Herriot and Pemberton 1995). These expectations are, firstly, what the organization perceives as a fair contribution from the employee, and secondly, what the organization will provide in return. Psychological contract fulfilment has positive impacts on expatriate work attitude and mediates the relationship between organizational practices and retention-relevant outcomes such as organizational commitment, intent to quit, and intent to return early to a domestic assignment (Guzzo et al. 1994).

The cycle of career planning and development for the expatriate (and his/her family) should start with the establishment of a mutual agreement, a psychological contract, which sets the type and style of future relationships for 'before, during and after' the expatriation.

Secondments

Secondment is the temporary assignment to another area within the organization, and sometimes even to another associated organization (such as a customer or supplier). In a way, expatriation is similar to a secondment within the organization, with prospects for mutual benefits for both the former unit and the operation where the expatriation takes place. Similarly to secondments, an impetus for expatriation can be derived from their manager, mentor, or from HR counselling and PA systems. There is a need for long-term HR planning and for mutuality, thus making it feasible mostly for large or well-established corporations. There is a risk of losing successful expatriates, either if they opt to stay abroad, or if their return is transformed into a bumpy road (Baruch et al. 2002). Of course, leaving the organization for good or being so disillusioned from the foreign experience that performance and motivation suffer substantially can be even more dangerous for the employer.

Intrapreneurship

People have different approaches to their life and career, and many look to fulfil their entrepreneurship desires. The employer should be able to identify those who possess the qualities needed to generate new business, as sometimes this is the major opportunity that expatriation provides. One way to achieve this is by intrapreneurship, i.e. entrepreneurship within the firm.

Written personal career planning for employees

This practice was considered to require reassessment for the 2000s, as suggested earlier (Baruch 1999). Yet, in particular as expatriation can take some three to four years, there is room for written documents to generate and reaffirm mutual commitment. While written personal career plans can be problematic in the sense of creating expectations, when making a long-term plan of expatriation it is justified to put certain career plans in writing.

Common career paths

A career path is the most preferred and recommended route for the career advancement of a manager in the organization. Such career paths can lead people through various departments and units within the organization as in the case of future top-level managers in multinational companies who will take a managerial role in an overseas subsidiary. The use of career paths spread rapidly in the 1970s and 80s among many organizations (Portwood and Granrose 1986). The use of career paths is more widespread in larger organizations, whereas more informal paths or a lack of paths might be found in smaller organizations. The base for career path planning is stability and a wide range of layers and positions. With traditional hierarchical structures flattening and diminishing and with the creation of boundaryless and virtual organizations, development of future career paths seems likely to decline. Yet, it is important to plan ahead a career path including international mobility. Good planning helps to avoid the 'out-of-sight, out-of-mind' phenomenon. It should be made clear what type of learning is required to be effective in the position abroad and which insights will prepare repatriates for a future career after their return.

Overview and integration

A wide number of career practices are available to plan and manage careers of the global workforce. This is particularly relevant to the management of expatriates' careers. The organization should bear in mind a need for an integrative system, where there exist vertical and horizontal career opportunities.

The career practices listed above were discussed separately, as if they are unrelated or disassociated practices. This is not the case of course, and appropriate HRM ensures a well-integrated, comprehensive system to put the practices into a coherent system. To achieve a fit and optimal utilization of such a system, it is necessary to apply a two-fold level of integration: 'internal', among the variety of practices, and 'external', integration between the career system and the organizational culture and strategy (Baruch 1999; Baruch and Peiperl 2000). Both internal and external integration are led by strategy: an HRM strategy that forms a part of the whole organizational strategy. Day-to-day management of the practices should be derived from the strategy (Baruch 2004a).

Internal integration relates to the existence or otherwise of harmony across the various practices. Specific practices relate to others, inputs from one practice (PA, for example) influence the use of others (e.g. high-flyers). As Baruch and Peiperl

(2000) suggest, career practices may appear in clusters where groups of practices are interrelated. The wide range of career management practices are clustered into groups according to their common use and interrelations among the practices. Further, these clusters are associated with certain characteristics of organizations such as size, age or culture and the clusters vary according to sophistication and involvement of the organization in the process of career management.

These systems require more integration and comparative analysis to understand and utilize the data. For example, creating reliable and valid succession planning depends on the use of IT systems to gather and analyse multi-sourced information. Internal integration will also enable flexibility and reflect the new type of psychological contract between employer and global employee, expatriate or local.

External integration

In terms of external integration, career systems that best fit the organization depend on the operational strategy of the whole enterprise. Sonnenfeld and Peiperl (1988) based their career system model on a Miles and Snow (1978) organizational strategic model, in line with the concept of strategic HRM. The career practices system should be developed in line with business objectives and needs (Tyson 1997; Purcell 1999). The types of practices carried out will depend on the culture of the organization and its overseas subsidiaries. In a bureaucratic system which is relatively stable (e.g. diplomatic service) common career paths can be applied for long-term career progress. In a dynamic, turbulent sector (e.g. IT sector), these will have to be revised on a continuous basis. For expatriates, career practices such as mentoring could become even more important, although it is difficult for mentors at the head office to keep in contact with the expatriate. Practices such as succession planning will be appealing to expatriates coming from individualistic cultures whereas those from group-oriented cultures will probably focus on developing induction programmes to the new environment. The local culture of the country and of the organization as a whole will help in shaping the career practices and their use, while in a complementary way, career management can help in the reshaping of organizational culture.

The cost of avoiding action

There is a certain debate in the literature regarding the success of international work. Some argue that there is no empirical support for the claims of high level of failure reported in earlier publications (Harzing 1995; Forster 1997). Yet, there is certain evidence in the literature to indicate that failure rates are high – some evidence suggests that more than 30 per cent of US corporate overseas assignments fail (Marquardt and Engel 1993; Solomon 1995), not only in terms of early departure but, most seriously, in poor performance during expatriation or in leaving the organization soon after repatriation. Indeed Baruch et al. (2002) pointed at a case of 50 per cent failure rate, which might be extreme, but yet a reality for certain firms, in line with the sparse indications from the literature claiming that between 30 and 40 per cent of expatriates leave their companies within two years of repatriation (cf. Dowling et al. 1994; Stroh 1995). Poor performance and departure soon after repatriation cause both a heavy expense burden and business risks (Selmer 1998).

Even if the actual numbers of success or failure of expatriation and repatriation are not exceeding the norm for any managerial assignment, it is agreed that expatriation assignment costs are much higher than traditional assignments, and thus there is a major need for risk management and for employing high-quality HRM. The outcomes of international work are explored in more depth in Chapters 8 and 9.

Summary and learning points

In this chapter we covered major career theories, from both the individual perspective and the organizational perspective in the global context. We further examined the mutual dependency in international careers between the individual and organization, as well as between the organization and the host nation. We then moved to cover the wide portfolio of career management practices and their relevance to global career management. Some of these practices may hold a crucial role for global careers, whereas others are more relevant for domestic operations.

Key learning points include:

- General career theories provide the background for the practice of managing careers in a global context.
- Global careers are more prevalent in the contemporary work environment.
- The way career concepts such as the boundaryless career and intelligent career are utilized by individuals and by organizations for IAs and their management.
- National-level implications, such as brain drain vs. brain circulation.
- HRM practices – how to employ these for effective management of global careers.

References

Altbach, P.G. and Bassett, R.M. (2004) 'The brain trade', *Foreign Policy*, Sept./Oct.: 30–31.

Altman, Y. and Baruch, Y. (2008) 'Global protean careers: a new era in expatriation and repatriation', paper presented at the *European Academy of Management* conference, Ljubljana, May 2008.

Arthur, M.B., Claman, P.H. and DeFillippi, R.J. (1995) 'Intelligent enterprise, intelligent careers', *Academy of Management Executive*, 9(4): 7–22.

Arthur, M.B., Hall, D.T. and Lawrence, B.S. (1989) 'Generating new directions in career theory: the case for a transdisciplinary approach', in M.B. Arthur, D.T. Hall and B.S. Lawrence (eds) *Handbook of Career Theory*, Cambridge: Cambridge University Press.

Ashkenas, R., Ulrich, D., Jick, T. and Kerr, S. (1995) *The Boundaryless Organization: Breaking the Chains of Organizational Structure*, San Francisco, CA: Jossey-Bass.

Bailyn, L. (1993) 'Patterned chaos in human resource management', *Sloane Management Review*, 34(2): 77–84.

Barley, S.R. (1989) 'Careers, identities and institutions: the legacy of the Chicago School of Sociology', in M.B. Arthur, T. Hall and B.S. Lawrence (eds) *Handbook of Career Theory*, Cambridge: Cambridge University Press.

Bartlett, C.A. and Ghoshal, S. (1989) *Managing across Borders. The Transnational Solution*, Boston, MA: Harvard Business Press.

Baruch, Y. (1995) 'Business globalization – the human resource management aspect', *Human Systems Management*, 14(4): 313–326.

Baruch, Y. (1999) 'Integrated career systems for the 2000s', *International Journal of Manpower*, 20(7): 432–457.

Baruch, Y. (2002) 'No such thing as a global manager', *Business Horizons*, 45(1): 36–42.

Baruch, Y. (2004a) *Managing Careers: Theory and Practice*, Harlow: FT-Prentice Hall/Pearson.

Baruch, Y. (2004b) 'Transforming careers – from linear to multidirectional career paths: organizational and individual perspective', *Career Development International*, 9(1): 58–73.

Baruch, Y. (2006) 'Career development in organizations and beyond: balancing traditional and contemporary viewpoints', *Human Resource Management Review*, 16: 125–138.

Baruch, Y. and Altman, Y. (2002) 'Expatriation and repatriation in MNCs: a taxonomy', *Human Resource Management*, 41(2): 239–259.

Baruch, Y. and Harel, G. (1993) 'Combining multi-source performance appraisal: an empirical and methodological note', *Public Administration Quarterly*, 17(1): 96–111.

Baruch, Y. and Hind, P. (1999) 'Perpetual motion in organizations: effective management and the impact of the new psychological contracts on "Survivor Syndrome"', *European Journal of Work and Organizational Psychology*, 8(2): 295–306.

Baruch, Y. and Peiperl, M.A. (2000) 'Career management practices: an empirical survey and theoretical implications', *Human Resource Management*, 39(4): 347–366.

Baruch, Y., Budhwar, P. and Khatri, N. (2007) 'Brain drain: inclination to stay abroad after studies', *Journal of World Business*, 42(1): 99–112.

Baruch, Y., Steele, D. and Quantrill, J. (2002) 'Management of expatriation and repatriation for novice global player', *International Journal of Manpower*, 23(7): 659–671.

Baugh, S.G., Lankau, M.J. and Scandura, T.A. (1996) 'An investigation of the effects of protégé gender on responses to mentoring', *Journal of Vocational Behavior*, 49: 309–323.

Bernardin, H.J., Kane, J.S., Ross, S., Spina, J.D. and Johnson, D.L. (1995) 'Performance appraisal design, development, and implementation', in G.R. Ferris, S.D. Rosen and D.T. Barnum (eds) *Handbook of Human Resource Management*, Cambridge, MA: Blackwell.

Bird, A., Gunz, H. and Arthur, M.B. (2002) 'Careers in a complex world: the search for new perspectives from the "new science"', *M@n@gement*, 5(1): 1–14.

Caligiuri, P.M. (2000) 'Selecting expatriates for personality characteristics: a moderating effect of personality on relationship between host national contact and cross-cultural adjustment', *Management International Review*, 40: 61–80.

Carr, S.C., Inkson, K. and Thorn, K. (2005) 'From global careers to talent flow: reinterpreting "brain drain"', *Journal of World Business*, 40: 386–398.

Carrington, W.J. and Detragiache, E. (1999) 'International migration and the "brain drain"', *Journal of Social Political and Economic Studies*, 24: 163–171.

Cavusgil, T., Yavas, U. and Bykowicz, S. (1992) 'Preparing executives for overseas assignments', *Management Decision*, 30(1): 54–58.

Conway, N. and Briner, R.B. (2005) *Understanding Psychological Contracts at Work. A Critical Evaluation of Theory and Research*, Oxford: Oxford University Press.

Creehan, S. (2001) 'Brain strain', *Harvard International Review*, 23(2): 6–7.

Crush, J. (2002) 'The global raiders: nationalism, globalization and the South African brain drain', *Journal of International Affairs*, 56: 147–172.

Derr, C., Jones, C. and Toomey, E. (1988) 'Managing high potential employees: current practices in thirty-three U.S. corporations', *Human Resource Management*, 27(3): 273–290.

Dickmann, M. and Harris, H. (2005) 'Developing career capital for global careers: the role of international assignments', Journal of World Business, 40(4): 399–408.

Doherty, N., Dickmann, M. and Mills, T. (2011) 'Exploring the motives of company-backed and self-initiated expatriates', *The International Journal of Human Resource Management*, forthcoming.

Dowling, P.J., Schuler, R.S. and Welch, D.E. (1994) *International Dimensions of Human Resource Management*, Belmont, CA: Wadworth.

Durkheim, E. (1933) *The Division of Labour in Society*, New York: Macmillan, first printed 1893.

Feldman, D.C. (2001) 'Career coaching: what HR professionals and managers need to know', *Human Resource Planning*, 24(2): 26–35.

Forster, N. (1997) 'The persistent myth of high expatriate failure rates: a reappraisal', *International Journal of Human Resource Management*, 8(4): 414–433.

Giddens, A. (1971) *Capitalism and Modern Social Theory*, Cambridge: Cambridge University Press.

Giddens, A. (1997) *Sociology* (3rd edn), Cambridge: Polity Press.

Glieck, J. (1988) *Chaos: Making a New Science*, London: Heinemann.

Guzzo, R.A., Nooman, K.A. and Elron, E. (1994) 'Expatriate managers and the psychological contract', *Journal of Applied Psychology*, 79(4): 617–626.

Hall, D.T. and Mirvis, P.H. (1995) 'The new career contract: developing the whole person at mid-life and beyond', *Journal of Vocational Behavior*, 47: 269–289.

Harvey, M. (1997) 'Dual-career expatriates: expectations, adjustment and satisfaction with international relocation', *Journal of International Business Studies*, 28(3): 627–658.

Harzing, A.W. (1995) 'The persistent myth of high expatriate failure rates', *International Journal of Human Resource Management*, 6(2): 457–474.

Herriot, P. and Pemberton, C. (1995) *New Deals*, Chichester: John Wiley.

Hiltrop, J.M. (1995) 'The changing psychological contract: the human resource challenge for the 1990s', *European Management Journal*, 13(15): 286–294.

Hofstede, G. (1980) *Culture's Consequences: International Differences in Work-related Values*, Beverly Hills, CA: Sage.

Holland, J.L. (1958) 'A personality inventory employing occupational titles', *Journal of Applied Psychology*, 42: 336–342.

Holland, J.L. (1959) 'A theory of vocational choice', *Journal of Counseling Psychology*, 6: 35–45.

Hughes, E.C. (1928) 'Personality types and the division of labor', *American Journal of Sociology*, 33: 754–768.

Hughes, E.C. (1937) 'Institutional office and the person', *American Journal of Sociology*, 43: 404–443.

Khapova, S.N., Arthur, M.B. and Wilderom, C.P.M. (2007) 'The subjective career in the knowledge economy', in H. Gunz and M.A. Peiperl (eds) *Handbook of Career Studies*, Los Angeles, CA: Sage.

Kotter, J. (1973) 'The psychological contract: managing the joining-up process', *California Management Review*, 15(3): 91–99.

Kram, K.E. (1985) *Mentoring at Work*, Glenview, IL: Scott, Foresman.

Larsen, H.H. (2004) 'Global career as dual dependency between the organisation and the individual', *The Journal of Management Development*, 23(9): 860–869.

Levinson, H., Price, C., Munden, K., Mandl, H. and Solley, C. (1962) *Men, Management, and Mental Health*, Cambridge, MA: Harvard University Press.

Mahroum, S. (2000) 'Highly skilled globetrotters: mapping the international migration of human capital', *R and D Management*, 30: 23–31.

Mainiero, L.A. and Sullivan, S.E. (2006) *The Opt-out Revolt: How People are Creating Kaleidoscope Careers Outside of Companies*, New York: Davies-Black.

Marquardt, M.J. and Engel, D.W. (1993) 'HRD competencies for a shrinking world', *Training and Development*, 47(5): 59–65.

Miles, R. and Snow, C. (1978) *Organizational Structure, Strategy and Process*, New York: McGraw-Hill.

Mitchell, A.M., Jones, G.B. and Krumboltz, J.D. (eds) (1979) *Social Learning Theory and Career Decision Making*, Cranston, RI: Carroll.

Moore, C., Gunz, H. and Hall, D.T. (2008) 'Tracing the historical roots of career theory in management and organization studies', in H. Gunz and M.A. Peiperl (eds) *Handbook of Career Studies*, Los Angeles, CA: Sage.

Morrison, A.M., White, R.P. and Van Velsor, E. (1987) 'Executive women: substance plus style', *Psychology Today*, 21: 18–26.

Morrison, E.W. and Robinson, S.L. (1997) 'When employees feel betrayed: a model of how psychological contract violation develops', *Academy of Management Review*, 22(1): 226–256.

Nicholson, N. and Johns, G. (1985) 'The absence culture and the psychological contract – who's in control of absence?', *Academy of Management Review*, 10: 397–407.

Parker, P. and Arthur, M.B. (2000) 'Careers, organizing and community', in M.A. Peiperl, M.B. Arthur, R. Goffee and Morris, T. (eds) *Career Frontiers: New Conceptions of Working Lives*, Oxford: Oxford University Press.

Parker, P. and Arthur, M.B. (2002) 'Bringing "New Science" into careers research', *M@n@gement*, 5(1): 105–125.

Perlmutter, H. (1969) 'The tortuous evolution of the multinational corporation', *Columbia Journal of World Business*, Jan.–Feb.: 9–18.

Portwood, J.D. and Granrose, C.S. (1986) 'Organizational career management programmes: what's available? What's effective?', *Human Resource Planning*, 19(3): 107–119.

Pryor, R.G.L. and Bright, J.E.H. (2003) 'Order and chaos: a twenty-first century formulation of careers', *Australian Journal of Psychology*, 55(2):121–128.

Punnett, B.J., Crocker, O. and Stevens, M.A. (1992) 'The challenge for women expatriates and spouses: some empirical evidence', *International Journal of Human Resource Management*, 3(3): 585–592.

Purcell, J. (1999) 'Best practice or best fit: chimera or cul-de-sac?', *Human Resource Management Journal*, 9(3): 26–41.

Robinson, S.L. and Morrison, E.W. (1995) 'Psychological contracts and OCB: the effect of unfulfilled obligation on civic virtue behaviour', *Journal of Organizational Behavior*, 16(3): 289–298.

Robinson, S.L., Kraatz, M.S. and Rousseau, D.M. (1994) 'Changing obligations and the psychological contract: a longitudinal study', *Academy of Management Journal*, 37(1): 137–152.

Rousseau, D.M. (1995) *Psychological Contracts in Organizations*, Thousand Oaks, CA: Sage.

Rousseau, D.M. (1996) 'Changing the deal while keeping the people', *Academy of Management Executive*, 10(1): 50–59.

Saxenian, A. (2006) *The New Argonauts: Regional Advantage in a Global Economy*, Boston, MA: Harvard University Press.

Scandura, T.A. (1998) 'Dysfunctional mentoring relationships and outcomes', *Journal of Management*, 24(3): 449–467.

Selmer, J. (1998) 'Expatriates: corporate policy, personal intentions and international adjustment', *International Journal of Human Resource Management*, 9(6): 996–1007.

Solomon, C.M. (1995) 'Success abroad depends on more than just job skills', *Personnel Journal*, 73(4): 51–54.

Sonnenfeld, J.A. and Peiperl, M.A. (1988) 'Staffing policy as a strategic response: a typology of career systems', *Academy of Management Review*, 13(4): 568–600.

Spindler, G.S. (1994) 'Psychological contracts in the workplace – a lawyer's view', *Human Resource Management*, 33(3): 325–333.

Stroh, L.K. (1995) 'Predicting turnover among repatriates: can organizations affect retention rates?', *International Journal of Human Resource Management*, 6(2): 443–456.

Sullivan, S.E. and Baruch, Y. (2009) 'Advances in career theory and research: critical review and agenda for future exploration', *Journal of Management*, 35(6): 1452–1571.

Sullivan, S.E. and Mainiero, L.A. (2007) 'Kaleidoscope careers: benchmarking ideas for fostering family-friendly workplaces', *Organizational Dynamics*, 36: 45–62.

Sullivan, S.E. and Tu, H.S. (1993) 'Training managers for international assignments', *Executive Development*, 6(1): 25–28.

Sullivan, S.E., Forret, M., Carraher, S.C. and Mainiero, L. (2009) 'Using the kaleidoscope career model to examine generational differences in work attitudes', *Career Development International*, 14: 284–302.

Sweeney, D.S., Haller, D. and Sale, F. (1989) 'Individually controlled career counselling', *Training and Development Journal*, August: 55–61.

Tung, R.L. and Lazarova, M. (2006) 'Brain drain versus brain gain: an exploratory study of ex-host country nationals in central and east Europe', *International Journal of Human Resource Management*, 17: 1853–1872.

Tyson, S. (1997) *Human Resource Strategy*, London: Pitman.

Tzafrir, S., Meshoulam, I. and Baruch, Y. (2007) 'HRM in Israel: new challenges', *International Journal of Human Resource Management*, 18(1): 114–131.

Van Mannen J. (1976) 'Breaking in: socialization to work', in R. Dubin (ed.) *Handbook of Work, Organization and Society*, Chicago, IL: Rand McNally.

van Rooyen, J. (2001) *The New Great Trek: The Story of South Africa's White Exodus*, Pretoria: Unisa Press.

Weber, M. (1965) 'Essay on bureaucracy', in F.E. Rourke *Bureaucratic Power in National Politics*, Boston, MA: Little, Brown and Company.

4   Cross-cultural working

Objectives

This chapter:

- focuses on cross-cultural issues faced by individuals and their employing organizations, underlying challenges and approaches to handling differences;
- identifies qualities needed for successful management of cross-cultural differences;
- describes organizational implications of cultural diversity;
- discusses 'cultural intelligence' and its relevance to global careers.

Introduction

In this chapter we explain the complex nature of global careers and the way in which different career theories and perspectives are relevant to different types of international work. Indeed we offer here a glossary of a variety of international work constellations and groups of international workers. This opens the global career framework far beyond the typical but limited perspective that global careers are involved with expatriation/repatriation. Several dimensions, such as the originator, the time frame, the connection to immigration, and the legality of the global move are relevant to the meaning of global careers.

We then focus on the subject of diversity management within global career systems, looking at several dimensions, in particular age and gender, factors which have both direct and indirect impact on issues such as career choice and timing of global career moves. These are not isolated from the role played by national business systems, as people management is a derivative of business management as a

Figure 4.1 A framework of global careers: different forms of careers across cultures

whole, and is connected and influenced by the national culture and the difference between the cultures of the home and host countries. Among the challenges HRM faces is the setting and development of multicultural teams. Such teams are increasing in prevalence and importance, and successful participation in a multinational team can have strong implications for global careers. Lastly, we discuss the importance of the so-called cultural intelligence to both individual and organizational management of global careers.

The complexity involved in global careers

Is the world indeed a 'global village', or a collection of separate entities? Cross-cultural and cross-national career moves (or moves associated and/or involved with global career progress) reflect a boundaryless career world (Arthur and Rousseau 1996; Baruch and Bozionelos 2010). The true meaning of boundarylessness in terms of career moves is not a total extinction of older boundaries. It is, rather, about making boundaries more permeable, not doing away with them (Gunz et al. 2002: 62). In a boundaryless world of career, people with non-traditional career attitudes (like the protean career, Hall 2004) will benefit from wider options of career moves, including moving to different cultures.

The big picture tells us about a change, and the progress overall is in a direction of globalization. Yet, there is much to overcome before we can call our planet Earth a true global village. Our focus in this book is on careers and their globalization, and the situation in this area has seen many boundaries breaking down, or, to use a more accurate metaphor, slowly melting. Even so, we would start with a caveat: most people on this planet have their career confined to a single country, where they were born, with very few being able or willing to leave. New developments include the availability of more options to interested people, and more organizations operate worldwide. In addition, there is higher tolerance than ever to global movement. Yet, the options are open mostly to the few people who were lucky enough to be born in the right (wealthy) country (see Chapter 1, for the big divide issue). While the option exists, a number of people are not too keen to embark on a global career, or merely not interested. Much of it is a matter of personal character, such as adventurousness and curiosity versus risk aversion and stability-seeking orientation.

In terms of the framework providing an overview of this book we will discuss the types and forms of international work and careers in this chapter. In so doing we draw up a framework of global work patterns. Having gained an understanding of the variety of international careers, we will discuss issues of diversity, different national contexts, work in multicultural teams and cultural intelligence. These reflections allow us to explore the implications of global career research for international careers.

Overall, this and the preceding chapters will have built a basis for further analysis of the stages of international work, ranging sequentially from the motivation to go, to the return and outcomes of global careers in further chapters.

Types of international work and groups of international workers

The basic types of cross-border career moves typically discussed in global career literature are expatriation (and repatriation), as organizational-oriented moves, and immigration, as individual-oriented moves. These, though, do not cover the full range of international work. Below we list the wider spectrum of international career or work involved with cross-border moves. We also list the populations characterized by these types of moves:

- expatriation (mainstream): firm- and self-initiated
- expatriation – flexpatriates
- expatriation – inpatriates/impatriates
- secondments overseas
- off-shore transfer
- short-term assignments
- globetrotting
- immigration (legal)
- immigration (illegal)
- asylum
- immigration (temporary)
- cross-border (commercial)
- government – diplomatic services
- government – armed services
- non-governmental organizations

- work experience, voluntary work, internships
- students/traineeships
- sabbaticals
- virtual global employees

The following section will discuss and elaborate on each of the options listed above.

Expatriation (mainstream)

Expatriation can be initiated by the employer, by the employee, or in collaboration (see Chapter 3 for a detailed discussion). It comprises a career period when an employee of the organization, usually a business firm, is posted to a subsidiary of the firm in a different country for a substantial time period. In the past, a typical expatriation period would last three to five years, but recent surveys (GMAC 2008) point out that the scope is reducing (see Chapter 1). Most of the expatriates are 'home' employees, but some are TCN – originated from a different country to that of the 'home' or 'host'. The expatriation deal accounts for a significant element in the psychological contract between the expatriated person and his or her employer (Yan et al. 2002).

Traditionally, most cases of organizational-based expatriation were initiated and managed by the organization. The organization chose and approached the individual manager and suggested/offered/informed them about the need/request/'offer one cannot refuse' to work internationally. Alongside corporate expatriation there were always cases of self-expatriation of people who decided to move and work in another country for a limited time period. A classic example is nurses working in the oil-rich countries (see Bozionelos 2009 for such a case). In recent years we have more variation in corporate expatriation with many more individuals having self-initiated their own expatriation as a desired career move (Dickmann and Harris 2005; Altman and Baruch 2008). Such career moves might be planned to achieve better career prospects within the organization, or in another one, or for pure self-development. Further elaboration on self-initiated expatriation is presented in Chapter 7.

Expatriation – flexpatriates

Flexpatriates are sent by their organizations to various parts of the world to perform short-term assignments and return 'home' soon after (Mayerhofer et al. 2004). This type of global traveller is typical of executives in MNCs (Welch et al. 2007). They can be the firm's lawyer, an IT expert, a negotiator, etc. Having the required knowledge and gaining the competence in performing across cultures, these 'frequent flyers' (Sparrow et al. 2004) will become a crucial asset for their employers. Yet, this mode of work is highly demanding and induces high levels of stress, which for some is energizing, but for others might be daunting. Moreover, it has a major impact on the private lives of frequent flyers with, for example, regular sports or social activities during the week being all but impossible.

Expatriation – inpatriates/impatriates

Inpatriation is the practice of developing host-country or third-country managers via a transfer to the corporate headquarters (Harvey et al. 2000). This has come as a response to an acute problem. In many cases, the action for firms willing to become global enterprises meant simply extending domestic core competencies to compete with global competitors (as discussed in Chapter 2). The cultural imprint of these core competencies is Western. MNCs that are willing to effectively differentiate in the global market realize they need to become more multicultural. One means of accomplishing this diversity of strategic perspective is to inpatriate foreign managers into the domestic management team on a permanent or semi-permanent basis (Harvey and Buckley 1997). This practice reflects investment in the inpatriates on a long-term basis, and would be instrumental in developing a future cadre of global managers for the firm.

Al-Rajhi et al. (2006) differentiate impatriates (foreign nationals hired for a fixed-term temporary employment) from inpatriates (subsidiaries' personnel sent for periods to work at the mother company). It relates to recruitment en-masse of foreigners by the mother company to work in-house for a limited period of time. An example of impatriation is the case of Saudi companies recruiting Bangladeshis to work for them on special contracts. The visa is confined to a five-year term by Saudi law and the positions are usually blue collar: low to medium skilled.

Short-term assignments

While typical long-term expatriation would last for a few years, and the duration of flexpatriate missions can be a few days, it sometimes happens that the firm has projects to fulfil that require a short period of time overseas. Short-term assignments – in contrast to extended business travel – can be from three months up to a year (Harris et al. 2003). Unlike expatriation, such moves will often not involve a family move, nor (from the individual point of view) a purchase of a house, car, placement of children in schools, etc. The implications for the work–family balance can be severe, particularly if this is not a one-off mission. The meaning of the situation and status implies that the organization requires the employees to make personal family-related sacrifices.

Short-term project-based working is especially common in professional service firms which compete through delivering knowledge-intensive services. For example, strategic and technological consulting firms, law and accountancy companies use international short-term assignments extensively.

Globetrotting

To be a frequent flyer and run a variety of missions in many places one does not necessarily have to be a firm flexpatriate. Many do that for themselves, as freelancers, self-appointed, self-employed, or delegates of others. The world is their oyster.

Box 4.1 Different patterns: the birds and the bees

The following metaphor builds on short vs. long time span in global careers and illustrates that different people will have different ways of enjoying (or otherwise) a global career. Bees fly from flower to flower, spend a short time sucking the nectar, hopefully have time to enjoy the flight and the scenery, and return to the beehive, just to go on another round (like the globetrotters).

Birds have different patterns. The majority of birds would stick to a specific area all their life (and, similarly, most employees never work abroad). Migrating birds are different. They will migrate to a different continent, stay there for a substantial time, and return home, in regular (seasonal) sequence. There is a certain similarity to the global career pattern of Foreign Office diplomats, though they would change destination country each time. Yet, unlike employees who may have a single expatriation period, or will move to different places if having multiple expatriation experiences, the pattern of the birds is regular and repetitive.

Box 4.2 Globetrotting

Celebrity globetrotting

Mark Twain is an example of a book author, who was a celebrity, and who travelled across the globe to give presentations, lectures and to sign his books. Modern authors follow the practice in a similar fashion, just much faster, using jets rather than ships. Author J.K. Rowling promotes her Harry Potter books widely. For humanitarian purposes, Nelson Mandela has promoted his message of freedom and equality by making high-profile global visits to numerous locations since his retirement.

The globetrotting diplomats

While many diplomats would work in their host country most of the time, people like Ban Ki Moon travel constantly from country to country, from crisis to crisis, to deal with them, as did his predecessor as UN Secretary-General, Kofi Annan. Travelling with the Secretary-General will be a host of journalists and their staff.

In-shoring

Increased globalization, but also crises such as the credit crunch that began in 2007, force firms to take major steps in cost-cutting, even when it comes at the expense of unemployment at the national level. Foreign firms who act as

Model work – work of models

In fact, it is not merely the model who travels. A team of photographers, make-up experts, dressers, hairstylists and others would join the photo-shooting in some of the most exotic places on earth.

Sport

Be it football, Formula 1 racing, boxing or tennis – teams or individuals will compete in various places, and with the team will travel media, technical support, coaches, trainers, public relations agents, and others (not to speak of certain dedicated fans and supporters who follow their heroes to most places).

subcontractors for local firms might be allowed to bring in employees to carry out work that was formerly conducted by a local workforce.

In 2009, it was estimated that some 35,000 foreign IT workers were brought into the UK via subcontract deals, practically replacing UK IT employees. One prominent case is of British Telecom, who have caused the redundancy of a substantial number of their IT-related project employees of UK subcontractors by replacing them with Indian people who were brought to the UK to work for about half the salary, as an exercise in cost cutting (BBC Radio 4, UK: 2 June 2009). This is essentially the reverse of off-shoring in which organizations relocate production or service delivery to cheaper locations. Instead, in this 'in-shoring' the firms encourage skilled but low-price people to come en masse to the high-price locations for a short time. People are not immigrating and yet they are distinct from traditional expatriation through their numbers and the replacement of the indigenous labour force in the developed country.

From business mobility to immigration-related mobility

Immigration (legal)

Immigration is not a new phenomenon, with a number of major reasons for each immigration decision (see Chapter 5 for elaboration). One significant cause of immigration is economic reasoning. The motivations include the need to find a job, and the belief that immigration would enable one to gain a well-paid job. This is a major push/pull factor for international moves (Baruch 1995). The procedure to gain an entry would usually start with a request for a work permit (e.g. visa) or a proof of enough money brought in to start a business. Applying for jobs in the host (target) country is a long process, and one significant hurdle to overcome is the protection laws in force to ensure local people have priority. For example, an applicant from outside the EU cannot legally be selected for a job in any EU firm if there are EU applicants who are qualified to fill the post.

Other factors exist too, adding further weight to the pressure on people to decide on a permanent move to a different country. Some of the major factors are:

- *Family factors* The will to join other family members who immigrated earlier, is a clear factor, in particular for extended families or when there are strong family ties. It can follow a case when one member has made the move and has become successful in the host country. It might be 'real success' but also relative success compared with the situation at the home country. Having made a successful transition, they may serve as role models for their siblings or cousins, for example, or a source of support to elderly parents or young nephews and nieces.
- *Desire for adventure*, which may go hand in hand with a risk-taking inclination. Many children read adventure books on global expeditions, on different and exotic locations. Some just read; others generate an urge to experience such excitement and just 'be different'. Individual factors such as seeking adventures, an interest, for example, in the history and culture of foreign countries or simply broad 'wanderlust' are explained in depth in Chapter 5.
- *Feeling marginal* and moving to a country or place where your group of reference is not marginal. An example would be black people in South Africa who looked for equality in countries where no apartheid existed.
- *Security*, for example, leaving war zones or countries where personal security is under threat. An individual does not have to be a refugee (see later) to feel insecure or under threat in their place of birth and residence. Many white people left South Africa and Zimbabwe after the changes in governance, much of it due to fear for their lives and their properties.

Our book focuses on global careers, and is thus work-related. Yet, often, more than one single factor determines an immigration decision. The reader interested in the wider scope is invited to revisit Chapter 1 and explore the literature on demography and immigration.

Immigration (illegal)

Some people decide to move even without entry visa or work permit. The routes to such immigrations vary, and imagination is the only limit for findings ways to enter a country. There is an industry of human trafficking, exploiting the dire needs of these immigrants. People are put in dangerous conditions, and a number of high-profile deaths have been reported – for example, when a ship sinks, or when a number of people hiding in a tanker or a container are suffocated. These immigrants are desperate and are ready to take desperate measures, but in most cases their intention is to work in lawful occupations. Many start working in occupations that have a low local labour supply, such as agriculture or unskilled basic jobs. Thus, while the immigration is illegal, the intention and hope of most such immigrants is to work their way into the legal labour market.

Another type of illegal immigration occurs when human trafficking takes place – including for sex exploitation. Unfortunately, networks of human traffickers exist that bring women, within the EU often from Russia and Eastern Europe, and (ab)use them within the sex trade. Unlike the former categories, this is a case of

> **Box 4.3 Other ways for illegal immigration**
>
> The human mind can be very inventive in finding ways to overcome regulations and authorities. Two examples are:
>
> * People sign up for pilgrimage tours to countries with special places of worship, gain a tourist visa, and then disappear upon arrival.
> * Young people gain acceptance for studying in universities in the US or the EU via legal means of passing an exam and applying to the course, arrive, then just disappear from the system. More 'black-market' operations are fictitious – shadow 'colleges' that 'sell' student visas.
>
> The price of these options can be cheaper than that paid for human traffickers. Now, governments have turned their attention to these possibilities and gaining a tourist or a student visa is not as simple as it once was.

forced or manipulated border crossing, to an 'industry' that is illegal and in many cases, resembles the slavery trade.

Immigration (temporary)

People who immigrate to another country for economic and financial reasons do not necessarily take this step aiming for a permanent change of citizenship. Many immigrate with the initial intention of working for a limited time, to collect enough money that will enable them to return to their home country with significant resources to re-establish themselves in better conditions (Winter-Ebmer and Zweimuller 1996).

A major wave of 'Polish plumbers' came to the UK after Poland joined the EU. A few years later, many of them had returned home. For them it was a short-term period for gaining financial benefits from working in a more affluent country. After that period they preferred to return to their homeland, their original culture and where they felt at home. Similarly, a large number of female Philippine care-workers are employed in other countries for a few years, far from their families, sending money home, but returning home once they have reached their target earnings. This mode of immigration might start as temporary, but can turn into a long-term arrangement, ending in permanent immigration.

Asylum seekers and refugees

The need to immigrate to another country might stem from political or physical threats, when people are persecuted or put in danger. Such people, if they are lucky (and have the means to escape) ask for asylum – typically in Western countries. When there they look for limited employment until their status is confirmed.

Sometimes it is in the interest of the target country not to enable them to work until their status is changed, and they are kept under confined conditions. Governments fail to realize that the experience, qualifications and skills asylum seekers bring can become an economic asset to their new country (Refugee Council 2005).

Cross-border (commercial) commuting

In a number of global locations people cross national borders to work in a different country, and return on a daily or weekly basis to their home. Examples are managers from Hong Kong crossing to China to manage operations and Palestinians crossing the border to work in Israel (many without work permits). Similar cases occur in many European adjacent countries. Many residents of Tijuana cross the border to work in San Diego but live in Mexico. Around the EU, crossing national borders is not much more than crossing borders between states within the USA, and residents of the EU often work in a country adjacent to their own. The Channel Tunnel shortens the travel time between the UK and the continent (from Folkestone to Calais takes 35 minutes, London–Paris is just over two hours) enabling cross-channel commuting.

Government – diplomatic services

The diplomatic service is perhaps the archetype for expatriation. For a very long time, countries have sent officials to other countries as their representatives. They work in a number of different countries as part of a long-term career commitment which involves staying in a foreign country for a specific term, e.g. three or four years. Their working lives can be a series of such appointments, in-between which they will work in the Foreign Office headquarters in their home country. The career ladder is fairly defined, with the position of 'ambassador' as the highest echelon (and with a clear order of priority in the different countries). At the highest level often a civil-servant diplomat official is replaced by a politician. An ambassador role in the USA or in the UN is almost always a political appointment, whereas an ambassador to a less prominent country would be manned by a civil servant from the diplomatic service.

Government – armed services

For most countries, army service means serving within the country borders, and keeping them secure – with the only exception of border crossing being during a war when invading another country's land. In distant history, wars (alongside religion-related missions) were a key form of global cultural 'exchange' (Appadurai 1990). Today, cultural exchanges take the form of economic and commercial transactions and global mobility of people is mostly done for non-military purposes. Yet, the major powers like the USA, Russia, the UK and France operate in various global locations, and the same applies to the peace-keeping forces where the personnel is recruited from many countries (van Emmerik and Euwema 2009). The US armed forces are a major global 'employer', with service men and women active in various locations; some are highly challenging (such as Iraq, Afghanistan) but others offer a calmer type of service.

INGOs and inter-governmental organizations

A number of organizations that are not commercial firms or governments send people for overseas operations. Not-for-profit organizations such as Greenpeace operate globally and send people to various missions, short- and long-term in many destinations.

NATO, the EU and the UN are other types of organizations who have political, humanitarian and economic operations in more than one country. Working or serving in any of them involves interaction with a number of nations and cultures, and almost guarantees physical mobility across borders.

Box 4.4 The United Nations World Food Programme (WFP)

With over 10,000 staff, the WFP is the UN's largest organization. It is in charge of providing food to the needy in more than 80 countries. It has a large range of regional, country and local duty stations and runs an impressive logistics network around the world, consisting of air, water, road and rail transports. On any given day WFP has an average of 5,000 trucks, 70 aircrafts and 30 ships delivering food across the globe (World Hunger Map 2009).

WFP has 1,200 permanently mobile professionals who move on average every four years (from one foreign duty station to another). An individual who works in insecure hardship locations will stay on average for two years in that duty station. It is common, however, for professional staff to be seconded for emergency relief, disaster aid and other catastrophes so that actual moves might be even more frequent.

Sabbaticals

Mostly confined to the academic profession, but employed also in some firms and organizations, is the practice of a sabbatical. Sabbatical programmes allow employees to self-learn, develop and grow professionally and personally when they are away from their permanent employer, and possibly working in a different country. Under this practice, once in about seven years, staff that prove worthy of this 'benefit' receive a year off from their normal duties, dedicated to their development. It will typically involve working as visiting scholars in other institutions, for cross-fertilization of ideas. Timing can vary, i.e. some institutions will allow a one-semester sabbatical after three years of productive work. Institutions will pose different levels of hurdles to academic staff, but excellence in research and teaching will be the major decisive factor. The value of a sabbatical is fundamental for renewal, reflection and the career progress of academics (Frost and Taylor 1996; Baruch and Hall 2004). The work of Richardson and Mallon (2005) indicates that key motivations for undertaking sabbaticals include career, family considerations and the exploration of new options.

Work experience, voluntary work, internships

A number of organizations offer volunteering work overseas. In some cases, people (usually, but not always, young people) will be ready to pay for gaining such experience. This can occur in a gap year, before or after university, but can also take place during a career break or at a later stage. There is a difference between global work for an MNC and overseas experience for a specific and limited time period (Inkson et al. 1997). At the intermediate level, people can look for one of the numerous opportunities for internship in a variety of organizations overseas. While an international internship is also an overseas experience, it is work-related, and can serve as an introduction for a global career. Alternatively, the first in-depth experience could result in the realization that the individual does not like, or regards himself/herself as not fit for, a global career. Indeed, many people do not feel comfortable in an environment which is very different from the one they are used to.

These voluntary work placements and internships offer a win-win possibility. For the organization, it benefits from a (cheap) internationally aware, globalized workforce. For the individuals, it helps in gaining an international perspective and unique experience that are essential ingredients for a successful career.

Box 4.5 Preserving the rainforest

A number of organizations build on the enthusiasm and goodwill of people who are looking to contribute to a good cause. While some are serious operations to support people in the Third World, others have become almost a travel agency offering 'adventure' for young people, for a significant payment. Young people are asked for several thousand dollars for the privilege of visiting and helping remote communities.

Groups such as the Rainforest Biodiversity Group are looking for people with an interest in volunteering in Costa Rica, for which one will only contribute towards living costs, but others demand thousands of dollars for volunteering/touring opportunities in exotic places such as Ecuador.

Students/traineeships

Students studying abroad are certainly crossing physical boundaries, and are put in a situation that forces them to cross, at least on a short time frame, certain cultural boundaries. The numbers are high and continue to grow, with some 600,000 in the USA (McCormack 2007). Other countries have substantial numbers too, for example, over 165,000 in the UK (Rao 2006), with a growing mobility of students across the EU following the Bologna agreement (Mechtenberg and Strausz 2008). Some will stay, either as they planned in advance, or because they have changed their mind, causing possible brain-drain or brain circulation (Baruch et al. 2007). The first of these occurs when countries lose their talent to other nations (brain drain) due to their emigration. Other authors argue that, in the long run people move around, return to their home country, and that this exchange is fruitful for many people as well as for countries at the national level (brain circulation – see Saxenian 2006; Baruch et al. 2007). Following their studies, the graduates can form the inventory of global talent for future employers in their homeland. This is true in particular for those coming from developing countries.

Secondments overseas

One career practice which is a developmental practice, but not in frequent use in organizations is secondments (Baruch 1999: 2003). Under this practice people leave their position in the organization and move to either another department or even another organization in order to acquire new knowledge and different, enriching perspectives. One example of secondment is when a new trainee lawyer has several 'chairs' in the induction process. One of these can take place in an overseas location of the firm.

Box 4.6 PricewaterhouseCoopers

At PwC, some partners are seconded to the UN for about five weeks. They bring their conceptual, methodological and process experience and share it with the UN organization. In turn, they come back to PwC with new insights, a deeper understanding of other people's needs and sensitivity to higher level communication skills (Harris and Dickmann 2005). Returned partners stressed in interviews afterwards that it gave them a new perspective on what they would do in their professional service occupation.

Traditional global occupation: overseas transportation

Since early history, seamen (and now seawomen too) worked mostly outside their national borders, staying at sea for long periods, and visiting/working in harbours and ports in other countries. Seamen, though, normally return to their home country, and the time they spend in a host country, mostly at the port town, tend to include merely short visits (i.e. to enable offloading and loading of stores and merchandise). These long-term voyages could last many months. Today, with much faster ships and advanced technology for loading and unloading, the cycles have become shorter (e.g. ships can now cross the ocean in a matter of days rather than months).

Also, the crew is not characterized by the 'home' country of the ship – for example, reports in 2009 on the captured Saudi supertanker that was seized by pirates indicate the multinational nature of current sea crews. The Sirius Star had a 25-strong crew – 19 from the Philippines, two from Britain, two from Poland, one Croatian and one Saudi. A hundred years ago, the length of sailing would be much longer; the nationality of the crew would mostly confined to the 'home country' of the ship, and the size of crew would be much larger (certainly when relative to the amount of goods taken on board).

These differences are even more significant when considering air transport, both of passengers and of cargo.

Virtual global employees

Unlike the above cases, all involving the physical move of people to and from different geo-locations, the virtual global employee can work from his or her office (even their home, if telecommuting), and be part of a multinational team, engaged in a global project, and/or collaborating with a number of contacts in various locations.

> **Box 4.7 Global virtual production**
>
> When one of the authors of this book co-edited a different book (Baruch et al. 2008), the team of four co-editors came from three different countries, and apart from one short face-to-face meeting at a conference, the project was run and managed fully via the net. The editors never met the representative of the publisher (who is located in the UK). A 'team' of 30 people from a number of countries wrote 25 different chapters. The written chapters were sent for proofreading and editing in India, printed in the UK, and sold across the globe.

Integrative framework

The above categories can be classified along a number of dimensions. One useful framework is suggested by Peiperl and Jonsen (2007) who offer a four-quadrant matrix with two dimensions to depict the types of global people. One dimension is actual time spent away from home culture or market, and the other is the amount of interaction across cultures and markets. They rightly claim that a 'real global citizen' is one that crosses both physical and cultural borders. Peiperl and Jonsen indicate that many cross physical borders but work within one culture, such as when travelling to work in the firm headquarters, or when expatriates live in enclaves detached from local people and their culture. Indeed, many employees of MNCs spend their entire career in a single country, while only some of their colleagues would do the actual travelling. Moreover, the rank-and-file employees of MNCs working in production in China, Malaysia or Thailand will probably never visit any other country. Only a handful of local employees, at the local executive level or possessing valuable professional skills, will have a global career. The majority cannot be considered truly global in their career. Others might stay in one country but interact with people from a variety of cultures, and might work virtually with a diverse workforce, the 'virtual global citizens'. In their classification, only those who encounter international work and have actual cross-cultural interaction – mental and physical – are true global citizens. Those who do neither are, nicely put, 'potential' global citizens. With the pace of change, indeed many who did not consider working outside their small town, village or country, may soon have a career change that will take them in the globalized direction.

To the two dimensions of Peiperl and Jonsen we would add that reality is more complex, and time and space dimensions are more complicated. Possible further dimensions might cover the intensity of the interaction, the number of countries/cultures involved, and the level of cultural gap between the home and host countries.

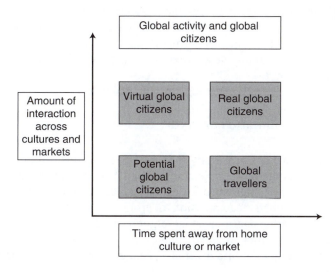

Figure 4.2 Different combinations of global movements and global interaction
Source: Peiperl and Jonsen (2007)

Acquiring global experience via IAs, be they short- or long-term, work-related or otherwise, helps individuals to gain and develop career capital (Dickmann and Harris 2005). Career capital refers to the intelligent career framework (Arthur et al. 1995), where global experience helps to re-shape the 'knowing-why', improves and enhances the 'knowing-how', and generates a new network of 'knowing-whom' for the person involved.

Reflection

There are manifold ways to work abroad and/or to acquire international experiences. These have an impact on global careers with regard to the depths and length

---

Box 4.8 Linguistic point

To be truly global, one should be able to speak English. Yes, the largest single-country population is that of China. Yes, one can manage very well in a large number of countries if one talks Arabic, Spanish or French. Yes, a single language cannot penetrate the nuances of many other languages. Yet, English is a key dimension of globalization (Phillipson 2003). It serves as the bridge across various languages, and is fully recognized as the global language. We do not say it is the most beautiful language (many would opt for Italian or French), certainly it is not the most logical language (Latin is far easier for logical understanding) and using English as the global language gives an 'unfair' advantage to native English speakers. But this is reality, business reality. Thus managers wishing to be global should practise their English.

of exposure to different cultures and work environments. People involved with such career trajectories gain global career capital, though this possibility is limited to certain individuals, mostly from affluent countries. The domestic context is instrumental in shaping these experiences and resulting opportunities. We will discuss these next.

Diversity within domestic contexts

There are a number of diversity sources: gender, ethnic origin, age, disability, sexual orientation, religion, to name the most prominent groupings. Other diversity bases were distinguished from the 'surface-level diversity' by Harrison et al. (1998), who coined the expression 'deep-level diversity', namely the diversity of values, norms and attitudes that might be different from that of the visible diversities. In addition, there are other factors, such as belonging to a special type of family, and 'hybrid diversity', i.e. belonging to more than one of these groups.

Most affluent Western countries benefit (or suffer) from a diverse population. Some 20 per cent of the population in the Netherlands comes from a variety of countries, not merely from adjacent Germany, but also from Indonesia, Turkey, Suriname, Morocco and more. Some countries have a concentration of specific immigration – e.g. people from Algeria tend to opt for France, Turkish persons focus on Germany – while other countries (Denmark, UK) are being targeted by a very wide diversity of sources.

In the USA, different waves of immigration occurred in the past, but the current situation witnesses many immigrants, a large proportion of which are illegal, coming from Mexico. It is interesting to note that in San Antonio, where the Alamo stands as a symbol of the fighting with Mexico over Texas many years ago, the majority of the population speaks Spanish as their first language.

The tolerance towards diverse workforces varies too. However, the general trend is of improving levels of diversity tolerance, even in countries notorious for their past segregation. An example would be that the caste culture in India is not diminishing, but its power and relevance has changed and reduced; women in Arab countries have gained an increasing number of rights – see, for example, Dalacoura (1998). Within MNCs, the largest of which are still mostly Western-based, there is substantial progress in managing diversity. The number of female expatriates is growing relative to past figures, but is not at the level of male expatriates, a difference noted earlier in Adler (1984, 1993). This imbalance continues to this day, because the pace of closing the gap is fairly slow (Altman and Shortland 2008). Altman and Shortland's review identifies a positive trend in the organizational view of women expatriates, though the gap remains significant. They argue that organizations have moved from the typical view of the 1980s debate whether to 'give women a chance' through attempts to identify and remove 'blockages' to women's progress (in the 1990s) up to the twenty-first-century practice of re-shaping the view towards women on global assignment. A reason, apart from legal and political correctness is because certain studies argue that women possess a superior affinity to operating internationally. We will present a wider discussion on the issue in Chapter 7.

There is less evidence about other types of diversity in the selection of expatriates. As language proficiency in the host country is a significant advantage (when it is not English), we would expect people with relevant cultural and linguistic knowledge of the host country to have preference in selection and to experience easier adjustment (see Bell and Harrison 2002). However, it was found that the role of cultural similarity between home and host is less important for a successful adaptation than an individual's ability to fit into the host culture (June and Gentry 2005). The cultural factor is a major element influencing the selection of employees for expatriate assignments (Franke and Nicholson 2002). An elaborated discussion on the issue is presented in Chapters 5 and 6. It is interesting to note that language capabilities do not seem to serve as a strong criterion in selection.

The age and family paradox of expatriation diversity

Another diversity-related issue in selection is the age and family status of the expatriate. Age discrimination is a topic of growing concern, but with regard to expatriation, the challenge is different, and may relate to family issues. Apart from very few technical roles and developmental assignments, expatriation will not be at an early career stage. Certain managerial experience and knowledge is required before embarking on representing the firm/organization overseas. At the other end of the age range are the top executives – again, unlikely to go for expatriation unless it is to lead a subsidiary of a very large organization in a major country. Such an exceptional example was the case of Akio Morita being expatriated to the USA by Sony (Morita et al. 1986). The typical age (career age) when expatriation takes place is in mid-career. At that age, in industrialized societies, it is common to have a dual-career family with young children, where both parents work, and expatriation poses a challenge of relocation of the family: both issues can prove to be a deal-breaker. Teenage children can be a major obstacle for relocation, and employment abroad of only one person can be a disaster for the career of her/his spouse. The issue is becoming relevant also in developing countries. With an increasing number of professional Chinese coming to Britain for further education and employment, Cooke (2007) compares the career experience of the 'trailing' wives of Chinese academic couples before and after their migration, identifying barriers that migrant Chinese professional women might encounter in Britain. The 2008 GMAC report identified a trend of reduction in duration of expatriation, which could be another indication of societal impacts on the nature of expatriation. This discussion is deepened in Chapters 5 and 6.

The age and family paradox in expatriation planning is that from the above discussion it implies that the best time from an age/family point of view might be very early or very late in a career. As we have seen in Chapter 2, firms increasingly choose early and late careerists for international work. Nevertheless, the highest expatriation flows are those that involve mid-career persons. It requires the HRM department to delve into wider family-related issues in the planning of expatriation (and repatriation), in particular as spillover effects between work and non-work issues are very strong during an expatriation period (Selmer and Fenner

2009). HRM can offer help such as in identifying an appropriate educational system for the children, and identifying employment opportunities for the spouse. Collaboration across firms can be fruitful: when several oil firms operate in the Gulf or in Aberdeen, for example, one might employ the spouse of an expatriate from a different firm, even a competitor, and vice versa.

Regarding diversity from another angle – that of training – diversity training is considered crucial in preparing people for their global career. Caligiuri et al. (2005) emphasize the role of training for successful global work. Chapter 6 will cover in depth the issue of training for expatriation.

National business systems, national cultures and HRM

Global career means working in a variety of countries, where values, norms and behaviours vary. One major factor for such variation is the national culture, and one of its derivatives – business system and business culture. Different features of business systems and national cultures can make the life of the global careerist more or less easy. Awareness and openness are crucial ingredients for success in the process. A simple example to manifest the challenge is the following question: 'Which are the most important criteria for managers to achieve success?'

According to Schneider and Barsoux (1997: 144), the answer depends very much on the culture in the relevant country. In the USA the right answer is drive and ability. In France it would be concerned with class and education, i.e. whether or not the manager attended one of the *Grand Écoles* for their studies. In Germany the underlying issue is technical and functional competence, whereas in the UK what often matters is a classical education and having a generalist approach. Further to the East, in Japan, people value qualification from top universities, compliance and loyalty. The diverse answers indicate that the assumptions and conventions that people have in their own country are not necessary applied elsewhere.

The meaning and nature of HRM varies across nations. Thus also the nature and the way certain practices are conducted. Selection, for example, might be competence based, but might rely on networks and nepotism. Even within the same country, the considerations for recruitment and selection can vary, for example, between the private and public sectors. In the Middle East context, the social and political networks (Wasta) can be influential in selection (Iles et al. in press). Within one country, practices within the public sector can rely on traditional systems whereas the private sector follows benchmarking with large global MNCs (Cohen and Baruch 2010). In some wealthy states in the Middle East, much of the private sector labour market is 'outsourced' to expatriates. For example, less than 20 per cent of the total population of the UAE comprises of native citizens (Economist Intelligence Unit 2008). Further, their share of the private workforce is estimated to be less than 1 per cent (Hafez 2009), as the majority are employed in the public sector (Forstenlechner 2009). This is despite official efforts to draw more local citizens into the workforce (Al Ali 2008). The deep roots of this phenomenon depend on the nature of the employment structure in the Gulf and, as a result, for the foreseeable future, we envisage the reliance on expatriates in the region will remain high.

> **Box 4.9 Professional and nationally segmented workforce?**
>
> The labour market of expatriates can be segmented based on various
> grounds. Professionally, the two distinct types of expatriation jobs are man-
> agerial vs. technical. Many MNCs will send people to their subsidiaries in
> order to manage them (and gain managerial development experience), but
> on other occasions, expatriates are sent to bridge a specific skill gap or pro-
> vide particular knowledge to the host country operation.
>
> Another segmentation, less accepted by Western measures, is the phenome-
> non in the Gulf where Europeans and Americans are the most desired
> expatriates for managerial roles (in particular, British citizens), while citi-
> zens of countries such as India or Bangladesh will be typically appointed to
> less desired, less well-paid jobs.

One of the most crucial roles of HRM is to recruit and select future employees, as
well as to select the right people from within the organization to be considered for
development and promotion. Within expatriation management, the selection is
usually of people within the organization (less so for the Professional strategy of
Baruch and Altman (2002) – see Chapter 3). The selection of a prospective expatriate varies according to several factors. The organizational strategy is a major
consideration, e.g. in a 'Global' system the selection will not be much different
from choosing a person to fill a new position; in the 'Peripheral' strategy the
choice will be who 'deserves' this perk. With more people self-initiating their
global assignment (Dickmann and Harris 2005; Altman and Baruch 2008), the
'selection' role might turn around, from identifying whom to approach, into
choosing between those who apply. Alternatively, the choice might be identifying
a high-potential employee, for whom expatriation is considered a crucial element
in their progress path.

Performance management is crucial for organizational effectiveness and success,
and this applies to global organizations too. Defining performance management,
Armstrong (2000) suggests it is 'a process which is designed to improve organizational, team and individual performance and which is owned and driven by line
managers'. Yet managers in a different culture would set different goals and performance measures. One typical difference is long-term vs. short-term gains;
another one is about profitability vs. market share as indicators of success. In an
organizational survey, including some two-thirds of MNCs, from 15 different
countries, most of the organizations (over 90 per cent) implemented a formal
performance management system, which helps organizations to outperform others
regarding financial outcomes and other outcomes including customer satisfaction,
employee retention and other relevant metrics (Cascio 2006). A major issue is the
difference between 'conventional performance management', as initiated in the
USA, and performance management in a global context, where the meaning of performance and its management varies across cultures. Discussing performance measurement in a cross-national context, Caligiuri (2006) presented a five-step process:

1 determine the broad content domain of performance – across countries for the same position;
2 determine if these jobs are comparable;
3 if so, create 'conceptual equivalence' that can be applied across cultures and countries;
4 determine 'how' the evaluations will be organized; and
5 'who' will conduct the appraisal(s).

All of these issues should gain considerable attention, as indeed cultural differences can be influential. It appears that 'objective task-based performance dimensions' are less influenced by differences in the nationality of the rater and the ratee than 'subjective contextual performance dimensions' (Caligiuri 2006). Yet, the subjective factor could count more for people's attitudes and should be considered while people from different social backgrounds meet.

Box 4.10, adapted from Baruch (2004) manifests the difference in understanding the meaning of evaluation (and in this specific case, discipline actions) taken across cultures.

Box 4.10 The hamburger discipline

An executive of a major US oil firm (Exxon-Mobil), who served as an expatriate in countries including Japan, Germany and the UK told me this metaphorical story. It illustrates what type of different metaphorical hamburger one might encounter when disciplined in different cultures.

When you work in the USA and make a mistake, your manager will call you up to his/her office. At first you will be told something along the lines, 'We know how good you are, valued by the company, and that usually your work is fine' (lower bun). Then will come the 'meat': 'Yesterday you acted in such and such manner, which is not according to our policy . . .', and so on. So a warning or comment will be entered into the file. Then the manager will say, 'We do know that it was a one-off event, and we value your work, and wish to leave this behind' etc. That is the upper bun. You got your 'balanced' hamburger.

What would happen if you work in Germany? Your manager will most probably call you up to his/her office, and will tell you exactly and straight to the point: 'Yesterday you acted in such and such manner, which is not according to our policy . . .' and so on. A warning or comment will be entered into the file. That's it. Pure 'meat'.

If, however, the event takes place in Japan, your manager will call you up to his (probably not her) office, and will tell you something along the lines, 'We know how good you are, valued by the company, and that usually your work is fine'. Then he will go on, praising your work, providing more nice positive comments, and will send you out (just the buns . . .). Nevertheless, you will know, you will know indeed why you were called up.

What implications may be taken from this illustrative case?

Cultures are different, but within each culture people can well recognize the method of the discipline action, its severity, and what lesson should be taken. Yet, when people from different cultures mingle with each other, such assumed common understanding and shared knowledge is not in place.

Imagine that a manager within a German culture orientation is placed in Japan. If he or she is called for a discipline procedure, they will probably never get the message. Or even a worse scenario, where a Japanese manager stationed in Germany is told off 'the German way' by the local manager – he might depart immediately, very upset, through the door, or worse, through the window . . .

While the Americans feel that their way is the right one (certainly it is a balanced approach), the question is not who is right. What matters is that the message needs to be delivered and understood, wherever the company operates. This is the challenge for people in global management.

As indicated earlier in the book, there are two challenges for MNCs in managing people across borders. Firstly, the general HRM system: how to keep a coherent HRM system that will be 'glocal' – keeping the home ethos of the firm's culture while responding to local needs and characteristics of the various subsidiaries. Secondly, the management of people movements across borders: how to manage resource movements, in particular expatriation and repatriation of key personnel.

The development of a career system for an MNC will thus have to take into account those differences: business-, cultural- and institutional-related. It is not just an issue of firm management. Sometimes the issue is wider, for example, when the legal system, economy and even religious inputs are concerned. When people opt to work in the Gulf, they will have to avoid alcohol, for example. Tolerance for drug use varies too, from the Netherlands, where some drugs can be purchased and consumed legally and openly (visits to a 'coffee-shop' in Amsterdam do not necessarily involve a drink of coffee). The other extreme case can be severe sentences, even the death penalty, for drug dealing.

A more conventional managerial issue can be dealing with performance appraisal (PA). Some decisions have to be made: which kind of system and what format (or forms) should be utilized? There is a variety of options to choose relevant types of criteria, and in a global context these would differ across countries. The system needs to be based on a proper type of measurement approach (instrument, scale). These can be ranking or behavioural appraisals (graphic rating scales, anchored rating scales, observation scales, to name a few), for the specific measurement of employees' inputs. A comprehensive managerial approach could include management by objective (Drucker 1974). Some PA systems fit well in individualist societies whereas others would match the needs of a collectivist society. The MNC has three options: (1) to apply the same system across the board; (2) to apply a multi-system with a different format for different operations; or (3) to opt for a compromise or a combination (Baruch 2004).

An example of the challenge is operating performance-related pay (PRP) PA, in which case the issue of remuneration is affected due to different cultures (cf. Kessler and Purcell 1992; Kessler 1994). Even within the same country, applying PRP in a subculture that opposes the idea can prove disastrous, as the case described by Popper (1997) of the 'glorious failure' in such intervention. The strategic, structural and application of IHRM issues have been discussed in more depth in Chapter 2.

The impact of the context and its cultural, institutional, political and economic impact factors is illustrated through the case of Miao running sales for SEL in Latin America.

Case study 4.1 Running sales for SEL in South America

'[T]his will never work!' Manolo told his boss Miao. How had this situation developed? After all, Chinese Miao was not used to being spoken to like this and felt that her authority was being challenged. Faced with open dissent, Miao thought for a moment. The history and context of the situation flashed through her mind.

Miao worked for Shanghai Enterprises Ltd (SEL), a multinational corporation that was founded in 1995 in China. It produces, markets and sells white goods around the world. The firm has ten factories (seven in China, one in Poland, one in Canada and one in Colombia) and employs approximately 45,000 staff. It operates in 87 countries, with sales of approximately €12 bn.

In South America SEL has sales of €1.4 bn and a staff of 3,500. Most of these work in Colombia. In the Caribbean coastal city of Baranquilla the firm has its factory, employing 2,800 persons. Miao, a 48-year-old sales executive from Shanghai was expatriated to head the sales operations throughout South America. She arrived 15 months ago, without her family who stayed in Shanghai. She missed her husband and her daughter but felt that she had an obligation to SEL to move abroad if her superiors asked her. One day in early May of last year Zang, the global sales and marketing director, had suggested that it would be good for her career to head the regional sales operations. She had reluctantly agreed to move.

Miao had not much knowledge of South America, let alone Colombia. While she had heard about Bogotá, Medellin and Cartagena, Baranquilla was unknown to her and it came as a surprise that the bubbly coastal city had more than 1 million inhabitants. Miao did not speak Spanish – in fact, her Spanish was still poor and only enabled her to order basic items in restaurants and get by in other situations – but she had read up on the history and politics of the South American country.

In late May Miao arrived in Baranquilla to meet her regional and local sales team. Joao was heading the Brazilian sales operations, Jaime, Enrique and Liliana different parts of Middle and Southern America while Manolo was in charge of Colombian sales. Miao had a strong persuasion that success is based on strong teams and felt that the key to stronger sales would be in learning from each other and cooperating across borders within sales. Her predecessor, a Colombian national (Jorge), had met her and briefed her about the sales staff. Manolo in particular was seen by Jorge as a key person who had single-handedly built an effective sales operation in Colombia. She was left with an impression that she was facing strong personalities who relished the authority they had to run their operations.

In August last year she had met with each of her top executives – Manolo, Liliana, Jaime, Enrique and Joao – to review their performance and to set objectives. The company's objectives were to increase sales from €12 bn last year to €20 bn in five years' time. To achieve this, she was cooperating with her counterparts in North America, Europe, Africa and the Middle East, Asia-Pacific (outside China) and China. She expected nothing less from her five sales executives and called them to a workshop regarding the future plans for the next five years. Imagine her surprise to find that each sales executive had brought detailed plans for the next 12 months – but no longer. Manolo laughed when she asked about longer plans and Liliana told her that there was no point in planning that long ahead given the dynamic environment they were in.

In the short workshop, Miao insisted that her executive team would develop five-year sales plans and operational activities to live up to the demanding goals. Moreover, she told her team that they had to factor in how to cooperate within the region. She noticed that especially Manolo and Enrique seemed to feel uncomfortable about this concept – although they had the geographically nearest regions with Venezuela and Colombia. However, the others did not seem keen on the idea either.

Considering these reactions, she decided that her evaluation of her team would be weighted at: 50 per cent for the achievement of overall regional sales targets for Middle and South America; 15 per cent for growing a second-line leadership pipeline in sales; 15 per cent for the cooperation with the after-sales and service departments; and 20 per cent for national sales growth.

The cooperation of sales and service departments turned out to be rather difficult. Sales personnel in most regions overpromised in terms of the reliability of their products so that service technicians often received hostile treatment when they went out to fix the washing machines and dryers in the customers' houses. The various heads of services had written a letter to Miao to reign in the sales teams but only Liliana and Manolo of the sales directors seemed to want to cooperate with this request.

The next year was also difficult for other reasons. Venezuela's president had decided to put up import duties on white goods and as a consequence sales suffered. Manolo had an open conflict with Enrique blaming him for Venezuela costing them all money. Joao's sales in Brazil, on the other hand, were increasingly strongly but he started to put pressure on Miao to change the national sales weight in the appraisal.

At the beginning of August things came to a head. Manolo had asked for a meeting and had told her that 'gagging' the sales team in terms of the way the products were described would cost them sales. Miao was shocked by the emotional, strong language Manolo used but pointed out that the long-term effect would pay off for SEL. This was the point when Manolo burst out that he thought that all her long-term plans would cost him money. He pointed out that he did not understand why poor sales in Venezuela should cost him money, that being handcuffed in terms of selling activities would cost him money and that she, Miao, would need more time to understand how the South American market in white goods really worked. 'The way things are now, this will never work!' With these words Manolo stormed out of her office.

This sort of open dissent and low respect had not ever happened to Miao. Her first impulse was to fire Manolo . . . and yet, he had built up the Colombian sales team and with great success over the last eight years. Miao started to think hard.

Case questions:

1. What are the key problems that Miao faces?
2. Why is Manolo so upset?
3. Which of these issues are down to organizational reasons? Please distinguish between structural, functional and cross-departmental issues.
4. What role do personality, national culture, history and politics play in the case?
5. What would you suggest as Miao's next steps? Why?

N.B. This case is fictional. All other cases in this book are based on organizational reality.

Another example can be found relating to the use of 360-degree feedback. This system is an excellent way of providing employees with rich feedback for their performance. Clear benefits have emerged in applying such a system in different cultures (Baruch and Harel 1993; Bernardin et al. 1995). For example, self PA (Baruch 1996) and upward PA (Bernardin 1986) can be valuable PA sources, increasing reliability and validity of the feedback. In other cultures, people might resent the use of this form of evaluation, for example, where there is a high level of 'power distance' (Hofstede 1980).

Bernardin et al. (1995) argue that any PA system should apply (1) legally defensible appraisal procedures, (2) legally defensible appraisal content, (3) legally defensible documentation of appraisal results and (4) legally defensible raters. As in many other issues in cross-border management, legal advice is important in adapting the global system to local considerations, including PA systems.

Multicultural teams

Even though we live in the age of individualism, there are very few organizational tasks that can be performed solely by single individuals. Teams are the building stone of organizations. They are at the centre of how work gets done in modern companies, and major changes in the structure of work and the interdependency and immediacy of life in a global society have only increased the importance of effective teams (Kozlowski and Ilgen 2006). Globalization and international integration of companies are inevitable, and thus it is no longer acceptable to proceed with the study of teams as if their members are isolated from their cultural and national heritage (Earley and Gibson 2008). Globalization has yielded a degree of multicultural diversity in team membership and structure, as members of the team come from various nations and cultures.

Teams take many shapes – small, large, ad hoc, permanent, task forces, self-managed teams, top management teams, and other forms. Some teams are formed within specific organizational departments, but many involve employees from a variety of departments, and sometimes these teams will include people associated with, but not employed by, the organization.

Teams are responsible for performance, for improvements in processes, for setting goals and fulfilling them. A work team can be defined as an 'interdependent collection of individuals who share responsibility for specific outcomes for their organizations' (Sundstorm et al. 1990: 12). In addition, working in teams is essential to fulfil social needs. Individuals are attached to the team, the team influences the way people work and interact, and influences the attitudes of the members in a way that they can develop or adopt certain norms and values. This is easier done within a specific culture where one can expect relative homogeneity of norms and values.

If a team comprises three or more individuals who interact directly or indirectly for the accomplishment of a common goal, then a multinational team is such a team where members come from more than a single national or cultural background (Earley and Gibson 2008). There is a difference between nationality and culture. Within the same nation many cultures can exist, and while there are many variations between different nations on several dimensions (Hofstede 1980), there is much variance within each nation.

Some factors do not change much with culture. Such is the issue of conformity and social influence, whereas differences exist across cultures in issues such as conflict handling and managerial styles (Earley and Gibson 2008: 4). Some features seem to apply in general for any human being whereas others are more concerned with different ways of 'programming the mind', which is the way culture is defined by Hofstede (1980). Even the acceptability of a team-based system varies across cultures (Kirkman and Shapiro 1997), and teamwork can be more harmonized in collectivist societies.

Multinational teams are necessary in MNCs, but exist also in other firms and organizations. Multinational teams are challenging to manage (Gibbs 2009). Global immigration, in particular of professionals, means that talented people working in one country could have come from a variety of countries. Some countries, and in particular the USA, provide a clear example for the ability of people from different cultures to work together and establish a successful team. The diversity of the workforce will inevitably be reflected in the diversity in the working teams within organizations (Earley and Gibson 2008).

Some multinational teams are virtual, offering new solutions and posing new challenges in managing across borders (Martins et al. 2004). Such is the case when a firm is required to provide 24/7 IT support to all its operations, and thus needs to have IT support teams throughout the day. Location issues might suggest having one team in Europe, one team in the Far East, and one in the USA, performing a daily 'handshake' of issues to be maintained in the various operations (Baruch 2004). The culture of work in these three global locations varies substantially in a number of dimensions.

The Earley and Gibson (2008) model provides an overview of a multinational team framework. The model rightly distinguishes between the individual level and the team level. They cover the main areas of relevance to the development and progress within multinational teams. In Figure 4.3 we present their model and we have added to the model the outcomes level for both individuals and teams. The

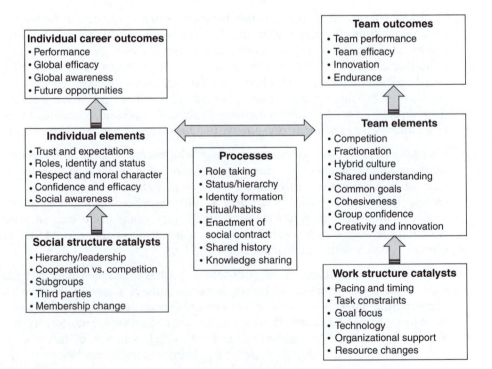

Figure 4.3 An overview of multinational team theory
Source: Adapted and enhanced from Earley and Gibson (2008: 52)

relevance of their model to global careers is concerned with the interaction processes between the individual and the team, where the diversity within the team can influence mutual learning and openness to other experiences.

Cultural intelligence

One necessity of global business is the need to interact with people who are culturally different (Thomas and Inkson 2004). The importance of cross-cultural people skills continues to grow as globalization expands, because effective management of people is key to individual, team and enterprise performance. And it is even more so for the global enterprise. Global managers need to have a number of qualities, and intelligence is certainly a crucial factor. Yet, recent developments in psychology point out that the nature of intelligence can be taken along a number of dimensions.

Possession of high intelligence quotient and emotional intelligence (IQ and EQ) is crucial for any manager, but for the global manager a new quality or capacity is essential – it is the cultural intelligence (CQ). The concept of CQ was developed and suggested by Earley and Ang (2003), with certain parallelism to other theories of intelligence.

> Definition: Cultural intelligence is an individual's capability to function and manage effectively in culturally diverse settings. It is a multidimensional construct targeted at situations involving cross-cultural interactions arising from differences in race, ethnicity and nationality.
>
> (Ang et al. 2007)

Global managers need to cooperate, collaborate and network with people from cultures different from their own – people holding a variety of beliefs, acquainted with different, sometimes opposing norms, who act using a variety of behaviours that are not customary in their homeland. People with high CQ possess cross-cultural people skills, which enable them to interact effectively with others who are different from them. CQ will enable people to employ appropriate behaviour, fit for the local culture, and adapt and adjust their behaviour as necessary under different cultural conditions. Cultural awareness is essential to understand why and how other people behave in the way that they do, and will enable effective communication with them.

Like any type of intelligence, possibly more so than other types of intelligence, CQ can be developed and people can train to improve their CQ. Earley and Peterson (2004) developed a systematic approach to intercultural training that links trainees' CQ strengths and weaknesses to training interventions. CQ can be developed through cognitive means: the head (learning about your own and other cultures, and cultural diversity); physical means: the body (using senses and adapting movements and body language); and motivational, emotional means.

General intelligence is 'the ability to grasp and reason correctly with abstractions (concepts) and solve problems' (Schmidt and Hunter 2000: 3). Thus intelligence can be measured. CQ can be measured too, and a number of scholars and practitioners have developed measurement scales (see Box 4.11 for one example) similar to those used for measuring personal IQ. People with a higher CQ are regarded as better able to successfully blend in to any environment, using more effective business practices, than those with a lower CQ (Ang et al. 2007). The academic literature discussed theoretical relationships between CQ capabilities and forming accurate judgements (Triandis 2006) and CQ as critical for expecting and addressing the unexpected during intercultural encounters (Brislin et al. 2006).

Although early research tended to view intelligence narrowly as the ability to solve problems in academic settings, there is now increasing consensus that intelligence can be displayed in places other than the classroom (Sternberg and Detterman 1986). This growing interest in 'real world' intelligence includes intelligence that focuses on specific content domains such as social intelligence (Thorndike and Stein 1937), emotional intelligence (Mayer et al. 2000) and practical intelligence (Sternberg et al. 2000). CQ acknowledges the practical realities of globalization (Earley and Ang 2003) and focuses on a specific domain – intercultural settings. Thus, following Schmidt and Hunter's (2000) definition of general intelligence, CQ is a specific form of intelligence focused on capabilities to grasp, reason and behave effectively in situations characterized by cultural diversity.

Box 4.11 Measuring CQ

Ang et al. (2007) suggested a five-dimensional measure for CQ, offering several items to test each one of them. Here are sample items for each dimension. Test yourself for your CQ (for a detailed evaluation you can log onto the web to identify a more specific evaluation test).

Below we list the dimensions suggested by Ang et al. and present a sample item of each from their questionnaire:

Metacognitive CQ

Sample item: I am conscious of the cultural knowledge I apply to cross-cultural interactions.

Cognitive CQ

Sample item: I know the rules for expressing non-verbal behaviours in other cultures.

Motivational CQ

Sample item: I am confident that I can socialize with locals in a culture that is unfamiliar to me.

Behavioural CQ

Sample item: I change my verbal behaviour (e.g. accent, tone) when a cross-cultural interaction requires it.

Ang et al. (2007) discuss CQ as a multidimensional construct, following Sternberg's (1986) integrative framework proposed different 'loci' of intelligence within the person. They refer to metacognitive intelligence as a control of cognition: the processes that individuals use to acquire and understand knowledge. Applying Sternberg's multiple-loci of intelligence, Earley and Ang (2003) conceptualized CQ as comprising metacognitive, cognitive, motivational and behavioural dimensions with specific relevance to functioning in culturally diverse contexts.

Implications of global HRM research for international careers

The new shape of careers calls for an understanding that it is not merely the organization but a combination of individuals and institutions sharing the responsibility for career's decisions (Hall 2004; Baruch 2006). Hall's logic suggests that the licence and incentive to experiment with new possibilities is granted by the individuals to themselves. Some decisions and career moves, such as expatriation, are risky and have much ambiguity inherent within them.

While much is subjected to the organizational plans, impetus and control, people are more open to take new paths and career options. Risk-aversion will be an obstacle for global moves, whereas for the risk-prone, expatriation acts as an enabler for such an attitude. Career proactivity is an essential ingredient for such an environment (Seibert et al. 2001) and the new career landscape calls for more self-reliance, internal focusing and self-initiation, either within the organization (Dickmann and Harris 2005), or outside it (Bozionelos 2009). Within this environment, expatriation provides the context for experimentation. Such experimentation enables people to respond with the intensity of a *calling* (Hall and Chandler 2005), though it requires more readiness to take risks and be resilient in terms of career future directions (Waterman et al. 1994).

Future global career research should identify and follow new trends, implications and outcomes for individuals and their employing organizations. We noted how, following the sharp increase in global work in the 1980s and 1990s, the scholarly work published in the 1990s presented a high volume of expatriation-based studies. When the wave of expatriation became a regular phenomenon, a new stream of repatriation literature emerged in the late 1990s and early 2000s. We now witness a new trend of expatriation studies in terms of their individualization. At a wider perspective the future of career research could become more fragmented, due to the multitude of global career options, as depicted in our 'glossary' at the beginning of this chapter. Each of these global career options deserves study and exploration. Further, new horizons are being opened constantly. The major one in recent years is the opening of China to capitalism, and the immense growth in global activity in China. Similarly, virtual global work will be a major field of a yet mostly unexplored area. We look with excitement for these future developments and the research that will unveil them.

Summary and learning points

We started by positing a variety of global career moves, moving the analysis beyond expatriation and repatriation moves. These show the variety of career trajectories available for developing global careers. Following our 'glossary' and analysis of the various types of global career moves, we presented an integrative framework together with the meaning of a 'real global citizen', and the different dimensions available for an analysis of the phenomenon.

We then discussed diversity within the local level and teams, moved to the national business systems, national cultures, and the relevance and implication of managing cross-cultural moves for HRM. The practice of HRM has high potential to deal with global moves in a positive way, as well as the potential to lead to disastrous outcomes. Lastly, we employed the Earley and Gibson model for multinational work teams to manifest different facets of global work and discussed the concept of cultural intelligence and its meaning for global careers.

Key learning points include:

• The existence of a variety of global career options, as reflected in the wide portfolio presented.
• The meaning of diversity management within global career systems.
• The role played by national business systems, national cultures and HRM.
• Multicultural teams and their impact on global careers.
• The importance of the concept of cultural intelligence to both individual and organizational management of global careers.

References

Adler, N. (1984) 'Women in international management: Where are they?', *California Management Review*, 26(4): 78–89.

Adler, N. (1993) 'Competitive frontiers: managing across borders', *Journal of Management Development*, 13: 24–41.

Al Ali, J. (2008) 'Emiratisation: drawing UAE nationals into their surging economy', *International Journal of Sociology and Social Policy*, 28: 365–379.

Al-Rajhi, I., Altman, Y., Metcalfe, B. and Roussel, J. (2006) 'Managing impatriate adjustment as a core human resource management challenge', *Human Resource Planning*, 29(4): 15–23.

Altman, Y. and Baruch, Y. (2008) 'Global protean careers: a new era in expatriation and repatriation', paper presented at the *European Academy of Management* conference, Ljubljana, May 2008.

Altman, Y. and Shortland, S. (2008) 'Women and international assignments: taking stock – a 25-year review', *Human Resource Management*, 47: 199–216.

Ang, S., Van Dyne, L., Koh, C., Ng, K., Templer, K., Tay-Lee, S. and Chandrasekar, N. (2007) 'Cultural intelligence: its measurement and effects on cultural judgement and decision making, cultural adaptation and task performance', *Management and Organization Review*, 3(3): 335–371.

Appadurai, A. (1990) 'Disjuncture and difference in the global cultural economy', *Public Culture*, 2(2): 1–24.

Armstrong, M. (2000) *Performance Management*, New York: Kogan Page.

Arthur, M.B. and Rousseau, D.M. (eds) (1996) *The Boundaryless Career: A New Employment Principle for a New Organizational Era*, New York: Oxford University Press.

Arthur, M.B., Claman, P.H. and DeFillippi, R.J. (1995) 'Intelligent enterprise, intelligent careers', *Academy of Management Executive*, 9(4): 7–22.

Baruch, Y. (1995) 'Business globalization – the human resource management aspect', *Human Systems Management*, 14(4): 313–326.

Baruch, Y. (1996) 'Self performance appraisal vs. direct manager appraisal – a case of congruency', *Journal of Managerial Psychology*, 11(6): 50–65.

Baruch, Y. (1999) 'Integrated career systems for the 2000s', *International Journal of Manpower*, 20(7): 432–457.

Baruch, Y. (2003) 'Career systems in transition: a normative model for career practices', *Personnel Review*, 32(2): 231–251.

Baruch, Y. (2004) 'Transforming careers – from linear to multidirectional career paths: organizational and individual perspective', *Career Development International*, 9(1): 58–73.

Baruch, Y. (2006) 'Career development in organizations and beyond: balancing traditional and contemporary viewpoints', *Human Resource Management Review*, 16: 125–138.

Baruch, Y. and Altman, Y. (2002) 'Expatriation and repatriation in MNC: a taxonomy', *Human Resource Management*, 41(2): 239–259.

Baruch, Y. and Bozionelos, N. (2010) 'Career issues', in S. Zedeck (ed.) *Industrial and Organizational Psychology Handbook*, APA publication, forthcoming.

Baruch, Y. and Hall, D.T. (2004) 'The academic career: a model for future careers in other sectors?', *Journal of Vocational Behavior*, 64(2): 241–262.

Baruch, Y. and Harel, G. (1993) 'Combining multi-source performance appraisal: an empirical and methodological note', *Public Administration Quarterly*, 17(1): 96–111.

Baruch, Y., Budhwar, P. and Khatri, N. (2007) 'Brain drain: inclination to stay abroad after studies', *Journal of World Business*, 42(1): 99–112.

Baruch, Y., Konrad, A., Aguinis, H. and Starbuck, W.H. (eds) (2008) *Opening the Black Box of Editorship*, Basingstoke: Palgrave-Macmillan.

BBC Radio 4 UK, 2 June, 2009.

Bell, M.P. and Harrison, D.A. (2002) 'Using intra-national diversity for international assignments: a model of bicultural competence and expatriate adjustment', *Human Resource Management Review*, 6(1): 47–74.

Bernardin, H.J. (1986) 'Subordinate appraisal: a valuable source of information about managers', *Human Resource Management*, 25: 421–439.

Bernardin, H.J., Kane, J.S., Ross, S., Spina, J.D. and Johnson, D.L. (1995) 'Performance appraisal design, development, and implementation', in G.R. Ferris, S.D. Rosen and D.T. Barnum (eds) *Handbook of Human Resource Management*, Cambridge, MA: Blackwell.

Bozionelos, N. (2009) 'Expatriation outside the boundaries of the multinational corporation: a study with expatriate nurses in Saudi Arabia', *Human Resource Management*, 48(1): 111–134.

Brislin, R., Worthley, R. and Macnab, B. (2006) 'Cultural intelligence: understanding behaviors that serve people's goals', *Group and Organization Management*, 31(1): 40–55.

Caligiuri, P.M. (2006) 'Performance measurement in a cross-national context', in W. Bennett, D. Woehr and C. Lance (eds) *Performance Measurement: Current Perspectives and Future Challenges*, Mahwah, NJ: Lawrence Erlbaum Associates, Inc.

Caligiuri, P., Lazarova, M. and Tarique, I. (2005) 'Training, learning and development in multinational organizations', in H. Scullion and M. Linehan (eds) *International Human Resource Management: A Critical Text*, Houndmills: Palgrave MacMillan.

Cascio, W.F. (2006) 'Global performance management systems', in I. Bjorkman and G. Stahl (eds) *Handbook of Research in International Human Resources Management*, London: Edward Elgar Ltd.

Cohen, A. and Baruch, Y. (2010) 'An agency theory perspective of the Israeli labor market segmentation: past, present, and future', *Human Resource Management Review*, forthcoming.

Cooke, F.L. (2007) ' "Husband's career first": renegotiating career and family commitment among migrant Chinese academic couples in Britain', *Work, Employment and Society*, 21: 47–65.

Dalacoura, K. (1998) *Islam, Liberalism and Human Rights*, London and New York: I.B. Tauris.

Dickmann, M. and Harris, H. (2005) 'Developing career capital for global careers: the role of international assignments', *Journal of World Business*, 40: 399–408.

Drucker, P. (1974) *Management: Tasks, Responsibilities, Practices*, New York: Harper and Row.

Earley, P.C. and Ang, S. (2003) *Cultural Intelligence: An Analysis of Individual Interactions across Cultures*, Palo Alto, CA: Stanford University Press.

Earley, P.C. and Gibson, C.B. (2008) *Multinational Work Teams: A New Perspective*, New York: Routledge.

Earley, P.C. and Peterson, R.S. (2004) 'The elusive cultural chameleon: cultural intelligence as a new approach to intercultural training for the global manager', *Academy of Management Learning and Education*, 3: 100–115.

Economist Intelligence Unit (2008) 'Country Profile 2008 – United Arab Emirates', Economist Intelligence Unit.

Forstenlechner, I. (2009) 'Workforce localization in emerging Gulf economies: the need to fine-tune HRMI', *Personnel Review*, 39(2): 178–194.

Franke, J. and Nicholson, N. (2002) 'Who shall we send? Cultural and other influences on the rating of selection criteria for expatriate assignments', *International Journal of Cross Cultural Management*, 2: 21–36.

Frost, P.J. and Taylor, M.S. (1996) *Rhythms of Academic Life: Personal Accounts of Careers in Academia*, California: Sage.

Gibbs, J. (2009) 'Dialectics in a global software team: negotiating tensions across time, space, and culture', *Human Relations*, 62: 905–935.

GMAC Global Relocation Services (2008) *Global relocation trends: 2008 survey report*. Oak Brook, IL: GMAC Global Relocation Services.

Gunz, P.H., Evans, M.G. and Jalland, R.M. (2002) 'Chalk lines, open borders, glass walls, and frontiers: careers and creativity', in M.A. Peiperl, M.B. Arthur and N. Anand (eds) *Career Creativity: Explorations in the Remaking of Work*, Oxford: Oxford University Press.

Hafez, S. (2009) 'Ministry confirms ban on sacking of Emirati workers', *The National*, Abu Dhabi, 17 February.

Hall, D.T. (2004) 'The protean career: a quarter-century journey', *Journal of Vocational Behavior*, 65(1): 1–13.

Hall, D.T. and Chandler, D.E. (2005) 'Psychological success: when the career is a calling', *Journal of Organizational Behavior*, 26: 155–176.

Harris, H. and Dickmann, M. (2005) *The CIPD Guide on International Management Development*, London: The Chartered Institute of Personnel and Development.

Harris, H., Brewster, C. and Sparrow, P. (2003) *International Human Resource Management*, London: The Chartered Institute of Personnel and Development.

Harrison, D.A., Price, K.H. and Bell, M.P. (1998) 'Beyond relational demography: time and the effects of surface- and deep-level diversity on work group cohesion', *Academy of Management Journal*, 41: 96–107.

Harvey, M.G. and Buckley, M. (1997) 'Managing impatriates: building global core competency', *Journal of World Business*, 32: 35–52.

Harvey, M., Ralston, D. and Napier, N. (2000) 'International relocation of inpatriate managers: assessing and facilitating acceptance in the headquarters organization', *International Journal of Intercultural Relations*, 24: 825–846.

Hofstede, G. (1980) *Culture's Consequences: International Differences in Work-Related Values*, Beverly Hills, CA: Sage.

Iles, P., Almhedie, A. and Baruch, Y. (2010) 'Managing HR in the Middle East: challenges in the public sector', *Public Personnel Management*, forthcoming.

Inkson, K., Arthur, M.B., Pringle, J. and Barry, S. (1997) 'Expatriate assignment versus overseas experience: contrasting models of international human resource development', *Journal of World Business*, 32(4): 351–368.

June, S. and Gentry, J.W. (2005) 'An exploratory investigation of the relative importance of cultural similarity and personal fit in the selection and performance of expatriates', *Journal of World Business*, 40: 1–8.

Kessler, I. (1994) 'Performance related pay: contrasting approaches', *Industrial Relations Journal*, 25(2): 122–135.

Kessler, I. and Purcell, J. (1992) 'Performance related pay: objectives and application', *Human Resource Management*, 2(3): 16–33.

Kirkman, B.L. and Shapiro, D.L. (1997) 'The impact of cultural values on employee resistance to teams: toward a model of globalized self-managing work team effectiveness', *Academy of Management Review*, 22(3): 730–745.

Kozlowski, S.W.J. and Ilgen, D.R. (2006) 'Enhancing the effectiveness of work groups and teams', *Psychological Science* Suppl. S: 77–124.

Martins, L.L., Gilson, L.L. and Maynard, M.T. (2004) 'Virtual teams: what do we know and where do we go from here?', *Journal of Management*, 30: 805–836.

Mayer, J.D., Salovey, P. and Caruso, D. (2000) 'Models of emotional intelligence', in R. Sternberg (ed.) *Handbook of Intelligence*, San Francisco, CA: Jossey-Bass.

Mayerhofer, H., Hartmann, L.C. and Herbert, A. (2004) 'Career management issues for flexpatriate international staff', *Thunderbird International Business Review*, 46: 647–666.

McCormack, E. (2007) 'Number of foreign students bounces back to near record high', *Chronicle of Higher Education*, 16 November, 54(12): A1.

Mechtenberg, L. and Strausz, R. (2008) 'The Bologna process: how student mobility affects multi-cultural skills and educational quality', *International Tax and Public Finance*, 15: 109–130.

Morita, A., Reingold, E.M. and Shimomura, M. (1986) *Made in Japan*, London: HarperCollins.

Peiperl, M.A. and Jonsen, K. (2007) 'Global careers', in H. Gunz and M. Peiperl (eds) *Handbook of Career Studies*, Los Angeles, CA: Sage.

Phillipson, R. (2003) 'English for the globe, or for the globe-trotters? The world of the EU', in M. Christian (ed.) *The Politics of English as a World Language: New Horizons in Postcolonial Cultural Studies*, Amsterdam: Rodopi.

Popper, M. (1997) 'The glorious failure', *The Journal of Applied Behavioral Science*, 33: 27–45.

Rao, H.S. (2006) *Five-Fold Increase in Influx of Indian Students to UK*, *Rediff.com* http://us.rediff.com/cms/print.jsp?docpath=/news/206/feb/07uk.htm (accessed 7 February 2007).

Refugee Council (2005) *The Forbidden Workforce: Asylum seekers, the Employment Concession and Access to the Labour Market*, London: The Refugee Council.

Richardson, J. and Mallon, M. (2005) 'Career interrupted? The case of the self-directed expatriate', *Journal of World Business*, 40: 409–420.

Saxenian, A. (2006) *The New Argonauts: Regional Advantage in a Global Economy*, Boston, MA: Harvard University Press.

Schmidt, F.L. and Hunter, J.E. (2000) 'Select on intelligence', in E.A. Locke (ed.) *The Blackwell Handbook of Principles of Organizational Behaviour*, Oxford: Blackwell.

Schneider, S. and Barsoux, J.L. (1997) *Managing Across Cultures*, London: Prentice Hall.

Seibert, S.E., Kraimer, M.L. and Crant, J.M. (2001) 'What do proactive people do? A longitudinal model linking proactive personality and career success', *Personnel Psychology*, 54: 845–874.

Selmer, J. and Fenner Jr, C.R. (2009) 'Spillover effects between work and non-work adjustment among public sector expatriates', *Personnel Review*, 38: 366–379.

Sparrow, P., Brewster, C. and Harris, H. (2004) *Globalizing Human Resource Management*, London: Routledge.

Sternberg, R. and Detterman, D. (1986) *What Is Intelligence?*, Norwood, NJ: Abley Publishing Corporation.

Sternberg, R.J., Forsythe, G.B., Hedlund, J., Horvath, J.A., Wagner, R.K. and Williams, W.M. (2000) *Practical Intelligence in Everyday Life*, New York: Cambridge University Press.

Sundstorm, E., De Meuse, K.P. and Futrell, D. (1990) 'Work teams: applications and effectiveness', *American Psychologist*, 45(2): 120–133.

Thomas, D. and Inkson, K. (2004) *Cultural Intelligence: People Skills for Global Business*, San Francisco, CA: Benett-Koehler.

Thorndike, R.L. and Stein, S. (1937) 'An evaluation of the attempts to measure social intelligence', *Psychological Bulletin*, 34: 275–284.

Triandis, H.C. (2006) 'Cultural intelligence in organizations', *Group and Organization Management*, 31: 20–26.

Van Emmerik, I.J.H. and Euwema, M.C. (2009) 'The international assignments of peacekeepers: what drives them to seek future expatriation?', *Human Resource Management*, 48:135–151.

Waterman Jr, R.H., Waterman, J.A. and Collard, B.A. (1994) 'Toward a career-resilient workforce', *Harvard Business Review*, 72(4): 87–95.

Welch, D.E., Welch, L.S. and Worm, V. (2007) '*International Journal of Human Resource Management*, 18(2): 173–183.

Winter-Ebmer, R. and Zweimuller, J. (1996) 'Immigration and the earnings of young native workers', *Oxford Economic Papers*, 48: 473–491.

World Hunger Map (2009) Rome: United Nations Food Programme.

Yan, A., Zhu, G. and Hall, D.T. (2002) 'International assignments for career building: a model of agency relationships and psychological contracts', *Academy of Management Review*, 27(3): 373–391.

Part II

Global career strategies and processes: individual and organizational approaches and career outcomes along temporal dimensions

5 | Resourcing and the motivation to go

Objectives

This chapter:

- distinguishes between organizational and individual perspectives in international resourcing;
- outlines the key organizational considerations in international mobility (IM);
- presents the main individual motivations and barriers to working abroad;
- develops a new framework for decisions on IM;
- discusses the diverse backgrounds and motivations of self-initiated and company-sent foreign workers;
- identifies gender differences in the staffing of global positions;
- explores considerations for organizational HR strategies, policies and practices;
- explicates general resourcing, selection and management implications;
- illuminates global career implications.

Introduction

Why do individuals work abroad? This chapter approaches this question from two key perspectives: the organization and the individual. The investment that companies undertake to send their staff overseas to work is substantial. Individuals tend to earn significantly higher salaries; there are costs associated with the international move; taxation and social security issues; family and other allowances are substantial (Dickmann et al. 2006) and expatriates are likely to earn more than their local peers (ORC 2004). In turn, individuals 'up sticks' to move across states and immerse themselves into foreign, unfamiliar cultures, moving away from the familiar and far from their wider families, endangering their social networks (Dickmann and Harris 2005; Richardson and Mallon 2005) and occasionally their security and health. There is a range of organizations that employ international assignees in 'hardship places' which have problems in areas such as security, infrastructure, child education, housing or health provision.

Box 5.1 Location classification in the United Nations

The UN distinguishes between hardship locations 'D' and 'E'. In a hardship location E conditions are regarded as so dangerous that the assignee is not permitted to bring his or her family. Normal assignment duration in hardship locations varies but for the UN World Food Programme it will last about two years. Moreover, in some duty stations, for instance in Sudan, field staff occasionally live in tents.

So why is it that a majority of organizations intend to increase IM (GMAC 2008) and self-initiated cross-country moves are frequent (Inkson et al. 1997; Bonache et al. 2007)?

Having presented a range of alternative ways to work abroad, this chapter will concentrate on traditional short- and long-term patterns of IM and will attempt to present a detailed picture that helps to answer the above questions in detail. In terms

Figure 5.1 A framework of global careers: resourcing and the drivers to stay or go

of orientation to the reader, Figure 5.1 shows where in the book we are and, at the same time, distinguishes other key areas that will be covered in subsequent chapters.

Some authors have argued that there is an especially high degree of mutual dependency between organizations and individuals in international work (Dickmann and Harris 2005). The organization depends on its international employees due to the scarcity of international staff resources and the criticality of these individuals (especially those in top managerial positions) for its success (Larsen 2004). In turn, individuals who work abroad are especially vulnerable due to potentially rapidly shifting national and legal contexts, a different health and natural environment (see also Chapter 10), diverse national and regional cultural and language circumstances, a 'new' start in the host work setting and for a variety of other reasons (Harris et al. 2003). Cappellen and Janssens (2005) maintain that the vulnerability of individuals working abroad is due to their needs for security, prestige and sense-making. Doherty and Dickmann (2008a) suggest a framework that explicitly takes account of this dual dependency. Figure 5.2 presents a simplified view of both perspectives on international careers in order to create an overview that incorporates key career actors over time. It shows global career

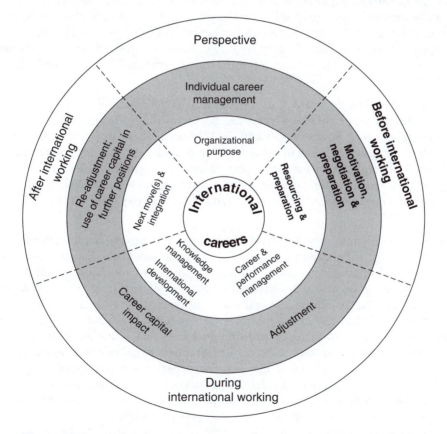

Figure 5.2 International career management from organizational and individual perspectives

Source: Dohesty and Dickmann (2008a)

management systems, processes and activities. The outer ring shows the time before, during and after international work. The next ring (inwards) outlines key stages that an individual goes through in expatriation. In the pre-departure phase individuals weigh up push and pull factors of international work (Baruch 2004). They make a decision as to whether they want to expatriate, one of the subjects of this chapter. In turn, organizations have conducted strategic planning in terms of their rationale for global staffing and employee selection approaches (Collings and Scullion 2008). Individual and organizational resourcing decisions are the key focus of this chapter.

In terms of the framework outlined in Figure 5.2, Chapter 6 discusses individual and organizational negotiation and preparation associated with global careers (cf. Dickmann et al. 2008). Chapter 7 focuses on individual cultural adjustment and career capital impact (Cappellen and Janssens 2005; Dickmann and Harris 2005; Jokinen et al. 2008). This chapter also outlines the organizational activities during work abroad and sets out interactions between staff and employer. Finally, Chapter 8 is devoted to the post-assignment phase. Individuals are likely to experience reverse culture shock. In their new role(s) within the organization they are likely to attempt to use and to continue to build on the career capital they have acquired while working abroad (Dickmann and Doherty 2008) and continue to refine their identities (Parker et al. 2009). The organization, depending on its context, is likely to strive to work on measures aimed to increase retention, performance and career progress of repatriates (Dickmann and Doherty 2010).

Figure 5.2 depicts the interaction of individuals with their employers. While individuals manage their own career capital, their work environment – mostly direct supervisors, business 'sponsors' and HR specialists – exerts an influence on the international careers of assignees. For instance, the 'expatriation contract' might have implications for the support during the assignment as well as effects after return in terms of job security, career progression and salary. For instance, a guaranteed job, a promotion and/or tie-over pay might have been negotiated.

The reader will notice that the dividers between the stages are not solid due to spillover effects. For example, pre-departure preparation (see Chapter 6) might be augmented by post-arrival preparations and learning. We use Figure 5.2 as it seems to be a good way to depict the long-term global career processes and inter-actions between the international assignee and the employing organization. However, reality is neither linear nor simple. For instance, an individual does not only use accumulated career capital after the IA but also during work abroad. One example may be the use of newly acquired networks to gain a new position in a different location before the official assignment period runs out. Equally, from an organizational perspective the international development of individuals does not only take place during their overseas assignment. Non-traditional international work patterns (Chapter 4) all add to the complexity of global careers. Nevertheless, Figure 5.2 is useful to identify broad trends in the literature and to sensitize the reader to the manifold interactions that take place between organizations and individuals.

The organizational purposes of international work

Organizations pursue a wide range of goals with their IM and global careers approaches (Harzing 1995; Harzing and Christensen 2004; McNulty and Tharenou 2004). These include transferring culture, filling open positions quickly and/or with a person possessing a better skill set than is deemed available locally, launching new initiatives, creating and/or transferring managerial and technical knowledge, building management or other expertise, establishing or improving managerial control, moving problem employees or increasing general organizational performance (Carpenter et al. 2001; Bossard and Peterson 2005; Shen 2006; GMAC 2008). Organizational reasons for international work can be split into strategic and operational considerations.

Strategic considerations

In a classic paper, Edström and Galbraith (1977) identified three major purposes of IM: two of these relate to strategic considerations, namely control and coordination as well as management development. The third category is operational, position filling. Their categorization has been very impactful and taken up by a variety of authors. This chapter will first explicate strategic considerations and will go beyond the ideas of Edström and Galbraith to incorporate knowledge creation, transfer and exploitation. It will also explore the operational categorization of position filling in more depth by discussing issues of quality, speed, career management and the launch of new initiatives.

Control and coordination

The first purpose identified by Edström and Galbraith is to help organizational control and coordination across borders. Ferner (2000) outlines bureaucratic control approaches such as standardized global reporting in order to create overview and transparency in MNCs. Delios and Björkman (2000) argue that Japanese MNCs operating in the USA and China give their international assignees a command and control function in order to align the subsidiary's operations to those of the Japanese head office. Dickmann and Müller-Camen (2006) link international assignees predominantly to coordination activities. In relation to Bartlett and Ghoshal's (1989) transnational configuration, expatriates are a means of personal coordination and can contribute to international cohesion (Holtbrugge and Berg 2004; Riusala and Smale 2004). Shen (2006) argues that Chinese MNCs recruit and select international managers using criteria such as trust and personal moral merits. Many studies have shown that organizations often use an array of motivations in their IM. Thus, it is no surprise that a study by Tharenou and Harvey (2006) found that Australian MNCs staff overseas posts to reduce risks from cultural friction and divergent goals as well as to battle asymmetry of knowledge between host operations and parent organization.

Knowledge creation, transfer and exploitation

Although the categorization of Edström and Galbraith (1977) does not have a separate segment for knowledge management, the general literature is so extensive as to merit a distinct section in the discussion of organizational mobility rationale (Zaidman and Brock 2009). Successful knowledge creation, transfer and exploitation do not simply occur (Kostova et al. 2004; Cabrera et al. 2006). It involves a specific set of psychological variables (e.g. self-efficacy, openness to experience, perceived support from colleagues) as well as significant internal coordination in the sense of organizational capabilities that are consistent over time and that facilitate linkages across units. These dynamic capabilities consist of specific strategic and organizational commitments to specific processes that enable the MNC to achieve new resource configurations (Eisenhardt and Martin 2000). With certain notable exceptions (Holtbrugge and Berg 2004; Riusala and Smale 2004; Bonache and Zárraga-Oberty 2008) little attention has been paid to the specific issues addressing international assignees in their knowledge-transfer function. Bonache and Zárraga-Oberty (2008) argue that HR practices such as emphasizing the cultural fit with the local environment in the selection of expatriates, extensive training, linking knowledge transfer to performance evaluation and rewards, de-emphasizing salary disparity and extensive socialization would create a more fertile relationship for knowledge transfers and aid the achievements of corporate goals in IM. Bonache and Dickmann (2008) provide an overview of key mechanisms for the international control, coordination, knowledge creation and transfer of HRM in MNCs (Table 5.1).

Global leadership development

Edström and Galbraith's second category of organizational purpose is management development. Expatriation, traditionally, has been an instrument in career management in order to 'build' the leaders of the future (Gregersen et al. 1998; Harris and Dickmann 2005). In the early years of this century Suutari (2002) outlined an emerging research agenda for global leader development and argued that companies typically do not have enough leaders with global competencies. The benefits of international work often include a better business acumen, improved understanding of different cultures and markets, a higher sensitivity to clear communication and higher self-confidence (Doherty and Dickmann 2005; Vance 2005). Bird and Osland (2004) distinguish between four building blocks of global competencies. They argue that first-level competencies consist of a range of threshold traits including integrity, humility, inquisitiveness and hardiness. The second-level competencies are described as a global mindset. These attitudes and orientations entail mastering cognitive complexity and possessing cosmopolitanism. The third level is interpersonal skills. Included are context- and culture-sensitive communication and an ability to create and build trust. Lastly, the fourth level is described as systems skills. Successful global managers are seen to be able to span boundaries – e.g. home–host; intra–extra organization – instigate change and build communities. In so doing they support the corporate goal of global cohesion and need to be able to make ethical decisions (Figure 5.3). The authors argue that managers need a wide range and depth of these various types of knowledge, skills, traits and attitudes to work effectively (Bird and Osland 2004: 66–74).

Table 5.1 Key mechanisms for HR knowledge management

Type	Mechanisms	Examples	Potential for	
			Knowledge transfer	Knowledge generation
Bureaucratic	*IHRM Planning*	Vision & mission, corporate culture, IHR strategy, HR principles, underlying competency frameworks, talent management approach etc.	Low	Low
	IHRM Reporting	Global, national, functional HR budgets, actual costs; outcomes	Low	Low
	HR Information Systems	Use of common approaches, forms, policy documents etc. that are for instance located on the intranet	High	Low
	Communities of practice	International management seminars on HR instruments such as appraisals, employees' opinion surveys, etc.	High	High
Social	*Globally distributed teams*	International project groups (including virtual teams)	Low	High
	Expatriation	Expatriation as a cultural coordination mechanisms (including international commuters)	High	Low
	HR Centre of Excellence	Expatriation as a cultural coordination mechanism (including international commuters).	High	High
Personal	*HR 'Line Manager' in Head Office*	International assignee who is leader/ line manager in host location and who also shapes some part of the 'organizational culture'	High	High
	Visits of IHR managers from HQ	Visits & other contacts with HR local professionals (including frequent flyers)	Low	Low
	Knowledge transferor	International assignees as introducing corporate systems and processes (e.g. in performance management) in local operations	High	Low

Source: Adapted from Bonache and Dickmann (2008: 76)

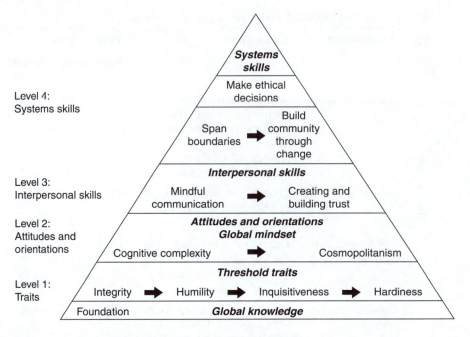

Figure 5.3 The building blocks of global competencies
Source: Bird and Osland (2004: 66)

Operational reasons

There is a plethora of operational reasons that organizations might have to send their employees abroad for work. While some less common ones include 'moving a problem employee', 'giving managerial incentives' or 'testing the hardiness and commitment of individuals', the more common operational reasons of quality of staffing, speediness of filling vacancies, management of global careers and launching new endeavours (ORC 2004; Dickmann et al. 2006; GMAC 2008) are outlined below.

Quality of resourcing

The third expatriation purpose identified by Edström and Galbraith refers to filling positions when qualified locals are not available. Industry surveys continually affirm that organizations send out a significant proportion of international assignees to fill positions in locations abroad driven by their inability to find local incumbents with equal or sufficient qualifications. For instance, the 2008 GMAC Global Relocation Survey (154 HR respondents representing 4.3 million employees) found that the most common assignment objective was filling a skills gap (29 per cent), followed by building management expertise (24 per cent) and launching new endeavours (15 per cent).

A variant of the quality of resource considerations with strong links to other motivations such as control and coordination is the international work that takes place in the armed forces and other governmental organizations. While in earlier centuries it was more common in the armed forces to send a relatively small cohort of the national army to a foreign country and then to recruit much of the fighting force locally, this has shifted to predominantly peripheral recruitment of support staff such as translators. The esprit de corps, extensive training and communication skills deemed necessary for modern warfare have meant that local skills filling and the trust levels needed for many activities has become more difficult.

Speed of response

The need for quick response times is intimately linked to the quality of staffing (Baruch and Altman 2002). The armed forces, many governmental organizations and charities such as Oxfam, Médecins sans Frontières or World Vision have an obvious need to be highly reactive in times of crises. However, many commercial organizations also perceive a strong need to staff vacant international positions more quickly than they deem it would be possible to hire, induct and train locally. For instance, capital investments in the oil and exploration industry are very high and delays can be extremely costly. Therefore, if Shell needs an experienced driller in the Niger Delta it is likely to use foreign, skilled labour. One expression of this perceived shortage of individuals with highly developed vocational and engineering skills and a willingness to relocate quickly is the existence of a company called Saipem, a service sector contractor in the oil and gas industry. At any time it has several thousand skilled expatriates who are on time-limited assignments working with other oil and gas firms.

Management of global careers

Some companies prescribe at least one long-term international sojourn if their managers want to reach certain hierarchical levels. For instance Dickmann (1999) outlines the case of Henkel where staff had to go through a 2 × 2 career framework if they wanted to reach a senior management position. In essence it meant that individuals were expected to work at least once abroad and in two different functions to climb the ultimate ranks of the managerial hierarchy. Jean-Luc Cerdin (2003) describes how LVMH's human resources function liked high-potential managers to change country, function and division at the same time. The case of CandyCo, described later in this chapter, outlines a company's policies in relation to their managers' performance and developmental potential. This book describes the diverse organizational career management approaches in more detail in Chapters 2 and 3.

Launching new initiatives

Starting major initiatives either in existing or newly founded subsidiaries of MNCs is a key operational rationale for companies (GMAC 2008). While this motivation is highly linked to the strategic considerations of control, coordination and knowledge exploitation, it is arguably often shorter term. The range of new initiatives – such as organizational expansion into a new market, launching a new product, establishing global reporting systems etc. – is wide. One example where a company has firm policy guidelines when it acquires other national or international companies is that of General Electric (Ashkenas et al. 1998). To aid integration around the GE model it sends a change management team including the new Managing Director and HR Director into the newly acquired company.

We will now turn to the key elements of the resourcing decision, distinguishing between organizational and individual perspectives. While the context and processes will shape the decisions of both parties (discussed below), we will now outline some of the most pertinent factors and considerations in the individual 'decision to go'.

Individual drivers for working abroad

The demand for competent global managers can be bigger than the supply (Quelch and Bloom 1999). Moreover, many potential expatriates do not seem willing to accept foreign assignments (Stahl et al. 2002; Dickmann and Harris 2005). There is an extensive literature on the reasons why individuals might be willing to work abroad which can be subsumed under the categories of antecedents and individual motivations (see below).

Key antecedents include an individual's family and social background, early experiences and personality. In terms of individual motivations, authors often distinguish as key motives: first, career and developmental considerations; second, organizational factors, including monetary and non-monetary elements of the contract to work abroad; third, individual interests, experiences and drives; fourth, family and partner considerations, including issues such as dual careers or influences of the extended family; as well as fifth, national and other location factors (Gregersen et al. 1998; Hammer et al. 1998; Tung 1998; Suutari and Brewster 2000; Mendenhall 2001; Stahl et al. 2002; Richardson and Mallon 2005; Dickmann and Mills 2010). The individual antecedents and motivations to seek and/or accept foreign work are outlined in Figure 5.4 and discussed below.

Individual		Organizational	
Antecedents	*Individual motives*	*Operational considerations*	*Strategic drivers*
• Family and social background • Early experiences • Personality	• Career and development • Organizational factors and inducements • Individual interest and drivers • Family and partner considerations • National and location-specific factors	• Quality of resourcing • Speed of response • Management of global careers • Launching new initiatives	• Control • Coordination • Global leadership development • Knowledge creation, transfer and exploitation

Figure 5.4 Individual and organizational resourcing considerations
Source: © Michael Dickmann, 2009

Antecedents

Some authors argue that a person's individual background, including early experiences of international travel or parental work (e.g. Third Culture Kids), the general family and social background as well as personality influence the willingness to proactively seek, reactively accept or reject foreign work (Doherty and Dickmann 2008b; Tharenou 2003). These antecedents will be discussed in more detail below.

Family and social background

Many key norms and values are acquired early in life through learning from one's immediate family context and wider social environment (Hofstede 1980; Trompenaars and Hampden-Turner 1997). Racial and cultural ethnicity, language(s) spoken from birth, norms and values acquired through family and environment, the national and international relationships of the family, the social background of the family and other influences that shape an individual's view of the world have an impact on the willingness to engage in international work and careers (Mayrhofer et al. 2004; Peiperl and Jonsen 2007). Tharenou (2003) argued that some of the most substantial barriers to developing an interest in international working for young people were family influence and partners, as a move abroad could include a physical separation from family and friends or entail dangers for a romantic relationship. The potentially strong influences of family or friendship ties in the decision to work abroad are explored in the motivation section below and the discussion is expanded in the following part of the book (especially Chapters 6 and 7).

Early experiences

There is a range of activities that individuals can engage in to gain international experience before expatriation. Vance (2005) distinguishes three phases. In the first phase – lasting until about the mid-twenties – individuals built an international business foundation through two types of experiences. A limited exposure to foreign cultures could be acquired through tourist travel, study abroad, learning foreign languages, or through attending courses in international business. A deeper immersion could be gained through activities such as international internships, working for the government abroad or missionary type service. During a second phase young people used networking, attempted to develop mentor relationships, acquired languages targeted for a specific region and developed interpersonal and communication skills for working abroad. Individuals secured overseas jobs during the third phase. The options individuals had ranged from immediate self-initiated foreign work experience to joining an organization's international career track. Vance implies that those individuals who actively engage in the first and second phases are more likely to have the opportunity for foreign work and to take it.

Personality

Bird and Osland (2004) indicate that personality traits such as integrity, humility, inquisitiveness and hardiness can increase the ability to successfully work abroad.

Self-confidence is often seen as increasing individuals' receptivity to international careers (Sparrow et al. 2004). Doherty, Mills and Dickmann (2006) researched youth mobility patterns in the EU and found that people who went to work internationally considered personal safety implications of being abroad as significantly less important compared to those remaining in their home countries. Among young graduates a range of individual variables such as self-efficacy, personal agency and positive expectations of outcomes contributes to a higher willingness to work abroad (Tharenou 2003). She recommended that MNCs should identify those graduates with the desire for an international career.

Individual motivations

Career and development considerations

Career advancement has been shown to be a key motivator for managers to accept an international posting (Altman and Baruch 2008; Dickmann et al. 2008; Baruch et al. 2009). Other authors argue that expatriates appreciate their international experience as an opportunity for personal and professional development and career advancement (Brett and Stroh 1995; Stahl and Cerdin 2004). Moreover, internationally mobile employees value the opportunity to learn unusual skills and gather foreign experiences (Tung 1998).

Considerations by individuals of their future job and the impact of foreign work on their own development and career opportunities are likely to be key considerations for company-sent internationally mobile individuals (Yan et al. 2002; Harris and Dickmann 2005) and self-initiated expatriates (Suutari and Brewster 2000; Richardson and Mallon 2005). The job offered in an IA together with the career opportunities that might arise from the posting, have a strong influence on the decision to accept the foreign work (Stahl et al. 2002). Age is a factor, too. Young people were more motivated than older individuals to pursue an international career (Tharenou 2003). The reasons were related to expectations about positive career outcomes, better job opportunities and higher pay.

Organizational factors and inducements

The likely financial impact of accepting an IA influences an individual's decision to accept an overseas post (Yurkiewicz and Rosen 1995). Stahl et al. (2002) argue that the importance of financial packages can vary according to the nationality of individuals, with their sample of German managers appearing to rate financial considerations as less influential compared to findings from American research (Yurkiewicz and Rosen 1995). Moreover, the 'package' that expatriates may expect also includes non-financial items such as the expected length of stay and the repatriation package (Dickmann et al. 2008). There is increasing evidence that expatriates are relatively discontented with the repatriation policies and practices of their corporations (Sparrow et al. 2004; Cerdin 2008). The effects of these issues on the acceptance of foreign work opportunities remain under-explored (cf. Chapter 11).

Individual interests and drives

Sometimes much planning and effort has already happened before individuals work abroad (Vance 2005). This allows the speculation that individuals often pursue personal interests by accepting international work, an argument that is supported by other researchers (Inkson et al. 1997; Tung 1998). Among the prominent motivators are personal challenge (Stahl et al. 2002), the desire for adventure, travel and life change (Richardson and Mallon 2005). Less frequent motivations are better work–life balance, a general desire to live abroad, personal health implications (Dickmann et al. 2008) or the desire to get away from a home-country problem (Cerdin 2003).

Family and partner considerations

There is increasing literature that addresses the families of internationally mobile professionals, expatriate couples and dual careers (Brett and Stroh 1995; Harvey 1995; Linehan and Walsh 2000). Stahl et al. (2002) argue that family- or partner-related motives are only moderately important in accepting IAs. Their data illustrates that family influences were in the bottom third of the 12 items that were ranked by German respondents for importance. Some studies which targeted individuals from other nations, however, come to other conclusions.

Researchers such as Cerdin (2008) and Sparrow et al. (2004) argue that in planning and selecting for an assignment, the willingness to relocate by both partners should be taken into account. Richardson and Mallon (2005: 414) and Richardson (2006) argue that family factors can be an incentive to expatriation. The reasons can often be found in the broad learning experiences and the opportunities for education that the prospective expatriates perceive for their families in the target location prior to working overseas. Therefore, general educational systems considerations together with opportunities for schooling or tertiary education might be important for the 'decision to go'.

Dual career and partner influence

A larger number of professionals find themselves in a family where both partners enjoy a full-time working career. A global move of one partner will mean a career change for the other partner. The chances that a similar role with similar position will be found for the 'trailing partner' are slim. A career break or embarking on a new type of job/career are the obvious options. As we will discuss in Chapter 6, one of the pre-departure considerations for the firm is to identify a possible position within the organization, or with another firm in the same location, that will be attractive enough for the partner.

The implications for the family which may be used to two income streams are severe, as the lack of suitable position might mean reliance on a single salary. At the personal level, the implication for each person's career is beyond the immediate loss of income. This is why the partner should be involved with the decision making (and take part in training too – see Chapter 6).

National and location-specific factors

Much of the research on international moves has focused on how expatriates adjust emotionally and intellectually to a new national cultural environment (Black et al. 1992; Bhaskar-Shrinivas et al. 2005; Haslberger 2005). The findings confirm the importance of companies' IM policies and practices (such as pre-departure preparation), and the influence of host culture, personal security, inter-cultural sensitivity and language compatibility. Other studies have concentrated on distinguishing the receptivity to international careers in relation to relocation to developed or developing countries (Tharenou 2003), looking at national factors such as the political stability of the host country, hostility to nationals from the parent country or general climate (Yurkiewicz and Rosen 1995). However, only recently has an interest arisen as to the role that cities and their specific context play in the decision to work abroad.

The literature on what influences the decisions of individuals to accept (seek or reject) a domestic relocation could give us valuable insights into decision factors in international moves. Intra-country moves have many parallels with international work as they also have career implications, affect social networks and can have significant family implications in terms of children's schooling etc. Noe and Barber (1993) looked at intra-country moves. In a US study of 270 employees the authors found that the destination has an impact in that respondents preferred to move to similar communities (e.g. from city to city or from rural to rural environments). Among others, career factors and community attachment influenced the location decision.

Dickmann and Mills (2010) explore the motivations foreign-born individuals have to go to London, UK. While in their sample of 347 expatriates career considerations are most important, location factors such as the reputation of London as a global centre for business and the desire to live in London, have a strong impact on individuals' willingness to be expatriated to the UK capital. Research conducted in Vienna by Haslberger and Zehetner (2008) also indicated that individuals distinguish between work and non-work factors when choosing an assignment location. Both research studies showed that expatriates distinguish between organization-focused career considerations and the location-focused professional environment in the respective cities. Moreover, the Dickmann and Mills research also identified wider issues such as London's reputation as a multicultural city, historical parallels to the participants' home countries or perceived tolerance of the city dwellers as some of the decision influence factors.

The decision to work abroad and new careers

Organization-sent expatriates

Some research has begun to contrast individual and organizational perspectives of aspects of IM more systematically. For instance, Dickmann et al. (2008) have identified individuals' reasons to go onto an IA and contrasted these with the organizational evaluation. The seven items with the most influence on the 310 individuals' decisions to accept expatriation were (in order of importance):

- position offered on assignment;
- willingness of spouse to move;
- potential for leadership skills development;
- career progression;
- children's education needs;
- potential for job skills development;
- professional challenge of working abroad.

For individuals in this sample career, development and family considerations were key. The authors contrasted this with the assessment of the individuals' 49 employers in a matched questionnaire. The assessment by the target HR directors and directors of IM of the importance of 11 of the 28 items was significantly different. For individuals it was important to have more developmental opportunities and a better work–life balance than organizations estimated. Corporations, however, overestimated the importance of dual-career issues and financial impact. These differences raise the question whether the IM proposition that is offered by organizations is satisfying the expectations of individuals. If companies significantly underestimate individuals' desire in areas such as job skills development, general professional challenge and leadership skills development, they are not likely to live up to the developmental promise they are giving before IAs. Research shows that organizational context influences the career behaviour of individuals working abroad (Richardson 2006; Dickmann and Doherty 2010). Based on this, individuals are likely to react to the corporate context, the implied psychological contract of working abroad and their own experiences of the 'deal' (Conway and Briner 2005; Lee 2005). These issues are outlined in more detail in the following chapters.

Immigration and self-initiated foreign work

The motivation to immigrate has a wide set of possible reasons. People might flee from dangerous areas, and might just look for a safe-haven. Others are seeking well paid positions not available in their home country. The aim might be to care for the future of one's own children. Many immigrants accept a decline in social status in the hope that the next generation will prosper and will benefit from chances they did not have. This is certainly the case when relating to illegal immigration.

Thus, whether career considerations in the decision to work abroad are a major factor or a marginal issue depends very much on the circumstances. Asylum seekers and refugees will think more of their life and survival. Others come to fulfil their dream of prosperity. For them a possible reality shock might be to experience that even after earning many times more than at home, the cost of living might be so high as to make it difficult to save.

Having immigrated, some foreign individuals aim to stay for good. But the reality means that sometimes those who planned to come for a short time stay longer, even permanently. Others who planned a stay a lifetime might decide to return or move on due to unfulfilled expectations or plans.

The major difference between immigrants and self-initiated foreign workers on the one hand, and company-sent expatriates on the other, is the lack of organizational support mechanisms. The former groups have to fend for themselves and their families (Min Toh and Gunz 2009). The discussion below will concentrate mostly on self-initiated expatriates who make the move across borders without organizational backing.

Many individuals seek work abroad of their own volition (Brewster and Suutari, 2005; Bonache et al. 2007). They have been referred to as people seeking overseas experience, self-initiated expatriates or self-directed international workers (Suutari and Brewster 2000; Inkson and Myers 2003; Myers and Pringle 2005). To some degree these 'titles' do matter in that they indicate some of the perspectives used in the literature. For instance, Inkson and Myers (2003) write about 'the big OE' describing the overseas experience of persons from New Zealand as essentially unplanned, improvisational working 'holidays' which can take a variety of forms. While the big OE has consequences for personal development and subsequent careers, authors who use the terminology of self-initiated or self-directed tend to concentrate less on Antipodeans where overseas work is often seen as 'rite of passage'. Instead, they explore the specific motivations for going abroad without the backing of an employer and tend to focus more on longer-term work, career and well-being effects.

As this chapter deals with motivation to live and work abroad, it will employ the terminology of self-initiated foreign work. Thorn (2008) has argued that individuals relocating within their company might also be seen as self-initiated as they might have taken their own decision to apply to an overseas vacancy. However, while this argument might apply to some individuals, it creates a range of methodological difficulties. We will concentrate on individuals going to work abroad independent of the auspices of an employing organization (Mayrhofer et al. 2008) and will see below that writers have identified a large range of differences in company-sent individuals.

While many company-sent expatriates have an envisaged return date and current expatriation patterns point to the use of shorter term assignments (Dickmann et al. 2006; GMAC 2008) this is less likely for self-initiated foreign workers. Some recent survey data indicates that average stays for individuals working in some major European countries are, at approximately six years, surprisingly long (Doherty et al. 2007) – and this was before these individuals had made their return or next move. This shows that in some cases the distinction between long-term foreign work – where individuals do not want to stay in the country until retirement or death – and migration, where 'indefinite' stays are possible, might be fluid. Many long-term foreign workers might start working abroad with the strong wish to return to their home country but might either change their minds or never have the realistic opportunity to do so. In contrast, the overwhelming majority of companies guarantee their expatriates the physical relocation to their home country as a minimum provision (Dickmann et al. 2006).

Traditional expatriation, of the company-sent variety, and self-initiated foreign work experience differ in many aspects. Inkson et al. (1997) argue that self-initiated expatriates acquire a different, and locally more attuned, knowledge, have richer experiences and might gain more for themselves from their work abroad. Because these people travel their international journeys in a less supported and often less organized way, they are more difficult to research. Therefore, Jokinen et al. (2008: 979) argue that they are an 'almost hidden aspect of the international labour market'. While we discussed drivers of organization-sponsored expatriation above, we now concentrate on the personality and motivations of self-initiated foreign workers.

The insights we have gained from looking at company-sent expatriates might only have limited relevance to the self-initiated (Jokinen et al. 2008). However, we have insufficient data with respect to this segment of the international labour force (Tams and Arthur 2007; Begley et al. 2008; Thorn 2008). Hudson and Inkson (2006) found that among self-initiated overseas development workers, the career anchors of pure challenge and dedication to a cause were prevalent. The authors also found that the overseas development workers showed high degrees of agreeability and openness. Self-initiated international workers might be more likely to be driven by a set of psychological and career factors that is distinct from company-sent expatriates.

Tams and Arthur (2007) argue that self-initiated international careers are based on diverse motivations. Inkson et al. (1997) point out that people undertaking overseas work experiences are more self-reliant and have more diffuse developmental goals. These individuals strive for personal and cultural experiences. Travel, work, developmental and career motives are key motivators (Inkson and Myers 2003; Richardson and Mallon 2005). Moreover, serendipity often played a strong role in the choice, timing and destination of foreign work with transience and risk being some of the contextual outcomes when working abroad (Richardson and Zikic 2007). Thorn (2008) looked at a large number of New Zealanders working abroad and identified key international drivers as culture and travel, career considerations, relationships, economic factors, the quality of life and the political context. Doherty and her colleagues (2007) analysed a set of data comparing self-initiated and company-sent foreign workers. Self-initiated individuals were more driven by

---

Box 5.2 Company-backed expatriates who initiated their moves within the organization

There is also a group of people who are highly willing to work abroad and push within their organization to be expatriated under the current IM policy. The organization needs to be aware of the motives for self-initiation of global work and act accordingly. If the employee sees it as a way to advance, a 'realistic career preview' (Baruch and Vardi 2009) should be presented to them to prevent disillusion and dissatisfaction after repatriation. If the aim is to gain experience 'on the way out', namely for career self-development in order to progress on a career path outside the organization, the organization needs to consider if this is the best career move for them. It will be hard, though, to realize in advance that this is the hidden agenda of the employee who volunteers to go on IAs.

a desire for adventure, to see the world, their confidence in their ability to adapt to life abroad, a desire to live in the host country, existing social networks and their personal skills development. In comparison to the company-sent expatriates who were seen as 'active careerists' who had embarked on a more traditional company career, self-initiated foreign workers emerged as 'career activists' driven by a more boundaryless career notion and attracted by holistic development.

Overall, self-initiated foreign workers seem to have a great personal interest in their foreign sojourn. They are driven by a more strongly developed sense of exploration, a desire for experimentation, adventure and excitement (Inkson et al. 1997). They are more self-directed and self-reliant but have less specific developmental goals. Moreover, they are often 'nudged' by social connections, moved to activity by serendipity, a poor employment situation or substantial social or political troubles, including persecution, at home (Suutari and Brewster 2000; Richardson and Mallon 2005; Min Toh and Gunz 2009). They often have rather idiosyncratic career, personal and cultural development experiences, support needs and aims which might be more holistic than those that company-sent individuals have (Myers and Pringle 2005; Doherty et al. 2007; Min Toh and DeNisi 2007).

Management and the new protean careers

While it appears that self-initiated foreign workers have distinct motivations, they are also likely to be substantially less expensive than company-sent expatriates. Mayrhofer et al. (2008) argue that this pool of global talent requires distinct attraction and retention processes. While self-initiated persons are clearly motivated by other factors, their interaction with locals is likely to be higher given that they have a wider local network at the outset of their international work (Doherty et al. 2007). Thus, global organizations which have a multitude of interests in this pool of global talent – be it to use them in their host countries, in international interface roles or after socialization and development in the corporate centre to repatriate them – might have to fine-tune their corporate branding and recruitment activities. One of these activities might be to create appropriate selection procedures and job planning so as to avoid the experience of underemployment among self-initiated foreign workers (Lee 2005). Because self-initiated foreign workers seem to be more self-directed and have a propensity to move of their own volition – and because they tend to 'go it alone' without the organizational backing, transcending not just geographical but also organizational boundaries – traditional retention mechanisms in organizations might have to be refined or more fundamentally rethought. Richardson and McKenna (2006) also outline that management might do well to factor in the importance of family and other networks in the home countries of self-initiated foreign workers. These might take the form of return trips, conscious building of global communities of practice, interests or excellence, or the encouragement of interactions with host-country nationals. Overall, the special background and interests of self-initiated foreign workers has substantial implications for HRM strategies, policies and practices in MNCs – not least with respect to the goals and patterns of IM and global careers. Differences between international and local hires might necessitate a more personalized career planning approach to accommodate diverse priorities and career strategies (Crowley-Henry 2007; Doherty and Dickmann 2008b; Chapter 2).

Selection of expatriates

Organizations can tell individuals to work abroad as in the case of the armed forces, or can ask staff to go on an international sojourn – with an array of likely consequences should individuals decide to say no – or can select among those persons who apply for an international vacancy. The organizational attraction and selection process is described below.

Organizations have a range of options to fill their international vacancies. Scullion and Collings (2006) distinguish between internal and external recruitment. Early studies have found that companies have a much higher propensity to use internal sourcing compared to external recruitment (Torbiörn 1982; Hogan and Goodson 1990). Internal international staffing is seen to have a number of advantages, including: cost effectiveness; the candidate's knowledge of the organization's processes, culture and goals; the prior existence of networks that can be useful for task accomplishment; and better insights into the candidate's family situation, performance track record, skills and personality (Finn and Morley 2002).

External recruitment sources include the use of (executive) search companies (head-hunters), open external advertising and internet recruitment (Scullion and Collings 2006). The GMAC (2008: 13) survey found that 14 per cent of companies reacted to cost pressures by hiring local employees to fill positions previously occupied by long-term assignees (and 20 per cent relied on localization). Evans et al. (2002) point out that MNCs that are active in recruiting high-potential local managers should stress the career prospects of host-country managers and outline their localization strategies and plans together with their impact on local career opportunities. This is a strategy that is being used by some international companies such as Standard Chartered Bank (Dickmann 1997).

There has been a long-standing interest in identifying variables that can contribute to an individual's success when working abroad. For instance, Tung (1981) suggests that technical competence, personal traits and related abilities, family situation and the ability to cope with a foreign context are highly pertinent. Studies have identified a range of behaviours that are linked to the effectiveness of international work (Hays 1974; Abe and Wiseman 1983; Jordan and Cartwright 1998; Black et al. 1999). These include the needs to be flexible, people-oriented and sociable, open to experiences, empathetic and non-judgemental and able to tolerate ambiguity. Moreover, success is facilitated if international assignees have clear goals and good communication skills. However, there seems to be a gap between the criteria that organizations should use to select their international assignees and those selection criteria that are being actually used. Brewster (1991) suggests that the three most important criteria are technical competence, previous track record and motivation. These are followed by less important selection variables such as language skills, stress resistance, independence, goal-oriented personality and communication skills. Not only do the lists of ideal and actual criteria vary, they also differ in ranking of importance.

We have seen earlier in this chapter the factors identified by Bird and Osland (2004) as global competencies. Dowling and Welch (2004) summarize the lists of specific items constructed by various authors and develop a list of six overarching competencies. Their general competencies can be categorized into three individual factors – technical ability, cross-cultural suitability and family requirements – and three situational factors – country/cultural requirements, MNC requirements and language.

The first of the *individual* factors is technical ability which is clearly linked to the operational rationale of staffing vacant positions with the highest quality person, as well as to strategic considerations of knowledge transfer and exploitation. There is a large body of literature that shows how highly valued technical ability is in selecting expatriates (Brewster 1991; Sparrow et al. 2004). However, technical excellence without adapting to local processes, customs and preferences might not be sufficient and Dowling and Welch caution us that success is related to how situations are being handled by individuals.

The second of Dowling and Welch's *individual* factors is cross-cultural suitability. In our framework it is related to the antecedents and individual interests and drives. Although personal characteristics associated with foreign work success are difficult to assess, some authors have linked these to the broad facets of Big 5 personality theory (Caligiuri 2000). Concentrating on more specific factors, authors have suggested cultural intelligence, adaptability, cultural empathy, openness and diplomacy as competencies facilitating cross-cultural work success.

The third of Dowling and Welch's *individual* factors is family requirements which are highly connected to the family and partner considerations in our framework (Figure 5.5). As we will further explore in Chapters 6 and 7, family requirements are not just an important factor in accepting international work but they also have a strong impact on individual adjustment and performance during an IA. Expatriates are no longer almost exclusively male (Adler 2002) and dual-career issues have emerged as important influence factors on the decision to go, as well as on the well-being of expatriates. The partner's willingness to relocate is an important decision variable (Konopaske et al. 2005), as are other contextual influences such as having elderly parents or the perceived quality of schooling. Family challenges – most prominent children's education, family adjustment and partner resistance – were seen as the most critical issues in IM (GMAC 2008: 43) and assessed as important reasons for turning down expatriation offers (GMAC 2006: 14) in recent surveys.

The first *situational* factor in Dowling and Welch's categorization is country/cultural requirements. These have their parallel in national and location-specific considerations and, to a lesser extent, in individual interests and drives in Figure 5.5. Thus, the national culture, security, climate, history etc. will be important to individuals when they evaluate personal risks and opportunities. Politically volatile, insecure or socially hostile countries might be considered as hardship postings and generally command a higher 'expatriation premium' to attract suitable candidates

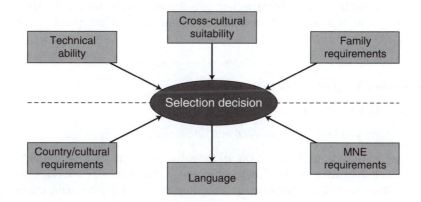

Figure 5.5 Factors in expatriate selection
Source: Dowling et al. (2008: 119)

(Doherty et al. 2006). With respect to selection criteria these hardship locations might also demand the use of different criteria which stress self-reliance, considered risk-taking, innovativeness and self-confidence.

The second *situational* factor relates to the requirements of the employing organization and is reflected in all the organizational considerations underlying IM approaches. Obviously, the organizational rationale should have an impact on the selection criteria used. For instance, global leadership development would need to factor in the learning capabilities of the individual and the ability to transfer acquired insights and to leverage expanded networks upon return. Control and coordination assignments have higher demands on diplomacy, communication and adjustment capabilities of individuals than pure skills-filling expatriation. Launching new initiatives will entail a much higher need for local understanding and flexibility compared to assignments driven by speed of response considerations. Lastly, knowledge creation, transfer and exploitation motivated assignments rely on highly developed cultural sensitivity and communication skills. Besides these different motives, the wider context of the planned assignment in terms of duration (family issues) or organizational power base (e.g. joint venture problems, subsidiary vs. head office power) will have an impact on selection criteria.

The last key *situational* factor for Dowling and Welch is language. While it is obvious that a good command of the local language can be helpful for expatriate adjustment and performance, it appears that language capabilities are to some degree neglected in expatriate selection (Björkman and Gertsen 1992). While this might be one of the effects of the growth of (predominantly English) global corporate languages, deciders within MNCs might underestimate the effects of rudimentary or better command of the local language in the host environment.

International selection in action

It has long been argued that there tends to be a divergence between international selection criteria that companies should use and those that are actually being used.

Harris and Brewster (1999) outline how the impetus to approach a specific candidate for foreign work can arise through chance encounters at the coffee machine (see Box 5.3).

Box 5.3 The coffee machine system

'How's it going?'

'Oh, you know, overworked and underpaid.'

'Tell me about it. As well as all the usual stuff, Jimmy in Mumbai has just fallen ill and is being flown home. I've got no idea who we can get over there to pick up the pieces at such short notice. It's driving me crazy.'

'Have you met that Simon on the fifth floor? He is in the same line of work. Very bright and looks like he is going a long way. He was telling me that he and his wife had a great holiday in Goa a couple of years ago. He seems to like India. Could be worth a chat.'

'Hey, thanks. I'll check him out.'

Source: Harris and Brewster (1999: 497)

What is likely to follow from this situation is that a 'pre-selection' has in effect taken place and the subsequent conversations and assessments of Simon (and his family) are undertaken in the spirit of risk-reduction and to legitimize the coffee-machine decision. Such an informal approach results in a highly restricted number of candidates who are often not evaluated against formal and agreed criteria. This is likely to result in a reactive rather than strategic management of IM.

	Formal	Informal
Open	• Formal decision to evaluate staffing needs • Clearly defined criteria • Clearly defined measures • Training for selectors • Open advertising of vacancy (internal/external) • Criteria-based discussions	• Less defined criteria • Less defined measures • Limited training for selectors • Open advertising of vacancy • Recommendations
Closed	• Formal decision to evaluate staffing needs • Clearly defined criteria • Clearly defined measures • Training for selectors • Criteria-based discussions • Nominations only (networking/reputations)	• Selectors' individual preferences determine selection criteria • Nominations only (networking/reputation)

Figure 5.6 Harris and Brewster's selection typology
Source: Adapted from Harris and Brewster (1999: 493)

Harris and Brewster (1999) distinguish between formal and informal as well as between open and closed expatriate selection systems. One of the key effects of the degree of formality is related to the quality of decisions – e.g. more informal processes have less-defined criteria and measures. In turn, open and closed selection has an impact on the pool of eligible candidates – open systems are likely to provide the organization with more persons to choose from – and career management. Open advertising of international vacancies is likely to lead to more applicants and puts the organization in a stronger negotiation position. Because a closed selection system means that the organization can nominate candidates it also has a better chance to manage local/global succession issues and individual as well as organization-wide career systems. With respect to Figure 5.7 this global leadership development might be very important to companies. The GMAC (2008: 39) survey states that building international management expertise and career development (one item) has moved in the history of this survey from fourth to second place in importance. In effect, many companies use a closed approach for some positions which are associated with key career steps while they advertise most of their international vacancies internally.

Case study 5.1 Organizational drivers, selection, performance and retention at CandyCo

The case firm is a fast-moving consumer goods organization that produces and globally distributes, among other products, well-known sweets and candy bars in more than 100 countries. Founded in the early twentieth century, it employed nearly 50,000 employees in 2008 and had a sales turnover of approximately $22 billion. A key objective of IM within it is the development of a broadly experienced group of employees that supports the needs of international expansion and successful operation. In line with this, the company's global assignment policy states that the key purposes to be satisfied through expatriation and other IAs are:

- skills-filling in emerging, developing and developed markets;
- coordination through skills and best practice in order to train local employees;
- improving cultural and national diversity;
- development of international assignees and transferees.

The assignment policy further requires that relocation policies and practices should be supportive of both business and employee needs. To this end principles have been developed that should be applied in a fair, consistent and reasonable way. These include a belief that international moves will be most successful where the firm provides adequate care and support to expatriates and their families, explains the economic consequences of an international move and honestly assesses and discusses potential career impacts, including risks.

Prior to any assignment a business case rationale form has to be filled in that lays out the business case for the organization, the development plan, potential and last performance rating of the employee, benefits of the move, the assignment/transfer objectives to be met by the individual, description of the position, and a verification that the sending and receiving units have been consulted and support the move.

In order to explore the business case rationale, a primary purpose for the assignment has to be defined in relation to the following matrix.

Development and personal growth through expatriation is seen as crucial within the organization in that a senior HR manager stated that there was, in effect, a 'glass ceiling' for the careers of managers who did not have international work experience.

Case questions

1 What are the key criteria inherent in the selection approach of CandyCo? How are the individual drivers accounted for?
2 Given the selection framework of Harris and Brewster (1999); what organizational purposes of CandyCo would be better served by open or closed resourcing approaches?
3 In general, what are the key strengths and problems with the IM policies in CandyCo?
4 What are the potential causes of problems?
5 What could possible actions be to tackle these problems?
6 What perspective(s) have you been using? What overlap between organizational and individual perspectives can you identify? What other considerations (head office, host, home, third-country, societal) might have an impact?

	1	**2**
Long	Transfer of knowledge Corporate culture; Local successor development	Development: Understand different perspective and culture and embed
TIME		
	3	**4**
Short	Crisis Management Project Management	Development: Intervention to see different perspective
	High Professional	High Potential

Figure 5.7 The primary purpose
Source: Adapted from International Mobility Policy of CandyCo

Gender issues

Recent surveys found that female expatriates constituted between 11.5 per cent (Dickmann et al. 2008) and 19 per cent (GMAC 2008: 23) of the total expatriate population. While the number of female managers varies between countries

(Rosener 1995; Caligiuri and Tung 1999), there have been many voices that have pointed out that female international assignees are underrepresented. For instance, International Labour Organization (ILO) data suggests that between 25 and 34 per cent of women had management jobs in various European countries (Kollinger and Linehan 2008). If this is so, what are some of the key reasons that women are not more frequently selected?

One possible reason could be prejudices among selectors that certain cultures – particularly those from Africa, the Middle East and Asia – inhibit the effectiveness of female managers (Adler 1984). Therefore, the perceived risk associated with sending females to certain destinations abroad would increase. Moreover, there might be a stronger reluctance of companies to send their female employees on 'hardship postings' where the perceived dangers to the security and health of staff are particularly high. Whilst female assignees are likely to differ in their professional status, actions and appearance from local women, therefore they are likely to be regarded and treated differently (Forster 1999). However, it is not clear that the majority of MNCs subscribe to this argument and being young or single might have more of an influence on the selection and work circumstances of female expatriates (Overseas Digest 2009). Overall, there is likely to be some organizational deselection with regards to female expatriation.

Moreover, a perception of a difficult host context might also lead to female self-deselection. The challenges might be related to the role of women in the host society, but they might also be related to the inherent risks associated with the foreign postings. Ryan and Haslam (2005) argue that women might be prone to be charged with precarious responsibilities and that they might face a 'glass cliff'.

Another reason for the underrepresentation could be simply that the pool of available female talent is not representative. Female international managers tend to work more frequently in the service sector (banking and finance, publishing, retailing) rather than in the industrial sector. Some industries, however, such as oil and gas exploration, heavy engineering and fast-moving consumer goods are particularly prone to use high numbers of international assignees. Often it is the case that the female intake in these industries – and especially the hiring of engineers who might have turned managers by the time an IA becomes a real possibility – is low. Then the higher numbers of male expatriates is understandable and especially true in the sense that many expatriates are middle or senior managers which is another area in which females seem to be underrepresented (Singh et al. 2002; Vinnicombe and Singh 2002). Given the trend to earlier international work the lower female numbers due to levels of hierarchical seniority are likely to become more equal over time (GMAC 2003; Collins-O'Sullivan 2005).

However, there might be also inconsistencies in the selection criteria of MNCs. An informal selection system, as outlined above with the coffee-machine example, is bound to favour highly networked individuals. The social capital of individuals is manifested through the number of contacts and used for mutual work benefits. These include collaboration, exchanging information, acquisition of tacit and other knowledge, developing alliances, creating visibility and gaining support

(Adler 1987; Barham and Oates 1991). While networking normally demands an exchange of reciprocal help and support, the building of major contacts is facilitated by similarity and a shared social background (Powell 1999). Women might sometimes be seen as non-typical (given their proportionate underrepresentation in management and among expatriates) and, therefore, as a networking investment with a risky return (cf. Kollinger and Linehan 2008). While there are instances of women-only networks (e.g. in PricewaterhouseCoopers, among female lawyers), Kollinger and Linehan argue that these are rare and that males have a superior access to informal networking facilities. Where women are not part of the informal backbone of the organization, this might have negative consequences for their influence, power and promotion prospects as well as for their chances of international career success.

Some organizations might also have a double standard in respect to marriage and children. Vinnicombe and Sturges (1995) argue that female married managers can be seen as a liability with the suspicion within some firms that they are likely to put their family first and, consequently, more likely to neglect their work and careers. In contrast, male married managers are viewed as an asset as they possess a support network at home that allows them to concentrate fully on their work and careers. In addition, female managers are more likely to face dual-career issues.

Organizational and individual implications

Sullivan and Arthur (2006) have developed a model of the boundaryless career that distinguishes physical and psychological dimensions on two continua. They maintain that boundaryless careers are not an either-or phenomenon but, rather, the degree of mobility shown by a career actor can be identified and measured. Physical mobility means movements where individuals tend to relocate in order to work in different organizations within their countries or to move across regions and states to live abroad. Not just the implied degree of mobility is different but also the interconnected degree of psychological mobility. Psychological mobility could range from a low degree where an individual pursues the same occupation that is relatively stable, to situations where persons are engaged in highly changing and demanding jobs (e.g. academics, consultants) or where people engage in radical change. For instance, individuals could decide to switch occupations, functions, employers and locations at the same time. International moves tend to be viewed as demanding both high physical and psychological mobility. One instance is the case of LVMH where managers were often asked to change function, division and country at the same time (Cerdin 2003). Movement in the model depends on a range of variables including career competencies, individual characteristics, organizational context, culture and demographic variables.

The discussion in this chapter would indicate that organizations need to match their strategic intent with their selection and management approaches in IM (see also Chapters 6, 7 and 11). It might be speculated that ceteris paribus organizations that pursue classical control and coordination, rapid response or resourcing quality reasons for their expatriation might need lesser psychological mobility of their global staff compared to those entities that use IAs to create, transfer and exploit knowledge, launch new initiatives or to develop the global leaders of the future. The reasons might lie in the degree of needed adaptability and openness to other approaches that expatriates would need and which varies with the assignment purpose. However, the organizational purpose would not, on its own, define the necessary psychological mobility as the organizational configuration, industry and other context factors would influence the required level of adaptability (cf. Chapter 2; Bartlett and Ghoshal 1989).

Arthur and Rousseau (1996) have outlined a variety of different meanings of the boundaryless career which have as a common factor the independence from traditional career arrangements. Therefore, where organizations have a requirement for individuals to work abroad before they can climb the next career ladder rung, or where persons go on an IA that is primarily designed to benefit their progress within a traditional company-designed career management system, the psychological mobility demands on career actors might not be as high as with other forms of IM. This fits well to the findings that self-initiated foreign workers are more likely to seek more holistic developmental experiences in which they are engaged in the host environment to a high degree (Doherty et al. 2007).

The discussion of individual drivers has shown that a large range of influence categories, including personality, family and social background, gender, early experiences, family and partner considerations, organizational context, regional, national and location-specific factors and individual interests and drivers have a strong impact on the needed psychological mobility when working abroad. It is through identifying the individual patterns of drivers and subsequently designing flexible policies and processes that organizations can manage some of the interactions with their staff and increase the quality of their IM approaches. The survey by Dickmann et al. (2008) shows that there is a range of individual or organizational goals that are not aligned to each other. Organizations might want to find out individual interests and – depending on the organization's vacant overseas positions, own goals and broader context – might be able to factor these in. For instance, individuals who have a strong wish to explore new things might be expatriated to culturally very distinct locations. In turn, people who have obligations to their parents might be offered nearer locations with frequent travel opportunities to come back and visit.

Possessing a high degree of physical and psychological mobility in the dynamic world of the twenty-first century is likely to be a career asset and will contribute to gathering new experiences and insights and to building new networks. As such, the high willingness to cross career boundaries might increase an individual's career capital (DeFillippi and Arthur 1994; Eby et al. 2003). Moreover, it might be speculated that organizations that identify the career drivers of persons working for them and are able to develop policies and practices that satisfy many of their assignees' expectations are likely to have more successful medium-term IM and long-term career and development outcomes. These issues are discussed in more depth in subsequent chapters.

Summary and learning points

This chapter has explored individual and organizational resourcing issues in global careers. It has concentrated on the point of making the decision whether to actively seek or to accept international work and has explored associated backgrounds, motivations and drivers.

Key learning points include:

- To understand global careers and IM a variety of perspectives is needed. Most importantly, there exists a dual dependency between individuals and their employers that is especially acute in international sojourns.
- There is a range of primary organizational drivers for IM. These include long-term strategic considerations such as control and coordination, knowledge creation, diffusion and exploitation and global leadership development.
- Operational reasons for organizations to use global mobility are related to the quality of resourcing, the speed of filling international vacancies, general management of global careers and the launching of new initiatives.
- Individuals are driven by many and diverse motives when seeking or accepting international work. Antecedents such as family and social background, early experiences and personality determine their receptivity to international experiences.
- Key individual motivations to work abroad include career and development considerations. Other important factors are individual interests and drives, family and partner considerations, organizational factors and inducements as well as national and location-specific factors.
- Understanding the individual and organizational perspectives and their interactions might enable employers to design and implement superior HR policies and practices. In turn, individuals benefit from realistically assessing the opportunities and threats associated with global careers.
- Traditional expatriation and self-initiated international experiences vary in many respects. Self-initiated foreign workers are more self-reliant, are driven by different career anchors, pursue more holistic work and life goals, value general culture, travel and quality of life considerations more and have a more strongly developed sense of exploration and adventure.
- While company-sent expatriates have been described as 'active careerists' due to their strong, organizational career orientation, self-initiated persons have been described as 'career activists'. They are likely to have a substantial degree of physical and psychological mobility in their search for a more holistic life.
- The 'dark side' of self-initiated foreign work includes more personal risks and transience and that individuals have a higher propensity than company-sent expatriates to accept a job that they view as being worse than the one they had in their home country. Normally, there is also no repatriation planning or support by the employer.
- Immigrants and self-initiated foreign workers represent a pool of global talent that is not yet sufficiently recognized by organizations, who often lack specific attraction and retention strategies for these individuals.

- There is a range of options that organizations have to attract and select candidates for expatriation. They can use external and internal labour markets and employ open, closed, formal and informal selection approaches. Many firms use informal and/or closed selection which has a number of drawbacks.
- Descriptions of global competencies that facilitate successful international work exist. The sometimes long lists of general global competencies can be categorized into technical ability, cross-cultural suitability, family requirements, country/cultural requirements, organizational requirements and language.
- Gender issues continue to impact on the selection of expatriates, with fewer women being sent on foreign assignments.
- Understanding and managing the various perspectives in IM and global careers might lead to the formulation of more realistic expectations and career activities by individuals as well as the design and implementation of more tailored and flexible expatriation and career strategies, policies and processes by organizations.

References

Abe, H. and Wiseman, R. (1983) 'A cross-cultural confirmation of the dimensions of intercultural effectiveness', *International Journal of International Relations*, 7: 53–67.

Adler, Nancy J. (1984) 'Women do not want international careers: and other myths about international management', *Organizational Dynamics*, 13(2): 66–79.

Adler, Nancy J. (1987) 'Pacific basin managers: a gaijin, not a woman', *Human Resource Management*, 26(2): 169–192.

Adler, N. (2002) 'Global managers: no longer men alone', *International Journal of Human Resource Management*, 13(5): 743–760.

Altman, Y. and Baruch, Y. (2008) 'Global protean careers: a new era in expatriation and repatriation', paper presented at the *European Academy of Management* conference, Ljubljana, May 2008.

Arthur, M.B. and Rousseau, D.M. (eds) (1996) *The Boundaryless Career: A New Employment Principle for a New Organizational Era*, New York: Oxford University Press.

Ashkenas, R.N., DeMonaco, L. and Francis, S.C. (1998) 'Making the deal real: how GE Capital integrates acquisitions', *Harvard Business Review*, Jan–Feb, 76(1): 165–178.

Barham, K. and Oates, D. (1991) *The International Manager*, London: Economist Books.

Bartlett, C. and Ghoshal, S. (1989) *Managing Across Borders*, London: Hutchinson Business Books.

Baruch, Y. (2004) *Managing Careers: Theory and Practice*, Harlow: FT-Prentice Hall/Pearson.

Baruch, Y. and Altman, Y. (2002) 'Expatriation and repatriation in MNC: a taxonomy', *Human Resource Management*, 41(2): 239–259.

Baruch, Y. and Vardi, Y. (2009) 'If it is so good, why are things so bad? The dark side of new careers', paper presented at the *EGOS Colloquium*, Barcelona, July 2009.

Baruch, Y., Altman, Y. and Adler, N. (2009) 'Topic: global careers and international assignments: the current discourse', *Human Resource Management*, 48(1): 1–4.

Begley, A., Collings, D.G. and Scullion, H. (2008) 'The cross-cultural adjustment experiences of self-initiated repatriates to the Republic of Ireland labour market', *Employee Relations*, 30(3): 264–282.

Bhaskar-Shrinivas, P., Harrison, D., Shaffer, M. and Luk, D. (2005) 'Input-based and time-based models of international adjustment: meta-analytic evidence and theoretical extensions', *Academy of Management Journal*, 48(2): 257–281.

Bird, A. and Osland, J. (2004) 'Global competencies: an introduction', in H.W. Lane, M.L. Maxnewski, M.E. Mendenhall and J. McNett (eds) *Handbook of Global Management*, Oxford: Blackwell Publishing.

Björkman, I. and Gertsen, M. (1992) 'Selecting and training Scandinavian expatriates', *Scandinavian Journal of Management*, 9: 145–164.

Black, J.S., Gregersen, H.B. and Mendenhall, M.E. (1992) *Global Assignments: Successfully Expatriating and Repatriating International Managers*, San Francisco, CA: Jossey-Bass.

Black, J.S., Gregersen, H.B., Mendenhall, M.E. and Stroh, L.K. (1999) *Globalizing People through International Assignments*, Reading, MA: Addison-Wesley.

Bonache, J. and Dickmann, M. (2008) 'Transfer of Strategic HR know-how in MNCs: mechanisms, barriers and initiatives', in M. Dickmann, C. Brewster and P. Sparrow (eds) *International Human Resource Management – A European Perspective*, London: Routledge.

Bonache, J. and Zárraga-Oberty, C. (2008) 'Determinants of the success of international assignees as knowledge transferors: a theoretical framework', *International Journal of Human Resource Management*, 19(1): 1–18.

Bonache, J., Brewster, C. and Suutari, V. (2007) 'Knowledge, international mobility and careers', *International Studies of Management and Organization*, 37(3): 5–21.

Bossard, A.B. and Peterson, R.B. (2005) 'The repatriate experience as seen by American expatriates', *Journal of World Business*, 40(1): 9–28.

Brett, J. and Stroh, L. (1995) 'Willingness to relocate internationally', *Human Resource Management*, 34(3): 405–424.

Brewster, C. (1991) *The Management of Expatriates*, London: Kogan Page.

Brewster, C. and Suutari, V. (2005) 'Global HRM: aspects of a research agenda', *Personnel Review*, 34(1): 5–21.

Cabrera, A., Collins, W. and Salgado, J. (2006) 'Determinants of individual engagement in knowledge sharing', *International Journal of Human Resource Management*, 17(2): 245–264.

Caligiuri, P. (2000) 'Selecting expatriates for personality characteristics: a moderating effect of personality on the relationship between host national contact and cross-cultural adjustment', *Management International Review*, 40(1): 61–80.

Caligiuri, P. and Tung, R. (1999) 'Comparing the success of male and female expatriates from a US-based multinational company', *International Journal of Human Resource Management*, 10(5): 763–782.

Cappellen, T. and Janssens, M. (2005) 'Career paths of global managers: towards future research', *Journal of World Business*, 40(4): 348–360.

Carpenter, M.A., Sanders, W.G. and Gregersen, H.B. (2001) 'Bundling human capital with organizational context: the impact of international assignment experience on multinational firm performance and CEO pay', *Academy of Management Journal*, 44(3): 493–511.

Cerdin, J.-L. (2003) 'LVMH: Career development through international mobility', *ECCH Case Collection*, 403-050-1.

Cerdin, J.-L. (2008) 'Careers and expatriation', in M. Dickmann, C. Brewster and P. Sparrow (eds) *International Human Resource Management: A European Perspective*, Abingdon: Routledge.

Collings, D.G. and Scullion, H. (2008) 'Resourcing international assignees', in M. Dickmann, C. Brewster and P. Sparrow (eds) *International Human Resource Management: A European Perspective*, Abingdon: Routledge.

Collins-O'Sullivan, C. (2005) 'Key issues in the repatriation of senior international female executives: a qualitative study in a European context', *Irish Business Journal*, 1(1): 62–69.

Conway, N. and Briner, R. (2005) *Understanding the Psychological Contracts at Work. A Critical Evaluation of Theory and Research*, Oxford: Oxford University Press.

Crowley-Henry, M. (2007) 'The protean career', *International Studies of Management and Organization*, 37(3): 44–64.

DeFillippi, R. and Arthur, M. (1994) 'The boundaryless career: a competency-based perspective', *Journal of Organizational Behavior*, 15: 307–324.

Delios, A. and Björkman, I. (2000) 'Expatriate staffing in foreign subsidiaries of Japanese multinational corporations in the PRC and the United States', *International Journal Human Resource Management*, 11(2): 278–293.

Dickmann, M. (1997) *The IPD Guide on International Management Development*, London: Institute of Personnel and Development.

Dickmann, M. (1999) 'Balancing global, parent and local influences: International human resource management of German multinational companies', unpublished thesis, Birkbeck College, University of London.

Dickmann, M. and Doherty, N. (2008) 'Exploring the career capital impact of international assignments within distinct organizational contexts', *British Journal of Management*, 19: 145–161.

Dickmann, M. and Doherty, N. (2010) 'Exploring organisational and individual career goals, interactions and outcomes of international assignments', *Thunderbird International Review*, 52(4): 313–324.

Dickmann, M. and Harris, H. (2005) 'Developing career capital for global careers: the role of international assignments', *Journal of World Business*, 40: 399–408.

Dickmann, M. and Mills, T. (2010) 'The importance of intelligent career and location considerations: exploring the decision to go to London', *Personnel Review*, 39(1): 116–134.

Dickmann, M. and Müller-Camen, M. (2006) 'A typology of international human resource management strategies and processes', *International Journal of Human Resource Management*, 17(4): 580–601.

Dickmann, M., Doherty, N. and Johnson, A. (2006) *Measuring the value of international assignments*, report for PwC UK Geodesy, Cranfield: Cranfield School of Management, England.

Dickmann, M., Doherty, N., Mills, T. and Brewster, C. (2008) 'Why do they go? Individual and corporate perspectives on the factors influencing the decision to accept an international assignment', *International Journal of Human Resource Management*, 19(4): 731–751.

Doherty, N. and Dickmann, M. (2005) 'Accumulating and utilizing the capital of global careers', paper presented at *British Academy of Management* conference, Challenges of Organizations in Global Markets, Oxford, September 2005.

Doherty, N. and Dickmann, M. (2008a) 'Capitalizing on an international career: career capital perspectives', in M. Dickmann, C. Brewster and P. Sparrow (eds) *International Human Resource Management – A European Perspective*, London: Routledge.

Doherty, N. and Dickmann, M. (2008b) 'Self-initiated expatriates – corporate asset or a liability', paper presented at *4th Workshop on Expatriation, EIASM*, Las Palmas de Gran Canaria, Spain, October 2008.

Doherty, N., Dickmann, M. and Brewster, C. (2006) 'Using the career capital of international assignments back home. The "career wobble"', paper presented at *British Academy of Management* Conference, Belfast, September 2006.

Doherty, N., Dickmann, M. and Mills, T. (2007) *Are you a hero or a heroine? An exploration of the expatriation journey*, research report for Expatica, Cranfield: Cranfield University.

Doherty, N., Mills, T. and Dickmann, M. (2006) *A study of the obstacles to transnational mobility of apprentices and other young persons in initial vocational training and of how these obstacles can be surmounted*, report compiled as part of the EU MoVE-iT project, Cranfield: Cranfield University.

Dowling, P. and Welch, D. (2004) *International Human Resource Management*, London: Thompson.

Dowling, P., Festing, M. and Engle, A.D. (2008) *International Human Resource Management: Managing People in a Multinational Context*, 5th edn, London: Thomson.

Eby, L.T., Butts, M. and Lockwood, A. (2003) 'Predictors of success in the era of the boundaryless career', *Journal of Organizational Behaviour*, 24(6): 689–708.

Edström, A. and Galbraith, J.R. (1977) 'Transfer of managers as a coordination and control strategy in multinational organizations', *Administrative Science Quarterly*, 22(2): 248–263.

Eisenhardt, K. and Martin, J.A. (2000) 'Dynamic capabilities: what are they?', *Strategic Management Journal*, 21(10): 1105–1126.

Evans, P., Pucik, V. and Barsoux, J.L. (2002) *The Global Challenge: Frameworks for International Human Resource Management*, London: McGraw-Hill.

Ferner, A. (2000) 'The underpinnings of "bureaucratic" control systems', *Journal of Management Studies*, 37(4): 521–539.

Finn, G. and Morley, M. (2002) 'Expatriate selection: the case of an Irish MNC', in M. Linehan, M. Morley and J. Walsh (eds) *International Human Resource Management and Expatriate Transfers: Irish Experiences*, Dublin: Oak Tree Press.

Forster, N. (1999) 'Another "glass ceiling"? The experiences of women professionals and managers on international assignments', *Gender, Work and Organization*, 6(2): 79–90.

GMAC (2003) *Global Relocation Trends Survey*, Warren, NJ: GMAC Global Relocation Services.

GMAC (2006) *Global Relocation Trends Survey*, Oak Brook, IL: GMAC Global Relocation Services.

GMAC (2008) *Global Relocation Trends Survey*, Woodridge, IL: GMAC Global Relocation Services.

Gregersen, H.B., Morrison, A.J. and Black, J.S. (1998) 'Developing leaders for the global frontier', *Sloan Management Review*, 40(1): 21–33.

Hammer, M., Hart, W. and Rogan, R. (1998) 'Can you go home again? An analysis of the repatriation of corporate managers and spouses?', *Management International Review*, 38: 67–86.

Harris, H. and Brewster, C. (1999) 'The coffee-machine system: how international selection really works', *International Journal of Human Resource Management*, 10(3): 488–500.

Harris, H. and Dickmann, M. (2005) *The CIPD Guide on International Management Development*, London: The Chartered Institute of Personnel and Development.

Harris, H., Brewster, C. and Sparrow, P. (2003) *International Human Resource Management*, London: The Chartered Institute of Personnel and Development.

Harvey, M. (1995) 'The impact of dual-career families on international relocations', *Human Resource Management Review*, 5: 223–244.

Harzing, A.W. (1995) 'The persistent myth of high expatriate failure rates', *International Journal of Human Resource Management*, 6(2): 457–474.

Harzing, A.-W. and Christensen, C. (2004) 'Expatriate failure: time to abandon the concept?', *Career Development International*, 9(7): 616–626.

Haslberger, A. (2005) 'Facets and dimensions of cross-cultural adaptation – refining the tools', *Personnel Review*, 34: 85–110.

Haslberger, A. and Zehetner, K. (2008) 'Cosmopolitan appeal: what makes a city attractive to expatriates and how do they benefit? The example of Vienna, Austria', paper presented at *4th Workshop on Expatriation, EIASM*, Las Palmas de Gran Canarias, Spain, October 2008.

Hays, R. (1974) 'Expatriate selection: ensuring success and avoiding failure', *Journal of International Business Studies*, 5(1): 25–37.

Hofstede, G. (1980) *Culture's Consequences*, London: Sage.

Hogan, G. and Goodson, J. (1990) 'The key to expatriate success', *Training and Development Journal*, January: 50–52.

Holtbrugge, D. and Berg, N. (2004) 'Knowledge transfer in multinational corporations: evidence from German firms', *Management International Review*, 44: 129–145.

Hudson, S. and Inkson, K. (2006) 'Volunteer overseas development workers: the hero's adventure and personal transformation', *Career Development International*, 11(4): 304–320.

Inkson, K. and Myers, B.A. (2003) 'The big OE: self-directed travel and career development', *Career Development International*, 8: 170–181.

Inkson, K., Arthur, M.B., Pringle, J. and Barry, S. (1997) 'Expatriate assignment versus overseas experience: contrasting models of international human resource development', *Journal of World Business*, 32(4): 351–368.

Jokinen, T., Brewster, C. and Suutari, V. (2008) 'Career capital during international work experiences: contrasting self-initiated expatriate experiences and assignees expatriation', *International Journal of Human Resource Management*, 19(6): 979–998.

Jordan, J. and Cartwright, S. (1998) 'Selecting expatriate managers: key traits and competencies', *Leadership and Organizational Development Journal*, 19(2): 89–96.

Kollinger, I. and Linehan, M. (2008) 'Women on international assignments', in M. Dickmann, C. Brewster and P. Sparrow (eds) *International Human Resource Management: A European Perspective*, Abingdon: Routledge.

Konopaske, R., Robie, C. and Ivancevich, J. (2005) 'A preliminary model of spouse influence on managerial global assignment willingness', *International Journal of Human Resource Management*, 16(3): 405–426.

Kostova, T., Athanassiou, N. and Berdrow, I. (2004) 'Managing knowledge in global organizations: a guide to managing complexity', in H.W. Lane, M.L. Maxnewski, M.E. Mendenhall and J. McNett (eds) *Handbook of Global Management*, Oxford: Blackwell.

Larsen, H.H. (2004) 'Global career as dual dependency between the organization and the individual', *Journal of Management Development*, 23(9): 860–869.

Lee, C.H. (2005) 'A study of underemployment among self-initiated expatriates', *Journal of World Business*, 40: 172–187.

Linehan, M. and Walsh, J. (2000) 'Work-family conflict and the senior female international manager', *British Journal of Management*, 11, Special Issue: 49–58.

Mayrhofer, W., Sparrow, P. and Zimmermann, A. (2008) 'Modern forms of international working', in M. Dickmann, C. Brewster and P. Sparrow (eds) *International Human Resource Management: A European Perspective*, Abingdon: Routledge.

Mayrhofer, W., Iellatchitch, A., Meyer, M., Steyrer, J., Schiffinger, M. and Strunk, G. (2004) 'Going beyond the individual. Some potential contributions from a career field and habitus perspective for global career research and practice', *Journal of Management Development*, 23(9): 870–884.

McNulty, Y. and Tharenou, P. (2004) 'Expatriate return on investment: a definition and antecedents', *International Studies of Management and Organization*, 34(3): 68–95.

Mendenhall, M. (2001) 'New perspectives on expatriate adjustment and its relationship to global leadership development', in M. Mendenhall, T. Kühlmann and G. Stahl (eds) *Developing Global Business Leaders*, Westport, CT: Quorum.

Min Toh, S. and DeNisi, A. (2007) 'Host country nationals as socializing agents: a social identity approach', *Journal of Organizational Behavior*, 28(3): 281–301.

Min Toh, S. and Gunz, H. (2009) 'Career-damaging relationships in the workplace: how new immigrants cope with social undermining', paper presented at *EGOS Colloquium*, Barcelona, July 2009.

Myers, B. and Pringle, J.K. (2005) 'Self-initiated experience as accelerated development: influences of gender', *Journal of World Business*, 40: 421–431.

Noe, R. and Barber, A. (1993) 'Willingness to accept mobility opportunities: destination makes a difference', *Journal of Organizational Behaviour*, 14: 159–175.

ORC (2004) *Worldwide Survey of International Assignment Policies and Practices*, London and New York: Organization Resources Counsellors Inc.

Overseas Digest (2009) *Interview with Grove, C. and Hallowell, W.* Online. http://www.over-seasdigest.com/odarticles/females.htm (accessed 30 June 2009).

Parker, P., Hall, D.T. and Kram, K.E. (2009) 'Peer coaching through learning teams', paper presented at *EGOS Colloquium*, Barcelona, July 2009.

Peiperl, M. and Jonsen, K. (2007) 'Global careers', in H. Gunz and M. Peiperl (eds) *Handbook of Career Studies*, Thousand Oaks, CA: Sage.

Powell, G. (1999) *Handbook of Gender in Organizations*, Thousand Oaks, CA: Sage.

Quelch, J. and Bloom, H. (1999) 'Ten steps to a global human resource strategy', *Strategy and Business*, 14: 1–6.

Richardson, J. (2006) 'Self-directed expatriation: family matters', *Personnel Review*, 35: 469–486.

Richardson, J. and Mallon, M. (2005) 'Careers interrupted? The case of the self-directed expatriate', *Journal of World Business*, 40: 409–420.

Richardson, J. and McKenna, S. (2006) 'Exploring relationships with home and host countries. A study of self-directed expatriates', *Cross Cultural Management*, 13: 6–22.

Richardson, J. and Zikic, J. (2007) 'The darker side of an international academic career', *Career Development International*, 12(2): 164–186.

Riusala, K. and Smale, A. (2004) 'Predicting stickiness factors in international transfer of knowledge through expatriates', paper presented at the *Workshop on Knowledge Transfer*, Copenhagen, 2004.

Rosener, J. (1995) *America's Competitive Secret: Utilizing Women as a Management Strategy*, London: Oxford University Press.

Ryan, M.K. and Haslam, S.A. (2005) 'The glass cliff: evidence that women are over-represented in precarious leadership positions', *British Journal of Management*, 16: 81–90.

Scullion, H. and Collings, D. (eds) (2006) *Global Staffing*, London: Routledge.

Shen, J. (2006) 'Factors affecting international staffing in Chinese multinationals (MNEs)', *International Journal of Human Resource Management*, 17(2): 295–315.

Singh, V., Kumra, S. and Vinnicombe, S. (2002) 'Gender and impression management: playing the promotion game', *Journal of Business Ethics*, 37(1): 77–89.

Sparrow, P., Brewster, C. and Harris, H. (2004) *Globalizing Human Resource Management*, London: Routledge.

Stahl, G. and Cerdin, J.L. (2004) 'Global careers in French and German multinational corporations', *Journal of Management Development*, 23(9): 885–902.

Stahl, G.K., Miller, E. and Tung, R. (2002) 'Towards the boundaryless career: a closer look at the expatriate career concept and the perceived implications of an international assignment', *Journal of World Business*, 37: 216–227.

Sullivan, S.E. and Arthur, M.B. (2006) 'The evolution of the boundaryless career concept: examining physical and psychological mobility', *Journal of Vocational Behaviour*, 69: 19–29.

Suutari, V. (2002) 'Global leader development: an emerging research agenda', *Career Development International*, 7(4): 218–233.

Suutari, V. and Brewster, C. (2000) 'Making their own way: international experience through self-initiated foreign assignments', *Journal of World Business*, 35: 417–436.

Tams, S. and Arthur, M.B. (2007) 'Studying careers across cultures. Distinguishing international, cross-cultural and globalization perspectives', *Career Development International*, 12(1): 86–98.

Tharenou, P. (2003) 'The initial development of receptivity to working abroad: self-initiated international work opportunities in young graduate employees', *Journal of Occupational and Organizational Psychology*, 76: 489–515.

Tharenou, P. and Harvey, M. (2006) 'Examining the overseas staffing options utilized by Australian headquartered multinational corporations', *International Journal of Human Resource Management*, 17(6): 1095–1114.

Thorn, K. (2008) 'Self-initiated international mobility: a force upsetting careers, organizations and nations', paper presented at the *EGOS Colloquium*, Amsterdam, July 2008.

Torbiörn, I. (1982) *Living Abroad: Personal Adjustment and Personnel Policy in the Overseas Setting*, New York: Wiley.

Trompenaars, F. and Hamden-Turner, C. (1997) *Riding the Waves of Culture: Understanding Cultural Diversity in Business*, New York: McGraw-Hill.

Tung, R. (1981) 'Selection and training of personnel for overseas assignments', *Journal of World Business*, 23: 129–143.

Tung, R. (1998) 'American expatriates abroad: from neophytes to cosmopolitans', *Journal of World Business*, 33: 125–144.

van Emmerik, I.J.H. and Euwema, M. (2009) 'The international assignments of peacekeepers: what drives them to seek future expatriation?', *Human Resource Management*, 48(1): 135–151.

Vance, C. (2005) 'The personal quest for building global competence: a taxonomy for self-initiating career path strategies for gaining business experience abroad', *Journal of World Business*, 40(4): 374–385.

Vinnicombe, S. and Singh, V. (2002) 'Sex role stereotyping and requisites of successful top managers', *Women in Management Review*, 17(3/4): 120–130.

Vinnicombe, S. and Sturges, J. (1995) 'European women in management', in S. Vinnicombe and N. Colwill (eds) *The Essence of Women in Management*, London: Prentice Hall.

Yan, A., Zhu, G. and Hall, D. (2002) 'International assignments for career building: a model of agency relationships and psychological contracts', *Academy of Management Review*, 27(3): 373–391.

Yurkiewicz, J. and Rosen, B. (1995) 'Increasing receptivity to expatriate assignments', in J. Selmer (ed.) *Expatriate Management*, Westport, CT: Quorum.

Zaidman, N. and Brock, D.M. (2009) 'Knowledge transfer within multinationals and their foreign subsidiaries: a culture-context approach', *Group & Organization Management*, 34: 297–329.

6 Pre-departure and post-arrival considerations in international work

Objectives

This chapter:

- depicts the individual and organizational considerations associated with pre-departure for international work;
- describes individual activities and actions to be taken before the assignment;
- identifies the key family and partner challenges associated with the preparation for the move;
- describes organizational policies and practices undertaken before international work;
- explores national and societal issues relating to work-related cross-border moves;
- outlines typical pre-departure preparations by organizations;
- investigates ways by which pre-departure preparations could impact performance and career while on assignment;
- covers post-arrival issues.

Introduction

In this chapter we explore the wide issues that need to be taken care of *after* a decision to make a global move has been taken, but *before* the actual move itself. The issues vary greatly, based on the type of global move (see Chapter 4 for elaboration), the length of anticipated stay, the family involved, the role to be carried out and a number of other factors.

We do not cover in this chapter the 'pre-departure' considerations of globetrotting or flexpatriates. For them, another away-from-home short visit is no more than yet another round of packing a small suitcase for a typical commute.

Figure 6.1 A framework of global careers: selection and development for international work

At the individual level, we will explore the career- and job-related preparation and the impact on the family – those members of the family who are moving with the assignee, and those staying, typically the extended family.

Issues include – short-term; long-term; variations from self-initiated and organizational-initiated considerations; different practices for different organizational strategies; organizational practices training, career planning and mentoring, including dual mentoring – in the host country and in the home country.

In the discussion we will differentiate between expatriates and immigrants. Some of the issues are relevant for both populations, whereas certain issues are limited to specific types. In immigration, each case is an ad-hoc one, and the fact that the cost of training (as well as other considerations, such as travel) is to be borne by the individual, has a major implication on the decision to train.

Work and family issues

Work

In the expatriation context, the move might be from managing a focused, specific department, to managing a national operation. The transition is typically from a practical to a strategic job, from dealing mostly with people within the organization, to dealing with a multitude of constituencies.

There are also exceptions, where the job change or change in roles performed is not major. An academic sabbatical is a fine example here: the university professor would run fairly similar courses, maybe even use the same textbook, would run a study, and interact with academics in the same discipline. Another exception, for the case of MNC expatriation can occur when the job comprises of technical support or simple knowledge transfer, which can be short, and is less involved with managerial duties.

Family

Two of the most significant and stressful events in an individual's life are a change of job and a move of a house. A global move, be it expatriation or immigration, incorporates both events. A global move typically means that each one of these changes becomes a major one.

The picture might be different for frequent travellers. First, typically there is no uprooting of the family, and one can actually enjoy travelling in both work and non-work aspects. One positive aspect of frequent business trips of flexpatriates/globetrotters was found by Westman et al. (2009). With high numbers of business trips the resources (trip control and trip satisfaction) were positively related to the traveller's stamina. No less important is that this resilience was matched by that of their spouse. This stands in clear contrast to the problems that 'conventional' expatriate dual-career couples face, where the expatriation of the main breadwinner, still typically the male, results in the trailing spouse losing out on (her) career, a forced sacrifice scenario.

The above discussion implies that the job and career change of a global move is significant in most cases. As a result, the people involved will feel a high level of career-related stress (Baruch 2009), and may need support. Even if no direct support is needed, the organization and its representatives should be aware that expatriation and repatriation are events associated with high stress potential.

Immigration context

In immigration, the future job might be unknown, or merely just aspired to. Sometimes the expectations far surpass the anticipated reality. In cases where a work permit is issued for an accepted job, there is less ambiguity, but sometimes there is no known job at all. For refugees, illegal immigrants and asylum seekers, employment in jobs for which they are overqualified should be expected and, even, appreciated, bearing in mind the high level of actual unemployment among these populations. Considering the low degree of available information, more is unknown than is clear in terms of understanding the local labour market, requirements for employment, and level of competition and regulation. In fact, the legal system often prevents this population from formal working, and many will find jobs at the fringe of society, mostly low paid and often in jobs less desired by locals.

In an immigration context, much depends on the circumstances. It might be a simple move, for conducting a similar job in a similar organization. When a chemical engineer moves from a refinery job in Indonesia to a similar job in the USA or Middle East or Europe, the major change will not be in the job (but expect much in terms of cultural and societal difference). Yet, when a person leaves his or her former country with no plan, sometimes no job, or in a profession where the qualification might not be recognized, they might have to be accept lower-status jobs. Anecdotal evidence present us with cases of medical doctors from Iraq who drive cabs in Toronto, of mechanical engineers from Malaysia who operate dishwasher machines in San Francisco, and many similar stories of professional immigrants working in lower-level jobs. And they are lucky, because refugees are sometimes not allowed to work at all and typically find themselves excluded from the local labour markets.

Practicalities – home

The other change is moving homes, which for the people involved is another major issue. Physically it is more demanding than a simple country-bounded move. It is not a relatively easy operation of a day or two, inviting removal firms to transport possessions to a new house that the family has visited and decided upon. It is travelling into the unknown, shipping can take weeks, and the person and family might need to use a temporary hotel stay. The future home or flat might belong to the firm, and thus might not be chosen by the expatriate. It could be a formal place, such as the ambassador's residency. Relocation can be performed either by in-house teams delivering such services (which might be efficient if the firm is large and has high volume of transfers) or it might be outsourced.

When deciding to outsource, there are a number of agencies, including global firms that focus their business at such opportunities. Such is SIRVA, which prides itself that half of the FORTUNE Global 500 choose them as their corporate relocation partner. In their web page (http://www.sirva.com), the firm claims that it 'conducts more than 300,000 relocations every year, transferring corporate and government employees and moving individual consumers. The company operates in more than 40 countries with approximately 2,600 employees and an extensive network of agents and other service providers in over 175 countries.' Other

---

Box 6.1 On-line cross-cultural pre-departure training: RW3

Like some other service firms, RW3 feel it is better to outsource the cross-cultural preparations for their expatriates. RW3 offers several on-line training modules, among these, the 'Intercultural Awareness Model' which provides consultants and participants with a framework for planning and preparing for their IA.

They claim that, through the use of various training tools such as action planning, role plays, critical incidents, strategy creation, etc., the participants will develop an in-depth and realistic understanding of what to anticipate during their assignment. During the entire course of their assignment they will have continuing access to the CultureWizard web site and, through it, to their Culture Coach to help them resolve cultural challenges as they arise.

Source: taken from http://www.rw-3llc.com

specialized organizations that give strategic, managerial and operational advice and offer other international relocation services, include ORC Inc. and ECA.

In sharp contrast to such services, immigrants will have to arrange all these relocation issues for themselves, to make sure that they have a new home in the host country. For the illegal immigrant, there will be no home at all, as they might come in a tanker, smuggled into a country in an overloaded boat, enabling them to carry no more than a small piece of luggage. The conditions they might live under were epitomized in the movie *Grow your Own* (2007).

Family issues

Most expatriation and immigration involve changes for the family. The close family – parent and children – will move, but the extended family stays behind. The issues associated with moving the close family vary. Whether the spouse has to give up their current employment is a major issue for a married couple, as the phenomenon of the dual-career family is widespread, in particular for professional middle-class people (Baruch 2004). Forcing teenage children out of their social environment is highly emotionally charged (cf. Metcalfe 2006). Even if the children are young, there is a need for them to identify and adjust to a new educational system. A different problem, which could co-exist alongside children considerations is the need to care for elderly relatives, the so-called 'sandwich generation' (Williams 2004). Moving overseas might involve either having to include an elderly parent with the family, or moving them to another sibling or to a residential home. None of these options is simple, and this adds stress and complication to the move.

Yet another family issue is the fact that expatriation and immigration tear apart the extended family. The severity of the problems depends much on the personal circumstances, but also on the national culture. In a tribal society the separation can be unacceptable. Even for modern families in Anglo-Saxon culture, it is hard not to be able to see members of the extended family for a year or more. Many firms offer a yearly 'home visit' to enable, alongside work visits, some time to spend with the family. Modern technology helps to close the time and space gap, with inventions like Skype (to enable free video-phone calls) helping people to connect to their homeland and extended family.

For the expatriate there is a great advantage – the firm will pay for many elements concerned with family issues. These will have to be taken care of individually by immigrants.

Organizational issues

We distinguish between global moves within an organization and those that are not related to specific organizational career systems. The former mostly involve expatriation moves, either organizational initiated, self-initiated or a combination, whereas the latter are self-planned and designed, and can be immigration, a work-related move for a limited time, or a number of options as detailed in Chapter 4.

What is success in terms of preparation to expatriation, and how may it be achieved?

These are probably the most fundamental issues which need clarification – for the organization and for the person involved. Certain targets will be fairly clear. There is an expectation for the expatriate to 'hit the ground running' – i.e. to quickly reach anticipated levels of performance, to manifest leadership, to deliver knowledge transfer and also fulfil ad-hoc aims.

There is an expectation that the assignee will fill a role for a certain time period. An appropriate preparation will make the expatriate and the family more resilient against early return, which is typically considered a failure in expatriation studies (but see Chapters 8 and 9 for a more in-depth discussion).

Going beyond professional and/or managerial performance, the expatriate is expected to gain considerable personal development, and for the organization it would be a desired aim to keep the talent and benefit from it. Deep understanding of cultural differences and how to bridge these is essential. Yet, the expatriate cannot, and should not, rely only on their employer to prepare them for the new role and new life. Proactive preparation will make their life much easier. The organization might know an internal employee who worked in the past in the destination country – but the expatriate could find such people by their own efforts, through networking, and make the most of it. Reading books and newspapers from the destination country can prove a great eye-opener. With the availability of newspapers on the internet, there is no excuse for limited access to knowledge of life and interests in the new environment.

Case study 6.1 It is tough being expatriated to the US!

According to the GMAC 2008 survey, the USA was the top international destination for expatriates, which is no surprise given the dominant role US corporations play in the global market. The USA was closely followed by China, signalling the growing recognition of China as an upcoming superpower industrial nation. However, when indicating the most challenging destinations, respondents listed China, India, Russia and the USA as the most challenging places to be expatriated to.

In the USA, respondents cited difficulties with immigration, obtaining work permits, tax preparation and safety concerns. Some would rather have these challenges than those presented in other locations.

Challenges presented in other global locations

Some of the global challenges in different countries are shared across the board whereas others are unique to specific countries. The level, of course, is different, and much is due to the met or unmet expectations.

In China, there are difficulties in finding suitable homes and schools, there is much bureaucracy represented in immigration formalities, coupled with general poor service orientation in the public service (e.g. complaints about unhelpful government officials). Help is needed in understanding tax laws and filing requirements. Added to this is the remoteness of certain destinations. Of course, like in any cross-country move, language and cultural differences are an issue – but the complexity of the Chinese language makes it harder. Salary differentials experienced by employees arriving from high-cost locations is another challenge. Indeed, in China prices are rising – no surprise due to the laws of supply and demand.

Some of these challenges are similar in India, where respondents cited administrative formalities during immigration, unclear tax and employment laws, a lack of acceptable services and accommodation, inadequate education facilities, security concerns, time-zone difficulties, and cultural challenges as major factors making the transition uneasy.

In Russia, legal and immigration complexities (including frequent changes in the law), poor-quality and uneconomical housing, the complex administration of work permits and taxes, and travel safety were cited.

Less prominent countries did not reach the top of the complaints list, but this is probably due to the scarcity of expatriation to such countries. Living and managing in a country where a significant share of the labour force suffers from AIDS is a major challenge and in some nations foreigners should have a weapon-carrying guard travelling with them. Even this might not be sufficient in Afghanistan or Iraq. Colombia, Mexico and South Africa are notorious for people being kidnapped. It is hard to prepare expatriates and their families for such conditions.

As for achieving success, in this chapter we focus on the pre-departure and actual move. Among the variety of factors that might influence success, we chose to focus on training, career planning and mentoring.

Discussing organizational issues, we will start with 'conventional' expatriation, where a person spends a considerable time in a global destination outside their home country. The actual action to be carried out pre-departure will not be different for expatriations initiated by the organization and those initiated by the individual. Some such preparations are mental cues, such as a clarification of expectations and the psychological contract between the expatriate and the organization (Guzzo et al. 1994), and others are practices to be undertaken by the organization (Black et al. 1999). Both types of preparation will depend greatly on the organizational culture and expatriation strategy.

In earlier chapters, especially in Chapter 2, we drew up a nuanced picture of strategic IM. Here, we present a simplified overview based on the theoretical framework of Baruch and Altman (2002). It offers five strategies for the management of expatriation and repatriation. Like other HR practices, the activities needed before expatriation vary. Each option implies different organizational approaches to the management of careers and the meaning of IAs, and thus a different set of considerations for expatriates. Some needs overlap and the related activities apply to all types of organizations; others are unique to each option.

The following discussion reflects how different organizational strategies presented earlier (Baruch and Altman 2002 model) are applicable to pre-departure considerations.

The Global (or Empire): In the Global organization, expatriation management is an integral part of the strategy. Because expatriation is fundamental to the organization and to careers within the organization, staff would anticipate expatriation at a certain career stage. It is 'part and parcel' of the role and, thus, an essential and unavoidable element within the career that has to be accepted. People will not be surprised or shocked. Because period(s) of expatriation are an inevitable part of career paths for any executive, managers will have former expatriates, sometimes those who served in the same destination, to provide advice and support. Because globalization is an inherent property and part of the organizational ethos, the company will have a comprehensive set of procedures and practices in place, including support and a 'to-do' list before the assignment.

The Emissary (or Colonial): The Colonial firm tends to count on its own people to manage its overseas operations, though expatriation will be a career stage for a few only. Some expatriates might go abroad out of obligation – a sense of duty backed with high commitment and loyalty, not due to a search of global experience. While they are not expected to refuse, the whole idea might be alien to them, and much persuasion and preparation will be needed, as well as providing specific training in each case. IAs are for other expatriates a valuable key to a global career as long as they preserve powerful networks at home (Dickmann and Harris 2005).

Peripheral: Here, expatriation experience is desirable for individuals and could be perceived as a benefit or reward for good service. People will be joyful to be expatriated, but will not be prepared for the hardship and culture shock of operating in a different country. While people will be queuing up for the chance of expatriation, it is necessary to present them with a 'realistic preview' and to make sure that business targets are to be met rather than taking it as a 'tour at the expense of the firm'. It will be perceived as a perk by both the individuals and the employer.

Professional: The Professional strategic option is based on buying-in knowledge and expertise. Relying on locals or on 'buying' expatriates and the outsourcing of people for cross-border activities, this delivery through people external to the company saves the need for 'conventional' expatriation. The company is, in effect, outsourcing the expatriation process. 'Pre-departure' activities become pre-employment actions. Possible future expatriates might visit the prospective employer to increase their understanding of the firm's culture and expectations.

Expedient: The emergent approach for newcomers to the global scene, meaning that the firm will not have established ethos and experience in expatriation or preparation for it. It might be at a stage where the process of developing policies and practices is not fully achieved. An ad-hoc and pragmatic approach, the expedient option, described in general (Chapter 3) as a 'mixed bag' will be so in preparation for expatriation too. Cases will be dealt with one at a time, and trial and error will pave the way for a more established procedure of preparation for expatriation.

Common ground?

The above discussion demonstrates that different expatriation strategies will yield different approaches for preparing for expatriation. Nevertheless, certain practices will be common, required for any type of expatriation; first and foremost is training (see below).

A major and related issue is the need for presenting a 'realistic role preview', in line with the 'realistic job preview concept' (Wanous 1992). It is important for both the future expatriate and their family. Family issues are mentioned as a major reason for failing expatriation or early return. While the expatriate might be fully occupied with actual work, the spouse will face issues of loneliness, hostility, boredom and frustration. Trying to find either employment or other activities for the expatriate's spouse can prevent these outcomes.

Pre-departure training

The benefits of receiving cross-cultural training prior to relocation are that it:

- mentally prepares the individual and the family for the move;
- removes some of the 'unknown';
- improves self-awareness and cross-cultural understanding;
- provides the opportunity for questions/anxieties to be addressed in a supportive environment;
- car motivate and excite;
- reduces stress and provides coping strategies;
- eases the settling-in process;
- overall, reduces the chances of relocation failure.

A number of reasons account for the need for pre-departure training. The GMAC (2008) report suggests that family and spouse issues are critical for the success of the relocation. Appropriate cross-cultural training can prepare both the expatriate and the family for the move, taking into account practical and mental issues.

The mental element is crucial. First, the training should provide knowledge about beliefs, norms and behaviours as practised in the target country. A clear example is the tendency of people holding monotheistic religions to presume that the Bible is well known around the globe, and using biblical metaphors would be useful. This is not the case in the Far East. Further, sometimes using Christian metaphors will not work well in Muslim societies.

Such knowledge transfer would reduce or eliminate misunderstanding and will certainly generate awareness of the local culture and the differences to be anticipated. Yet, knowledge transfer is an insufficient factor in itself for ensuring smooth transition. Learning by doing, action-learning, will be more appropriate than simple knowledge transfer. Exercises such as simulations and scenario analysis/discussions will prompt much more in-depth realization of 'what needs to be done' when in a new and different place. Examples of cases, of meeting with people who were there and, in particular, employees who served there as expatriates, are an invaluable preparation for future expatriates and their families.

Training and, in particular, cross-cultural training before taking up an expatriation appointment has often been viewed as a way to increase the likelihood of success during the assignment. This view is shared by some academics (e.g. Tung 1987; Bolino and Feldman 2000; Hurn 2007) and practitioners (e.g. Laroche 1999; Bennett et al. 2000). However, the impact of pre-departure training programmes for expatriates seems to vary. Some studies appear to delineate a strong and positive impact on cross-cultural skills development, cross-cultural adjustability, and job performance of individuals (Deshpande and Viswesvaran 1992). A more recent meta-analysis by Morris and Robie (2001) similarly found a weak but positive relationship between cross-cultural training before expatriation and general adjustment of expatriates. In contrast, Hechanova et al.'s (2003) meta-analysis identified a weak negative relationship between attendance at cross-cultural training and expatriate adjustment in the host workplace. Bozionelos (2009) did not find significant impact at all for nurses working in the Middle East. Overall, empirical evidence on the effectiveness of cross-cultural training is far from compelling, and there is little evidence that cross-cultural training had a long-term positive effect on successful outcomes for expatriates (Kealey and Protheroe 1996).

Box 6.2 The United Nations World Food Programme II

The World Food Programme (WFP) is a UN agency. WFP responds to emergencies and strives to prevent hunger. In 2008, UNWFP operations reached over 102 million people in approximately 80 countries with food assistance.

The nature of WFP's activities means that the organization sends people into many of the world's most dangerous places. Most international moves are into non-family duty stations where individuals stay approximately two years. Individuals can get extensive country and security briefings aimed to make their professional staff more effective on the ground and to enable them to behave appropriately.

Analysis of training needs

The analysis of training need is the first step in the training cycle of expatriation preparation (Baumgarten 1995). The analysis of training needs should be followed by determination of training goals, answering the 'What' question. Then comes the 'How' question, to which the key factors are the content, method, media and sequence (Baumgarten 1995), which influence the training design. Then comes the implementation stage which can be in-house, external or hybrid. Firms who look for immediate and direct impact could be disappointed, as the impact might be indirect, and not immediate (van Eerde et al. 2008). Yet, there is clear evidence for positive impact of HRM, and in particular general and technical training, on organizational performance (Pfeffer 1998; Combs et al. 2006; Tharenou et al. 2007).

The need for training varies between individuals and is subject to the target culture. At the simplest level, language preparation will not be needed for people who already speak the host-country language. Legal systems can be similar, like some aspects of the British, Commonwealth and US legal systems. Training preparation for expatriation to a similar operation, e.g. that of an oil rig, will be similar in technical terms (apart from issues related to temperature), but very different regarding the culture, if the target country is Venezuela compared with Norway or Nigeria.

At a more sophisticated level, global training forms part of the efforts by global organizations to increase their coordination capabilities in order to gain and maintain competitiveness (Prahalad and Doz 1987; Gregersen and Black 1992). Managers at headquarters need to overcome their predominant orientation towards local conditions and develop a holistic perspective of the objectives and conditions of the entire MNC (Pucik 1992). The need for providing cross-cultural training increases with the level at which a manager works within a different culture, and also for managers at headquarters who deal with all the subsidiaries.

Case study 6.2 Preparation for expatriation – the dream and the wake-up call

Below we tell the story of a family and the challenges they faced in moving to a different country.

The Shalom family moves from Israel to the US

The Shalom family learnt about the anticipated move to Fort Worth, Texas three months before it was due to take place. Dan was an engineer in a major aviation industry corporation in Israel (IAI). IAI is a large Israeli employer with some 25,000 employees, and operations in R&D, manufacturing and maintenance of avionic products. Dan was sent by the IAI for a three-year period, to work on a guided missile research and development project. Dana, his wife, was a teller in the local branch of a large Israeli bank in their town near Tel Aviv.

Dan was chosen for the role following his success in software programming, and at IAI in Israel he managed a small team of five programmers. In Fort Worth he will need to manage the operation, with seven programmers, five electronic engineers and five mechanics, as well as collaborating and coordinating with the US plan in which the project was a joint venture between IAI and AirSmart, the US guided missiles manufacturer. The new role represented a clear promotion, but also new responsibilities in terms of people and budget management, for which Dan had no relevant experience. Dan had joined the guided missile division only two years before and did not have direct work experience with his future team. He only knew two good friends who live in Arlington. He saw that there is a train line from Dallas to Fort Worth, and assumed that he could use public transport within Arlington.

Their children, a seven-year-old daughter Rina and four-year-old son Ron were excited, although Rina realized that after one year in her primary school in Israel, she would have to start school in the US in English. Dan and Dana were not sure if Rina should repeat the first year, stay one more year in the kindergarten, or just continue to the second year after an intensive English language course. Ron was less of a problem in terms of education, but he had the skin problem of psoriasis, and had to stay for about two weeks each spring in a Dead Sea resort to cure the symptoms. Added to this was the fact that while not overly religious, the Shalom family kept to a kosher food tradition, and had no idea how they would manage to keep to Jewish life. They knew that a small Israeli community exists there, many of them are the future co-workers of Dan, but were not sure of the availability of food or if a synagogue existed.

They knew that Dallas area's climate is fairly warm, desert like, but were not sure how cold the winter would be.

Issues – which of them will Dan and Dana discover before departure? What can be done about them that IAI should deal with?

- Winter in mid Texas can be freezing.
- The synagogue is likely to be Reformist, which many Israelis will not find appropriate because the services and norms are different. A parallel problem for Christians would be to realize that in the host country there is no branch of their specific church denomination – e.g. no Lutheran, Anglican, Methodist etc.
- What level of knowledge is required for Rina to cover if she is not to lose one year of her studies?
- What are the prospects of finding alternative work for Dana in a local bank? How much will they suffer financially from the three years of non-earnings?
- What impact might moving to Texas have for Dana's future career?
- There is no public transport system in Arlington (the largest US city with no public transport) and the trains are merely freight operations.
- The IAI will cover one home visit for Dan and Dana each year, but it might not fit the period of stay in the Dead Sea that is necessary for Ron's treatment.

The analysis of training needs will take into account current knowledge of the prospective expatriates and the requirements in their roles in the host country. Certain competencies are generic.

Type and depth of training

Rigour of training is expressed by the issues covered and time dedicated to the training. Black et al. (1999: 100) suggest the following three levels: low, moderate and high training rigour. The level will depend on time available before the assignment date, resources available to the organization (or, if it is a personal immigration decision, to the individual himself/herself), and the actual need.

- *Low training rigour* duration involves 4–20 hours, and typically includes lectures, films, books and area briefing.
- *Moderate training rigour* will take 20–60 hours, and typically includes, in addition to the low training programme, role-plays, cases, assimilators and 'survival-level' language.
- *High training rigour* will need 60–180 hours, and typically includes the activities from the low and moderate programmes plus assessment centres, simulations, field trips and in-depth language training.

What are the typical contents of pre-departure training? Kupka et al. (2008) list the following method used by German MNCs for preparing expatriates and their spouses for an overseas assignment, under their programmes of intercultural communication training:

- area briefings
- lectures
- books
- movies
- foreign language training in the classroom
- case studies
- culture assimilator
- interactive foreign language training
- role plays
- field trips
- simulations
- others (cartoons, pictures, poems, jokes)

These, Kupka et al. (2008) claim, focus mostly on the culture of the target country/region. One challenge in preparing and sending people to pre-departure training is the need to plan ahead, versus the actual timeframe left between the selection of the expatriate and actual departure. The average was found to be less than four and a half months, but the extremes ranged between three days and over two years.

HRM activities – training, career planning, mentoring – should make the induction and transition smooth, delivering a short time to performance following the expatriation. Having a local mentor to provide support in learning local customs, a social club or other support for the trailing spouse, clear preparation for enlisting the children into an appropriate school – all these are factors that will make the transition manageable. Having a mentor 'at home' to keep contact and update about the situation in the parent firm will help in future career moves. Understanding the language is a basic element, and even simple attention to the need to manage and enable self-expression in contact with locals will make a very positive impression on the local people, managers and the wider community.

Another dimension added by Black and Mendenhall (1989) is the modelling process involved. The modelling dimension is presented in Figure 6.2 and below, where the horizontal dimension starts with symbolic – verbal as basic, and moving to observational – and ends with the more advanced, participative (again, starting with verbal and moving to behavioural). Adding the rigour dimension on the vertical axis, we can note how training methods vary from basic ones like briefing, lectures, books (which are *Factual*), films, class language training, case studies, culture assimilators and sensitivity training (which are *Analytical*), and at the higher end, interactive language training, role plays, field trips and simulations (*Experiential*).

The training media is also an issue. Looking at future trends in the early twenty-first century, Mendenhall and Stahl (2000) identified three: (1) in-country, real-time training; (2) global mindset training; and (3) CD-ROM/internet-based training. The training media corresponds with the rigour and timing to be devoted to this crucial factor in preparation for the assignment. A lot of training has moved to virtual media, and much can be gained in this low-cost but non-customized type of training. Yet, to gain a real grasp of cultural, emotional and contextual issues, it is important to benefit from direct contact with people with first-hand knowledge and experience of the culture in the host country. It can be people from the firm's operation in that country, former expatriates that served there, or an expert from the country.

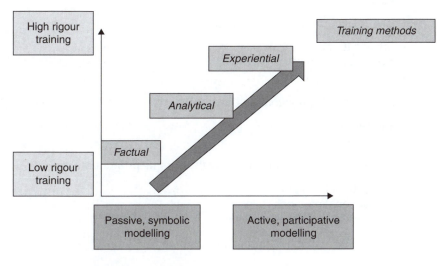

Figure 6.2 Training method model
Source: Adapted from Black and Mendenhall, 1989

Cross-cultural training

Cultural training in general, and specific cross-cultural training, are fundamental for working in a multicultural environment. Culture-general training provides knowledge about cultural norms, values, and anticipated behaviours. Participants can acquire understanding about potential differences in values, and ways to deal with intercultural conflict situations (Gudykunst and Hammer 1983; Brislin and Yoshida 1994). Culture-general training increases managers' awareness of the general issues that need to be addressed in order to effectively deal with people and situations under various cultural environments. One problem is how in-depth such training can be and, accordingly, what might be the impact. Major global corporations utilize cross-cultural training. However, such training often appears to have a rather low level of sophistication. Moreover, it tends to be short in length (i.e. two to three days) and is, therefore, of limited impact (Mervosh and McClenahen 1997).

Where should the training take place? For practical and cost considerations, firms tend to provide training in the home country, before the departure. Running the training in the destination country can generate clear advantages, as was the case of European managers selected for a cross-cultural training programme in Japan (Lievens et al. 2003).

Some cross-cultural training can be specific, such as those for working in multi-cultural teams (Earley and Gibson 2002) or for intercultural communication training (Brislin and Yoshida 1994). Tarique and Caligiuri (2004) suggest the following five-phase process for a global training programme:

- Phase 1: Identifying the type of global assignment:
  - technical
  - functional
  - developmental
  - strategic
- Phase 2: Determining training needs
  - organizational analysis
  - expatriate analysis
  - assignment analysis
- Phase 3: Establishing goals and measures
  - short-term
  - long-term
- Phase 4: Developing and delivering the training programme
  - instructional content
  - instructional methods
  - sequence of training sessions
- Phase 5: Evaluating the training programme
  - short-term goals
  - long-term goals

Their framework emphasizes the cyclical nature of the process, which explores both short- and long-term analysis, and evaluation which provides feedback for future management of the training programme.

The design and delivery of a training programme could involve several constituencies. The headquarters, the subsidiary in the host country, the training vendor, and the future assignees, all of these are stakeholders and participants in the process. The training should aim to ensure a smooth operation across borders, and the various parts of the organization, typically an MNC. Interaction activities and coordination between headquarters and subsidiaries are crucial for integrated transnational networks. To achieve better performance on these dimensions, experiential intercultural training was suggested as an effective tool, as it reduces cognitive and emotional barriers of cross-border interactions (Gudykunst et al. 1996; Landis and Bhagat 1996; Cushner and Brislin 1997).

Evaluation of pre-departure/post-arrival preparation

Studying the effects of cross-cultural training on the effectiveness of expatriate managers, Deshpande and Viswesvaran (1992) have identified five effectiveness criteria: (1) self-development; (2) perception; (3) relationship; (4) adjustment; and (5) performance. Cross-cultural training improves managers' cross-cultural effectiveness and performance, and reduces failure rates (Black and Mendenhall 1989, 1990; Bhawuk and Brislin 2000).

The impact of pre-departure/post-arrival preparation can be a make or break process. Preparing for the unknown will reduce stress and possible anxiety of the future expatriate and his or her family. Acculturation is a process that takes time. It is explored in depth in Chapter 7.

Training for whom? Don't forget the partner

Apart from training the future expatriate, partner inclusion is another issue to consider. Inclusion of the partner in the training would improve the prospects of the assignment's success. Neglecting to note the needs of the partner can cause expatriation failure. Unprepared partners, stepping into the unknown, could be a recipe for disaster. In fact, an unwilling partner might cause the expatriate to reconsider or withdraw from the post, another disastrous outcome for the organization. A supportive partner could prove essential for a successful assignment. They might be expected or required to take part in ceremonies and other events. Adler (1993) pointed out that the partner, usually a wife, could face the most difficult role of the family. While the expatriate has extensive work to carry out, performing to a schedule and routine, the spouse has to contend with family, managing a household, surviving in the new environment – market, banks and schooling – to name a few challenges. They have to leave behind their social networks and friends, their daily activities and, often, their careers.

One thing the organization can do is to offer a position to the trailing spouse, though employment of partners within the same workplace might be problematic.

If there are a number of other firms, even competitors, operating at the same desti-nation, a win-win possibility for HRM is to arrange a pool of jobs which spouses can fill.

If trailing expatriate spouses face difficulties in securing the work permit required for employment in their destination country, they might opt to become a house-wife or house husband. Some of those who give up work and career will be happy with the freedom (but might not like the loss of career and income); others will just become upset. A spouse's unhappiness can impinge upon the success of the expa-triate, with growing frustration which might lead to family crises or early return.

Career planning

We have argued throughout this book that global moves – be they short or long-term expatriation, and certainly immigration, are major career steps, and should be part of a wider career planning scheme (Baruch and Altman 2002). For organiza-tions, sending employees on an IA serves as more than just filling positions. It is a way to test and train managers on their path to executive roles. In a truly global firm, having international experience is a major advantage to both executives and the organization as a whole (Sambharya 1996; Tsang 1999).

Clarifying expectations and transparency

When people decide to emigrate they should clarify for themselves what their aim is. It is a basic element of communication within the family – the close family that will accompany the migrant, and the family that is left behind. Sometimes the immediate family is left behind. In Israel there are a number of foreign male work-ers employed in the construction and agricultural sectors, sending much of their salary to their homes in Romania, Thailand or China. Similarly, many female care workers from the Philippines send much of their salary to their husbands back home. Both timeframe and level of anticipated income should be determined in advance, though these will always be subject to changing circumstances.

When talking about organization-based expatriation, the need for clarified expec-tations is no less important. The candidate for expatriation should learn the time-frame for the assignment (start and end dates), the required preparations, the salary and other benefits while on assignment, arrangements for the family, etc. These issues are discussed in detail in Chapter 10. Beyond these, the assignee and HRM representative should consider the options and the expected career stage that will follow the assignment. These are just the basics, with a number of other less prominent but important issues emerging.

In Chapter 1 we introduced the intelligent career framework (Arthur et al. 1995). Exploring the training and its impact on the expatriate in terms of 'social capital', we can benefit from reference to the *knowing-how*, *knowing-why* and *knowing-whom* of the intelligent career framework. Here it would be crucial to especially consider the *knowing-when*, later added to the framework by Jones and DeFillippi (1996). The expatriate arriving in a new place should know the 'why' – the reasons why the organizations sent him or her, and why they agreed (or why they have initiated the move).

In terms of *knowing-whom*, there is a need to act fast and interact with totally new networks, many of which will be substantially different from those in the home HQ. Further, staying in the host country will reduce the ability to maintain the original connections at 'home'.

The *knowing-when* is crucial in terms of career stage. There is no single answer about the optimal timing for a global assignment. Heading an operation in a small subsidiary can be a great preparation for a promotion back at the HQ, heading a major subsidiary can be the step before becoming a CEO at home. At the same time it can take people off the track if the assignment ends in a sideways move. Timing is also important in terms of preparation and the level of training (and time they last).

What next? In a perfect world, there would be enough time for the required pre-departure preparations, in particular for comprehensive and rigorous training as described above. There would be a proper overlap with the former expatriate who served in the role, or, for new ventures, a clear business plan to follow upon arrival. There should be a set plan for communication while the assignment lasts, and there should be a repatriation role waiting for the assignee upon return.

Life is never perfect, and it is rare to expect the above scenario to materialize. In reality, sometimes an expatriation will be needed on the spot due to an early return of the former post-holder. Training might not be comprehensive or rigorous, and coordination and communication during the assignment might be less than desired. Yet, the issue of repatriation is possibly the most worrying. Studies point out the lack of planning for repatriation. The dynamic current business environment could mean that upon returning, the original department might have changed, moved, or dispersed or disappeared altogether. Being out of sight could also mean being out of mind of the HRM and direct managers. We will discuss these issues in more detail in Chapter 8.

The self-initiated global mover, who moved as a career strategy or action on their own will have even less resources to provide for planning, and even less so in considering the return. The return could be a vague decision of 'one day we will be back' or, alternatively, people might aim to have a permanent move of immigration, but three years or so in the new country might persuade them that there is no place like home. Illegal immigrants might be deported, with their dream of a new-found land shattered. The best career advice for the global assignee is to make a contingency plan, a Plan B, in case they need to return early, to return to the unknown, or to move in a different direction.

Mentoring

Mentoring is a career practice that has gained wide and compelling evidence for its effectiveness (Kram 1985; Allen and Eby 2007). An expatriation period should be no exception, and might require even more mentoring. In expatriation, there are at least two kinds of mentoring. The expatriate (with the help of HR) can identify a home mentor who will be there to keep track of current affairs within the organization back home, will help with advice (and earlier international experience of the mentor is a major advantage in this case), and help the protégé upon return, in their re-adjustment back home.

A second kind of mentor might be one in the host country; someone whose advice will be concerned with overcoming the culture shock, in helping adjustment, understanding clues and other communications, opening doors for networking in the host country, and even some activities such as where to buy food and where to enjoy entertainment in a safe environment.

A further kind of mentor might be a personal-life mentor in the local community. The partner could be in need of such support, and it can be done in an informal manner, or organizationally arranged (see Box 6.3).

Box 6.3 Welcome to New Zealand, welcome to UC

The University of Canterbury at Christchurch, New Zealand, benefits from a generous financial support of the Erskine Fellowship, inviting some 70 academic scholars each year to attend the university.

While the expatriate (mostly academics on sabbatical) works in the university, the spouse will be invited to the 'club', where a number of spouses of permanent university staff will arrange tours, visits and other social activities.

The social involvement is extended by inviting the whole family of the visitor to frequent events in the university social club.

Gender is a clear issue of concern for career planning. It has long been recognized that in MNCs or any global organization, a service 'away from home' is important in the development of future executives. Avoiding appointing female assignees would mean that women are deprived of this option for developmental roles, potentially creating a 'glass ceiling'.

Post-arrival

HR and the general management might wish to have immediate performance from the expatriate. Yet, there will be a substantial period between landing in a foreign destination and actual delivery of performance. 'Hitting the ground running' is a nice metaphorical expression, but reality dictates allocating time, energy and effort for the transition to be as smooth as possible. Issues to be considered or to be dealt with are:

• Reception in the destination. The consideration will vary depending on the type of global move.
• For commercial-based assignments, make sure someone is waiting for the assignee and his or her family at the airport.

- For diplomatic service, deal with security issues.
- For immigrants, check that the papers are valid (illegal immigrants will skip this issue!).

Global relocation firms (see, for example, SIRVA, RW3 or Brookfield) claim they can handle the whole operation of relocating people across borders. This can be an easy and convenient solution for firms that can pay for such services. Yet the local operation might be able to offer much more effective ways for induction and acculturation.

Other considerations are:

- *Jet lag*: do not expect much on the first couple of days. For those who are not frequent flyers, allow more time.
- *Whom to meet*: A series of meetings should be arranged for the arriving person, as in any new appointment, but bear in mind the time/space/culture gap. They will need to meet the head of the operation (and if the expatriate is the new head – then s/he should meet the former head or, if they have left already, the deputy).
- *Where to stay, for how long*: Initial accommodation, transportation and communication means should be arranged (the Blackberry could save some of the latter).
- *Checking up*: schooling, permanent accommodation etc. that was (supposed) to be arranged and hopefully waiting for them.

Expect a crisis or two. Again, using a specialist relocation consultant can ease the burden. In some cases legal advice will be worth the investment. Most global firms will provide tax checks and social security. Their interest, though, is not always best for the individual. For example, the cost of social security varies substantially: in France the level of such costs are about 40 per cent compared with some 13 per cent in the UK and less than 8 per cent in the US. This means that the employer would aim to set an arrangement where they will be paying lower social security contributions, whereas for the individual more benefits will emerge if s/he is paid in a different country. We explore the issues of international remuneration and social security in Chapters 10 and 11.

Throughout the chapter we have referred explicitly or implicitly to the processes of physical and psychological preparation for the assignee. At the same time, a global career move is not restricted to expatriation, and people can self-initiate a career move beyond existing organizational boundaries. For example, by starting a new business or a new career with different employers in the new country. We discussed the relevance to the general global careers in earlier chapters. The next chapter will explore the changes in behaviours, attitudes and emotions of global workers while they work in their host environment.

Summary and learning points

This chapter has explored the issues concerned with 'what needs to be done' (and why) before the actual assignment or new life begins in the destination country. A number of processes are recommended, and special caution should be exercised, as many ambiguities exist.

Key learning points include:

- There is a multitude of different contingencies and various constituencies for moving to work abroad. Due to the diverse legal, cultural and economic contexts as well as due to the high degrees of complexity, substantial preparation is needed to give individuals a good start to their work abroad.
- Therefore, there is a range of individual and organizational considerations when preparing for work abroad. These include pre-departure training, administrative preparation and gaining clarity of business goals and individual drivers.
- Family issues impact individual drivers and the preparation to move abroad. Employers might consider aiding the partners of their international assignees.
- The organization would benefit from exploring:

  - defining success and ways to achieve it;
  - different strategies to employ under different organizational cultures and norms;
  - training and, in particular, cross-cultural training.

- Career planning for the individual and the organization is extremely important. There is a risk that individuals are 'off the career radar screen' when working abroad.
- Mentoring can be powerful in preparing individuals for a move and in giving them more focus and confidence in their work.
- Post-arrival preparation can address emerging issues and utilizes the first experiences of individuals. It can, therefore, be highly specific and might deal with issues that have been overlooked before.

References

Adler, N. (1993) 'Competitive frontiers: managing across borders', *Journal of Management Development*, 13: 24–41.

Allen, T.D. and Eby, L.T. (2007) *The Blackwell Handbook of Mentoring: A Multiple Perspective Approach*, Malden, MA: Blackwell.

Arthur, M.B., Claman, P.H. and DeFillippi, R.J. (1995) 'Intelligent enterprise, intelligent careers', *Academy of Management Executive*, 9(4): 7–22.

Baruch, Y. (2004) *Managing Careers: Theory and Practice*, Harlow: FT-Prentice Hall/Pearson.

Baruch, Y. (2009) 'Stress and careers', in C.L. Cooper, J.C. Quick and M. Schabracq (eds) *Work and Health Psychology Handbook*, 3rd edn, London: Wiley/Blackwell.

Baruch, Y. and Altman, Y. (2002) 'Expatriation and repatriation in MNC: a taxonomy', *Human Resource Management*, 41(2): 239–259.

Baumgarten, K. (1995) 'Training and development of international staff', in A. Harzing and J. van Ruysseveldt (eds) *International Human Resource Management: An Integrated Approach*, London: Sage.

Bennett, R., Aston, A. and Colquhoun, T. (2000) 'Cross-cultural training: a critical step in ensuring the success of international assignments', *Human Resource Management*, 39: 239–250.

Bhawuk, D.P.S. and Brislin, R.W. (2000) 'Cross-cultural training: a review', *Applied Psychology: An International Review*, 49: 162–191.

Black, J.S. and Mendenhall, M. (1989) 'A practical but theory-based framework for selecting cross-cultural training methods', *Human Resource Management*, 28: 511–539.

Black, J.S. and Mendenhall, M. (1990) 'Cross-cultural training effectiveness: a review and a theoretical framework for future research', *Academy of Management Review*, 15: 113–136.

Black, J.S., Gregersen, H., Mendenhall, M.E. and Stroh, L.K. (1999) *Globalizing People through International Assignments*, Reading, MA: Addison-Wesley.

Bolino, M.C. and Feldman, D.C. (2000) 'Increasing the skill utilization of expatriates', *Human Resource Management*, 39: 367–379.

Bozionelos, N. (2009) 'Expatriation outside the boundaries of the multinational corporation: a study with expatriate nurses in Saudi Arabia', *Human Resource Management*, 48: 111–134.

Brislin, R.W. and Yoshida, T. (1994) *Intercultural Communication Training. An Introduction*, Thousand Oaks, CA: Sage Publications.

Combs, J., Liu, Y., Hall, A. and Ketchen, D. (2006) 'How much do high-performance work practices matter? A meta-analysis of their effects on organizational performance', *Personnel Psychology*, 59(3): 501–528.

Cushner, K. and Brislin, R.W. (1997) *Improving Intercultural Interactions. Module for Cross-cultural Training Programmes*, Thousand Oaks, CA: Sage.

Deshpande, S.P. and Visweswaran, C. (1992) 'Is cross-cultural training of expatriate managers effective? A meta analysis', *International Journal of Intercultural Relations*, 16: 295–310.

Dickmann, M. and Harris, H. (2005) 'Developing career capital for global careers: the role of international assignments', *Journal of World Business*, 40: 399–408.

Earley, P.C. and Gibson, C.B. (2002) *Multinational Work Teams: A New Perspective*, New Jersey: Lawrence Erlbaum Associates.

GMAC (2008) *Global relocation trends survey*, Oak Brook, IL: GMAC Global Relocation Services.

Gregersen, H.B. and Black, J.S. (1992) 'Antecedents to commitment to a parent company and a foreign operation', *Academy of Management Journal*, 35: 65–90.

Gudykunst, W.B. and Hammer, M.R. (1983) 'Basic training design: approaches to intercultural training', in R.L. Wiseman (ed.) *Intercultural Training*, 2nd edn, New York: Pergamon.

Gudykunst, W.B., Guzley, R.M. and Hammer, M.R. (1996) 'Designing intercultural training', in D. Landis and R.S. Bhagat (eds) *Handbook of Intercultural Training*, 2nd edn, Thousand Oaks, CA: Sage.

Guzzo, R.A., Nooman, K.A. and Elron, E. (1994) 'Expatriate managers and the psychological contract', *Journal of Applied Psychology*, 79(4): 617–626.

Hechanova, R., Beehr, T.A. and Christiansen, N.D. (2003) 'Antecedents and consequences of employees' adjustment to overseas assignment: a meta-analytic review', *Applied Psychology*, 52(2): 213–236.

Hurn, B.J. (2007) 'Pre-departure training for international business managers', *Industrial and Commercial Training*, 39: 9–17.

Jones, C. and DeFillippi, R.J. (1996) 'Back to the future in film: combining industry and self-knowledge to meet the career challenges of the 21st century', *Academy of Management Executive*, 10(4): 89–103.

Kealey, D.J. and Protheroe, D.R. (1996) 'The effectiveness of cross-cultural training for expatriates: an assessment of the literature on the issue', *International Journal of Intercultural Relations*, 20: 141–165.

Kram, K.E. (1985) *Mentoring at Work: Developmental Relationships in Organizational Life*, Glenview, IL: Scott, Foresman & Co.

Kupka, B., Everett, A.M. and Canthro, V. (2008) 'Home alone and often unprepared – intercultural communication training for expatriated partners in German MNCs', *International Journal of Human Resource Management*, 19: 1765–1791.

Landis, D. and Bhagat, R.S. (1996) *Handbook of Intercultural Training*, 2nd edn, Thousand Oaks, CA: Sage.

Laroche, L. (1999) 'Relocating abroad: a high stakes venture', *Engineering Dimensions*, 20(1): 32–35.

Lievens, F., Harris, M.M., Van Keer, E. and Bisqueret, C. (2003) 'Predicting cross-cultural training performance: the validity of personality, cognitive ability, and dimensions measured by an assessment center and a behavior description interview', *Journal of Applied Psychology*, 88: 476–489.

Mendenhall, M.E. and Stahl, G.K. (2000) 'Expatriate training and development: where do we go from here?', *Human Resource Management*, 39: 251–265.

Mervosh, E.M. and McClenahen, J.S. (1997) 'The care and feeding of expats', *Industry Week*, 246(22): 68–72.

Metcalfe, A. (2006) "It was the right time to do it": moving house, the life-course and kairos', *Mobilities*, 1: 243–260.

Morris, M.A. and Robie, C. (2001) 'A metaanalysis of the effects of cross-cultural training on expatriate performance and adjustment', *International Journal of Training and Development*, 5: 112–125.

Pfeffer, J. (1998) *The Human Equation: Building Profits by Putting People First*, Boston, MA: Harvard Business School Press.

Prahalad, C. and Doz, Y. (1987) *The Multinational Mission: Balancing Local Demands and Global Mission*, New York: Free Press.

Pucik, V. (1992) 'Globalization and Human Resource Management', in V. Pucik, N.M Tichy and C.K. Barnett (eds) *Globalizing Management. Creating and Leading the Competitive Organization*, New York: Wiley.

Sambharya, R.B. (1996) 'Foreign experience of top management teams and international diversification strategies of U.S. multinational corporations', *Strategic Management Journal*, 17: 739–746.

Tarique, I. and Caligiuri, P. (2004) 'Training and development of international staff', in A.-W. Harzing and J. van Ruysseveldt (eds) *International Human Resource Management*, 2nd edn, London: Sage.

Tharenou, P., Saks, A.M. and Moore, C. (2007) 'A review and critique of research on training and organizational-level outcomes', *Human Resource Management Review*, 17: 251–273.

Tsang, E.W.K. (1999) 'The knowledge transfer and learning aspects of international HRM: an empirical study of Singapore MNCs', *International Business Review*, 8: 591–609.

Tung, R.L. (1987) 'Expatriate assignments: enhancing success and minimizing failure', *Academy of Management Executive*, 1(2): 117–126.

van Eerde, W., Tang, K.C.S. and Talbo, G. (2008) 'The mediating role of training utility in the relationship between training needs assessment and organizational effectiveness', *International Journal of Human Resource Management*, 19: 63–73.

Wanous, J.P. (1992) *Organizational Entry: Recruitment, Selection, Orientation, and Socialization of Newcomers*, 2nd edn, Reading, MA: Addison-Wesley.

Westman, M., Etzion, D. and Chen, S. (2009) 'Crossover of positive experiences from business travelers to their spouses', *Journal of Managerial Psychology*, 24: 269–284.

Williams, C. (2004) 'The sandwich generation', *Perspectives on Labour and Income*, 5(9): 9. September, Statistics Canada Catalogue 75–001-XIE.

During global assignments

Objectives

This chapter:

- depicts the organizational and individual behaviour during international work, assesses underlying philosophies, patterns and approaches;
- describes organizational activities for international assignees;
- outlines international management and leadership development;
- investigates performance, retention and career management;
- discusses strategic and operational issues in knowledge management;
- explores the process of psychological adjustments when individuals are immersed in a host-country culture;
- identifies the key family and partner challenges when working abroad;
- distinguishes gender issues;
- presents the career and career capital impact of working abroad;
- illuminates some of the darker sides of working abroad.

Introduction

How do organizations plan and organize foreign sojourns? How do they try to ensure that their employees are productive, learn from their foreign stay, diffuse their own knowledge, acquire useful networks and insights and progress in their careers?

This chapter will concentrate on company-sent international assignees and their experiences while working abroad as well as the organizational activities to manage these staff members in their special situations. In earlier chapters we have identified many other forms of international work and have distinguished also especially self-initiated expatriates who have moved to another country without the help of any employer (including immigration). While there is some evidence that covers their experiences (see Inkson and Myers 2003; Richardson and Mallon 2005; Doherty and Dickmann 2009; Min Toh and Gunz 2009), the key focus of this chapter lies on the organizational and organization-initiated individual phenomena related to the time that expatriates work abroad.

Beyond the formal administration of the actual move across borders, there is a range of work-related activities to support the assignee, including the attention organizations will give to security issues, the help they give to partners and family in terms of setting up accommodation, schooling, bank accounts etc. The international development, performance and knowledge management, as well as career activities that organizations have developed for people on an IA will be presented in this chapter (see Figure 7.2).

Career progression is often at the heart of the decision to work abroad by individuals and organizations (see Chapter 5). Given the rise in developmental assignments (see Chapter 2), career issues are of particular importance for individuals and organizations. Oddou et al. (2000) and Kakabadse and Kakabadse (1999) outline the challenges that individuals have to go through in order to become their organization's future global leaders.

Figure 7.2 depicts the key issues for individuals, which range from the psychological process of cultural adjustment, to family issues and career capital, as well as general career activities and outcomes. This framework goes beyond the more

Figure 7.1 A framework of global careers: attitudes and actions during international work

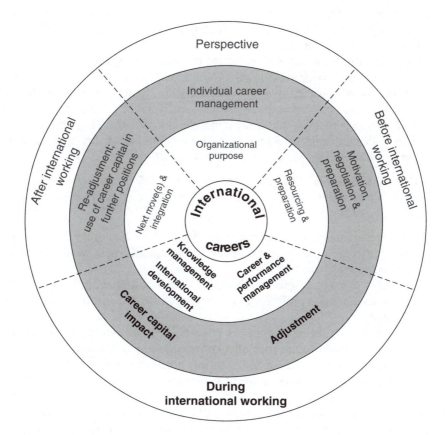

Figure 7.2 International career management from organizational and individual
perspectives
Source: Doherty and Dickmann (2008a)

established expatriation cycle (Harris et al. 2003) as it explicitly distinguishes
individual and organizational perspectives and allows us to contrast these during
the different phases of the expatriation journey. Some of the strategic considerations as well as activities to increase 'security' and 'guidance' that organizations
have developed are outlined below.

The organizational perspective: knowledge management

The old dictum 'knowledge is power' is highly applicable within international competition. Bartlett and Ghoshal (1989) have further developed Michael Porter's
thoughts and proposed that a key to future success is innovation. These authors
viewed international knowledge flows as so important that they would propose that
a firm needs to be highly innovative in order to survive in the long term. Innovation
consists of the creation of new ideas and their development, the communication,
absorption and application of these ideas (Asakawa and Lehrer 2003). The

determinants of international knowledge exploration and exploitation are manifold, including organizational strategy, resource flows, resources of local affiliates, information processing capabilities, cultural distance of subsidiaries from their parent, the local affiliate's embeddedness in the local business system and the control and coordination approaches of the MNC (Gupta and Govindarajan 1991; Ferner 2000; Birkinshaw et al. 2002; Edwards et al. 2004). Dickmann and Müller-Camen (2006) condense the discussion of organizational configurations of international strategies, structures and processes and apply it to the realm of HRM. They define two dimensions – standardization and knowledge networking – which serve to depict the configurational choices that organizations make (see Chapter 2).

This links well to Bartlett and Ghoshal's (1989, 2003) typology of global managers. These authors distinguish the following types of managers for highly international companies:

- Business managers (strategists + architects + coordinators) with the responsibility to increase worldwide efficiency and competitiveness while coordinating the companies' approaches.
- Country managers (sensors + builders + contributors) with the responsibility to sense local market preferences and to react to local institutional and regulatory changes.
- Functional managers (scanners + cross-pollinators + champions) with the responsibility to access specialist knowledge and functional expertise, to link knowledge of technical, manufacturing, human resources, marketing and financial advances and to create worldwide learning and support innovation.
- Corporate managers (leaders + talent scouts + developers) responsible for worldwide operations, the scouting of talented individuals, the overall leadership of the organization and the support of key individuals who champion new approaches.

Having discussed the different international configurations of MNCs (see Chapter 2 for an in-depth exploration) and the key types of managers and their roles, we will now concentrate on knowledge management associated with and conducted through international assignees. One of the key tasks of international assignees is to transfer skills from the parent organization to the subsidiary they work in (Bonache and Brewster 2001).

Wang et al. (2004) have developed a model of knowledge transfer into a local subsidiary. Given the above discussion, this would be especially applicable in MNCs with a global configuration. Wang et al.'s model distinguished two steps. The first step is the knowledge contributed by the MNC to the subsidiary. Wang et al. (2004) discuss the capacity to transfer, and the willingness to transfer, knowledge to the subsidiary. The capacity to transfer depends first on the knowledge base of the organization – including whether the knowledge is tacit or explicit (Nonaka 1994) – and, second, on expatriate competencies to be able to transfer the knowledge. Where the knowledge to be transferred is tacit, human interaction becomes more important.

We have seen above (especially in Chapter 5) that the selection of international assignees should ideally factor in 'soft' competencies such as interpersonal skills and communication abilities. Moreover, the assignee's willingness to learn and adapt to the culture environment (see below) will have an influence on his or her capability to diffuse knowledge locally originating from elsewhere. For instance, research assessing the necessary skills that expatriates need to transfer knowledge in Nigeria and using the Kühlmann and Stahl (2005) list of intercultural competencies found that individuals needed the following personal competencies to be successful (Oku 2007):

- tolerance for ambiguity;
- religious sensitivity;
- behavioural flexibility;
- sociability and interest in other people;
- empathy; *and*
- well-developed communication skills.

Given that more and more companies stipulate that expatriates need to develop local successors (see also Chapter 10), international assignees ideally should impart their hard-earned professional knowledge to locals and, in the process, might work themselves out of a job (Rogers 1999).

Black et al. (1999) describe four types of expatriates based on their allegiance to their country of origin and their local links. 'Free agents' have low links to either, while 'dual citizens' with dual allegiance have strong links to both home and host countries. Expatriates who have their 'heart at home' display low local allegiance and a strong parent-country orientation while those individuals who 'go native' identify very much with their host culture and environment and show less allegiance to their home country. While these four types are more or less adequate for different international configurations and goals of organizations, selection, socialization, training, reward and performance management approaches might be used by organizations to impact or guide these 'knowledge transferors'. Bonache and Zárraga-Oberty (2008) suggest that the following HR practices can be used to target (potential) international assignees and to promote the success of knowledge transfer between international workers and local staff:

- extensive screening of prospective employees (beyond technical qualifications);
- extensive training of expatriates, requiring interaction with locals;
- emphasis of the importance of knowledge transfer, especially in performance evaluation criteria;
- reward systems linked to knowledge transfer;
- selecting intrinsically motivated persons;
- establishing psychological contracts based on emotional loyalties and participation.

It seems that knowledge management is important in all stages of international work. The above list includes the phase before an individual is chosen to work abroad, in the preparation to move to a foreign country, and during the assignment. Moreover, it seems important that repatriate knowledge transfer and application in the home country is also beneficial (Bonache and Dickmann 2008). Unfortunately, the transferability of acquired competencies or insights is often seen as low and the appreciation of home-country colleagues might also be far from high (Dickmann et al. 2006).

Wang et al. (2004) argue that the willingness to transfer knowledge depends on the importance of the subsidiary. Among the reasons are that knowledge transfer costs can be substantial (Teece 1977) and that subsidiaries have different strategic roles in the implementation of the parent company's strategic goals (see above, also Gupta and Govindarajan 1991). A further influence factor is the ownership type, with firms being less willing to share sensitive and commercially valuable intellectual property when working in joint ventures or under licensing agreements. When operating in international joint ventures, the quality of relationships and the ability to develop contractual safeguards will also influence the parent's willingness to share knowledge.

Wang et al.'s second step is related to the absorptive capacity of the subsidiary and, again, consists of two sub-themes: the capacity and intent to learn of the foreign affiliate. The capacity to learn is related to the qualification of local employees and the formal development, investment and emphasis on training in the subsidiary. Jaw et al.'s (2006) study of 130 Taiwanese affiliates supports the latter point and proposes that the best learning effects are to be achieved in earlier stages of subsidiary establishment. The intent to learn, in turn, depends on the individual local staff members but may be influenced by reward mechanisms. This leads us into the realm of HRM management.

Bonache and Zárraga-Oberty (2008) implicitly build on these insights and have developed a micro-perspective of individuals in their work environments and their motivations to share knowledge. Crucially, they develop propositions as to how HR practices might promote a fertile relationship between expatriates and local staff for knowledge transfer. Among their suggestions are to emphasize the cultural fit with the local environment in the selection and training of assignees, to de-emphasize salary disparity, to promote a sense of egalitarianism and to develop processes to encourage extensive socialization. These HR practices are seen to promote easier communication, increase interpersonal sensitivity and perceived reliability of the partners and to foster a good team spirit.

In further work, Bonache and Dickmann (2008) explored the international knowledge management mechanisms in a major German MNC. They compiled an overview geared to the strategic configuration and control/coordination discussion which is further explicated in Table 7.1.

Knowledge is power – for organizations, individuals and nations. Therefore, international corporations often strive to encourage the worldwide exploration and exploitation of knowledge. The role of expatriate managers is highly important in the knowledge diffusion process (Riusala and Suutari 2004). Individuals, however, might aim to safeguard their positions, earning-power and other benefits associated with being the 'expert' on specific topics and corporate processes. Moreover, the culture and politics of an organization should be geared to effective knowledge management, not least by creating suitable HR policies and practices to encourage the willingness to diffuse and to absorb new ideas. While the temptation might be high to ring-fence knowledge on the part of the individual, Au and Fukuda's (2002) study of 232 expatriate showed that those persons who were more effective boundary-spanners experienced higher job satisfaction and more power within their organizations. Among the approaches to manage the knowledge

Table 7.1 Mechanisms for international knowledge management

Type	Mechanisms	Examples	Knowledge generation & transfer	A key mechanism in:
Bureaucratic	IHRM planning	Vision & mission, corporate culture, IHR strategy, HR principles, underlying competency frameworks, talent management approach etc.	Low, Low	Global and transnational MNCs
	IHRM reporting	Global, national, functional HR budgets, actual costs; outcomes	Low, Low	Global, transnational & cognofederate MNCs
	HR information systems	Use of common approaches, forms, policy documents etc. that are for instance located on the intranet	Low, High	Global, cognofederate & transnational MNCs
	Communities of practice	International management seminars on HR instruments such as appraisals, employees' opinion surveys, etc.	High, High	Global and transnational MNCs
	Globally distributed teams	International project groups (including virtual teams)	High, Low	Especially transnational, also global and cognofederate MNCs
Social	Expatriation	Expatriation as a cultural coordination mechanisms (including international commuters)	Low, High	Global and some multidomestic MNCs
	HR centre of excellence	Units (with cross-border collaboration) responsible for the design of HR practices, to be exported and standardized across the whole organization.	High, High	Global and transnational MNCs
	HR 'line manager' in head office	International assignee who is leader / line manager in host location and who also shapes some part of the 'organizational culture'	High, High	Global MNCs
Personal	Visits of IHR managers from HQ	Visits & other contacts with HR local professionals (including frequent flyers)	Low, Low	Global MNCs
	Knowledge transferors	International assignees as introducing corporate systems and processes (e.g. in performance management) in local operations.	Low, High	Global and transnational MNCs

Source: Based on Dickmann and Müller-Camen (2006) and Bonache and Dickmann (2008)

transfer and the willingness of individuals to share knowledge is international management development.

The organizational perspective: international management development

Strategic international management development (IMD) incorporates influences from the business environment, corporate and people management areas (Dickmann 1997). As outlined above (see also Chapter 2) it uses the ideas or corporate configurations to identify and enhance individual and group capabilities that further its strategic goals. These, in turn, are followed by structure considerations (Chandler 1962). Bartlett and Ghoshal (1989), in their ground-breaking work, have defined four organizational configurations. Chapter 2 and the section above on knowledge management have outlined further theoretical developments and the application of their ideas to IHRM (Dickmann and Müller-Camen 2006; Dickmann et al. 2009). There appear to be some generic managerial capabilities that are applicable for both domestic and international settings (Baruch 2002). However, some capabilities that global managers need are linked to the chosen configuration of their organization. For instance, while global firms aim to create one consistent and strong organizational culture, multidomestic companies strive to be as locally responsive as possible. The subsequent skills sets and knowledge fields of managers working in these organizations vary dramatically.

Harris and Dickmann (2005) point out that the creation of an IMD strategy needs to have the buy-in of the chief executive and the senior team. In order to achieve this, the IMD needs to reflect the global business strategy that factors in the competitive environment of the organization. Dickmann (1997: 18) identifies '4C' factors used in the strategic planning of international management development. These are:

- *competitive advantage*, which is linked to the corporate strategy and structure of the organization and its competitive environment;
- *control*, which is related to the adequate balance of control and degrees of freedom within the network of international operations and defines what issues are decision-relevant and should be monitored;
- *coordination*, which refers to more informal international communication processes and might relate to the sharing of 'best' or 'good' practice; and
- *costs*, which relate to the efficiency and effectiveness of IMD approaches.

Moreover, the IMD strategy needs to be sensitive to HR and line capabilities. For instance, the core competencies of the UN's senior management network relate to UN executives being able to lead change, to get the best out of people, being results driven, capable of building lasting partnerships, good communicators and sophisticated decision-makers (Harris and Dickmann 2005). These are, as outlined by Baruch (2002), essential for many national and international managers.

Much IMD, beyond the preparatory training or seminars given to assignees (see Chapter 6), seems to be rather informally embedded in international work. In fact, the distinction between general management development and more specific *international* development initiatives is rarely made by firms or in the academic literature. Thus, few tailored activities geared to the organizational knowledge diffusion activities of international assignees can be identified. However, there are some companies that have developed unusual programmes geared at working as a manager in an international organization. These relate more to the generic global management capabilities outlined by Bartlett and Ghoshal (1989) or Jokinen et al. (2008) but seem not to relate specifically to the chosen international configuration of the organization. One example that covers all three areas of career capital is PricewaterhouseCoopers' Genesis Park.

Case study 7.1 International development of high potentials in PwC

PricewaterhouseCoopers (PwC) has a goal of creating 'thought leadership'. This means that the organization strives to create innovative ideas and approaches – internally, this is described as 'clear, blue water' between PwC and its competitors. Within PwC IMD has significantly increased in importance during the last decade, not least due to the increased complexity of national and international regulations. In February 2001, this led the organization to create a centre for leadership development called Genesis Park (in Washington, DC, USA). The firm aims to build the future leaders of PwC, increase retention of top performers, drive its globalization, and to refine its worldwide strategy.

The eight to 16 Genesis Park participants come from a large range of countries. They are selected after about five years with the firm. The selection criteria include the performance track record and the leadership potential of the individual, especially in the areas of innovation, influencing skills and generation of commitment in others. New Genesis Park participants will be greeted by their predecessors and there is an overlap built into their five-month period in order to learn from the outgoing cohort and to take over some of their projects. These projects have topics such as 'New Industry Model', 'The Future of Advisory Services' and 'Advisory Quality Framework'. During the months in the centre, participants receive training and coaching sessions, discuss general professional service ideas and business cases, listen to internal and external speakers, have many interaction opportunities with senior partners of the firm to build their internal networks and work on strategic projects. Upon return, Genesis Park participants in larger offices have access to a network of Genesis Park alumni that meets regularly. Early indications are that the retention rate of Genesis Park alumni is much higher than that of their peers.

Questions for discussion

- How does Genesis Park increase the knowing-how, knowing-why and knowing-whom of participants?
- How can such an initiative support a global culture and the globalization of the company?

> • How important might be the 'symbolic' element of having attended Genesis Park for the further career of participants?
> • What skills, insights and networks is such an initiative likely to foster? Do these serve more the demands placed upon international assignees, global managers or corporate leaders?
>
> Source: based on Harris and Dickmann (2005)

In essence, many international development initiatives of organizations primarily serve one of five key aims:

1 They might aim at a corporate control or coordination goal – e.g. achieving a specific culture aim such as Henkel's strive for transnational thinking of its German managers (Dickmann 1997). As Ferner (2000) outlines, there is a range of control and coordination mechanisms, some of which are financial and accountancy related; others are cultural, where the firm aims to disseminate, even impose, the home culture onto the subsidiaries.

2 They might strive to advance the corporate expansion strategy. One driving factor could be international differences in resource cost or access to inexpensive labour. Other reasons include the search for new markets for existing products. Moreover, there might be local laws that stipulate or encourage domestic content in products (e.g. the US automotive manufacturing regulations). These issues are explored in more depth in Chapter 2.

3 They might be geared up to drive on a project of key importance. For instance, the management might have decided that the organization needs to balance its risks geographically and, therefore, needs a global spread of activities. Other key projects might be linked to knowledge generation within organizations. Some IT companies have purposefully moved their R&D departments to Silicon Valley in the USA in order to have easier access to a highly skilled workforce and professional networks.

4 Their prime objective might be to instil international capabilities, including cross-cultural and other management skills that are perceived to be globally applicable, as in the case of PwC's Genesis Park. This could be a key initiative to prepare them to become the future global leaders of the organization (Harris and Dickmann 2005).

5 A further aim can be getting to know key global staff and to build one's own international networks for purposes of better cross-national insights, performance and careers.

There are, of course, myriad further potential reasons which are, however, less frequently key drivers of IMD.

The special needs of the chosen *international* corporate configuration and the subsequent special demands on international assignees are relatively neglected. IMD is, therefore, often geared up to expose national or global managers to other ways of thinking and behaving but is not specifically focused on international assignees. The exception to this is the preparatory training and cross-cultural seminars that some assignees get shortly before and/or after their relocation. Normal training and development while individuals are working abroad is, therefore, either local or simply a functional or management intervention that is aimed at both non-expatriated and expatriated staff (for elaboration, see Chapter 6).

Doherty and Dickmann (2009) outline the business case for organizations to look at an international resource that might be more cost-effective than traditional expatriation: self-initiated expatriates, including immigrants (see Chapters 4 and 5). Many of these highly qualified persons are being underemployed. Ethnic immigrants in the USA and other minority workers tend to be channelled into secondary-sector jobs and immigrant workers face initial disadvantages in labour force assimilation (De Jong and Madamba 2001). However, immigrants and self-initiated expatriates might provide a very valuable addition to staff, especially when working across borders with their home countries. Doherty and Dickmann (2008) argue that this target group of international workers is neglected and that organizations do not use special recruitment or development approaches to gain and utilize immigrants or long-term self-initiated foreign workers.

The organizational perspective: performance management and retention

International performance management is a difficult issue to tackle for MNCs. It is one of the areas where the global–local dilemma of creating worldwide standards for efficiency, control, coordination purposes vs. the local pressures to conform to national cultures, preferences, the wider institutional context and the local competitive demands is most clearly evident. The case 'The evaluation' (Butler and de Bettignies 1996) paints a vivid picture of the practical difficulties when a British manager attempts to establish global appraisal standards in Thailand. The underlying strategic and operational considerations, advantages and drawbacks have been discussed extensively in Chapter 2.

The organizational configuration and outcomes of the struggle between globalizing and localizing forces are important for performance management. For instance, they will determine whether the original objectives that an assignee agreed in the country of origin are valid and relevant in the host country. Sometimes expatriates are informed upon arrival that 'the wind blows differently here' and that they will have to work towards different goals. Performance evaluation will then depend very much on who (a local or a global superior) will assess the individual. A second operational problem arises from differences in assessment processes, timeframes, criteria and local customs and expectations. The more varied these are, the more difficult it becomes to really understand the assignee's performance and to compare it to those of others. Highly differentiated local performance approaches can make comparative equity even more difficult to achieve than it normally is, and might result in barriers to management development and international careers for those individuals who either are not highly connected to powerful persons, or who work in an organizational unit where the performance management system is less trusted or less understood by the corporate centre. In effect, less standardized appraisal approaches might result in a career 'glass ceiling' for local managers.

A research initiative undertaken by Cranfield School of Management together with PricewaterhouseCoopers and Saratoga (Dickmann et al. 2006) examined performance implications of working abroad. It analysed the performance data of 3,450 expatriates over time, using the globally integrated performance management systems of nine large MNCs. Additionally, it contrasted the performance data with those of non-expatriated peers in these organizations at similar levels. Almost a third of the companies' expatriates were what these companies regarded as their top performers in the year of the commencement of the IA. This percentage dropped slightly during the assignment and the first year of return (to about 29 per cent). It seemed that top performance is slightly harder to deliver when working abroad or during the upsetting time of resettling in the home environment. In turn, looking at performance for all the 3,450 expatriates, it increased during the assignment (6 per cent more assignees had improved their performance than had worsened it) but performance levelled off during the year of return. Thus, this study challenges the negative performance effects envisaged in many academic papers. It has, of course, the usual caveats of the performance management systems of companies, their limitations and the potential trend to be especially lenient in the evaluation of current or recent assignees.

While Dickmann et al. (2006) found a high level of expatriate retention during assignments (only 2 per cent of their sample left their employers), churn is reported to be higher in other studies. Suutari and Brewster (2003) report that 11 per cent of Finnish expatriates in their study left during the assignment and Stahl et al. (2002) indicate that even more consider leaving.

The organizational perspective: international career management

While much of the recent career literature has focused on how individual careerists can be masters of their own destination, organizational career planning is not dead (Baruch 2006; Lips-Wiersma and Hall 2007). In fact, the 'war for talent' discussions, employer of choice activities and leadership development programmes all point to substantial and often sophisticated HR and career planning that goes on within organizations. While it might be sometimes the case that individuals on IAs slip off the radar screen (Dickmann and Doherty 2008), many organizations integrate international sojourns into their general career planning. As we have seen in early chapters of this book, the propensity to have one worldwide, overarching career system for managers is related to the international configuration of the organization and their career strategies. The global career approaches are often related to the four types of firms described by Heenan and Perlmutter (1979).

Where executive leaders have chosen a polycentric approach to managing the organization, the focus will be on the local development of capabilities, networks and motivational energies of their employees. Therefore, global career planning will be less important and infrequently done, as it is not aiming to 'spread' the home culture and ways of performing. Expatriates will need to adopt local strategies and practices. In contrast, the centrality of global career systems is much higher in ethnocentric entities. Firms and other organizations, such as the foreign service organizations of national governments, tend to select and send country-of-origin nationals to many key local positions abroad. Key reasons, as we saw above in Chapter 5, include control and coordination goals, skill-filling assignments, knowledge transfer and individual development aims. The expatriates from the home country are expected to instigate the home culture globally. Therefore, the career prospects and opportunities of head office and other home country employees tend to be better than those of local staff.

Regiocentric and geocentric management concentrates on identifying individuals with the best talent and performance irrespective of their national backgrounds. Capabilities and performance are key in this transnational approach which is associated with intensive knowledge flows and the search for approaches that are based on principles, values and norms that can be applied across a large range of countries. Companies often choose to have moderate configurations (Dickmann and Müller-Camen 2006) and might combine different career and expatriation planning approaches geared to different target groups and linked to diverse objectives. Case 7.2 outlines one of these configurations in action.

Case study 7.2 Managing international assignments in an FMCG corporation

The firm SweetsCo is a globally operating FMCG organization employing more than 25,000 employees. One of the key corporate objectives is international growth. Therefore, a major goal of IM is the development of a broadly experienced group of employees that support the needs of international expansion and successful operational activities. The key purposes to be satisfied through assignments include skills filling in emerging, developing and developed markets, coordination through skills and best practice transfer in order to train local employees, improving cultural and national diversity and the development of international assignees and transferees.

SweetsCo has drawn up two different patterns of developmental IAs. Interestingly, the firm distinguished between the international development of good individuals in order that they gain cross-border experience. The company believes that these individuals gain cross-cultural sensitivity through a short-term assignment within their own geographical region. There is a conscious decision that there will be limited investment into these persons who would move for instance from France to Spain or from the UK to Germany. The business case for their very best employees is different in that these are encouraged to go on a long-term assignment outside of their region. For example, this would lead an Italian to China or an American to South Africa or an Australian to Hungary. The company is willing to invest substantially into these individuals, hoping that they will move beyond cross-cultural sensitivity to global capability and will become the senior executives of the firm in the future.

An internal SweetsCo document shows that only the best of their talent and professionals are eligible to international moves and, therefore, that it would be important to retain repatriates. Moreover, the career impact is important since a senior HR manager stated that there is, in effect, a 'glass ceiling' for the careers of managers who did not have international work experience. Thus, one would expect that IAs create substantial career capital (and symbolic kudos for progression within the firm) so that repatriates have an incentive to stay with the company.

Internal data indicates a good performance of current expatriates with 40 per cent being among the top performers. Despite a good performance during an IA, SweetsCo experiences substantial problems with reintegration and retention of international assignees – in some years the expatriate churn is up to 40 per cent. Given SweetsCo's aim to have 80 per cent of developmental assignments (in 2006 two-thirds of its expatriates were abroad for developmental purposes), this created an urgent need to tackle the problem.

The FMCG Corporation internally acknowledges that its preparation process for repatriation is poor. An internal document outlines that part of the explanation is due to a 'low career planning awareness on both the associates as well as the business side'. In order to counter this, a new process has been set up that goes beyond the initial career conversations prior to expatriation. Three to six months before the end of an assignment, the international assignee, line management and a person from HRM should have a conversation to determine the next career steps. New policies are also considered with respect to a 'global talent pool' and activities to monitor expatriates and to keep them in the career planning loop.

Case questions:

1 Why does the company distinguish between short- and long-term developmental IAs? What might the associated benefits and drawbacks be?
2 What are the possible reasons that individual returnees decide to leave the organization?
3 How could the company react to decrease expatriate and repatriate 'churn'?
4 With reference to responsible and ethical management, how do you evaluate the 'glass ceiling' that seems to exist for individuals with little or no international work experience?
5 What international HRM configuration does this company seem to have?

It is not simply the importance and centrality of expatriation and other forms of international work in the general career planning, development and succession system of an organization that determines the progression chances and other outcomes for individuals. The underlying context of how careers really work in organizations, the competitive environment, new strategies and structures, sometimes happenstance, and the decisions of key individuals and peers who might compete for the same vacancies and promotion opportunities, have a substantial impact.

The relevance and importance of expatriation vary in different organizations. In terms of individual career paths, much depends also on the profession/occupation. For instance, expatriation might be an essential part of the careers of general and operational managers in MNCs. For specific professionals such as IT experts, who are assigned to cover skill gaps for a limited time period, such IA means a separation from the knowledge base and might mean a deviation from their desired path of progress. Thus, an IA could pose dangers to their career progress and they might have to find ways to analyse their organization's career management approaches and to react to perceived shortcomings (Dickmann and Doherty 2010). Conversely, some professionals will not be expecting expatriation, as their knowledge and competence is locally based or not needed for a global assignment. For example, HR managers will typically not move overseas, but operation managers have a higher chance to do so.

The individual perspective: cultural adjustment

The need to adjust is a recurring phenomenon in our lives. Changing employers, finding a new partner and friends and moving house will trigger the need to adjust. Moving abroad is simply one form of adjustment that is likely to need significant and multiple changes, depending, among other factors, on the cultural distance that the individual has from the host culture. National culture, however, is only one of the many facets that might vary. Haslberger (2008) distinguishes between macro-economic variables that cannot be altered and micro-economic factors that might be malleable.

Macro-level factors include the institutional and cultural context shaping business practices, the religious and political system, levels of socioeconomic development and the health and medical system (Hofstede 1980; Trompenaars and Hampden-Turner 1997; Dickmann 2003; Edwards et al. 2004). To these we would add the legal system, and the level of importance it has (some societies are more litigious than others). The level of unionization is a related issue, as industrial relations vary across countries, and much of it is regulated or legislated. For example, different countries have employment relations systems that create a need to have collective bargaining or other forms of conciliation before workers can go on strike. Unionism can be more political (France, Spain, Italy) or less political (Germany) and workers' rights can be more or less juridified. Moreover, governments can choose to interfere to different degrees in the employment relationship. Some of the immediate effects are preferred ways to interact and interpret behaviour in business, administrative burdens on individuals and organizations (e.g. degree of difficulty to obtain work permits, bank accounts etc.), access to emergency medical attention, housing standards, quality of water supply and so on. Other macro-level factors include climate, weather patterns, environmental pollution and the level of security, although these might vary with the specific location within countries (Dickmann and Mills 2010).

Micro-level variables relate to both work and private lives, and the interplay, sometimes spillover, between both. Many of the work variables we have come across above when discussing how to improve expatriate adjustment and success. These include the IM policies and practices of firms in relation to determining the job design in areas such as role discretion, job novelty, role conflict and clarity of work objectives and reporting lines. The literature on POS (Perceived Organizational Support) indicates that organizational mechanisms aiming to help individuals at work generate positive outcomes for individuals and their employers (Eisenberger et al. 1986, 1990). Other support structures including mentors, coaches, logistical back-up and host-country help by supervisors and co-workers are also quoted by Haslberger (2008). The private life micro-economic factors are broad. They start with partner and family considerations (e.g. the motivational structure to move to and to stay in the host country, resilience of family members, relationship with the extended family and friends in the home country) and extend to the wider social network such as friends and local acquaintants. Moreover, aspects such as the specific schooling situation of own children, shopping facilities, cultural interests of the family or availability of desired food or spare-time activities all play a role. Overall, these and other idiosyncratic factors can be either a driving or restraining force in the adjustment of individuals (see Baruch's 1995 push-pull model).

Having illuminated the many factors that have an effect on our adjustment in a foreign country, let us explore what adjustment actually is. Haslberger (2008: 132) defines expatriate adjustment as a 'lasting change in behaviour or behavioural tendencies that originates in relevant past experiences and enables the expatriate to be more effective in the new environment'. What is 'effective' will relate to the corporate demands in relation to its international configuration, specific role and objectives, the degree of cultural and business system understanding needed in the expatriate's role, the control, coordination and knowledge management function the individual is responsible for and a variety of other influence factors (see above). The evaluation of effectiveness is also in the eye of the beholder: the expatriates themselves, their families, work colleagues, other international assignees and the wider network of social contacts in the country might all hold different opinions – and these might, again, differ from those evaluations being made by superiors in the country of origin or work colleagues elsewhere. Yet, from the organizational perspective, effectiveness would mean the ability to fulfil the role – usually meaning the management of the operation.

Adjustment, sometimes called acculturation, is important because the lack of understanding of the host-country environment and inappropriate behaviour triggers a variety of wrong cognitive impressions, misinterpretations and wider problems (Trompenaars and Hampden-Turner 1997; Black et al. 1999). Highly adjusted international workers, however, are seen to avoid these problems and to perform better at work – a meta-study has shown that a significant percentage of the variance in performance is explained by their adjustment (Bhaskar-Shrinivas et al. 2005). However, this relationship is sometimes seen to be weak and factors such as organizational commitment, strain or job satisfaction might moderate it (Hechanova et al. 2003; Thomas and Lazarova 2006).

The dominant approach to research adjustment was developed by Black and his associates (Black 1988; Black and Mendenhall 1991; Black et al. 1999) who distinguish between work, interaction and general adjustment. Adjustment to work is seen as the easiest adaptation, aided by those policies, practices and task requirements that are similar in the host country to those that are familiar to the expatriate (Black et al. 1999: 109). Yet, sometimes the role of the expatriate would be to instil such policies and practices that exist in the home country and not in the host country, and locals might resent or take time to accept the ways the parent organization expects them to use. Interaction adjustment is regarded as the most difficult. It consists of interacting (verbal and non-verbal) with host nationals inside and outside of work. The difficulties originate from conscious and unconscious differences in mental maps, behavioural scripts, rules and interpretations showing up in the process. Lastly, the adaptation to the general non-work environment relates to the changes that individuals and their families might need to make in response to differences in the general context outside work. This is a broad category including climate, security situation, housing, transport, cost of living, different ways to spend one's spare time, entertainment etc. (see above).

Generally, individuals have gone through a process of anticipatory adjustment before they leave their country to work abroad. Realistic job previews are a good means to create more applicable expectations and should be given in preparation for such a major change. Getting mentally involved with the prospective host country and already making a number of adjustments, focusing on adapting to important aspects of the new culture and environment and refining the changes to improve accuracy are seen to aid anticipatory adjustment and, along the line, actual adjustment (Black et al. 1999: 115). Previous overseas experience is likely to have a positive, if somewhat moderate, impact on adjustment. As seen from the above discussions, a range of individual, job-related, organizational, family-member, individual situation-specific and non-work factors have an impact on the ability, quality and speed of personal adjustment.

While there is much supportive research evidence (Hechanova et al. 2003; Bhaskar-Shrinivas et al. 2005), there are voices that critique the Black et al. conceptualization of adjustment. Three weaknesses are identified by Thomas and Lazarova (2006) due to the development of the original survey items. Key critique points include that the approach is not rooted in theory and is weakened by insufficient specification of mutually exclusive categories, measures loosely defined, overlapping facets of adjustment (interaction–work adjustment). Moreover, as Haslberger also conceptualizes, it measures adjustment as a unidimensional construct while adjustment might be a multidimensional phenomenon.

Haslberger (2008) explains that adjustment has three components: behaviour (or a preference for certain behavioural patterns), information processing (including memory and learning from experience) and emotions. The case of meeting Omar in Bogotá might manifest some of the adjustment processes involved (see Case study 7.3).

Many people who come to work in another country feel initially very excited and highly positive about the move, so that this state is often described as the 'honeymoon period' in the literature. During the first few weeks Mark felt happy,

Case 7.3 Meeting Omar in Bogotá

After studying for a Masters at the London School of Economics, 24-year-old Mark decided to take a year out. Mark, a German, had always dreamt of seeing South America and, having made a Colombian friend at university (Ernesto), decided to go to Bogotá to learn Spanish and to find work. Mark arrived in the Colombian capital and shared an apartment with Ernesto's cousin, Daniel. Daniel decided to give a welcome party the Friday after Mark's arrival and during that evening he got to know Omar, another cousin of Ernesto. They struck up a conversation about Colombian culture, history and politics and Omar offered to show Mark around the following day.

They had agreed to meet at a street corner (Calle 72, Carrera 15) in Bogotá at 3 pm and Mark made sure he would be there with plenty of time to spare. Unfortunately for Mark, Omar did not arrive on time – in fact, he was three hours late. Mark, therefore, had enough time to analyse the differences in punctuality between Germany and Colombia. He used it to develop a plan for how to handle what he saw as 'Colombian (un)punctuality'. In future, he said to himself, he would never meet on a street corner. Instead, he would opt to either meet in his apartment or in cafés or other places where he could sit down and read. Moreover, he would never be so punctual again. In the following weeks he would implement his plan but despite being late he would find himself waiting for other persons. During this wait he had plenty to read but still did not feel happy about the lack of punctuality.

In fact, after the first excitement of being in Colombia had diminished, a lot of what was going on puzzled him. At first, things had seemed very interesting and delightfully different. Now, they simply seemed different and confusing. He started to feel 'drained' and wished for the old certainties. Not only did he feel inadequate in expressing himself in Spanish, he also thought he did not quite get to the point of many of the observed differences. While he had started to tolerate 'Colombian time' and many of the other differences, and while he had developed ways to deal with these, he had not yet accepted the cultural differences.

With respect to punctuality, this acceptance happened after an incident several weeks later. By then he had a Colombian girlfriend and they were invited to a dinner party starting at 9 pm. As 9 pm was approaching, his girlfriend went into the bathroom to take a shower. Mark's reaction was to indicate his frustration of surely arriving late at the dinner party. However, his girlfriend simply answered that if they were to leave now and arrive near 9 pm that would positively be regarded as rude. In fact, she speculated, the hosts would probably just now take a shower. So, Mark enquired in desperation as to what the appropriate time to arrive was. The answer was that they would be expected to be about 45 minutes late. Arriving 30 minutes late would be okay, arriving one hour late would be still tolerated but later than that would not be acceptable. Upon hearing this Mark reflected on the inherent advantages of this arrangement. As a German it would be easy to hit a time corridor of 30 minutes to arrive. In fact, it would take out much of the stress he had experienced in Germany or the UK to arrive punctually. From then on he was much happier with 'Colombian punctuality' and would enquire with his new local and international friends on 'what time' they were working to when specifying meeting hours.

Questions:

- What cultural values did Mark feel were challenged at his first meeting with Omar? Might these be an expression of deeper held basic norms and beliefs?
- How do Mark's emotions change over time?
- What happened to his cognitive confidence?
- How did he adjust his behaviour and what impact do you think this will have had on its effectiveness?
- What is the outcome of his changes? How would you think he would be likely to behave when he returns to his native Germany?

sometimes bordering on euphoria. Occasionally, he was unsure about what to do and how to act but the negative feelings associated with this did not last long. But as time goes on, these negative impressions and emotions came to last longer. In fact, what was seen as excitingly different came to be viewed as disturbingly distinct due to Mark's inability to intellectually decipher and understand, adequately respond with his behaviours and emotionally accept the cultural and contextual differences. These emotional patterns have come to be called 'culture shock' (Oberg 1960). Over time, Mark's behaviour became more adequate as he slowly deciphered his context. While Mark's cognitive insights increased in the host environment, at first his confidence decreased. In the long term, however, his cognitive confidence returned as he realized that his behaviour became more and more adequate and as he increasingly gained positive feedback from his local contacts and expatriated peers. Figure 7.3 shows the adjustment curve (including culture shock) and depicts how all three curves of emotions, behavioural effectiveness and cognitive confidence develop over time.

The reader will notice that neither the level of adjustment, the levels of confidence, effectiveness of behaviour, emotions or time are specified in Figure 7.3. This has to do with it simply attempting to illustrate some possible dynamic processes. However, there are likely to be many variations between individuals and the adjustment process is also dependent on the level of cultural gap experienced. Sometimes, we might expect a smooth adjustment with individuals not necessarily going through a culture shock. This might be the case where individuals go to countries that are culturally rather similar to their country of origin. For instance, Haslberger (2008) quotes moves from the USA to English-speaking Canada or from Germany to Austria. Nevertheless, there is some potential for serious cultural ineffectiveness of behaviour and understanding through seemingly

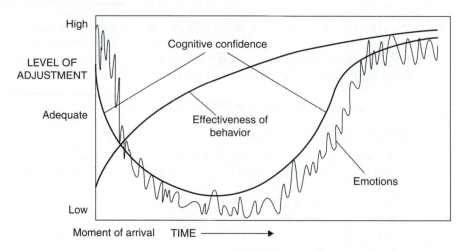

Figure 7.3 Adjustment curve, including culture shock
Source: Haslberger (2008: 138)

similar patterns having different roots or interpretations. For instance, the use of formal titles is seen to be more important and adequate in Austria compared to Germany. Moreover, the statement 'that is interesting' might invite a very distinct interpretation of the speaker's evaluation of the situation in the UK compared to the US. In the US something being 'interesting' might be exciting while in the UK something interesting might indicate that the speaker finds a situation peculiar or that s/he cannot or does not want to say anything else about it.[1] Further, expatriates who have had recent experience with the host country might experience a lesser culture shock (Takeuchi et al. 2005).

Adjustment, therefore, is an intellectual and emotional learning process that takes place in a variety of life's domains over time. It might progress at a different pace in relation to these different domains – work, spare time, social environment, interaction with the state, shopping, schooling, sport etc. Moreover, it is not assured that the individual will adjust sufficiently to be emotionally content and behaviourally effective. What seems to be sure, however, is that cultural adjustment constitutes an identity change that means that the expatriate returns a different person. Further, the distant and especially closer environment of the expatriate can have a substantial impact on the process of adjustment – in that, the assignee's partner, family and close friends are likely to have a leading role.

Other key qualities that would be crucial for managing expatriation issues are concerned with the different facets of intelligence and, in particular, cultural intelligence (see an in-depth introduction in Chapter 4). The term 'cultural intelligence' (CQ), refers to the capability of an individual person to function and manage effectively in culturally diverse environments (Earley and Ang 2003; Earley et al.

1 If the reader wants to explore more of the semantic and cultural differences that exist in the English culture, the book 'Watching the English' by Kate Fox (2004) will give further insights.

2006). CQ is viewed as an individual's property, which is based on a wide range of individual attributes including personality, capability, skills and interests. While some may see parallels between CQ and cognitive ability (IQ) or emotional intelligence (EQ), all being individual qualities, the CQ focuses on culturally related capabilities, and as such is of specific relevance to working in different cultures. This claim does not come to undermine the need for high cognitive ability for expatriation. IQ is an essential quality for any manager, and so, too, is the need to have a strong EQ. EQ is the ability to use emotional information in reasoning and behaviour (Mayer and Salovey 1997). Current literature on emotional intelligence suggests that individuals with high levels of EQ are generally successful in inter-personal relationships (e.g. Mayer et al. 2004; Mayer et al. 2008), certainly an issue when landing in a new role. The multiple requirement of not merely per-forming a role, but conducting it effectively in a different culture and under differ-ent conditions will require the expatriate to have a combination of high IQ, EQ and CQ. Developing these capabilities is challenging. IQ is typically determined for individuals and training is not expected to improve an adult's IQ. EQ and even more, CQ, could be subjected to training that will, at least, improve awareness and provide tools for better dealing with unfamiliar situations.

The individual perspective: family and partner issues while on assignment

Traditionally, one of the key reasons for early return has been stated by expatriates to be the lack of family adjustment (GMAC 2006). While it could be true that fam-ilies might experience most difficulties to adjust, it could also be that blaming family members allows the international assignee, local bosses and other signifi-cant decision-makers in the firm to save face. This allows the career fall-out for the individual assignee to be minimized.

In this chapter we have consciously concentrated on company-supported expatria-tion. Immigrants, including those who come to a foreign country due to work-oriented reasons, have little or no 'organizational support' or safety nets. While the cognitive and emotional processes of adjustment are the same, they face bureau-cratic hurdles for themselves and their families which they often have to overcome on their own. While, therefore, the 'plunge' into the new country culture, institu-tions and reality is more immediate, the learning needs are often more acute. A more in-depth discussion of the drivers and the situation of immigrants can be found in Chapters 5, 8 and 9.

Career capital accumulation, interaction and other outcomes

By now, this book has drawn a vivid picture of many facets of international work. This serves to remind us that no two foreign work assignments or self-initiated work experiences abroad are the same. There is a large range of organizational, individual, institutional, situational and other contextual factors that will influence the shapes, displayed behaviours and outcomes of international work. In a situation where the mutual dependency of foreign-born workers and organizations is especially high, there is a large potential for 'darker' outcomes of working abroad. Richardson and her associates have published a stream of research looking at dysfunctional and non-positive career results for foreign workers (Richardson and Mallon 2005; Richardson and Zikic 2007). Some of the self-initiated academics experienced a drain on their emotional and physical energies due to the transience and precariousness of their situation. However, most expatriates found ways to manage this darker side of IAs, an indication of high levels of resilience. Overall, it should be clear by now that the concept of career success has multiple definitions (Arthur et al. 2005) and what might be considered as a success by organizations might not be seen as such by individuals and vice versa (Lazarova and Cerdin 2007; Dickmann and Doherty 2008). For the immigrant, a typical issue is underemployment. Often, professionals need to give up their former high-status professions because they are not allowed to practise these in their new country. For instance, most teaching qualifications acquired abroad will not be accepted in Germany. In turn, medical degrees from abroad are normally not accepted in Canada. There is a lack of a global system of recognition for overseas diplomas, even when talking about medical doctors. In other occupations, there is a need for adjustment. A lawyer will have to re-qualify, even if moving within states in the USA, not to speak of a move from a developing country to a developed one.

Richardson and her co-writers stress that assignees react to some of the darker developments in their employment status or careers. Looking at some of the institutional pressures that assignees and self-initiated expatriates face – for instance, their research isolated these for academics working in the Middle East – it seems that individuals working abroad react to these by developing copying strategies and mechanisms that factor in dysfunctional and threatening developments. The work of Dickmann and Doherty (2010) explores more of the dynamics. It shows that where expatriates noticed that their organization did not facilitate the acquisition or preservation of their career capital they would become active and attempt to compensate for the identified gap. In turn, if organizations noticed dysfunctional outcomes or the lack of individual activities, they would work on targeted IHRM policies and practices.

Dickmann and his associates have used the intelligent career framework (DeFillippi and Arthur 1994) within the domain of IM extensively. In the early part of the twenty-first century they investigated the career capital impact of working abroad. On average, they found a positive career capital effect for individuals who worked abroad (cf. Stahl et al. 2002). In one study, 98 per cent of respondents claimed to have increased their capabilities; 90 per cent to have built social networks; and 92 per cent to be motivated while working abroad (Dickmann et al. 2005). However, they identified certain individuals embedded in specific organizational contexts who seemed to have suffered a loss in their *knowing-whom* capital. Moreover, many international assignees underwent a substantial change to their motivations and identities which made them reassess their relationship with their employers (Lazarova and Cerdin 2007; Dickmann and Doherty 2008). This led to an in-depth investigation of individual and organizational reactions to perceived dysfunctional effects during IM in a fast-moving consumer goods firm.

In terms of *knowing-whom* most individuals wanted to expand their social capital and aimed to build host-country and international networks. While 'being in' with powerful people was seen as important by the organization, the networking process was not managed extensively. It seemed that the firm was, in fact, worried about potential external networking of junior and middle managers (they expected this from senior managers). While at the time of the research the organization considered building expatriate expert networks and implementing a sponsor approach for IM, assignees had already acted. Expatriates have the challenge to build their local and often their international networks at the beginning of an assignment. Towards the end of their foreign sojourns they concentrate on strengthening or re-establishing their home links. Many of the returned expatriates felt that their own performance in the last year of foreign work had suffered but that this behaviour had made a positive difference with respect to having a job to return to (Dickmann and Doherty 2010).

With respect to *knowing-how*, the goals of individuals and organization were relatively similar. They included the acquisition of a broader business perspective, intercultural sensitivity and relationship skills, the improvement of general skills and the application of the broad set of capabilities to improve performance. Expatriates, however, felt that the firm did not do enough to enable them to acculturate and learn from the local environment in the first part of their assignment, and also thought that they did not have sufficient access to general management training (often at the head office). They explored their local environment through a range of self-initiated activities and used their old and new contacts to gain access to international development initiatives. The firm, in turn, was dissatisfied with the application of international learning in the next job (see Chapter 8 for a more in-depth discussion). It had reacted by drawing up specific assignment goals in relation to the vacancies, prescribed that a business case had to be established for international work, used more inpatriation and strove to expatriate individuals to centres of excellence which made a knowledge application after return more likely.

Lastly, HR managers in the firm's head office were persuaded that IAs would give clearer career goals to individuals and that foreign work would bestow symbolic career capital which had the potential to increase individual commitment to the FMCG organization (cf. Doherty and Dickmann 2009). Individuals, however, had much more varied and personal factors to explain why they wanted to embark on a foreign sojourn. Some of these were related to the organizational culture and global context of their employer and some to long-range career goals. Repatriation, however, was considered by both sides as being handled ineffectively and this situation led to the organization planning to implement expectation management before the return. Individuals, however, had consciously or unconsciously often started to reassess their relationship with the company given the disappointment and insecurity that they felt.

This research confirmed some earlier findings, such as the need to manage repatriation better and to treat IA as a part of long-term career planning on behalf of organizations (Lazarova and Caligiuri 2001). By showing how individuals react flexibly to their organizational context and specific expatriation situation, it indicates that individuals behave as career capitalists. Therefore, organizations need to understand the expectations of their expatriates to cover more specific career capital areas. In terms of *knowing-how*, organizations should consider how to ensure that expatriates gain relevant skills, insights and knowledge so that these can be used after repatriation. With respect to *knowing-whom* the crucial role of home and international networks needs to be recognized and organizations might consider a range of activities to link expatriates more closely to their home base. In terms of *knowing-why*, organizations are well advised to tailor their approaches to the specific international assignees and to understand and manage specific rather than general expectations. This is why Dickmann and Doherty (2010) call for an individualization and personalization of organizational IM management.

Diversity issues during working abroad

Like many areas of management, women entered the scene of corporate IAs lagging behind their male counterparts. When expatriation started to become an issue, women were practically absent from the map (Adler 1984). Many barriers have been diminished, and while there is still a significant gender gap in international expatriation, much progress has been made (Tung 2004; Altman and Shortland 2009). Such a gender gap is not surprising, with ample empirical evidence for it in the career literature (Sullivan 1999; Sullivan and Baruch 2010).

Reviewing the history of women expatriates, Altman and Shortland (2009), point out that following an almost non-existence of women expatriates in the 1970s, to a very minor start in the 1980s, the trend in the 1990s identified that more women were offered IA opportunities but they remained a negligible minority compared to men. The current trend is for a gradual increase in the number and visibility of women in IAs, where more women also opt for self-initiating their expatriation (Altman and Baruch 2008). The debate, they argue, has moved from the question of whether to 'give women a chance' through attempts to identify and remove 'blockages' to women's progress to, most recently, structural changes in the expatriate assignment and claims for women's superior affinity to operating internationally. Apart from corporate expatriation, a large number of women can be found in care roles (Bozionelos 2009).

The continuous entry of women to the expatriation roles is an important step in terms of future career prospects, because in most large, multinational corporations, overseas assignments are becoming a crucial stage for career progress into the executive ranks.

Most of the issues of concern for expatriation exist for both males and females, though some are more problematic for women: for example, it is easier to make a move decision based on the needs and career prospects of the main breadwinner – the majority of which are still males. The burden of family care (not merely child care, but care for elderly parents) falls on women more than on men, again, working against gender equality in terms of agreeableness for global move. Other HR issues might present either paternalistic view, prejudice, or real care, as discussed by Caligiuri and Cascio (1998). Indeed, some cultures (e.g. in the Middle East) will not be open to females in managerial roles. For the young generation (X and Y generations), though, and in particular in the early career stage, we witness a more balanced view of expatriation and readiness to expatriate.

Summary and learning points

This chapter has explored individual and organizational issues in relation to pertinent issues during IAs. The key organizational activities to foster successful international adjustment are outlined in Table 7.2.

Because the risks and investments associated with international work are more substantial than those linked to working at home, the emerging career picture is complex and subject to many initiatives and intensive individual emotions. The mutual dependency of individuals and their international employers seems to indicate that the traditional discipline of career and succession planning is still very relevant and important.

Key learning points include:

- Organizational configurations and the particular tasks that an international assignee is charged with will have a substantial effect on the expatriate experience, function and power.
- Knowledge management is one of the key organizational goals associated with IAs. It varies with the organizational strategy, structure and wider context. The organizational activities and networking patterns will determine much of tacit knowledge management.
- There is a large range of organizational activities that can foster successful IAs. Organizations can use sophisticated approaches to selection, training and development, job design, career planning, administrative and logistical support and influencing the social environment of expatriates. A wide range of individual characteristics also exert an important influence.
- IMD can serve both individual and corporate goals. Some firms have designed approaches that link into a variety of career capital areas, strengthen the globalization of the entity and aid the development of more international strategies and policies.
- Retention during an assignment can be a problem for organizations. Strategic and operational international career management contributes to the fulfilment of assignees' expectations and goals. Developing frameworks to address *knowing-why* issues in terms of expectation management and career and values dialogues, to support the development of *knowing-whom* through social interaction and further the augmentation of individuals' skills, knowledge and capabilities is likely to increase retention.
- Expatriate adjustment is a learning process which will be different for diverse individuals. Assignees will experience large dynamics with regards to their emotions, behavioural effectiveness and cognitive confidence. Over time the performance of individuals and their cognitive confidence is seen to steadily improve, while their emotions might have to go through a honeymoon period and a substantial dip before showing high levels of adjustment. Not all assignments

Table 7.2 Organizational activities to foster successful international adjustment

Area	Organizational action	Some characteristics that would help
Selection	• Sophisticated selection factoring in personality factors, soft competencies, performance and potential • Involve partner in selection and consider extended family responsibilities • Use psychometric and other instruments and give feedback to candidate and partner regarding cross-cultural strengths and weaknesses • Match candidate's profile to intercultural job demands of organization and international vacancies • Provide realistic job, local team and country previews (and also 'look-see visits')	*Individual characteristics:* • Self-confidence • Willingness to learn about different cultures and business environments • Interpersonal orientation • Good communication skills • Willingness to critically review own values and norms • Openness
Training and development	• Provide rigorous training for increased job demands; ideally linked to organizational configuration • Provide intercultural training (pre-departure and post-arrival) and language classes • Include partner in the training • Provide team-building initiatives together with new team • Provide (where useful) extensive briefings to local employees regarding role and function of assignee • Enable interaction with repatriates from assignment region/area	*T&D considerations:* • Distinguish between local position requirements, global or international control, coordination and innovation responsibilities • Distinguish between general communication skills and development of personality of individual • Distinguish between work and social environment • Encourage local interaction as much as possible
Job design	• Give discretion in the job • Clarify job expectations and responsibilities • Gain agreement as to job objectives between individual, home and host country • Provide overlap with incumbent to facilitate 'hitting the ground running' • Align any other conflicting expectations regarding performance standards, job, working environment etc.	*Job design choices:* • In most cases, choose a job that the candidate will find only a slight stretch. Adjustment to a new team and new culture is already a challenge • For earmarked top leaders the stretch might be larger. This might include changing divisions, functions or more radical job content alterations

Administrative and logistical support	• Provide effective administrative support in relation to the international mobility framework, compensation and benefit questions • Provide good logistical support and high quality in terms of moving abroad, accommodation (abroad and at home), health insurance, banking, schooling, return visits etc. • Guarantee security as much as possible and provide protection in high-risk areas • Monitor own and service-provider activities and gain expatriate feedback for improvements	*Administrative issues:* • Set an end-of-assignment date in order to avoid assignments that 'drag on' • Consider periodically whether the assignment objectives have been fulfilled and, therefore, keep the option of early return open • Provide support through corporate sponsor, mentors and coaches who proactively approach the assignees in regular intervals
Social environment	• Encourage local national employees to provide support to new assignees and families • Collect and provide information regarding social, religious, sport, cultural organizations and enable expatriates and their families to join these • Develop social support networks • Provide an Employee Assistance Programme (EAP) for people experiencing culture shock and train local manages to recognize symptoms	*Social facilitation:* • Consider setting up local 'buddies' for expats and partners • Support partners in carving out meaningful roles for themselves
Career issues	• Link selection to individual's long-term career plan and organizational career management (avoid 'out of sight, out of mind' syndrome) • Foster the acquisition of knowing how, knowing why and knowing whom capital • Design support mechanisms such as business sponsors, formal and informal networks, shadow career planning	*Career planning:* • The mutual dependency of individuals and organization is especially strong during an IA. There is a case for more long-term career planning which looks likely to aid retention • Consider NOT promoting on the way out – instead, actively consider promoting upon repatriation • Consider expatriation to centres of excellence and ways how to apply insights and use social capital in the job upon return

Source: Table based on Black et al. (1999); Harris, Brewster and Sparrow (2003); Lazarova and Caligiuri (2001); Dickmann et al. (2005); Dickmann et al. (2006); Dickmann and Doherty (2008); Haslberger (2008)

will lead to culture shock; there might be a smooth adjustment. Not all international sojourns will require high levels of adjustment and cognitive confidence.

- Family and partner issues are important in international work and have an influence on the adjustment of individuals. These should be factored into selection processes and criteria as well as a range of other supporting activities during the IA.
- Gender continues to be an issue in decision making, and while the gap between women and men is declining, the trend is slow, and the outcome can be detrimental for women's careers in the long run.
- IAs, the behaviours and attitudes of individuals as well as the policies and processes of organizations are dynamic. There are strong interaction effects which determine the range of organizational and individual outcomes of the foreign sojourn.

References

Adler, N. (1984) 'Women in international management: where are they?', *California Management Review*, 26(4): 78–89.

Altman, Y. and Baruch, Y. (2008) 'Global protean careers: a new era in expatriation and repatriation', paper presented at the *European Academy of Management* conference, Ljubljana, May 2008.

Altman, Y. and Shortland, S. (2009) 'Women and international assignments: taking stock – a 25-year review', *Human Resource Management*, 47(2): 199–216.

Arthur, M., Khapova, S. and Wilderom, C. (2005) 'Career success in a boundaryless career world', *Journal of Organizational Behavior*, 26: 177–202.

Asakawa, K. and Lehrer, M. (2003) 'Managing local knowledge assets globally: the role of regional innovation relays', *Journal of World Business*, 38(1): 31–42.

Au, K. and Fukuda, J. (2002) 'Boundary spanning behaviors of expatriates', *Journal of World Business*, 37: 285–296.

Bartlett, C. and Ghoshal, S. (1989) *Managing Across Borders*, London: Hutchinson Business Books.

Bartlett, C. and Ghoshal, S. (2003) 'What is a global manager?', *Harvard Business Review* (1992), reprinted in *A Changed World* edn of *Harvard Business Review*, August 2003.

Baruch, Y. (1995) 'Business globalization – the human resource management aspect', *Human Systems Management*, 14(4): 313–326.

Baruch, Y. (2002) 'No such thing as a global manager', *Business Horizons*, 45(1): 36–42.

Baruch, Y. (2006) 'Career development in organizations and beyond: balancing traditional and contemporary viewpoints', *Human Resource Management Review*, 16: 125–138.

Bhaskar-Shrinivas, P., Harrison, D., Shaffer, M. and Luk, D. (2005) 'Input-based and time-based models of international adjustment: meta-analytic evidence and theoretical extensions', *Academy of Management Journal*, 48(2): 257–281.

Birkinshaw, J., Nobel, R. and Ridderstrale, J. (2002) 'Knowledge as a contingency variable: do the characteristics of knowledge predict organizational structure?', *Organization Science*, 13(3): 274–289.

Black, J.S. (1988) 'Work role transition: a study of American expatriate managers in Japan', *Journal of International Business Studies*, 30(2): 277–294.

Black, J. and Mendenhall, M. (1991) 'The U-curve adjustment hypothesis revisited: a review and theoretical framework', *Journal of International Business Studies*, 22(2): 225–247.

Black, J.S., Gregersen, H.B., Mendenhall, M.E. and Stroh, L.K. (1999) *Globalizing People through International Assignments*, Reading, MA: Addison-Wesley.

Bonache, J. and Brewster, C. (2001) 'Knowledge transfer and the management of expatriation', *Thunderbird International Business Review*, 43(1): 145–168.

Bonache, J. and Dickmann, M. (2008) 'The transfer of strategic HR know-how in MNCs: mechanisms, barriers and initiatives', in M. Dickmann, C. Brewster and P. Sparrow (eds) *International Human Resource Management – A European Perspective*, London: Routledge.

Bonache, J. and Zárraga-Oberty, C. (2008) 'Determinants of the success of international assignees as knowledge transferors: a theoretical framework', *International Journal of Human Resource Management*, 19(1): 1–18.

Bozionelos, N. (2009) 'Expatriation outside the boundaries of the multinational corporation: a study with expatriate nurses in Saudi Arabia', *Human Resource Management*, 48: 111–134.

Butler, C. and de Bettignies, H.-C. (1996) 'The evaluation', *Insead Euro-Asia Centre*, ECCH case collection: 497-012-1.

Caligiuri, P.M. and Cascio, W.F. (1998) 'Can we send her there? Maximizing women on global assignments', *Journal of World Business*, 33(4): 394–416.

Chandler, A. (1962) *Strategy and Structure: Chapters in the History of American Industrial Enterprise*, Cambridge, MA: MIT Press.

DeFillippi, R. and Arthur, M. (1994) 'The boundaryless career: a competency-based perspective', *Journal of Organizational Behavior*, 15: 307–324.

De Jong, G. and Madamba, A. (2001) 'A double disadvantage? Minority group, immigrant status and underemployment in the United States', *Social Science Quarterly*, 82: 117–130.

Dickmann, M. (1997) *The IPD Guide on International Management Development*, London: Institute of Personnel and Development.

Dickmann, M. (2003) 'Implementing German HRM abroad: desired, feasible, successful?', *International Journal of Human Resource Management*, 14(2): 265–284.

Dickmann, M. and Doherty, N. (2008) 'Exploring the career capital impact of international assignments within distinct organizational contexts', *British Journal of Management*, 19: 145–161.

Dickmann, M. and Doherty, N. (2010) 'Exploring organisational and individual career goals, interactions and outcomes of international assignments', *Thunderbird International Review*, 52(4): 313–324.

Dickmann. M. and Mills, T. (2010) 'The importance of intelligent career and location considerations: exploring the decision to go to London', *Personnel Review*, 39(1): 116–134.

Dickmann, M. and Müller-Camen, M. (2006) 'A typology of international human resource management strategies and processes', *International Journal of Human Resource Management*, 17(4): 580–601.

Dickmann, M., Doherty, N. and Johnson, A. (2006) *Measuring the Value of International Assignments*, London: PricewaterhouseCoopers and Cranfield School of Management.

Dickmann, M., Müller-Camen, M. and Kelliher, C. (2009) 'Striving for transnational human resource management – principles and practice', *Personnel Review*, 38(1): 5–25.

Dickmann, M., Wigley-Jones, R. and Wignall, D. (2005) *Understanding and Avoiding the Barriers to International Mobility*, London: PricewaterhouseCoopers.

Doherty, N. and Dickmann, M. (2008) Self-initiated expatriates – corporate asset or a liability, paper presented at 4th *Workshop on Expatriation, EIASM*, Las Palmas de Gran Canaria, Spain, October 2008.

Doherty, N. and Dickmann, M. (2009) 'Exploring the symbolic capital of international assignments', *International Journal of Human Resource Management*, 20(2): 301–320.

Earley, P.C. and Ang, S. (2003) *Cultural Intelligence: An Analysis of Individual Interactions across Cultures*, Palo Alto, CA: Stanford University Press.

Earley, P.C., Ang, S. and Tan, J. (2006) *CQ: Developing Cultural Intelligence at Work*, Palo Alto, CA: Stanford University Press.

Edwards, T., Colling, T. and Ferner, A. (2004) 'Comparative institutional analysis and the diffusion of employment practices in multinational companies', paper presented at *Multinationals and the International Diffusion of Organizational Forms and Practices* conference, Barcelona, Spain, July, 2004.

Eisenberger, R., Fasolo, P. and Davis-LaMastro, V. (1990) 'Perceived organizational support and employee diligence, commitment and innovation', *Journal of Applied Psychology*, 75(1): 51–59.

Eisenberger, R., Huntington, R., Hutchison, S. and Sowa, D. (1986) 'Perceived organizational support', *Journal of Applied Psychology*, 71(3): 500–507.

Ferner, A. (2000) 'The underpinnings of "bureaucratic" control systems', *Journal of Management Studies*, 37(4): 521–539.

Fox, K. (2004) *Watching the English: The Hidden Rules of English Behaviour*, London: Hodder & Stoughton.

GMAC (2006) *Global Relocation Trend Survey*, Warren, NJ: GMAC Global Relocation Services.

Gupta, A. and Govindarajan, V. (1991) 'Knowledge flows and the structure of control within multinational corporations', *Academy of Management Review*, 16(4): 768–792.

Harris, H. and Dickmann, M. (2005) *The CIPD Guide on International Management Development*, London: The Chartered Institute of Personnel and Development.

Harris, H., Brewster, C. and Sparrow, P. (2003) *International Human Resource Management*, London: Routledge.

Haslberger, A. (2008). 'Expatriate adjustment: a more nuanced view', in M. Dickmann, C. Brewster and P. Sparrow (eds) *International Human Resource Management – A European Perspective*, London: Routledge.

Hechanova, R., Beehr, T.A. and Christiansen, N.D. (2003) 'Antecedents and consequences of employees' adjustment to overseas assignment: a meta-analytic review', *Applied Psychology*, 52(2): 213–236.

Heenan, D.A. and Perlmutter, H.V. (1979) *Multinational Organizational Development: A Social Architecture Perspective*, Reading, MA: Addison-Wesley.

Hofstede, G. (1980) *Culture's Consequences*, London: Sage.

Inkson, K. and Myers, B.A. (2003) 'The big OE: self-directed travel and career development', *Career Development International*, 8: 170–181.

Jaw, B.-S., Wang, C. and Chen, Y.-H. (2006) 'Knowledge flows and performance of multinational subsidiaries: the perspective of human capital', *International Journal of Human Resource Management*, 17(2): 225–244.

Jokinen, T., Brewster, C. and Suutari, V. (2008) 'Career capital during international work experiences: contrasting self-initiated expatriate experiences and assignees expatriation', *International Journal of Human Resource Management*, 19(6): 979–998.

Kakabadse, A. and Kakabadse, N. (1999) *Essence of Leadership*, London: Thompson International Business Press.

Kühlmann, T. and Stahl, G. (2005) 'The development of multicultural competencies', in M. Connerly and P. Petersen (eds) *Leadership in a Diverse and Multicultural Environment: Developing Awareness, Knowledge and Skills*, London: Sage.

Lazarova, M. and Caligiuri, P. (2001) 'Retaining repatriates: the role of organizational support practices', *Journal of World Business*, 36(4): 389–401.

Lazarova, M. and Cerdin, J.-L. (2007) 'Revisiting repatriates concerns: organizational support vs career and contextual influences', *Journal of International Business Studies*, 38: 404–429.

Lips-Wiersma, M. and Hall, D.T. (2007) 'Organizational career development is not dead: a case study on managing the new career during organizational change', *Journal of Organizational Behavior*, 28: 771–792.

Mayer, J.D. and Salovey, P. (1997) 'What is emotional intelligence?', in P. Salovey and D. Sluyter (eds) *Emotional Development and Emotional Intelligence: Educational Applications*, New York: Basic Books.

Mayer, J.D., Roberts, R.D. and Barsade, S.G. (2008) 'Human abilities: emotional intelligence', *Annual Review of Psychology*, 59: 507–536.

Mayer, J.D., Salovey, P. and Caruso, D.R. (2004) 'Emotional intelligence: theory, findings, and implications', *Psychological Inquiry*, 15: 197–215.

Min Toh, S. and Gunz, H. (2009) 'Career-damaging relationships in the workplace: how new immigrants cope with social undermining', paper presented at *EGOS Colloquium*, Barcelona, July 2009.

Nonaka, I. (1994) 'A dynamic theory of organizational knowledge creation', *Organization Science*, 5(1): 14–37.

Oberg, K. (1960) 'Cultural shock: adjustment to new cultural environments', *Practical Anthropology*, July–August: 177–182.

Oddou, G., Mendenhall, M. and Ritchie, J. (2000) 'Leveraging travel as a tool for global leadership development', *Human Resource Management*, 39: 159–172.

Oku, A. (2007) *Intercultural Competencies Required by International Managers in Managing Intercultural Teams*, unpublished thesis, Cranfield: Cranfield University.

Richardson, J. and Mallon, M. (2005) 'Careers interrupted? The case of the self-directed expatriate', *Journal of World Business*, 40: 409–420.

Richardson, J. and Zikic, J. (2007) 'The darker side of an international academic career', *Career Development International*, 12(2): 164–186.

Riusala, K. and Suutari, V. (2004) 'International knowledge transfers through expatriates', *Thunderbird International Business Review*, 46(6): 743–770.

Rogers, B. (1999) 'The expatriate in China – a dying species', in L. Lee (ed.) *Localization in China: Best Practice*, Hong Kong: Asia Law and Practice.

Stahl, G.K., Miller, E. and Tung, R. (2002) 'Towards the boundaryless career: a closer look at the expatriate career concept and the perceived implications of an international assignment', *Journal of World Business*, 37: 216–227.

Sullivan, S.E. (1999) 'The changing nature of careers: A review and research agenda', *Journal of Management*, 25(3): 457–484.

Sullivan, S.E. and Baruch, Y. (2010) 'Advances in career theory and research: critical review and agenda for future exploration', *Journal of Management*, forthcoming.

Suutari, V. and Brewster, C. (2003) 'Repatriation: empirical evidence of a longitudinal study from careers and expectations among Finnish expatriates', *International Journal of Human Resource Management*, 14(7): 1132–1151.

Takeuchi, R., Tesluk, P., Yun, S. and Lepak, D. (2005) 'An integrative view of international experience', *Academy of Management Journal*, 48(1): 85–100.

Teece, D. (1977) 'Technology transfer by multinational firms: the resource costs of transferring technological know-how', *Economic Journal*, 87: 242–261.

Thomas, D.C. and Lazarova, M.B. (2006) 'Expatriate adjustment and performance: a critical review', in G.K. Stahl and I. Björkman (eds) *Handbook of Research in International Human Resource Management*, Cheltenham: Edward Elgar.

Trompenaars, F. and Hampden-Turner, C. (1997) *Riding the Waves of Culture: Understanding Cultural Diversity in Business*, New York: McGraw-Hill.

Tung, R.L. (2004) 'The model global manager?', *Organizational Dynamics*, 33: 243–253.

Wang, P., Tong, T. and Koh, C. (2004) 'An integrated model of knowledge transfer from MNC parent to China subsidiary', *Journal of World Business*, 39: 168–182.

After global assignments

Objectives

This chapter:

- outlines key organizational and individual considerations associated with moving on from an international work assignment;
- explores organizational repatriation support practices and their effects;
- discusses knowledge transfer and management implications of returning from international work;
- identifies and reflects on global career management approaches by organizations;
- explores psychological effects in repatriation;
- explores considerations for organizational HR strategies, policies and practices;
- illuminates organizational, individual and societal global career implications.

Introduction

As organizations have gathered long-term experiences with large flows of internationally mobile workers to and from countries, it has become increasingly clear that the return to one's home country is full of pitfalls. Many surveys (Dickmann et al. 2005; GMAC 2008) and much of the academic literature (Lazarova and Caligiuri 2001; Lazarova and Cerdin 2007) as well as the business press, point out the manifold challenges that individuals and organizations encounter. In short, repatriation can be the 'toughest assignment of all' (Hurn 1999).

So far, we have covered a broad picture of IHRM strategies, structures and processes, diverse forms of international work and careering, have focused on the

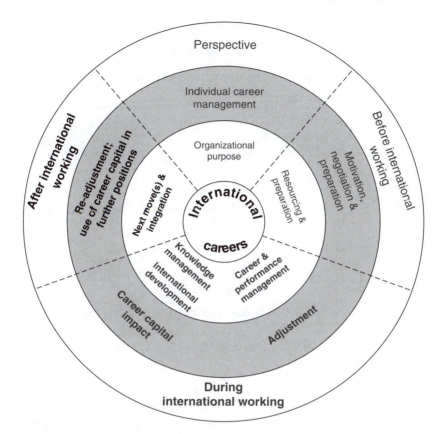

Figure 8.1 International career management
Source: Doherty and Dickmann (2008a)

motivation for global careers, pre-departure issues and the complex interactions of actors, organizations and their contexts during international work. We are now at the stage where global careerists make their next move – either home, which is still the most common form, or on to another foreign assignment. This and the next chapter are devoted to explicating the issues associated with 'moving on' from working abroad.

The attentive reader will notice that the next chapter is entitled 'Outcomes of global work'. The distinction we have drawn is that the current chapter looks predominantly at short- to medium-term issues while the next one concentrates on longer-term career, identity, career capital, organizational and national effects.

We have now reached the last 'segment' of our diagram outlining the intensive interaction of organizations and individuals within global careers. By now, the reader is familiar with our preferred approach to outline both individual and organizational considerations, behaviours and interactions. We will do so again in this chapter, exploring repatriation, retention and knowledge management elements of the 'next move'. In turn, we will describe repatriate psychological effects and their consequences. Moreover, the chapter will outline organizational policies and

Figure 8.2 A framework of global careers: activities and insights into the completion of international work stages

practices, as well as proactive individual behaviour. Because changes in the organizational, national and cultural context have an impact on repatriation, these are also discussed. The overall location in the book is indicated in our overview framework depicted in Figure 8.2.

This chapter focuses strongly on the short- and medium-term outcomes of individuals who work abroad under the auspices of their employing organizations. Issues of self-initiated migration or self-sponsored foreign sojourns for educational purposes are discussed in Chapter 9.

The organizational perspective

Repatriation and retention

During a positive economic climate when firms expand, individuals have better chances in the labour market and might have a higher propensity to leave after international work, in contrast to times of recession or low growth (Huang et al. 2006). Thus, one would expect that during the difficult economic situation that began after August 2007 – i.e. the banking crisis that spread to engulf the wider service and manufacturing sectors – repatriate turnover would be lower. While this might be heavily influenced by the particular industry and capability set of individual returnees, the economic situation in the home country can be considered as one of the factors influencing repatriate turnover and career prospects. In general, however, in the global economy, internationally experienced professionals have become more marketable (Tams and Arthur 2007). Thus, we witness the phenomenon of international migration, influencing HRM practices that need to focus on attraction, development and retention of international talent within multicultural contexts (Dickmann et al. 2008).

Chapter 5 outlined the various organizational drivers to utilize global managers. MNCs often use a combination of reasons, such as control and coordination, knowledge creation, transfer and exploitation, leadership development and quality of resourcing, to staff global management positions. These have different implications for the likely time of 'pay-back' and the importance of retention of global managers (Suutari and Brewster 2000; Dickmann et al. 2006). Moreover, the competitive context, industry and business environment have an impact on organizations' willingness and ability to continue to employ staff returning from IAs or other forms of global work (cf. Chapter 4). Thus, in very volatile times, with staff numbers being reduced by many organizations (as happened in 2008 and 2009 with Citigroup alone announcing more than 70,000 job losses), the risks for individuals in terms of continued employment increase. Moreover, even in 'good times', firms might decide to reorganize with subsequent implications for returning assignees. For instance, Dickmann and Doherty (2006) present a case study of a tobacco firm which had gone through a restructuring and which asked 40 per cent of repatriates to leave the organization.

Moreover, the expectation from expatriation might not live up to its anticipated career benefits. Evidence suggests that expatriates receive fewer intra-organizational promotions compared with their counterparts who did not acquire expatriate experience (Benson and Pattie 2008). Kraimer et al. (2009) found that repatriates reported that they had been demoted and promoted at very similar levels (15 per cent and 17 per cent, respectively). It is thus not surprising that repatriates express dissatisfaction with their intra-organizational career prospects, and voice intentions to leave (Bossard and Peterson 2005) or do actually leave (e.g. Black and Gregersen 1999; Baruch et al. 2002). Repatriate turnover can be approximately double the rate of the rest of the workforce (GMAC 2008).

Reality offers a wide range of options for the outcomes of repatriation. Four categories exist for identifying where people who have gone on an IA have ended up (Borg 1988). Borg found that only 38 per cent of the 200 managers in his study have had a single global assignment and just returned. The rest have either stayed in the country where they were sent (25 per cent), continued their global careers with several consecutive global assignments (22 per cent were still abroad), whereas 15 per cent returned home after such multiple assignments.

Generally, the international experience of global workers is seen as rare, valuable and hard to imitate (Lazarova and Caligiuri 2001). Typically, therefore, MNCs attempt to keep repatriate turnover low. Research analysing 3,450 expatriates found that 15 per cent left their employer in the first reporting period after their assignment (Dickmann and Doherty 2006). A range of activities that are seen by various authors to serve repatriation retention is outlined in Table 8.2 towards the end of this chapter. The various reasons underlying these will be discussed below.

Table 8.1 Distinguishing single and multiple global assignments

	Single assignment abroad	Multiple global assignment
Staying abroad	Naturalized	Cosmopolitan orientation
Returning home	Local orientation	Unsettled

Source: Adapted from Borg (1988)

Lazarova and Caligiuri (2001) suggest 11 organizational HR practices that can lead to successful outcomes of repatriation activities. These are:

1 Pre-departure briefings on what to expect during repatriation

2 Career planning sessions

3 Guarantee/agreement outlining the type of position expatriates will be placed in upon repatriation

4 Mentoring programmes while on assignment

5 Reorientation programmes about the changes in the company

6 Repatriation training seminars on the emotional response following repatriation

7 Financial counselling and financial/tax assistance

8 Lifestyle assistance and counselling on changes likely to occur in expatriates' life upon return

9 Continuous communications with the home office

10 Visible signs that the company values international experience

11 Communications with the home office about the details of the repatriation process

The authors lament that despite widespread awareness about the importance of retaining internationally experienced individuals, companies often fail to capitalize on these resources (Lazarova and Caligiuri 2001). A few years later, research in over 50 companies presented a similar picture with approximately 80 per cent of IM directors viewing repatriation support as important, but only 20 per cent claiming that their organization is good at it (Dickmann et al. 2005). Stahl and Cerdin (2004) indicated in their French-German sample that a large percentage – especially of their French repatriates – were concerned or highly concerned about their career advancement upon repatriation, responsibility and autonomy on the job, compensation package upon repatriation, and their opportunities for using new knowledge and skills. Most organizations indicate that they wish to keep most of their repatriates. However, the authors found that 51 per cent of their German expatriates and 33 per cent of their French expatriates were willing or highly willing to leave their company for a better job in another company. Given that the developmental aspect of IM is growing (see Chapter 5; Kühlmann 2001; Harris and Dickmann 2005; GMAC 2008), this constitutes a major problem.

Case study 8.1 The retention challenge

CigaretteCo, a major international tobacco company, decided in 2003 to consolidate the various mobility approaches that its different divisions had into a single global policy. By 2005 it had established global processes and communicated the policies and approaches to key HR and business managers. The company distinguishes between these key reasons for IM:

- *control and coordination*: business or new opportunities development, extra profit creation, management control or cultural integration;
- *skills transfer*: skills and know-how transfer or training local people (including succession planning); and, in a few cases
- *development*: opportunities for future leaders.

CigaretteCo uses a performance/potential matrix for appraisal purposes. The key target group to go on an assignment would be high performers. Only in exceptional cases – for instance when people are new in the job – managers who were assessed as having high potential but low performance might also be expatriated. There is, therefore, not a strong link into development and talent management. Its Global Policy for Long Term International Assignments, drawn up in 2006, specifies that expatriation purposes include skills transfer and the training of local successors but not any talent management or central development purpose.

While there are international commuters and transferees – this case concentrates on their 100 'true expatriates'. In an interview with an international compensation and benefits manager it was verified that one of the key aims of CigaretteCo is to have cost-effective IM.

Internally, CigaretteCo raises concerns about the long-term effects of their IAs, pointing out that both in career and development they might provide a deal that is below the market average. The company distinguishes three predominant outcomes of expatriation: career progression, a new assignment or redundancy. Company HR managers argued that it would be effective to provide two different 'deals' to expatriates. First, where assignees are likely to get promoted, it focuses on development and performance during the assignment. However, where managers are likely to be made redundant after expatriation, it suggests moving to a transactional relationship with the employee and a focus on the financial package.

There was a high percentage of expatriate redundancies initiated by CigaretteCo in the early years of the twenty-first century. Up to 40 per cent of repatriates were made redundant due to a conscious evaluation of whether everybody who was on an assignment was really needed in the home organization. Further reasons were related to the strong acquisition activity of the firm that led to reorganizations and continued integration activities. In turn, the organization saw some people go to other firms (including competitors) who they would have liked to have kept.

> *Case questions*
>
> 1 What IHRM strategy does CigaretteCo pursue? Given this strategy, what IHRM configuration would suit the firm?
> 2 What advantages are associated with this IM approach? What disadvantages would you identify?
> 3 What are the consequences for global careers? What could be done to strike a balance between the dynamic corporate context, efficiency considerations and global career and retention pressures?
>
> > Case based on information found in Dickmann and Doherty (2006)
> > Cranfield Report for PwC, and follow-up research.

The case shows the need for corporate activities to decrease voluntary repatriate turnover. Ceteris paribus, those companies that are seen as being relatively successful in this seem to integrate their IM within a general career system and to manage the knowing-how, knowing-why and knowing-whom aspects of career capital (Riusala and Suutari 2000; MacDonald and Arthur 2005; Dickmann and Doherty 2008).

A case in point is HSBC, the global bank. The organization distinguishes between long-term development of future leaders and its short-term business needs. The bank strives to increase diversity by having a local manager either as the managing director or the main direct-report to head office in the UK. The local manager should have foreign experience. In terms of long-term leadership planning, all group talent pool incumbents are meant to have at least one international job posting as part of their individual career development. Long-term planning is seen by HSBC as crucial, and the bank draws up plans each year to assess the demand for international assignees for the next year, factoring in business plans, leadership development needs and expected repatriations (HSBC 2005).

With respect to career planning, the role of home sponsors within HSBC can be crucial. The home sponsors are high-ranking bank executives (business heads, chief executives or general managers) who need to establish a good contact with the assignee. Among their responsibilities are to sign off the secondment letter, oversee that international assignees are not slipping off the 'career radar screen' but are instead closely career managed. In terms of *knowing-whom*, these home sponsors are meant to enable superior home–host country networking for expatriates. Further, they are charged with keeping regular contact with the international assignees. Moreover, in terms of *knowing-why* they, and other HSBC professionals, are likely to conduct pre-return conversations with assignees to 'manage expectations'. In addition, they are charged with ensuring that an adequate new role will be found for returnees. This position should ideally allow the returned manager to work with his or her new international capabilities (knowing-how) and networks (knowing-whom). Overall, all three forms of career capital investments are being managed by HSBC (Harris and Dickmann 2005).

While this organizational perspective is useful in outlining some of the activities that firms can engage in to increase their repatriate retention, it is insufficient to explore repatriation fully. First, the organizational context varies substantially and diverse forms of global career and IM policies and practices might be suitable and are practised (Dickmann and Doherty 2008). There is no single best organizational approach to repatriate retention, and various strategies are applied in practice (Baruch and Altman 2002). Second, the decision to remain with an employer also depends on environmental influences (Yan et al. 2002) and the broader economic context (Huang et al. 2006). Third, Lazarova and Cerdin (2007), while acknowledging the organizational perspective of the 'frustrated expatriate' leaving the organization, present a persuasive case that in terms of the 'new career', repatriates can be highly proactive, might engage in boundary-spanning activities, seek to build internal and external networks and attempt to increase their individual exposure to career opportunities. Thus, repatriates have a career agenda of their own which might not necessarily involve their current employer. Lazarova and Cerdin find that both organizational and individual perspectives help to explain repatriate retention. This argument is also put forward by Stevens et al. (2006). In their Japanese sample they investigated repatriate job satisfaction and job attachment. While HR policies and practices could increase repatriate job satisfaction and attachment, the self-adjustment of returning expatriates was found to be more important. This points to the importance of psychological factors in the selection of international assignees in the first place, and indicates the limited impact that organizational practices purely designed to focus on the repatriation phase might have. Moreover, concepts such as 'career activism' might carry different implications depending on whether individuals focus their attention on activities internal or external to the organization. We will return to individual considerations after discussing knowledge management implications of repatriation and further career issues below.

Knowledge transfer

Bartlett and Ghoshal (1989) have argued that the strengths of transnational corporations would be to be locally responsive, globally efficient and worldwide innovative (see Chapter 2). To achieve this, sophisticated knowledge management and the sharing of best practice is highly important (Dickmann and Müller-Camen 2006; Mir and Mir 2009; Zaidman and Brock 2009). However, there are many barriers to knowledge management, which according to Briscoe et al. (2009: 230) include:

- ignorance and lack of relationships;
- lack of a system for sharing;
- belief that knowledge is power;
- lack of trust;
- lack of understanding the value of knowledge;
- fear of negative consequences;
- belief that best practices in one country are not applicable elsewhere;
- language and translation issues;
- superiority and/or condescending attitudes;
- intra-organizational competition.

Many of these barriers might also apply to international working and expatriates. Issues such as intra-organizational rivalry, lack of trust, or knowledge as a source of power are likely to be linked into the perceived reasons why an international assignee is working in the host country. Based on the well known categorization of Edström and Galbraith (1977), Hocking et al. (2004) build a model of principal categories of assignment purposes and link these to role objectives. Knowledge creation, transfer and application are key purposes and are reflected in each of their three categories. Within the business applications category, they list managerial and professional know-how application and technology innovation transfer. Within their organization applications category they count policy transfer/control, best practice systems transfer and coordination. Lastly, within their expatriate learning category, they point to international business/professional experience and the development of a global company perspective, all of which would suffer if the repatriate is not able to use the acquired capabilities in the new location. In short, the creation, transfer and exploitation of knowledge is extremely important for organizations in IM – and continues to be so when individuals return.

Bender and Fish (2000) have pointed out that competition in the learning and innovation environment requires organizations to manage repatriation in a way that it results in the assignees' ability to effectively use acquired skills and experiences throughout the organization. To facilitate this and to increase learning, Bonache and Zárraga-Oberty (2008) have argued that organizations can implement a range of HR policies and practices in order to increase the transfer of knowledge during IAs (see Chapter 7). As we saw, their model basically assumes that an efficient knowledge transfer through expatriates during the assignment needs three conditions: the abilities and motivation of international assignees; the abilities and motivation of local staff; and a good interrelationship. These factors might also be important for repatriate knowledge transfer with an added proviso that the acquired knowledge is perceived to be useful in the working environment upon return. Unfortunately, this 'utility gap' might be rather large. Research by Dickmann et al. (2005) shows that while more than 90 per cent of their surveyed expatriates thought they acquired relevant skills, insights, capabilities and networks during their work abroad, less than half felt that they could use their new capabilities or enhanced social capital. Interviews indicated that respondents linked this to work factors, but also to the scepticism and lack of interest from their immediate colleagues. Clearly, this limits the 'forward' and 'reverse' knowledge transfer upon the end of an assignment and has prompted some commentators to suggest that individuals, if possible, should strive to go to perceived leading-edge locations or centres of excellence within their firms in order to gain new capabilities that are also symbolically seen as useful (Doherty and Dickmann 2009).

Retention, performance and immediate career effects of repatriates

In an ideal organizational world, the performance of repatriates would be relatively high. While there is a honeymoon period when individuals go to work abroad (see Chapter 7), maybe one could expect another honeymoon period of individuals who are happy to return to work 'at home'. Certainly, one might expect a high degree of cognitive confidence of individuals returning home with some appreciation of the chance to show how they have developed and what they can use in terms of their new capabilities and networks.

Unfortunately, the reality looks radically different. International assignees return and often suffer a range of emotional readjustment problems that are described in more detail below. One of the contributory factors is that they perceive they have lost some of their special status or, as one respondent described to one of this book's authors: 'Here I am somebody. When I return, I am a nobody.' Moreover, most repatriates earn significantly less upon return. While some companies have introduced tie-over pay to alleviate the most immediate financial shock of returning, this is often either a lump sum or some additional payment lasting for up to one year. In nine detailed case studies in engineering, fast-moving consumer goods and professional service companies, researchers from Cranfield School of Management teamed up with PwC and Saratoga to analyse more than 3,000 expatriates' career, performance, compensation and retention data over time (Dickmann and Doherty 2006).

All case companies had a long-term IA policy document which typically set out the basic ground rules for international moves. In the majority of cases, individuals' practices were designed to leave the individuals no worse off in their destination country – in fact, calculating direct compensation effects (50 per cent), costs for additional long-term benefits (11 per cent) and other assignment-related allowances (32 per cent) revealed that firms paid almost twice as much to their expatriates than before. Typically, the direct pay increase would be massively curtailed and the long-term benefits and assignment-related allowances stopped altogether upon return.

These effects were moderated by promotion. In the Cranfield, PwC and Saratoga sample, 24 per cent of returners were promoted during their year of return, thus enabling the organization to take away the expatriate financial benefits and yet increase 'base pay' due to the career move. In comparison to their non-expatriated peers, this promotion rate was significantly higher. Retention, on the other hand, was much lower than the average management retention data in each of the nine companies. Repatriates had a higher than 15 per cent likelihood of leaving the organization – in most cases this was voluntary turnover.

Performance development was measured over time and, with respect to performance during the assignment, commented upon in Chapter 7. Long-term performance effects – those that emerged after repatriation – were on aggregate positive. Of companies' 'top performers', 32 per cent were expatriated, and while the percentage of repatriates in the top evaluation category dropped slightly shortly after return (to about 29 per cent), it increased to 38 per cent in the long term. Long-term performance effects of IAs might be positive, possibly one of the reasons why those CEOs of Fortune 1000 companies who had been on an IA in their careers happened to earn more on average than their CEO colleagues who did not have longer term foreign work experience (Hamori and Kakarika 2009).

Overall, for most organizations and in many circumstances it will be important to retain repatriates, not only due to the large investment they have undertaken but also because of an additional range of reasons. These include most prominently the development of global leaders, knowledge transfer and exploitation, and the symbolic message they are giving to potential future and current expatriates, which has the power to influence their psychological contract. There are many activities that an organization can undertake to manage global careers and, in particular, the repatriation phase. Lazarova and Caligiuri's 11 policies and the approaches of HSBC and other firms can give valuable insights into ideas that might have to be tailored to the specific organizational environment. However, taking a German proverb that stresses that the 'bill has to be settled with the inn-keeper' we have to take the individual perspective as key to repatriation success.

The individual perspective

Reverse culture shock

Considering the repatriation process, HR managers, line managers and colleagues often underestimate the problems that might arise from returning home. While some problems might be due to managerial and career issues, it has become clear that a major factor is the reverse culture shock (RCS). It refers to the surprise and shock people encounter upon their return home. The reasons are due to multiple changes. Some of the key ones are noted below.

People change The expatriate has changed; the people who stayed 'at home' have changed. The foreign sojourn provided the expatriate with an invaluable experience. He or she might have been faced with the challenging role of the head of operation, possibly for the first time in their career. They had to make strategic decisions, be in charge, and hold extensive responsibility. Returning home typically means serving as a 'cog in the machine', and the experience gained is not, or little, appreciated (Baruch 2003).

Firms change While the expatriate is away, many changes occur in the firm. The most striking one may be a full collapse or disappearance of the company. Mergers and acquisitions change the shape of the firm, and can cause full sections to be outsourced or closed. Even more subtle changes would have a strong impact – restructuring, downsizing, new market focus, are just some types of change that would surprise or cause the repatriate certain upset. Some of these are outlined in detail above.

Cultures change People learn to do things differently, sometimes in better ways. They can realize that others utilize improved ways than those applied at home. Can they persuade their former colleagues to improve according to the newly acquired experience?

Being away means being disconnected from one's original networks, and missing out on important and less important events. It creates 'black holes' of knowledge

---

Box 8.1 Driving

In some Mediterranean countries, flashing your light when approaching a junction means 'I am entering the junction – look out'. When an expatriate from such a country visits the UK they realize that flashing your light when approaching a junction means 'I see you – go ahead, I will wait'. Assuming they survived the first 'almost-accident' that might follow from such discrepancy in driving culture, they might learn that being polite and considerate in driving can be useful to the general flow of traffic, and the inner feelings of the driver.

Upon returning home they might find that some of their local old habits are not as good as the ones in the country they have just spent some time in, adopting new norms and ways of behaviour.

---

about what has happened at home while being away. People might become out of touch, feeling disconnected from their former culture, yet do not really feel part of the new culture that has now been left behind.

What can be done about the RCS? The model in Figure 8.3 and Baruch (2004: 234) lists possible impact factors that might influence the existence and level of RCS.

Baruch's (2004) model considers antecedents, moderators and outcomes of the RCS. We will discuss each one below.

Success on the assignment will set the mental state of the repatriate, and will determine his or her reputation within the organization as someone who achieved much or a little. It is taken that success leads to further success, whereas failure might lead to negative outcomes, including simply leaving the firm.

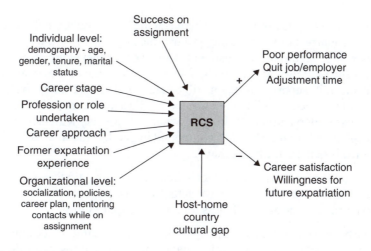

Figure 8.3 Reverse culture shock
Source: Baruch (2004)

Personal demography includes factors that were widely studied in the literature, and can influence adjustment to a change. A supporting family, in particular the spouse, will make the process smoother than, for example, a single parent, who will have to handle a number of family issues upon return.

More than age, the career stage is a factor influencing the repatriation. More senior expatriates, in particular those for whom the expatriation was a preparation to an executive role, are likely to know exactly what they are coming to, while others might have little idea.

The profession is another factor – if the expatriate works in a technical role, the geography and culture are of less relevance, and the major factor is whether or not s/he managed to keep track of the technological progress 'at home'. The destination country can be a moderator – staying in an IT role in a third-world country might mean staying behind whereas moving to a country with advanced technology could improve the human capital of the expatriate, and the repatriation will be much easier.

Career approach or attitude is an essential factor, and we envisage people who hold a protean career attitude to find it much easier to repatriate. Lastly, past experience can be instrumental in shortening the adjustment period.

At the organizational level, much depends on the strategies, policies and practices. For example, global firms should recognize that repatriation requires attention and perhaps introduce repatriation programmes. Part of it should start while assignees are still working abroad. As described in the case above, having a home mentor or sponsor is one element. Home visits can be another one, and having succession planning helps in setting out a realistic repatriation process. Much is also up to the firm's strategy of managing expatriation (see Chapter 7), where the 'Global' firm will have well-tried routes; the 'Emissary' will need much individual support; the 'Professional' may have no problem as the expatriation is 'bought-out', and the 'Peripheral' will have the task of reality crisis management (Baruch and Altman 2002).

An interesting factor is the gap between the home country culture and that of the host country. Logic would suggest that the larger the gap, the tougher it will be to overcome repatriation adjustment. The reason is that while on expatriation the person and their family got used to the local culture, adapted to it, and adopted elements of it – upon returning it will be challenging to re-adjust. Yet, when the gap is very large, people might not even try to adjust and relate to it. For example, there are cases of expatriates' 'villages', where people stay with their home country colleagues and friends (e.g. in a compound in Saudi-Arabia), and for them returning home is to the same home they knew.

The outcomes one might expect to be influenced by are factors like time for adjustment, tendency to quit (or actually quit), performance level, and, relating to expatriation, the agreeableness for a future expatriation.

We have argued at the beginning of the book that careers – despite having become more boundaryless – are a relational phenomenon (Rousseau 1995; Baruch and Altman 2002). While transactional work arrangements have a more stringent focus on immediate or short-term pay-back and an emphasis on economic issues, relational contracts are longer term and contain economic and socio-emotional exchanges (Stroh et al. 2000; Conway and Briner 2005). Expatriation and repatriation are more relational than transactional (Harvey 1997; Doherty et al. 2008).

Hyder and Lövblad (2007) outline a longitudinal model of the repatriation process concentrating on the organizational goal of retention. In parallel to the structure of last chapters, they distinguish between motives and other factors before repatriation takes place. These are principally based on earlier international work experiences and information as well as distinguishing work, interaction and general expectations. These are similar variables to the 'anticipatory adjustment' variables that Black et al. (1992) identified. Hyder and Lövblad (2007) suggest that experiences and expectations before repatriation influence what happens during repatriation. During the repatriation process they distinguish work and organization, training and support and non-work issues. Moreover, demographic factors and cultural identity changes influence the repatriation experience and retention.

Case study 8.2 Retention of returnees through general career and job needs focus

Due to a lack of data because of limited measurement systems, many organizations continue to make the often very expensive 'leap of faith' that IAs will result in pay-offs in terms of business benefits and individual career impact. For example, a range of issues has been highlighted in the literature critiquing the received wisdom of the utility, particularly longer-term, of expatriation (Stahl and Cerdin 2004; Doherty and Dickmann 2005). If companies are to reap the benefits of IAs then short- and, particularly, longer-term issues such as repatriate performance, retention over the longer term and promotion as a proxy for added value to the organization become important factors.

Company Black is a globally operating service organization with more than 100,000 employees. Within Company Black IAs are business driven not developmental, and objectives are set for the role not the individual or the assignment. This clearly articulated business rationale means that IAs are not considered a must for career progression per se, however, it does generate a focus on how IAs fit within talent management. The succession planning process considers the experiences required by individuals to facilitate their progress and maintain a talent flow within the company. Thus, IAs are positioned as one of the critical experiences valued within the general career structure of the organization as a whole.

Since assignments are business driven and role based, the push comes via the job evaluation system. Promotion during assignment is regularly attained and a number of expatriates come back to a promoted role. Data on internal promotion of expatriates shows a consistent trend of around a third being promoted on return. Although there is no guaranteed return home for expatriates (because positions are role-vacancy driven) the organization reports a consistently high retention rate over time. Combined with longer-term (more than 2 years returned) consistently improving performance, these data would indicate the potential for good longer-term utilization of skills within the organization with benefits to both company and individual potentially accruing.

From Dickmann and Doherty (2005)

Lazarova and Cerdin (2007: 423) outline a theoretical repatriation framework that distinguishes the traditional (organizational) from an emerging (proactive individual and environmental context) perspective.

The organizational perspective – most obviously the IM strategy, policies and practices linked to repatriation – have been discussed above. These include the repatriation approach of the organization, knowledge management and transfer outcomes, retention, performance and hierarchical career effects. Many of the available insights use the perspective of what would serve the organization's goals. In contrast, Lazarova and Cerdin (2007) add two further perspectives. What they describe as a proactive perspective includes the environmental context, which looks at the available employment opportunities for the repatriate. While the macro-economic situation has an impact on the availability of opportunities

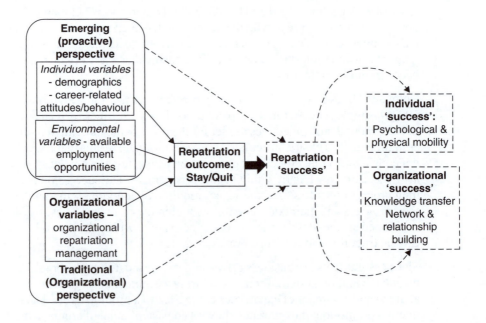

Figure 8.4 Proposed theoretical framework for repatriation success

(Huang et al. 2006), factors residing in the individual will shape the repatriation outcome. Lazarova and Cerdin point out demographics and career-related attitudes and behaviours.

Individuals often suffer stress within their families upon return, perceive a financial loss and lower social esteem (Dickmann et al. 2005). Sometimes, they accept a demotion in order to stay with their company which results in less important jobs at lower salaries or wages. Lazarova and Cerdin (2007) direct our attention to individual success factors which include psychological and physical mobility. In terms of physical mobility a large majority of repatriates consider leaving their employer (Stahl and Cerdin 2004). A considerable number leave their employer within one year of repatriation (Suutari and Brewster 2003). Older figures indicate a 10–25 per cent repatriate turnover (Black 1992; Solomon 1995) and more recent data from 881 returnees indicates a repatriate turnover that is twice as high as that of their non-expatriated management peers (Dickmann et al. 2006). For most companies – and especially those that have a high instance of developmental assignees – this level of attrition is seen as too high and a potential waste of investment. The one piece of good news for organizations in repatriation – the 'toughest assignment of all' (Hurn 1999) – is that Dickmann et al. found that those repatriates who stayed with their employer in the first year after return are very likely to stay several more years. Their cumulative churn rate is so low that within three years the retention differences between former expatriates and non-assigned peers were not significant.

Summary and learning points

This chapter has focused on organizational and individual perspectives associated with the immediate period before, during and after returning from an IA. It has developed an overview of some of the pertinent issues and drawn up a recommendation for good organizational policies and practices as depicted in Table 8.2.

Table 8.2 summarizes the key organizational activities that can be designed to further expatriate retention. It builds on a range of academic and professional insights and depicts the manifold considerations, strategies, policies and practices that organizations can employ. There are two issues that are difficult to 'list' in such a table. First, the 'gestalt' of the organizational approach, its communication and perceived acceptability to key stakeholders will be important in shaping the expectations and the 'international repatriation-related psychological contract' between global careerists and their employers. Second, the broader, probably dynamic, context of the organization and the returning individuals is not depicted and might pose serious challenges to the success of retention practices. The following chapter will shed further light on these issues.

Key learning points include:

• The area of repatriation is perceived to be one of the most difficult to manage for organizations and individuals.

Table 8.2 Good practices in expatriate retention

Area	Policies and Practices such as:
Organizational strategy and structure	• Clear and attractive strategy to internationalise • Attractive degree of existing internationalisation • Little or no significant gap between statements of top management and implementation • Adequate organizational configuration • High kudos of international work
IM policies and practices	• Staffing policies are perceived to be fair or advantageous • Selection looks at a range of factors, including personality factors linked into adjustment and self-adjustment upon return • Pre-return preparation for the job • Ongoing support for time after return • Long-range planning for repatriation • Networking opportunities • Continuous communication with home
Career	• Long-term career planning • Re-entry planning • Career advancement • Mentor system/international work sponsor system
Development	• Systematic development of professional skills • Systematic development of personal skills • Systematic development of leadership skills • Repatriation seminars on the emotional response • Financial and tax counselling, advice and help for time after return
Job variables	• Job challenge • Ability to use new global capabilities • No reduced responsibility and autonomy
Financial impact	• Rewards for pursuing an IA • Rewards for developing an international perspective • Rewards for developing a worldwide network • Rewards for developing global skills, abilities and knowledge • Tie-over pay
Personal drivers & expectations	• Pre-return and after return dialogues to manage expectations/ build realistic pre-return expectations • Briefing and update regarding organizational structure, goals, politics and changes in the new locations
Family	• Help for partner to find meaningful activity such as job and career re-entry • Help for family to (re)settle

Source: Based on sources such as: Stahl et al. (2002); Lazarova and Caligiuri (2001) (see also Lazarova and Cerdin (2007)); Dickmann et al.,(2008); Hocking et al. (2004); Doherty et al. (2008)

- Organizations aim at increasing the retention of returnees, especially those who are seen as high performers and future organizational leaders. They are also keen on demonstrating to potential future international assignees that working abroad has positive pay-offs.
- Firms also strive to have good knowledge management in all aspects associated with their IM approach. This includes the generation, diffusion and exploitation of knowledge before, during and also after an assignment. In a highly globalized world this aspect is increasingly important.
- Individuals want good management of their return, help during the repatriation phase for resettlement of themselves and their families and, above all, a meaningful job.
- The existence and extent of the reverse culture shock (RCS) has a substantial impact on performance, career satisfaction, retention and willingness for future expatriation. This chapter presents organizational activities how to manage RCS (see also Figure 8.3).
- Writers have used several perspectives when considering repatriation. These include the organizational management of IM, the proactive management by individuals of their own career paths, the subjective perspective regarding psychological elements of mobility and long-term views of repatriation as the middle of careers rather than the end of an assignment.
- The chapter has presented several viewpoints on how organizations and individuals can manage IM and has provided case study evidence for real-life examples.

References

Bartlett, C. and Ghoshal, S. (1989) *Managing Across Borders*, London: Hutchinson Business Books.

Baruch, Y. (2003) 'Career systems in transition: a normative model for career practices', *Personnel Review*, 32(2): 231–251.

Baruch, Y. (2004) *Managing Careers: Theory and Practice*, Harlow: FT-Prentice Hall/ Pearson.

Baruch, Y. and Altman, Y. (2002) 'Expatriation and repatriation in MNC: a taxonomy', *Human Resource Management*, 41(2): 239–259.

Baruch, Y., Steele, D. and Quantrill, J. (2002) 'Management of expatriation and repatriation for novice global player', *International Journal of Manpower*, 23(7): 659–671.

Bender, S. and Fish, A. (2000) 'The transfer of knowledge and the retention of expertise: the continuing need for global assignments', *Journal of Knowledge Management*, 4(2): 125–137.

Benson, G.S. and Pattie, M. (2008) 'Is expatriation good for my career? The impact of expatriate assignments on perceived and actual career outcomes', *International Journal of Human Resource Management*, 19(9): 1636–1653.

Black, J.S. (1992) 'Coming home: the relationship of expatriate expectations with repatriate adjustment and job performance', *Human Relations*, 45(2): 177–192.

Black, J.S. and Gregersen, H.B. (1999) 'The right way to manage expats', *Harvard Business Review*, 77(2): 52–63.

Black, J.S., Gregersen, H.B. and Mendenhall, M. (1992) 'Toward a theoretical framework of repatriation adjustment', *Journal of International Business*, 2(4): 737–760.

Bonache, J. and Zárraga-Oberty, C. (2008) 'Determinants of the success of international assignees as knowledge transferors: a theoretical framework', *The International Journal of Human Resource Management*, 19(1): 1–18.

Borg, M. (1988) *International Transfer of Managers in Multinational Corporations*, Stockholm: Almqvist and Wiksell Int.

Bossard, A.B. and Peterson, R.B. (2005) 'The repatriate experience as seen by American expatriates', *Journal of World Business*, 40(1): 9–28.

Briscoe, D., Schuler, R. and Claus, L. (2009) *International Human Resource Management: Policies and Practices for Multinational Enterprises*, 3rd edn, Routledge: New York.

Conway, N. and Briner, R. (2005) *Understanding the Psychological Contracts at Work: A Critical Evaluation of Theory and Research*, Oxford: Oxford University Press.

Dickmann, M. and Doherty, N. (2006) *Measuring the Value of International Assignments*, report for PwC UK Geodesy: Cranfield School of Management, England.

Dickmann, M. and Doherty, N. (2008) 'Exploring the career capital impact of international assignments within distinct organisational contexts', *British Journal of Management*, 19: 145–161.

Dickmann, M. and Müller-Camen, M. (2006) 'A typology of international human resource management strategies and processes', *International Journal of Human Resource Management*, 17(4): 580–601.

Dickmann, M., Doherty, N. and Johnson, A. (2006) *Measuring the Value of International Assignments*, London: PricewaterhouseCoopers and Cranfield School of Management, UK.

Dickmann, M., Doherty, N. and Mills, T. (2008) 'Exploring differences of drivers of company-sent and self-initiated expatriates', paper presented at the *Academy of Management Symposium* 'New global nomads: Examining diverse forms of international mobility', Anaheim, CA, August.

Dickmann, M., Wigley-Jones, R. and Wignall, D. (2005) *Understanding and Avoiding the Barriers to International Mobility*, London: PricewaterhouseCoopers.

Doherty, N. and Dickmann, M. (2005) 'The symbolic capital of international assignments: linking career capital accumulation to human capital utilization', paper presented at the *21st EGOS Colloquium*, Berlin, Germany, 29 June–2 July.

Doherty, N. and Dickmann, M. (2009) 'Exploring the symbolic capital of international assignments', *International Journal of Human Resource Management*, 20(2): 301–320.

Doherty, N., Brewster, C., Suutari, V. and Dickmann, M. (2008) 'Repatriation: the end or the middle?', in M. Dickmann, C. Brewster and P. Sparrow (eds) *International Human Resource Management – A European Perspective*, London: Routledge.

Edström, A. and Galbraith, J.R. (1977) 'Transfer of managers as a coordination and control strategy in multinational organizations', *Administrative Science Quarterly*, 22(2): 248–263.

GMAC Global Relocation Services (2008) *Global Relocation Trends: 2008 Survey Report*. Oak Brook, IL: GMAC Global Relocation Services.

Hamori, M. and Kakarika, M. (2009) 'External labor market strategy and career success: CEO careers in Europe and the United States', *Human Resource Management*, 48(3): 355–378.

Harris, H. and Dickmann, M. (2005) *The CIPD Guide on International Management Development*, London: The Chartered Institute of Personnel and Development.

Harvey, M. (1997) 'Dual-career expatriates: expectations, adjustment and satisfaction with international relocation', *Journal of International Business Studies*, 28(3): 627–658.

Hocking, J.B., Brown, M. and Harzing, A.-W. (2004) 'A knowledge transfer perspective of strategic assignment purposes and their path-dependent outcomes', *International Journal of Human Resource Management*, 15(3): 565–586.

HSBC (2005) 'Group international secondment policy', Internal document. February.

Huang, I., Lin, H. and Chuang, C. (2006) 'Constructing factors related to worker retention', *International Journal of Manpower*, 27(5): 491–508.

Hurn, B. (1999) 'Repatriation: the toughest assignment of all', *Industrial and Commercial Training*, 31(6): 224–228.

Hyder, A. and Lövblad, M. (2007) 'The repatriation process: a realistic approach', *Career Development International*, 12(3): 264–281.

Kraimer, M.L., Shaffer, M.A. and Bolino, M. (2009) 'The influence of expatriate and repatriate experiences on career advancement and repatriate retention', *Human Resource Management*, 48: 27–47.

Kühlmann, T. (2001) 'The German approach to developing leaders via expatriation', in M. Mendenhall, T. Kühlmann and G. Stahl *Developing Global Business Leaders: Policies, Processes and Innovations*, Westport, CT: Quorum.

Lazarova, M. and Caligiuri, P. (2001) 'Retaining repatriates: the role of organizational support practices', *Journal of World Business*, 36(4): 389 401.

Lazarova, M. and Cerdin, J.-L. (2007) 'Revisiting repatriation concerns: organizational support versus career and contextual influences', *Journal of International Business Studies*, 38(3): 404–429.

MacDonald, S. and Arthur, N. (2005) 'Connecting career management to repatriation adjustment', *Career Development International*, 10(2): 145–158.

Mir, R. and Mir, A. (2009) 'From the colony to the corporation: studying knowledge transfer across international boundaries', *Group and Organization Management*, 34: 90–113.

Riusala, K. and Suutari, V. (2000) 'Expatriation and careers: perspectives of expatriates and spouses', *Career Development International*, 5(2): 81–90.

Rousseau, D.M. (1995) *Psychological Contracts in Organizations*, Thousand Oaks, CA: Sage.

Solomon, C.M. (1995) 'Repatriation: up, down or out?', *Personnel Journal*, 74(1): 28–37.

Stahl, G. and Cerdin, J.-L. (2004) 'Global careers in French and German multinational corporations', *Journal of Management Development*, 23(9): 885–902.

Stahl, G.K., Miller, E. and Tung, R. (2002) 'Toward the boundaryless career: a closer look at the expatriate career concept and the perceived implications of an international assignment', *Journal of World Business*, 37: 216–227.

Stevens, M., Oddou, G., Fuquay, N., Bird, A. and Mendenhall, M. (2006) 'HR factors affecting repatriate job satisfaction and job attachment for Japanese managers', *International Journal of Human Resource Management*, 17(5): 831–841.

Stroh, L., Gregersen, H. and Black, J.S. (2000) 'Triumphs and tragedies: expectations and commitments upon repatriation', *International Journal of Human Resource Management*, 11(4): 681–697.

Suutari, V. and Brewster, C. (2000) 'Making their own way: international experience through self-initiated foreign assignments', *Journal of World Business*, 35: 417–436.

Suutari, V. and Brewster, C. (2003) 'Repatriation: empirical evidence of a longitudinal study from careers and expectations among Finnish expatriates', *International Journal of Human Resource Management*, 14(7): 1132–1151.

Tams, S. and Arthur, M. (2007) 'Studying careers across cultures: distinguishing international, cross-cultural and globalization perspectives', *Career Development International*, 12(1): 86–98.

Yan, A., Zhu, G. and Hall, D. (2002) 'International assignments for career building: a model of agency relationships and psychological contracts', *Academy of Management Review*, 27(3): 373–391.

Zaidman, N. and Brock, D.M. (2009) 'Knowledge transfer within multinationals and their foreign subsidiaries: a culture-context approach', *Group and Organization Management*, 34: 297–329.

9 The outcomes of global work

Objectives

This chapter:

- describes various approaches geared to assess the outcomes of global careers and international work;
- outlines five principles to evaluate international work experiences;
- identifies repatriation as the middle of global careers and depicts the 'career wobble' that some people experience upon returning from working abroad;
- develops a contextual framework of international work experiences and associated outcomes;
- investigates the longer-term impact of international work on individuals, organizations and nation states;
- depicts reasoned actions for immigration;
- summarizes organizational activities before, during and after expatriation to facilitate positive outcomes such as retention, the acquisition and use of career capital, career satisfaction and adequate employment;
- illuminates some of the key challenges associated with managing global careers in a dynamic environment.

Introduction

This chapter looks at individual, organizational and national outcomes of global careers. It is intimately linked to the preceding chapter that illuminated the short and medium-term effects of working abroad. Here, we want to widen the perspective and depict the interactions between organizations, individuals and their wider

Figure 9.1 A framework of global careers: long-term individual, organizational and societal outcomes

context in more depth. The shaded part of Figure 9.1 gives the reader an overview of where we are in our exploration of global careers.

The outcomes of global mobility will be discussed at several levels. We will deal with the outcomes for the individual and his or her family. We will discuss the outcomes for the employing organization – both the home and host operations – and, finally, we will refer to the outcomes in the wider context.

The expatriation literature that attempts to evaluate the outcomes of IM and global careers often refers to high costs (Sparrow et al. 2004), expatriate failure (Mendenhall and Oddou 1985), early return (Dowling and Welch 2004), poor or insufficient adjustment (Black et al. 1992; Haslberger 2005) and repatriate turnover (Bolino 2007). These expressions used by academics carry negative connotations. In turn, IM practitioners seem to focus on the cost implications of working abroad and find it hard to assess the benefits associated with global careers. This chapter will outline some of the considerations and principles involved in exploring the outcomes of international work (cf. Dickmann and Doherty 2008) before drawing up a conceptual model.

For other types of global mobility and international work, such as globetrotting, virtual careers and immigration, the outcomes vary and involve a wide range of outcomes to the individuals and their families.

At the organizational level, the implications for employers occur at both the home HQ and in the subsidiaries. The implications relate to having more developed and trained employees with improved cultural intelligence (see Chapter 4). Host countries become acquainted with representatives from the centre and, at the same time, can influence the centre too.

National outcomes such as the brain drain and brain circulation issues have captured much attention in the academic literature as well as with the media. We argue that the brain drain phenomenon is not simple and has a number of implications.

Brain drain – the Industrial Revolution at a global scale?

In the eighteenth and nineteenth centuries, Europe underwent a significant change. National economies transformed themselves from agrarian, where the majority of the population were working the land, to industrial economies. There was a massive migration from villages to cities. Industry became the magnet which brought individuals from the villages, leaving there a tiny fraction of the population. Many were attracted to the wealth and opportunities of the towns and cities. The phenomenon of today might resemble a similar trend – at an international level. However, legal implications often prevent a mass move from one country to another, e.g. from Mexico to the USA.

In essence, we want to address the question of what are the outcomes of global careers and argue that it is important to use an integrative perspective, to factor in organizational and individual goals, to be sensitive to time, to explore costs and benefits and to take account of various context factors. These five conditions are discussed below before we draw up a framework of international experiences and outcomes that explicate individual, organizational and national effects.

Principles for assessing the outcomes of international work

Assessing the outcomes of global careers depends on the perspective. Much of the available literature has concentrated either on individual or organizational factors in relation to the outcomes of global careers. Therefore, studies used discrete approaches to measuring the outcomes of global work, either focusing on individual versus organizational elements or looking only at expatriation or repatriation (Yan et al. 2002). An example is Harzing and Christensen's (2004: 622) treatment of expatriate failure which concentrates on the organizational perspective. They saw it as 'the inability of the expatriate or repatriate to perform according to the expectations of the organisation'. Moreover, it is tempting to just concentrate on IM policies and practices that organizations use. A range of articles, e.g. those by Caligiuri and Lazarova (2001) or McCaughey and Bruning (2005) describe good IM policies and practices as outlined in other parts of this book. In turn, many writers concentrate on how international workers themselves evaluate the outcomes of working abroad (Richardson and Mallon 2005; Kohonen 2005; Cappellen and Janssens 2005).

However, we have consistently argued in this book that in traditional expatriation arrangements there is a high dependency of individuals on organizations due to the substantial risk the individual and his/her family are taking. In turn the costs to the firm are especially high, and the dependency of the organization on the individual is substantial, due to the scarcity and criticality of employees who work abroad (cf. Larsen 2004). Thus, the assessment of the outcomes of global careers needs to incorporate both an individual and an organizational perspective. Moreover, as we outline in the latter part of this chapter, wider perspectives such as that of a nation state are useful to consider.

Assessing the outcomes of global careers depends on goals

The contexts of each organization employing people who work abroad and each individual who has an international career are different. We discussed the individual reasons for IM extensively in Chapter 5. Whether key drivers are individual careers, family, adventure, learning and development, security or monetary incentives, to name but a few, they will have a strong impact on the person's own evaluation of the outcomes of working in a foreign country. The goals of individuals are highly diverse.

Equally, there is a large range of organizational reasons in terms of what staff should achieve when working abroad (cf. Chapters 2 and 5). While the achievement of specific objectives will be important to the employer, HR instruments such as performance management will depend on other staff with whom the person interacts. Moreover, retention activities have a high dependency on the market environment and possible organizational changes such as a restructuring. To assess the outcomes of global careers for an organization, the specific context and underlying causes for the development of environmental factors will be important (Harzing and Christensen 2004; Dickmann et al. 2006). Again, the possible objectives of organizations display many variations. They are likely to include generic goals such as the retention of expatriates and repatriates, high performance and good promotion prospects as an indication of the development of future global leaders.

Assessing the outcomes of global careers needs to be time sensitive

Bonache et al. (2001) claim that the outcomes of expatriation need to be measured at different times, depending on the various purposes of the assignments. For instance, if Shell sends a drilling expert to Nigeria because it cannot find local expertise, the 'pay-off' is likely to take place during the assignment. In contrast, a developmental assignment for Mars with the aim to build the future leaders of the corporation is likely to experience much of the 'pay-off' in the years after the return of the individual. In a similar vein, McNulty and Tharenou (2004) and McNulty et al. (2009) claim that a long-term perspective is needed if one is to evaluate the outcomes of international work. The authors hold that return on investment for organizations is not widely used in firms. Where it is used it is poorly calculated; and it is not widely researched by academics. Overall, if we look at the outcomes of global careers we would do well to incorporate a temporal element in the assessment.

Assessing the outcomes of global careers needs to incorporate benefits and costs

Assessing the outcomes of global careers needs to capture both positive and negative effects. While this principle looks very obvious, there seems to be a tendency of organizations to think in terms of expatriation costs – which they find easier to assess – and less so in terms of the benefits associated with individual staff working abroad. Articles dealing with expatriate failure often concentrate on the cost involved in early return (Black et al. 1992). However, it is also important to assess the costs of underperformance during IAs (Bolino 2007). And yet, early returners might move because they have fulfilled their objectives before the planned time or because there are other career options suddenly available (and they were asked to come 'home'). There are tentative indications that early returners might experience a more rapid career advancement (Dickmann et al. 2006). It seems appropriate to assess both the perceived benefits of global careers by individuals and their employers and contrast these with associated costs. This would allow us to move beyond an efficiency perspective towards looking at effectiveness.

Assessing the outcomes of global careers needs to be relative

Measures of expatriate performance, retention or career advancement are proposed above. Although some 'benchmark' might be available through the work of organizations such as Saratoga, data is likely to differ according to sector, managerial hierarchy, function etc. Therefore, it is difficult to say whether a 5 per cent expatriate churn or a 20 per cent promotion rate of returnees is good or not. However, Dickmann and Doherty (2007) argue that if this data is compared with a non-expatriated, matched peer group it becomes more sensitive to the organizational context and, thus, more meaningful. Case study 9.1 depicts a strategic view on IM with measurements comparing international mobile staff with non-expatriated peers.

Case study 9.1 Measuring the outcomes of international mobility

The strategic and operational context of Green

The case company 'Green' employed more than 30,000 people in over 60 countries. Worldwide, it is among the top five companies in its industry. One of its strategic objectives was to increase international activity, often through acquisitions. The company's HR strategy is centred around David Ulrich's ideas of what an HR function should entail and focuses especially on the role of being HR Business Partners and supporting employees. Within Green, an increasing number of global or regional opportunities are arising and, therefore, the company aims to 'build a cadre of managers who have multi-culture and multi-country experience'. Foreign work experience in at least two countries outside one's own home country is now seen to be a necessary condition to become a senior manager. The long-term assignment policy is based around the principles of fair treatment, development of international leaders, encouragement of mobility and competitive efficiency.

The length of an IA is normally up to three years but may be extended to a total of five years. After this, the assignee would be most likely localized. The host company is responsible for bearing all the cost of an IA. Green pursues a flexible approach to expatriate selection in that either individuals can 'push' or the organization can 'pull' for international experience. All positions above junior management are advertised internationally on the company's intranet. Approximately 70 per cent of expatriates have the primary purpose of skills-gap filling, about 20 per cent serve coordination and control purposes, with the remainder being developmental assignments.

The organization used IM to build knowing-how competencies as part of its career progression system. The company planned the movement of people into key roles. The competencies gained as part of an IA fed into the global Performance Management process. Performance patterns over the span of the IA and beyond stood out.

Performance during and after an IA

While a reasonable or good performance is paramount to be selected for an IA, only 2.4 per cent of all expatriates are in the high performance category. This number is, at 1.5 per cent, even lower during their first year in the foreign location, a pattern that points to the culture shock and other challenges that arise for new expatriates.

During the international work, which lasted on average three years, 7.2 per cent of assignees improved their performance while only about 0.5 per cent received lower performance ratings. An HR interviewee explained that while an IA is seen as an 'opportunity to prove yourself' there was still a perception that international experience per se was not much valued in the organization. She concluded that 'only performance during an international assignment is your ticket back'. Another HR expert added that 'Green has a strong, harmonic culture'. This social coordination might enable people working abroad to find their bearings more quickly and, subsequently, aid performance. Lastly, both interviewees pointed to the ongoing support from the home country. Given that Green has forced performance rankings and has had the same performance and appraisal system over the reporting period, expatriate performance figures are indeed developing better than their non-expatriated peers.

Returnees displayed even more positive performance evaluations. Twenty per cent improved their performance ratings in the first year after return and none of the 20 returnees in 2005 had received a lower performance assessment. With 17.6 per cent rated top performers, this was comparable to their non-expatriated peers in 2005 and constituted a substantially higher figure than that for current expatriates (2.4 per cent). Given that generally returnees are placed in 'bigger roles', this is a positive development.

Reflecting on the whole expatriate and repatriate performance over time, an HR executive summarized the success factor as having a clear career path geared to the individual's expectations, the use of a mentor and/or coach and a high degree of pro-activity by the individual assignee coupled with intensive networking.

Case questions

1 With 60 possible destinations for expatriates, some more desirable than others, what will be the guideline for identifying the best match between prospective expatriates and their destination country?
2 What factors will you use to persuade and negotiate with people needed in less-desired destinations?
3 What variations in the repatriation process will be needed to reflect the differences upon returning from those 60 subsidiaries? How can you involve former expatriates in the selection, mentoring and advising for new expatriates? How can you intervene to support repatriation?

Case based on Dickmann and Doherty (2006) report for PricewaterhouseCoopers, own additions.

Assessing the outcomes as seen by individuals in relation to other indicators is more problematic. One of the key problems is that the individuals have chosen their personal career – e.g. by working abroad – and researchers would have to rely on individuals' speculations.

Towards a framework of international experience and outcomes

The challenge in incorporating all five principles for the assessment of the outcomes of global careers is in the complexity of the necessary model. Moreover, the demands on the data gathering approach of any study are enormous. For this reason, most research studies focus on elements of the overall picture.

Bolino's conceptual framework

For instance, Bolino (2007) draws up a conceptual framework of repatriate career success and decides to focus on objective rather than subjective career success. Moreover, the contextual and cost elements are not defined in depth. In a latter work, the author – together with two colleagues – refines and focuses the model into postulating and measuring antecedents and consequences of career advancement upon repatriation (Kraimer et al. 2009). The model outlines antecedents in depicting international experiences – focusing on the number of IAs, the developmental purpose of the IA, managerial and cultural skills acquired, the completion of the assignment objectives and organizational career support for repatriation. These antecedents are hypothesized to have an effect on career advancement upon repatriation, perceived underemployment by the individual and resulting turnover intentions.

The findings included that employees who perceived to be promoted following their repatriation were less likely to experience feelings of underemployment (Kraimer et al. 2009: 40). While there are very few companies that promise expatriates an automatic promotion upon return (GMAC 2008), it has been argued that organizations should consider moving away from promoting newly sent international assignees in favour of promoting them when they move on/go home (Dickmann et al. 2006). A second finding was that there was a positive relationship of career support practices and repatriate retention. More surprising results included that multiple assignments had a less positive career effect (within the employing organization) than working abroad only once. A further finding was highly surprising in that those returnees who built their managerial skills while working abroad were less likely to perceive that they had been promoted in comparison to those individuals who had acquired less managerial skills. While the data might point to organizations not adequately valuing the increase in managerial skills – or doubting the applicability of these in a new context – larger-scale and longer-term research might illuminate and explicate these findings.

A framework of international context, experiences and outcomes

Building on the work of Bolino, Kraimer et al. and other authors who have been covered in earlier chapters, we suggest a framework of international context factors, experiences and outcomes of global careers. These three areas are interrelated (with the strongest influences going from context to experience to outcomes) and distinguish between individual and organizational elements. This is depicted in Table 9.1 which only gives a few examples in the different categories.

Like the work of Bolino (2007) our framework focuses on intra-organizational career success, albeit with some wider effects with regards to the individual level. With regard to the organizational context of global careers, the importance of SIHRM configurations has been discussed in Chapter 2. These organizational HR strategies and structures lead to a range of IHRM policies and practices which cover the IM area. Policies that the organization applies such as:

- guaranteed promotion on starting to work abroad,
- sophisticated repatriation practices that enable individuals to gain a job that they regard as 'good',
- career chances of repatriates, or
- the range of preparation and support mechanisms,

will shape the organizational context and will have an impact on the individual assignee's impressions. A fuller account of the manifold options that organizations have is given in Chapters 4–8. The last example outlined is that of the global importance of the host location which is interlinked with the configuration discussion. Gupta and Govindarajan (1991) distinguish between global innovators, integrated players, local innovators and mere implementers as subsidiary roles. The profound effects of these diverse roles for knowledge networking, standardization, resource flows (including staffing decisions) and global careers have been discussed elsewhere (especially in Chapter 2). Some subsidiaries have a more important role within the network of interlinked operating units in MNCs (Bolino and

Table 9.1 International context factors, experiences and outcomes

Organizational and individual assessment of international work/careers	Organizational and individual context	International experience	Outcomes of international work/careers
Organizational examples	SIHRM configurations	Global importance of international project	Costs of IM and willingness to support IM
	IM strategies, structures and processes	Importance of organizational goal of specific IA	Degree of completion of organizational assignment objectives
	Global importance of host location		Willingness of other employees to accept IAs
			Retention
Individual examples	Key individual goals for IA	Development of career capital	Use of career capital and individual performance
	Individual context	Completion of personal assignment objectives	Objective promotion and subjective perceived career success/satisfaction (including career wobble)
	Extent of international experience/number of IAs		Perceived under-employment

Feldman 2000) and it would be important for global careerists to be assigned to these locations.

The organizational context has an influence on the international experience. For the organization, the importance of both the international project or post that an individual is engaged in, and the objectives associated with a specific international work assignment, will shape the value and respect attached to this particular international work and the person's experiences (Doherty and Dickmann 2009). In some companies the kudos of working on specific projects or in specific locations has a signalling effect and influences the outcomes of working abroad.

The organizational outcomes of individuals working abroad, in separation, as well as the collective outcomes of the IM programme, relate to both individual repatriates and those staff who consider working abroad in the future. Retention over time of repatriates is a key challenge for corporations and has been shown to be one of the most difficult nuts to crack (Stahl et al. 2002; Lazarova and Cerdin 2007). While a case might be made that not all expatriates must be kept on by their organizations – especially when their competitive environment has changed dramatically, in times of crisis or during corporate restructuring – most organizations seem to want to keep repatriate churn to a minimum. Moreover, it is likely that people who went on to a developmental assignment are encouraged to stay with their employers and some data indicates that they are more likely to remain (Kraimer et al. 2009). A further element is the degree of completion of assignment objectives, which is an outcome factor in itself and will have repercussions with other outcomes such as promotion prospects or the organization's willingness to further support IM. Moreover, the cost of IM – direct costs such as increased salaries, social costs, benefits and travel as well as indirect costs related to the administration and management of IM programmes (Dickmann et al. 2006) – will be an organizational outcome and will have an impact on future numbers of international workers and the extent of support for global mobility. A final example of outcomes of international work listed is the willingness of other employees to accept IAs. GMAC (2008) lists international resourcing issues as one key problem in MNCs, and Cranfield University in combination with PricewaterhouseCoopers has done research into how to identify the reasons for 'barriers to mobility' and how to address these (Dickmann et al. 2005). Among the key reasons for people to turn down IA offers are individual context factors and the outcomes associated with international work of their predecessors in their organizations. These are explicated below.

The individual context, experiences and outcomes are explored in the lower half of Table 9.1. As discussed in Chapter 5, the context is shaped by the key goals of individuals for working abroad and their specific context. These might include factors associated with career and development, monetary and non-monetary incentives, general and specific location factors, individual drives and family issues (Dickmann and Mills 2010). The extent of international experience (Bolino 2007) – be it the number of IAs that an individual has gone through (Kraimer et al. 2009), extensive travel (Inkson and Myers 2003) or international experience accumulated during youth (Vance 2005) – is also an antecedent to organizational and employee outcomes.

Individuals are interested in the completion of their personal objectives – normally related to the formal objectives but often going beyond these – during and after their work abroad. Often, the accumulation of career capital – international capabilities, global and host-country networks as well as the development of their identity and drivers (see Chapters 3, 5 and 7) – is one of the core interests of expatriates (Stahl et al. 2002; Dickmann et al. 2008). The fulfilment of individual interests is related to the organizational context as well as to individual actions.

The outcomes of international work experiences are related to objective and subjective criteria. Among the objective criteria are actual vertical promotions and (relatively) better performance appraisals in the short term (during and immediately after an IA, see Chapters 7 and 8) and in the long term. More subjective career outcomes relate to the individual's perception of career success, his or her ability to use the career capital acquired in a domestic context and the evaluation of the current position or job as challenging, adequate or as a form of underemployment (Dickmann et al. 2005; Kraimer et al. 2009). The individual and organizational experiences and outcomes are further outlined in the two sections below.

Individual effects

There are manifold individual long-term effects of global careers. While this chapter concentrates on 'traditional expatriation' and, to some extent, immigration, the diverse forms of international experiences introduced in Chapter 2 all carry distinct outcomes. Some of these are briefly introduced below.

Globetrotting can enrich the individual cultural experience – whereas the family is less affected compared with the expatriation situation, and is fairly 'sheltered' from the upheavals of mobility, unless a significantly high level of frequency of international visits takes it toll on the ability of the family to cope. Virtual careers can have little impact on family life, though the need to work through various time zones might impede some sleeping. The most striking impact on careers – well, on life – is that of immigration. People can progress and realize endless opportunities which may be unavailable in their home country; yet for many the fruits of the transformation might become a reality only for the next generation, whereas the parents' generation sacrifices much and has to compromise through underemployment or permanent unemployment. Immigration issues are explored more thoroughly through the terms of brain drain, gain and circulation below in this chapter.

The intelligent career framework (DeFillippi and Arthur 1994) that was used in earlier chapters can shed light on processes during and after repatriation. Research by Dickmann et al. (2005) indicates that the overwhelming majority of individuals perceived to gain career capital in all three ways of knowing while they were on assignment. However, the repatriation experience, including the effects of reverse culture shock, often combined with a lack of immediate opportunities within their employing organization, meant that less than half the respondents thought that they could use their accumulated skills, knowledge, abilities and expanded networks in their new roles. This is despite the fact that career arrangements are a very prominent concern among repatriates (Riusala and Suutari 2000; Stahl et al.

2002). Many felt demotivated and perceived their career to be in a 'wobble' (Doherty and Dickmann 2007). A typical case is outlined below.

Case study 9.2 Surviving a career wobble

Anna had worried for a while what would happen when she returned with her family from China to Germany. She had asked for two meetings with the IM manager in charge of Asia-Pacific and the HR director to clarify her future role. During these meetings she was assured of the continuing support of her employer and that HR would look for a suitable position for her upon return. However, even while her worries grew during the last month in China she only got non-committal responses even though she felt herself to be very valuable for her organization, especially given its strategic intent to expand in East Asia.

On her first day back in the Munich head office she had a short meeting with the HR director who politely apologized because there was no immediate vacancy available. Instead, he offered a place on a project team and continued support in her search for a permanent position. Anna thought about the project and although she was not terribly keen on it decided to join the project. The reasons she later quoted in an interview were related to a continued trust in her employer as an organization that would still feel a strong obligation to its staff, especially if a person was seen to be committed. She felt that she surely had demonstrated this commitment.

In the following months it emerged that colleagues on her new project team (and elsewhere) had little interest in her China experiences. In fact, while she was eager to share her new insights regarding a different business and cultural context and new ways how to focus communication with diverse people, she registered polite disinterest. Anna felt frustrated and believed that her career was not going anywhere. She even considered accepting a position that was slightly lower than the job that she had before going on the IA. She also began applying to other companies.

Now, two years after her return, she is still with the company and occupies a hierarchically higher role. She explained that the turning point for her was to utilize some of her international contacts that she had acquired while working in Shanghai. When a position became vacant that had some interface activities with China she was recommended and finally selected for this job. Anna reflected that she had felt that for 15 months her career was in a wobble and that she did not seem to be able to use much of what she had learnt abroad. In fact, her insights and new capabilities did not seem to be appreciated until she was able to move into her current role.

Case questions

1 Why was Anna frustrated?
2 What organizational/managerial responses could have alleviated the situation? Please distinguish between pre- and post-return policies and practices.

3 What risks does an organization incur if it does not respond effectively to repatriation complications and problems?
4 What are the limits to what the organization can do to keep repatriate labour turnover low?
5 In what situations does the organization not want to keep repatriates?

While in our example Anna stays with the organization, she was considering leaving during her 'career wobble'. Dickmann et al.'s (2005) sample indicated that the key reasons to leave included a higher marketability to competitors (85 per cent), the expansion of their external networks (67 per cent) and the loss of internal networks (55 per cent); the latter being supported by several other studies (Dickmann and Harris 2005). Other reasons include the lack of career opportunities or clarity, and missed opportunities during the time abroad (Doherty and Dickmann 2008). The authors suggest that organizations use a range of HR approaches to improve retention (compare also the list by Lazarova and Caligiuri 2001 presented in Chapter 8). Moreover, they recommend that individuals become clear about what goals they pursue and that they base their decisions to seek a particular IA on how it furthers these goals. Moreover, they advise individuals to consider long-term career issues (e.g. using a time horizon of five years and factoring in the next work after return) and to strive to go to centres of excellence if possible.

While physical, inter-organizational mobility is often viewed as detrimental by organizations, this is often not the case for individuals. Research that tracks leavers is sparse due to the difficulty in accessing these individuals. A non-published master's thesis conducted at Cranfield University's School of Management seems to indicate that changing employers after an IA was viewed as predominantly positive by the individuals. Respondents argued that they would be able to use two of their three career capital areas more in their new places of work. They said that they were able to use their acquired capabilities (knowing-how) to a greater extent and felt that the motivational drivers, insights, their evolved identities and ideas of work–life balance could be better fulfilled. In essence, they indicated that they were happy with the decision to change employers. While there might be some reduction of cognitive dissonances, these impressions make uncomfortable reading for companies. The area of psychological and physical mobility merits more research attention.

Organizational effects

Many of the short- and medium-term organizational outcomes of international working have been presented in Chapter 8. These include predominantly the issues of retention, knowledge transfer and exploitation and symbolic effects of (un)successful IAs. Longer-term outcomes relate to global leadership planning for the future and, with a lot of expatriate churn, the lack of successor options, in-depth international understanding and potentially negative consequences in terms of corporate branding and recruitment activities.

The reader of this book will have noticed that we advocate a broad view on organizational activity for the management of global careers. Therefore, it should not come as a surprise that we see a wide array of organizational approaches that can facilitate positive outcomes of global work. It is also clear that these effects are substantially interlinked between individuals and organizations which, in turn, will have an impact on the immediate environment of individual global careerists (e.g. their family, friends etc.) as well as on a societal level.

Table 9.2 builds on our arguments presented in Chapter 8 in terms of good organizational strategies, structures, policies and practices located in their specific contexts. It expands our thoughts, for instance by distinguishing between the periods before, during and after international work. In so doing and in relation to our framework depicted throughout the book (e.g. in Figure 9.1 in this chapter) it addresses a range of organizational and individual levels.

The first level outlined is the meta-level of organizational strategies and structures (Dickmann and Müller-Camen 2006). While credibility and attractiveness of the international strategies and structures of the organization are highly important at all times, the kudos associated with international work will be most important for the decision to seek or accept expatriation before undertaking to work abroad or afterwards (as a sign for others).

Moving from the business meta-level more to the HR realm, it will be important to create sophisticated, fair, motivating and long-term IM policies and practices. Table 9.2 gives a range of details and distinguishes when these approaches are most important, i.e. when they either influence decisions or exert their strongest impact.

More specific HR sub-area policies – career, development, job design – are important for all phases of working abroad. This long list (which could be extended substantially) includes many 'generic' HR activities which are seen as 'good practice' (Pfeffer 1998). Some activities are, however, very specialized (such as financial and tax counselling) and will be designed for a time-bounded effect (see Chapter 11). In this case it might help returnees to reintegrate and suffer less reverse culture shock.

Our perspective on global careers as a long-term phenomenon for individuals has meant that we suggest giving the rewards of working internationally towards the end of IAs. Moreover, we recommend giving incentives to stay on in the next job. This attitude can be challenged, depending on how difficult it is for organizations to find willing individuals to work abroad. We believe that the key problems for organizations are often to be found after the work abroad ends, that developmental assignments become more frequent (and, therefore, their pay-off is delayed) and that many expatriates move from developed to developed countries (or from developing to developed countries) with little country insecurity or other hardship involved. Thus, it is at the tail-end of international work that we see the need for creative thinking about incentives. Moving from Germany to, say, France does not

Table 9.2 Good organizational policies, practices and created perceptions for expatriate retention

Area	Policies, practices and perceptions such as:	Before IA	During IA	After IA
Organizational strategy and structure	Clear and attractive strategy to internationalize	•		•
	Attractive degree of existing internationalization	•		•
	Little or no significant gap between statements of top management and implementation	•		•
	Adequate organizational configuration		•	•
	High kudos of international work	•	•	•
IM policies and practices	Staffing policies are perceived to be fair or advantageous	•		•
	Selection looks at a range of factors, including personality factors linked into adjustment and self-adjustment upon return	•		•
	Pre-return preparation for the job		•	•
	Ongoing support for time after return		•	•
	Long-range planning for repatriation		•	•
	Networking opportunities with home		•	•
	Continuous communication with home	•	•	•
Career	Long-term career planning	•	•	•
	Re-entry planning		•	•
	Career advancement	•		•
	Mentor system/international work sponsor system		•	•
Development	Systematic development of professional skills	•	•	•
	Systematic development of personal skills	•	•	•
	Systematic development of leadership skills	•	•	•
	Repatriation seminars on the emotional response			•
	Financial and tax counselling, advice and help for time after return			•

Job variables
Job challenge
Ability to use new global capabilities
No reduced responsibility and autonomy

Financial impact
Rewards for pursuing an IA
Rewards for developing an international perspective
Rewards for developing a worldwide network
Rewards for developing global skills, abilities and knowledge
Tie-over pay

Personal drivers and expectations
Pre-return and after return dialogues to manage expectations/build realistic pre-return expectations
Briefing and update regarding organizational structure, goals, politics and changes in the new locations

Family
Help for partner to find meaningful activity such as job and career re-entry
Help for family to (re)settle

Based on sources such as: Lazarova and Caligiuri (2001) (see also Lazarova and Cerdin (2007)); Stahl et al. (2002); Hocking et al. (2004); Dickmann et al. (2008); Doherty et al. (2008).

Note: The points indicate when organizational activities might be most valued by international assignees.

normally (in our minds) constitute hardship – in fact, we believe that more and more firms will see this as a normal career step and will do away with most expatriate incentives. In turn, it is ironic that in many not-for-profit organizations where professionals go into really dangerous hardship locations the incentives to do so are meagre (cf. WFP staff working in Sudan, Iraq, Afghanistan).

Helping individuals – for instance through understanding their personal goals with respect to working abroad – and their families can improve the outcomes not only for the persons but also for their employer. While Chapters 5 and 6 have explored intensively the core issues, Table 9.2 outlines possible organizational activities to support repatriates and their families during their transition back into their home country. Overall, therefore, there is a range of activities – beginning with pre-departure and extending to post-return – that employers can design and implement to increase the positive effects of global work.

The interaction of individuals and organizations

Individuals are embedded in their personal environment and we have seen the impact of their own goals, desires, drivers, family, love and friendship considerations as well as their own material, political and security situation on their willingness to seek international work, how they feel and adapt when working in a foreign country and a range of potential outcomes when returning 'home'. Organizations are, of course, also part of a wider context that offers globalization chances, but also one that exerts competitive pressures and results in dynamic developments such as reorganizations or new strategies.

Dickmann and Doherty (2010) have investigated the interaction of organizations and individuals using the intelligent careers framework in an international setting. They outline in two case studies how expatriates acted to increase their own knowing-why, how and whom when they perceived a lack in their organization's HRM practices. For instance, in one organization it was perceived that social networks were highly important for gaining a meaningful job upon return and for having a positive career trajectory (knowing-whom). Expatriates, however, thought that the company was not helping them to preserve their home-country networks. Therefore, they began to travel more frequently 'home' during their last year of assignment, started to get involved in 'home'-country project groups and initiated a series of meetings that would keep them on the 'radar screen' of important people in the centre of power. One of the less desirable effects was that assignees were seen as 'taking their eyes off the ball' and not concentrating sufficiently on their foreign work in the end-phase of their sojourn.

In turn, organizations started to learn when they perceived dysfunctional outcomes of not covering one of the career capital areas sufficiently. In order to increase expatriate retention one company introduced tie-over pay and repatriation conversations (knowing-why). Moreover, the firms aimed to utilize the acquired international competencies more effectively (knowing-how) through assignment-specific objectives and long-term career/job planning that took account of these when deciding on the post to fill after return.

Overall, the research of Dickmann and Doherty (2010) indicates that organizations and individuals are in a dynamic interaction with both parties reacting to the other. The firms were vigorously pursuing organizational aims and refined their IM and career policies and practices to motivate specific kinds of individual behaviour. In turn, in order to gain more career capital, individuals seem to compensate for perceived inactivity in organizations. The international experience of individuals is strongly linked to their own context, their own expectations and organizational IM strategies, policies and practices.

National effects of international work

Brain drain is a phenomenon in which people with a high level of skills, qualifications and competence, leave their countries and emigrate. Although the phenomenon of brain drain (BD) is not new, it has gained much attention over the last decade or so. The increased interest in the topic can be due to rapid globalization, and a host of political, economical, sociological and technological factors. Its scope is growing steadily (e.g. Carrington and Detragiache 1999; Mahroum 2000). Most of the BD at a national level occurs when immigrants move from developing countries to developed countries, most notably from Asia to North America and Europe (Creehan 2001; van Rooyen 2001; Crush 2002; Altbach and Bassett 2004). A specific group of talented people are those who come to study in developed countries, and of these there is a growing number who opt for business management studies, partially due to the nature of the labour markets in the developing countries (see Nichols et al. 2004).

Globalization has fundamental implications for the mobility of people across geographical and cultural boundaries (Baruch 1995; Koser and Salt 1997; Stalker 2000; Iredale 2001; Shenkar 2004). An increased level of mobility is an important manifestation of the internationalization of professions and professional labour markets (Iredale 2001; Ackers and Bryony 2005; Carr et al. 2005). Indeed, Carr et al. (2005) suggested the term 'talent flow' to replace the brain drain label as a fairer representation of the phenomenon of people movement across borders. A complementary approach is offered by Tung and Lazarova (2006), which contrasts brain drain with brain gain (see Chapter 3).

The considerable competitive advantage in the labour market of some countries, most notably the USA and some Western European countries, makes them clear winners (although recently the US experience might be losing its competitive advantage in attracting such talented people – see Florida (2005)). Yet, the causes of such moves, the role of the educational institutions, and analysis of specific populations for their vulnerability to the phenomenon has not been the focus of many academic studies. Such an analysis would have major implications at three levels: individual, organizational and regional/national level. The BD could make developing countries less competitive than developed countries by increasing the human capital of developed countries at the expense of developing countries (e.g. Gessen 1998).

Much research has been conducted on the trend of people coming to study in affluent countries. The scope of the trend is substantial, and is mostly based on the East–West or the South–North divide (Gatley et al. 1996).

Factors affecting brain drain

The factors contributing to the BD can be put under two broad categories – 'push' and 'pull' factors. The 'push–pull' model was developed by Lewin (1951) and it has clear relevance for cross-border movements (Baruch 1995, see Figure 9.2) and, in particular, for students' global movement (Mazzarol and Soutar 2002).

The push–pull model offers a framework for analysing the decision to move (or not move) across borders. The employee will be subjected to two forces, one operating in a pushing direction, influencing the employee to move; the other is pulling the employee back, employing pressure against the move. Any final decision is due to the strength of these conflicting forces. These forces operate in the realms of economy, law and culture. Employers can increase the push factor by offering a high level of remuneration and benefits (see Chapter 10) or by offering clear future career progress based on successful completion of the assignment. A pull factor can be the career of the spouse, the education opportunities for the children in the host country, or issues such as risks (war – Iraq; health – Africa), or even the physical climate (too warm or too cold for the preference of the person). The legal constraints might be decisive – in particular if the employee cannot be issued with a work permit. Cultural forces can push or pull people – depending on their inclination to try an adventurous life versus a tendency to look for stability and easiness within the well known. Some exotic destinations might have great appeal to certain people, whereas others will perceive the same 'attractions' as a deterrent. The difference between a condition perceived as appealing and appalling will surprise

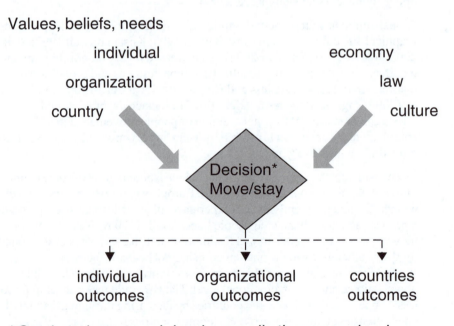

Figure 9.2 Factors affecting brain drain
Source: Baruch (1995: 315)

many HR managers. Some people would love to visit Las Vegas; others will resent the idea (subject to their liking or otherwise of gambling).

Baruch suggested a number of factors at the individual, organizational and national levels that can explain the nature and direction of the forces. A host of factors – economic, social or legal – influence an individual's decision to stay abroad, some of these push people towards a move, other factors pull people back. In many cases, even when decisions about expatriation are concerned, it is the individual choice that influences the final decision. Self-directed expatriation is increasingly recognized as a common career choice (Suutari and Brewster 2000; Richardson and Mallon 2005), and much of it is about improving life style and looking for new career opportunities. The expatriation career concept fits well with the 'boundaryless career' approach (Stahl et al. 2002), where, among other physical boundaries, national borders are no longer rigid (Arthur and Rousseau 1996). For overseas students, in a similar way to expatriates (see Tung and Lazarova 2006), international experience might enhance internal rather than external careers within the context of global movements across borders (Tung 1998).

While the standard of living in Europe and the USA is much higher than that in developing countries, this could be one of the factors, but not necessarily the only one. Quality of teaching is a major factor stimulating students to study in developed countries. Social and cultural factors such as family ties, social networks, and socialization processes could have a strong impact too. Social and cultural factors are crucial in the integration processes as students moving from one culture to the other encounter cultural complexities (Tsuda 1999; Osland and Bird 2000).

The BD can also be studied at organizational and national levels. Understanding of the BD at the organizational level can be extended to enhance understanding at the national level (Rosenblatt and Sheaffer 2001; Dhanaraj et al. 2004; Frey 2004; Simonin 2004). At the organizational level, Reingold and Brady (1999) noted the emergence of age-related BD. Their major finding was that BD results in the loss of knowledge in organizations. As indicated above, extending this finding to the national level means that developing countries could lose their most promising human capital to developed countries (Gessen 1998).

Education policy might counter the adverse effect of BD on economic growth (Kar-yiu and Chong 1999). Studying students from developing countries who attend educational institutions in wealthy countries and their inclinations to remain there, Baruch et al. (2007) re-emphasized the BD risks of such a case. Yet they have pointed out the prospects of brain circulation, as many return to their home country, immediately after studies, or at a later career stage.

The expatriation period causes people to challenge their common beliefs, the relevance of norms of behaviours, and even their values. Experiencing different culture, alternative ways of thinking, feeling and behaving, can cause changes in their attitudes – towards work, employer, even life (Figure 9.3). They might like, even 'fall in love' with the new country; they might dislike it and its customs. They could actually fall in love with a local person.

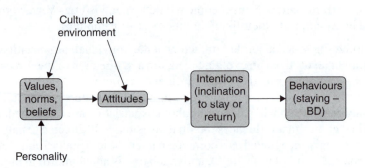

Figure 9.3 Theory of reasoned action for immigration
Source: adapted from Fishbein and Ajzen (1975)

As a result, their intentions might be a solid decision to return home and never return to that destination, maybe even never agree to another expatriation. They might decide to stay, either permanently working for their home firm, but also to become the 'perpetual expatriate', moving from firm to firm, conducting similar jobs, and enjoying their new country. Some might choose to become naturalized citizens – much depends on the gap between income (and pension) between home country and the host, possible new country.

Summary and learning points

This chapter has looked at a wide spectrum of outcomes of global careers, distinguishing individual, organizational and national effects and interactions. It has depicted the difficulties of assessing career and other outcomes of international work.

Key learning points include:

- There are five principles that need to be incorporated in order to assess the outcomes of international work. These are the use of multiple perspectives, the understanding of diverse goals, applying time sensitivity, the factoring in of both costs and benefits and the sensitive and contextual utilization of comparators such as non-expatriated peer groups.
- Key organizational consideration upon repatriation is the retention of returnees, especially those who are seen as high performers, knowledge experts and future organizational leaders. While repatriate churn is high in the first year after the assignment ends, those individuals who stay have a high propensity to work for the organization in the long term.
- Ideally, organizations would want repatriates to be able to apply their internationally acquired capabilities and use their networks for the benefit of the employer. Many individuals have identified substantial barriers to doing so and feel unable to use their new skills, knowledge and abilities or their foreign/international networks.
- Many returnees experience a career wobble in which they feel undervalued and

frustrated. Their interest in seeking alternative employment is generally high during this phase.

- A framework that can be helpful in assessing the outcomes of global work is proposed. It factors in the international context and dynamic work experiences during international careers.
- This chapter has drawn up a list of organizational activities that can be used to improve the outcomes of global work and careers.
- Organizations and individuals have their own international agendas. These lead to a dynamic interaction in which employers and international assignees adjust to each others' approaches, and develop strategies as well as behaviours to maximize their beneficial outcomes.
- The diverse flows of international workers lead to a talent flow that is often labelled brain drain. It might, however, also constitute brain gain – especially for the recipients of highly skilled or educated workers from abroad. These are often from developing countries, which raises a range of ethical and political considerations.

References

Ackers, L. and Bryony, G. (2005) 'Attracting and retaining "early career" researchers in English higher education institutions', *Innovation: The European Journal of Social Sciences*, 18: 277–299.

Altbach, P.G. and Bassett, R.M. (2004) 'The brain trade', *Foreign Policy*, Sep/Oct: 30–31.

Arthur, M.B. and Rousseau, D.M. (eds) (1996) *The Boundaryless Career: A New Employment Principle for a New Organizational Era*, New York: Oxford University Press.

Baruch, Y. (1995) 'Business globalization – the human resource management aspect', *Human Systems Management*, 14(4): 313–326.

Baruch, Y., Budhwar, P. and Khatri, N. (2007) 'Brain drain: inclination to stay abroad after studies', *Journal of World Business*, 42(1): 99–112.

Black, J.S., Gregersen, H.B. and Mendenhall, M.E. (1992) 'Towards a theoretical framework of repatriation adjustment', *Journal of International Business Studies*, 23(4): 737–758.

Bolino, M. (2007) 'Expatriate assignments and intra-organizational career success: implications for individuals and organizations', *Journal of International Business Studies*, 38: 819–835.

Bolino, M. and Feldman, D. (2000) 'The antecedents and consequences of underemployment among expatriates', *Journal of Organizational Behavior*, 21(8): 889–911.

Bonache, J., Brewster, C. and Suutari, V. (2001) 'Expatriation: a developing research agenda', *Thunderbird International Business Review*, 43(1): 3–20.

Caligiuri, P.M. and Lazarova, M. (2001) 'Strategic repatriation policies to enhance global leadership development', in M. Mendenhall, T. Kuhlmann and G. Stahl (eds) *Developing Global Business Leaders: Policies, Processes, and Innovations*, Westport, CT: Quorum Books.

Cappellen, T. and Janssens, M. (2005) 'Career paths of global managers: towards future research', *Journal of World Business*, 40(4): 348–360.

Carr, S.C., Inkson, K. and Thorn, K. (2005) 'From global careers to talent flow: reinterpreting "brain drain"', *Journal of World Business*, 40: 386–398.

Carrington, W.J. and Detragiache, E. (1999) 'International migration and the "brain drain"', *Journal of Social Political and Economic Studies*, 24: 163–171.

Creehan, S. (2001) 'Brain strain', *Harvard International Review*, 23(2): 6–7.

Crush, J. (2002) 'The global raiders: nationalism, globalization and the South African brain drain', *Journal of International Affairs*, 56: 147–172.

DeFillippi, R. and Arthur, M. (1994) 'The boundaryless career: a competency-based perspective', *Journal of Organizational Behavior*, 15: 307–324.

Dhanaraj, C., Lyles, M.A., Steensma, H.K. and Tihanyi, L. (2004) 'Managing tacit and explicit knowledge transfer in IJVs: the role of relational embeddedness and the impact on performance', *Journal of International Business Studies*, 35: 428–442.

Dickmann, M. and Doherty, N. (2006) *Measuring the Value of International Assignments Report*, Cranfield: Final Research Report for PricewaterhouseCoopers.

Dickmann, M. and Doherty, N. (2007) 'Assessing the success of international assignments in three fast-moving consumer goods organizations', paper presented at the *EGOS Colloquium*, Vienna, July 2007.

Dickmann, M. and Doherty, N. (2008) 'Organisational and individual perspectives on success in developmental international assignments', paper presented at the *Academy of Management conference*, Anaheim, CA, August 2008.

Dickmann, M. and Doherty, N. (2010) 'Exploring organisational and individual career goals, interactions and outcomes of international assignments', *Thunderbird International Review*, 52(4): 313–324.

Dickmann, M. and Harris, H. (2005) 'Developing career capital for global careers: the role of international assignments', *Journal of World Business*, 40(4): 399–408.

Dickmann, M. and Mills, T. (2010) 'The importance of intelligent career and location considerations: exploring the decision to go to London', *Personnel Review*, 39(1): 116–134.

Dickmann, M. and Müller-Camen, M. (2006) 'A typology of international human resource management strategies and processes', *International Journal of Human Resource Management*, 17(4): 580–601.

Dickmann, M., Doherty, N. and Johnson, A. (2006) *Measuring the Value of International Assignments*, report for PwC UK Geodesy, Cranfield: Cranfield School of Management.

Dickmann, M., Wigley-Jones, R. and Wignall, D. (2005) *Understanding and Avoiding the Barriers to International Mobility*, London: PricewaterhouseCoopers.

Dickmann, M., Doherty, N., Mills, T. and Brewster, C. (2008) 'Why do they go? Individual and corporate perspectives on the factors influencing the decision to accept an international assignment', *International Journal of Human Resource Management*, 19(4): 731–751.

Doherty, N. and Dickmann, M. (2007) 'Managing the career wobble of repatriates', *Developing HR Strategy*, 13 July 2007.

Doherty, N. and Dickmann, M. (2008) 'Capitalizing on an international career: career capital perspectives', in M. Dickmann, C. Brewster and P. Sparrow (eds) *International Human Resource Management – A European Perspective*, London: Routledge.

Doherty, N. and Dickmann, M. (2009) 'Exploring the symbolic capital of international assignments', *International Journal of Human Resource Management*, 20(2): 301–320.

Doherty, N., Brewster, C., Suutari, V. and Dickmann, M. (2008) 'Repatriation: the end or the middle?', in M. Dickmann, C. Brewster and P. Sparrow (eds) *International Human Resource Management – The European Perspective*, London: Routledge.

Dowling, P.J. and Welch, D.E. (2004) *International Human Resource Management: Managing People in a Multinational Context*, London: Thomson.

Fishbein, N. and Ajzen, I. (1975) *Belief, Attitude, Intention and Behavior: An Introduction to Theory and Research*, Reading, MA: Addison-Wesley.

Florida, R. (2005) *The Flight of the Creative Class: The New Global Competition for Talent*, New York: HarperCollins Publishers.

Frey, W.H. (2004) 'Brain gains, brain drains', *American Demographics*, June: 19–23.

Gatley, S., Lessem, R. and Altman, A. (1996) *Comparative Management: A Transcultural Odyssey*, London: McGraw-Hill.

Gessen, M. (1998) 'Brian haemorrhage', *The New Republic*, 219(16): 14–16.

GMAC (2008) *Global Relocation Trends Survey*, Woodridge, IL: GMAC Global Relocation Services.

Gupta, A. and Govindarajan, V. (1991) 'Knowledge flows and the structure of control within multinational corporations', *Academy of Management Review*, 16(4): 768–792.

Harzing, A.-W. and Christensen, C. (2004) 'Expatriate failure: time to abandon the concept?', *Career Development International*, 9(7): 616–626.

Haslberger, A. (2005) 'Facets and dimensions of cross-cultural adaptation – refining the tools', *Personnel Review*, 34(2): 85–110.

Hocking, J.B., Brown, M. and Harzing, A.W.K. (2004) 'A knowledge transfer perspective of strategic assignment purposes and their path-dependent outcomes', *The International Journal of Human Resource Management*, 15(3): 565–586.

Inkson, K. and Myers, B.A. (2003) 'The big OE: self-directed travel and career development', *Career Development International*, 8: 170–181.

Iredale, R. (2001) 'The migration of professionals: theories and typologies', *International Migration*, 39(5): 7–26.

Kar-yiu, W. and Chong, K.Y. (1999) 'Education, economic growth, and brain drain', *Journal of Economic Dynamics and Control*, 23: 699–725.

Kohonen, E. (2005) 'Developing global leaders through international assignments: an identity construction perspective', *Personnel Review*, 34(1): 22–36.

Koser, K. and Salt, J. (1997) 'The geography of highly skilled international migration – Research review', *International Journal of Population Geography*, 3: 285–303.

Kraimer, M.L., Shaffer, M.A. and Bolino, M. (2009) 'The influence of expatriate and repatriate experiences on career advancement and repatriate retention', *Human Resource Management*, 48(1): 27–47.

Larsen, H.H. (2004) 'Global career as dual dependency between the organization and the individual', *Journal of Management Development*, 23(9): 860–869.

Lazarova, M. and Caligiuri, P. (2001) 'Retaining repatriates: the role of organizational support practices', *Journal of World Business*, 36(4): 389–401.

Lazarova, M. and Cerdin, J.-L. (2007) 'Revisiting repatriation concerns: organizational support versus career and contextual influences', *Journal of International Business Studies*, 38: 404–429.

Lewin, K. (1951) *Field Theory in Social Science*, New York: Harper and Row.

McCaughey, D. and Bruning, N.S. (2005) 'Enhancing opportunities for expatriate job satisfaction: HR strategies for foreign assignment success', *Human Resource Planning*, 28(4): 21–29.

McNulty, Y. and Tharenou, P. (2004) 'Expatriate return on investment: a definition and antecedents', *International Studies of Management and Organisation*, 34(3): 68–95.

McNulty, Y., De Cieri, H. and Hutchings, K. (2009) 'Do global firms measure expatriate return on investment? An empirical examination of measures, barriers and variables influencing global staffing practices', *The International Journal of Human Resource Management*, 20(6): 1309–1326.

Mahroum, S. (2000) 'Highly skilled globetrotters: mapping the international migration of human capital', *R & D Management*, 30: 23–31.

Mazzarol, T. and Soutar, G. (2002) '"Push-pull" factors influencing the international student destination choice', *International Journal of Educational Management*, 16(2): 82–90.

Mendenhall, M.E. and Oddou, G.R. (1985) 'The dimensions of expatriate acculturation: a review', *Academy of Management Review*, 10: 39–47.

Nichols, T., Cam, S., Chou, W.-C.G., Chun, S., Zhao, W. and Feng, T. (2004) 'Factory regimes and the dismantling of established labour in Asia: a review of cases from large manufacturing plants in China, South Korea and Taiwan', *Work, Employment and Society*, 18: 663–685.

Osland, J.S. and Bird, A. (2000) 'Beyond sophisticated stereotyping: cultural sensemaking in context', *Academy of Management Executive*, 14: 65–79.

Pfeffer, J. (1998) *The Human Equation: Building Profits by Putting People First*, Boston, MA: Harvard Business School Press.

Reingold, J. and Brady, D. (1999) 'Brain drain', *Business Week*, Issue 3647: 112–119.

Richardson, J. and Mallon, M. (2005) 'Career interrupted? The case of the self-directed expatriate', *Journal of World Business*, 40(4): 409–420.

Rosenblatt, Z. and Sheaffer, Z. (2001) 'Brain drain in declining organizations: toward a research agenda', *Journal of Organizational Behavior*, 22: 409–424.

Riusala, K. and Suutari, V. (2000) 'Expatriation and careers: perspectives of expatriates and spouses', *Career Development International*, 5(2): 81–90.

Shenkar, O. (2004) 'One more time: international business in a global economy', *Journal of International Business Studies*, 35: 161–171.

Simonin, B.L. (2004) 'An empirical investigation of the process of knowledge transfer in international strategic alliances', *Journal of International Business Studies*, 35: 407–427.

Sparrow, P., Brewster, C. and Harris, H. (2004) *Globalizing Human Resource Management*, London: Routledge.

Stahl, G., Miller, E. and Tung, R. (2002) 'Toward the boundaryless career: a closer look at the expatriate career concept and the perceived implications of an international assignment', *Journal of World Business*, 37: 216–227.

Stalker, P. (2000) *Workers without Frontiers: The Impact of Globalization on International Migration*, Boulder, CO: Lynne Reiner.

Suutari, V. and Brewster, C. (2000) 'Making their own way: international experience through self-initiated foreign assignments', *Journal of World Business*, 35: 417–436.

Tsuda, T. (1999) 'The motivation to migrate: the ethnic and sociocultural constitution of the Japanese-Brazilian return-migration system', *Economic Development and Cultural Change*, 48: 1–31.

Tung, R.L. (1998) 'American expatriates abroad: from neophytes to cosmopolitans', *Journal of World Business*, 33: 125–144.

Tung, R.L. and Lazarova, M. (2006) 'Brain drain versus brain gain: an exploratory study of ex-host country nationals in central and east Europe', *International Journal of Human Resource Management*, 17: 1853–1872.

van Rooyen, J. (2001) *The New Great Trek: The Story of South Africa's White Exodus*, Pretoria: Unisa Press.

Vance, C. (2005) 'The personal quest for building global competence: a taxonomy for self-initiating career path strategies for gaining business experience abroad', *Journal of World Business*, 40(4): 374–385.

Yan, A., Zhu, G. and Hall, D. (2002) 'International assignments for career building: a model of agency relationships and psychological contracts', *Academy of Management Review*, 27(3): 373–391.

Part III

Global career management: social security, risk, structural and remuneration considerations and global careers in the future

Social security considerations in global careers

MICHAEL DICKMANN AND JOOST SMITS

Objectives

This chapter:

- describes a range of strategic and operational approaches to social security and other regulatory issues;
- charts a brief history of social security systems and depicts general provisions;
- introduces a key supra-national social security regulation that applies in the EU and explores its key provisions and their effects;
- presents key social security challenges and how organizations deal with these; the options for organizations – home-based, global approaches and a mixture of these are outlined;
- identifies the impact of the regulatory context and the organizational and individual reactions to these;
- discusses the impact on global careers, distinguishing between company-supported and self-initiated international careerists.

Introduction

The management of social security aspects of global work is highly complex and subject to dynamic developments. The regulatory environment is strongly linked to local labour laws and other stipulations and many MNCs opt to seek external

Michael Dickmann, Cranfield University, School of Management, UK and Joost Smits, Ernst and Young, Human Capital, The Netherlands

help from law firms. Conferences, web-based publications and masterclasses from organizations such as the Global Forum for Cross-Border Human Resource Experts (XBHR)[1] underline the scope and complexity of issues. Companies also need to be expert at national cultures and customs, specific employment practices, the diverse use of allowances, security situations and local/national politics. Therefore, it is no wonder that many companies additionally seek advice from/or outsource activities to the global mobility divisions of accounting firms – such as Ernst and Young – and specialized consultancies (e.g. ORC Worldwide, ECA). A recent study has shown that three-quarters of IM administration costs were spent on outsourcing and external advice (Dickmann et al. 2007).

The framework presented in Figure 10.1 outlines the importance of these national social security factors. Together with remuneration considerations, social security and other regulatory factors form a basis that determines some of the context in which careers unfold. More specifically, migration patterns (discussed in Chapter 2) and IAs will be substantially influenced by residence and work permit regulations as well as social security stipulations. These issues are discussed below, using historical, sociological, institutional and managerial perspectives.

Figure 10.1 A framework of global careers: regulations and social security

1 XBHR The Global Forum of Cross-Border Human Resources Experts is a multi-disciplinary, global forum for professional advisors and academics who are experts in cross-border HR issues. XBHR's key objective is to create a think-tank of HR experts across the globe who are interested and involved in cross-border HR issues.

General social security considerations

The concept of social security

One of the challenges that companies face while employing international workers relates to social security. Social security was defined by Pieters (1993: 2) as: 'The body of arrangements shaping solidarity with people facing (the threat of) a lack of earnings or particular costs.' While not always high on the agenda of an MNC, social security is very important for an individual. This is due to issues such as benefits and entitlements being covered by social security which determine the support an individual is entitled to in areas such as illness, disability or pension.

The following example shows the importance of social security regulations. A French resident is working partly in Italy and Spain for an Italian company. Based on the European legislation, s/he will be socially insured in Italy. In case s/he starts working regularly in France, his or her social security position changes towards the French social security. Thus, the international worker becomes socially insured in another country (i.e. from Italy to France) with other entitlements than were previously part of the employment deal. Therefore, the question arises whether s/he is entitled to compensation due to this change in the social security position. Moreover, what obligations occur for the employer? The Italian employer should then pay French rather than Italian social security contributions. Furthermore, the French social security benefits might not compare very well with the Italian employment conditions the French employee is subject to.

The key questions that different national, bi- or multinational social security arrangements and contracts influence are:

- In which country is a person socially insured while working abroad?
- In which country is a person socially insured while working in several countries?
- In which country does the company have to register itself and pay the contributions?
- Does the international worker have any gaps in his social security position while moving from one social security scheme to another scheme?

One of the challenges for international organizations is that the concept of social security is interpreted in very diverse ways throughout the world. A lot of countries do not have a legal description of social security. Each country, in which a social security system exists, has different schemes of benefits with varying contents. Furthermore, the way that social security schemes are structured differs throughout the world. In the following, we will describe diverse social security approaches.

Different social security approaches

Social security schemes have strong roots in history. Key ideas were often developed in Europe which then evolved over time. Increasingly, other nations have analysed the different social security systems and have adopted some of these ideas while developing their own approaches in other areas.

Historical schemes

The origin of social security dates back to the nineteenth century. Germany was the first nation in the world to adopt a retirement insurance programme. Bismarck introduced social insurance in Germany to promote the well-being of workers. Characteristics of this approach are that the working population, specifically employees, are covered mandatorily. The amount and sometimes duration of the benefits relates to the length of working time and the income earned.

A second major approach was introduced by Beveridge in the UK. Characteristics of this approach are that the entire population is covered for social security whether or not they are working. Benefits are, in principle, paid out as lump sum amounts while some might be means-tested. Table 10.1 summarizes these fundamental distinctions.

While social security systems hardly exist in the pure forms outlined above, one can trace the impact of these influential thinkers and politicians in today's social security approaches in many countries. A good example of a mixture of Bismarck's and Beveridge's approaches is the social security system of the Netherlands. While all residents of the Netherlands are socially insured for some parts of the social security scheme, employees are also covered for further parts. The social security system in the US was developed relatively late and is strongly influenced by the Bismarck approach.

New approaches

In the traditional approach, persons contribute to the social security system while payments are only made to the insured person in case an event arises which gives rise to entitlements. For instance, when a person becomes disabled, the paid contributions will be paid to the disabled person via disability benefits. If such an event does not arise, the money stays in the social security system.

Recently, new developments can be seen in this regard, which can influence international workers and companies. A good example is the Indian social security system where employers and employees pay contributions towards the Provident Fund. If an employee leaves the country (and is no longer compulsorily socially insured in the country), s/he can take the paid contributions out of the social security system. Furthermore, the money can be taken out upon reaching retirement. This approach is therefore akin to a savings system with an insurance element. After having explained the different approaches which currently exist, we will discuss different options to structure a country's social security scheme below.

Table 10.1 Social security systems based on Bismarck and Beveridge compared

Approach	Persons covered	Benefits
Bismarck	Working population, in employment	Amount and sometimes duration relates to time period of working and income earned
Beveridge	Entire population, working or not	Benefits are in principle lump sum and means tested

Different options to structure a country's social security system

In general, one can distinguish between (state) compulsory social security schemes and non-compulsory social security schemes. For international workers and international companies it is important to be aware of the differences while determining the social security position of an individual, so they can implement it in their policies accordingly.

State compulsory social security schemes

Compulsory social security schemes are often supported by the government and are based on the solidarity systems. If a member of the solidarity network is affected by a social risk, the person can be provided with a social benefit. Participation in the schemes is normally compulsory for residents. An example for a scheme based on Beveridge is the national health system in the UK. An example for a state social security scheme geared not to the whole population – ergo based on the Bismarck approach – is the mandatory coverage of all employees in the US disability insurance.

Non-compulsory social security schemes

Coverage in the schemes is not compulsory, but persons can choose to opt-in to the insurances. Different forms of coverage exist.

Occupational social security schemes

Some of the occupational social security schemes are linked to collective labour agreements. Employees in a certain industry or occupation can choose (or are sometimes obliged) to participate in the occupational pension scheme or other types of supplementary insurance.

Voluntary social security schemes

Voluntary social security schemes of a country are, in principle, more or less comparable with the state compulsory social security schemes. These schemes are open to persons who do not fall under the personal scope of the state compulsory scheme. For instance, if a person is expatriated and therefore does not fall under the personal scope of the state pension as mentioned before, the person can decide to take out the insurances on a voluntary basis. After opting for the voluntary insurances, the person is also entitled to the benefits comparable to the state system. For instance, if an international worker is assigned from country A to country B and, as a result, cannot remain covered by the compulsory social security system of country A, by opting for the voluntary social security scheme of country A, he will most likely not lose any benefits to which he was originally entitled.

Individual social security coverage

Instead of opting for a voluntary social security scheme to build up entitlements, persons can decide to ensure their social security entitlements in another way. For instance, if an international worker wants to be able to receive cash entitlements upon retirement, s/he can decide to take out a private insurance with an insurance company. Another option is via personal savings. Furthermore, the tendency can be seen that companies decide to be 'own risk bearers'. This means that private insurance is not taken out, but the company pays benefits to an employee in case of disablement or unemployment.

All the above-mentioned schemes can be considered to be part of the social security scheme. In the remainder of this section we will mainly focus on the state social security scheme.

An overview of social security legislation

General

Now that the reader has accompanied us through the general concept of social security and the different forms which exist throughout the world, we will focus more on the different legislation that exists in relation to social security. For both the international worker and the international company it is important to be aware of the international rules. Once the international rules are known, international companies can draft their policies in relation to social security. MNCs and international workers act in a world with several layers of legislation. Compliance with all relevant legislation is important.

In case a worker performs activities in two or more states and the social security position has to be determined, first of all community legislation needs to be considered to verify whether the social security position can be determined. Once community legislation has been verified, it should be investigated whether on an applicable multilateral or bilateral level (special) arrangements are made to determine the social security level. Finally, national legislation of the relevant states needs to be checked. In the following we will specify the four different levels.

Community legislation

This level contains social security legislation which is concluded by a community such as the EU. A key feature is that each individual state does not have to agree upon the legislation as soon as the community has agreed to the rules. A regulation which is concluded between the member states of the EU and those of the European Economic Area, including Switzerland, Regulation 1408/71, is an important example of community legislation. This was replaced by Regulation 883/2004 in May 2010.

Multilateral level

This level contains social security legislation which has been concluded between more than two states. In Europe, one can think of treaties which have been concluded between the Rhine states. This treaty determines in which country an international worker who is working in one of the Rhine states is socially insured. Another example is the International Transport Treaty. In North America, social security legislation has been discussed between the USA, Canada and Mexico, the NAFTA countries.

Bilateral level

This level contains social security legislation which has been agreed between two different states. More and more states are, in the same way as with tax treaties, currently entering into social security treaties ('totalization agreements') to determine the social security position of an international worker. We will show the relevance and the importance of the totalization agreement with an example. For instance, consider the treaty which is concluded between the US and Germany. This treaty determines in which country a person is socially insured while living in one country and working in another country. If the totalization agreement did not exist, both (or none) of the national laws of US and Germany might be applicable to the person.

National level

This level contains the social security legislation which exists in a country. An example is of the national legislation which determines the social security contributions and benefits position of an individual in respect to the state, unemployment and disability benefits. National social security systems differ throughout the world.

It is important to note that all international treaties or arrangements determine in which country an international worker is socially insured. If the legislation of a country is determined as applicable based on international rules, the national legislation of the specific country will determine the position (coverage, benefits and contributions) in more detail. Therefore, for a global worker international legislation always has to be considered together with national legislation.

The structure of social security legislation: supra-national Regulation 883/2004

The content of legislation can differ substantially. However, in general, most social security legislation has common structural elements. To provide the reader with an overview, we will describe the structure of one of the most important community legislations which exists, namely Regulation 883/2004. Regulation 883/2004 was concluded between the following member states of the EU (Table 10.2).

Table 10.2 Country applicability of Regulation 883/2004

Austria	Belgium	Bulgaria
Cyprus	Czech Republic	Denmark
Estonia	Finland	France
Germany	Greece	Hungary
Ireland	Italy	Latvia
Lithuania	Luxembourg	Malta
Netherlands	Poland	Portugal
Romania	Slovakia	Slovenia
Spain	Sweden	UK

Its predecessor, Regulation 1408/71 is also applicable to nationals of the European Economic Area (Norway, Iceland and Liechtenstein) and Switzerland. However, Regulation 883/2004 is, at the time of publication of this book, not yet applicable to nationals of the European Economic Area. The respective treaties first need to be changed, which is expected in due course.

Goal of Regulation 883/2004

International social security legislation has as one of its key objectives the coordination of social security legislation. The main importance of the legislation is to prevent an international worker being double insured (i.e. in more than one country) or not being socially insured at all.

The impact of international social security legislation can best be described with an example. An international worker has always been working in the Netherlands. In the Netherlands, a person is socially insured for part of the social security system if they can be considered a resident. The international worker will now start working in France, but remains resident in the Netherlands. Based on French social security legislation, a person is socially insured when the person is working in France. If no international social security legislation existed, the international worker would be partly socially insured in the Netherlands (based on residency) and in France (based on work place). Double social security is not in line with the freedom of workers. Therefore, Regulation 883/2004 determines in which country a person is exclusively socially insured.

Personal scope

This part of the regulation determines which persons are covered under the regulation and can, as a result, evoke the rules of legislation. Regulation 883/2004 is applicable to employees or self-employed persons and students to which the legislation of one or more member states is, or has been, applicable. The regulation is also applicable to their family members.

Material scope

This part determines which section of social security legislation falls under the material scope of the EC Regulation 883/2004.

• Illness and maternity entitlements
• Disability entitlements
• Old age entitlements
• Entitlements due to occupational diseases
• Survivor's entitlements
• Death benefits
• Unemployment entitlements
• Family allowances

In principle, all state social security legislation falls under the scope of the EC regulation. Social assistance, however, is an exception and does not fall under the scope of the regulation. It is therefore part of national regulations.

Rules of conflict

The rules of conflict are an important part of the regulation since they provide guidance to determine in which state a person is exclusively socially insured while working internationally.

The main rule is that a person is socially insured in the work state even if they are a resident of another state.

Three exceptions to this exist, namely assignment, working in several countries and some special cases. First, if a person is assigned to another country, s/he can remain socially insured in the home country while working (and sometimes living) in another state. In order to apply this important exception to the main rule as stated before, the following conditions need to be met:

- An organic link with the home employer exists. One can think of the following criteria to verify whether the organic link still exists with the home company: who has the authority to instruct, who is paying the wages, who determines the employment conditions (termination of contract)?
- Employer who assigns the individual performs substantial activities in the country of assignment.
- Individual can remain insured in home country if s/he was prior to the assignment insured in the home country.
- Initial period of 24 months or less but an extension is possible (in most cases up to five years).

The second exception to the main rule is that a person is socially insured in her or his work state when working in several countries. The person is then socially insured in the state of residency when s/he is working partly in the state of residency or where multiple employment contracts exist with different employers.

Thirdly, specific exceptions exist for special groups. In Table 10.3 we provide an overview of the applicable legislation for the most important groups. We distinguish between the rules that were applicable under Regulation 1408/71 and those that are now applicable using Regulation 883/2004.

Entitlements to benefits

This part of the Regulation provides important rules regarding:

- how to determine the amount of benefit in case a person has been socially insured in more than one country;
- rules to determine from which country or countries the calculated benefits will be paid while a person has been socially insured in more than one country;
- summation of insurance periods – a country needs to take into consideration the number of insurance years in another country while calculating the benefits to which the international worker is entitled based on the national law;
- export of benefits.

We will highlight the main rules with an example in relation to health care and state pension.

Table 10.3 Social security position

Group	Social security position under EC Regulation 1408/71	Social security position under EC Regulation 883/2004
Working simultaneously in more countries	• Insured in state of residence if working there regularly or in case two employers exist • Insured in state where company is established if not working at least one day per month in state of residence	• Insured in state of residence if working there at least 25% of the time (or income) or in case two employers exist • Insured in state where company is established if not working at least 25% of the time (or income) in state of residence
Assignment	• Insured in home country for an initial period of 1 year, maximum 5 years. • Assignment conditions (like organic link) need to be fulfilled	• Insured in home country for an initial period of 2 year, maximum 5 years. • Assignment conditions (see before) need to be fulfilled
Working as employee in country A and self employed in country B	• Insured in country where working as employee • However, in case the country in which the person is working as self-employed person is listed on a special annex (Annex VII), the person is also socially insured in the country where the person is working as self-employed person	• Insured in country where working as employee
International transport	• Insured in country in which the transport company is established • However, insured in country of residency in case the person is mainly working in country of residency	• Insured in state of residence if working their at least 25% of the time or in case two employers exist • Insured in state where company is established if not working at least 25% of the time in home country

Example in relation to health care

A person is on assignment from the UK to France. S/he remains socially insured in the UK during the assignment while moving to France. The individual is still entitled to UK health care. Based on the regulation s/he can export this benefit to France. As a result, when in France, the individual is entitled to health care benefits while the costs of the entitlements are paid by the UK. The same applies to the non-working family members of the individual.

Pension entitlements

The rules to determine the pension entitlements are very complex. We will therefore only focus on the key regulations. On reaching retirement age, an individual can be entitled to state pensions from different countries if s/he was socially insured in several countries. The regulation states that the individual is entitled to benefits from more than one country, pro rata according to length of insurance periods. The same applies in principle to disability entitlements.

Above, we have explored the history of social security systems, their diverging approaches and provisions and given an in-depth description of a supra-national social security arrangement. In the two sections below we focus on new developments and political considerations.

New social security developments

General

We have argued throughout the book that internationalization and globalization become increasingly important. As a result, the number of international workers is also growing. Legislation and practices change accordingly. As a consequence, new developments can also be seen in social security. For MNCs it is important to be aware of these new developments so that policies, remuneration and international structures can be adjusted accordingly. In this part of the chapter, important developments within the social security field will be addressed.

New totalization agreements

Due to the rise of IM, the necessity of international rules to coordinate the social security position of international workers is more important. If international coordination rules do not exist, undesirable events can occur. Until recently, many countries in, for instance, Asia and Africa neither had a very well developed social security system nor had they concluded totalization agreements. As a result, when a person is assigned from a country in which social security legislation exists, to a country in which there is no social security legislation, one can imagine this would have a major impact on the social security position of the international worker.

In order to make this career move for an international assignee more secure, MNCs had high costs through concluding expensive insurances to ensure that the international worker would not have a gap in her or his social security entitlements. The following example can stress the importance of totalization agreements.

Case 10.1 Shaun working in India – the effects of not having totalization agreements

Shaun, a US American, is assigned from the US to India. A totalization agreement to coordinate the social security position of an employee does not yet exist. Shaun was always socially insured in the US prior to the assignment. Moving to India, he might not remain compulsorily socially insured in the US social security system and would therefore lose some entitlements, e.g. with respect to his old age pension. Shaun, therefore, might be faced with large voluntary payments in the US or with negative consequences once he comes back to the USA or retires. Moreover, during his assignment, Shaun is liable to contribute to the social security system of India. This system, however, is different to the US system.

Recognizing Shaun's problems, the MNC might opt to insure the expatriate on a voluntary basis or to conclude private insurances to guarantee that Shaun remains in the same social security position as prior to his assignment. Once leaving India, Shaun can take out the money which was contributed to the Indian scheme. If additional US coverage has been taken care of, this could lead to a double entitlement of the expatriate. Arrangements between the MNC and the employee should be made to determine who (employee or employer) is entitled to the Indian refund.

As soon as a totalization agreement is concluded between the US and India, all international workers can remain socially insured in the US during their assignment. As a result, only US social security contributions are due (practical for the MNC) and international workers have no change in their social security entitlements (beneficial for international assignees).

Case questions

1 In terms of social security, what are less complex locations?
2 What elements of a social security system would you assess when sponsoring a move from one country to the next?
3 What are the key pitfalls that individuals should look out for when they move abroad?

Note: India has recently concluded several new totalization agreements and has also introduced new social security legislation. As a result, if an employee is assigned from India to Germany, the individual can remain covered by the Indian social security scheme while being exempted from the German scheme.

The case shows that if no totalization agreement exists, this can have negative effects on the personal situation of an employee (for instance, coverage which differs from the home scheme or high social security contributions). As a result, countries try to keep up with the changing international environments and enter into more and more social security agreements. During the past years a large number of new totalization agreements have come into effect. It is therefore important that MNCs are aware of developments with regard to new totalization agreements coming into force so they can adjust their policies and remuneration accordingly.

Trends: the shift from state social security to additional social security schemes

Traditionally, MNCs tried to keep the international worker home-base insured. This meant that international workers should, during their entire international career, stay in the same social security provision as prior to their work abroad. For this, coverage under the home social security system was generally continued.

Recently, a change in this approach can be seen. Companies investigate, due to cost-saving pressures, whether the same or comparable 'home-based' coverage can be achieved by either bearing certain risks themselves (e.g. disability risks) or seeking private coverage on a par with the state provision. For instance, companies tend to enter into voluntary insurance contracts, since the contributions are sometimes lower than the state contributions, while the benefits are the same. For instance, in France, voluntary social security contributions are, in general, not due on expat allowances and, as a result, the costs of social security coverage can be lowered substantially. Moreover, other cost-saving approaches can be identified. For example, some MNCs try to understand the health systems in the host countries so that they might not have to pay expensive international health insurance in places such as the Netherlands or Germany where inexpensive and good public health provision is accessible.

Policies in relation to social security

General

As described in the previous part of this section, MNCs have to cope with different social security schemes and rules while employing international workers. They not only have to be familiar with the international and national legislation that exists in relation to social security, they also have to ensure that they are aware of the social security developments that are happening throughout the world. MNCs need to be compliant with the rules but also have to ensure that the social security position of international workers is assured while working internationally. The remuneration policy of a company needs to be adjusted accordingly. Previously in this chapter, the importance of policies has been addressed. We will focus on the items MNCs can think of while drafting a policy in relation to social security. This is often included in the expatriate policy.

We will distinguish between assignments to countries with which a totalization agreement is concluded and to countries with which no totalization agreements exist.

Home-based and host-based approaches in the company's policy

While employing international workers, companies should determine whether to use a home-based approach or the host-based approach to social security provision. Based on a home-based approach, an international worker will remain, during his international career, covered for social security as if he was working in his home country. MNCs have a preference to choose this approach because international workers are thereby ensured that the international career will not have a detrimental influence on their social security position. Characteristics of the home-based approach are the following:

* Assumption of a temporary assignment
* To prevent changing the social security position of the individual the home coverage is continued
* Employer and employee continue to pay the same contributions as prior to the assignment
* Additional employment conditions are in line with the home social security
* In principle, coverage for family members is also included

Under the host-based approach, the international worker will be covered based on the social security legislation applicable in the host country. Main characteristics of the host-based approach are:

* Long-term assignments or localizations
* Host social security coverage. Legislation of host country is applicable. Other conditions and benefits will be applicable during the assignment
* Once returned to the home state, host social security benefits, in principle, can be exported to the home country
* Insurance periods abroad can in general be used by calculating the entitlement to benefits in the home country

While the home-based approach is commonly used, combinations of both approaches are being applied more often. This enables MNCs to optimize social security costs and reduce administrative costs in the most flexible way.

In the following part, we will describe certain important items which should be taken into consideration in the expat policy which is based on the home approach.

Important items to take into consideration in the policy

It is important to describe in the policy which approach the company is taking. In the following we will describe items that can be taken into consideration while drafting policy.

Assignment to treaty countries

Home benefits can often be exported to the host country if a home-based approach is applied. The following items are to be taken into consideration while drafting a policy for social security. If a home-based coverage is followed:

- It is important that the assignment contract is well structured. An international worker can only remain covered in the home social security system if certain criteria, as described previously are met.
- Apply for relevant certificates to the authorities (e.g. E101AI Certificate or Certificate of Coverage) to ensure home-based coverage.
- Determine whether family members are meant to be covered under the social security approach of the company. For instance, should additional insurances also be concluded for the family members?
- Conduct detailed cost planning.

The social security contributions in different countries vary throughout the world. MNCs should therefore take into consideration that paying social security contributions in the host country might be more beneficial. The home-based approach can then be reached by concluding additional (voluntary or private) insurances in the home country. In Figure 10.2, we have depicted the estimated social security contributions in five different countries due on an income of €100,000 gross per year.

Figure 10.2 shows that the likely social security contributions vary significantly with both employee and employer having to pay rather diverse amounts in the five countries. The employee contribution is lowest in the UK, while both employer and employee contributions in France are substantially higher than in the other four countries.

Below, we describe social security and taxation implications for individuals. Another important challenge that companies encounter while employing international workers relates to the lack of coordination between tax and social security (international) law. Therefore, it often happens that the international worker is taxable in country A while socially insured in country B (see Table 10.4).

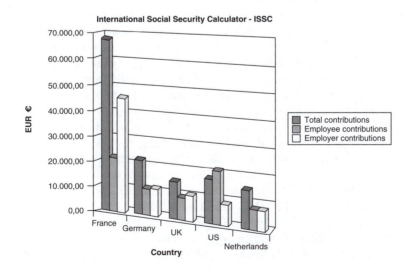

Figure 10.2 Estimated social security contribution in five developed countries on a €100,000 salary

Table 10.4 Income effects of location of social security determination

	Dutch tax and social security (€)	Dutch tax and Belgium social security (€)	Difference (€)
Gross annual income	120,000	120,000	
Taxes	45,144	45,144	
Social security	7,974	15,685	
Net annual income	66,882	59,171	7,711

Source: Ernst and Young calculations

Not only does this bring huge challenges to companies in relation to compliance and administrative rules, it might also cause differences to the net wage of employees. An employee with the same gross income who is not taxable and socially insured in the country as another employee, might have a lower net income while performing exactly the same activities in the same environment. Companies should think whether they want to compensate the employee for the lower net income. The taxation implications from working in different countries are described in more detail in the next chapter.

Assignment to non-treaty countries

Large MNCs often have operations in well over 50 countries, among these several non-treaty states. Important items to take into consideration while drafting an assignment policy to non-treaty countries are:

- Which insurances should be concluded to ensure the employee keeps home-based coverage or is not worse off? Among the options are voluntary, private, or own-risk company approaches.
- The MNC should be compliant with host and home social security legislation. For which insurances is the employee covered in the host system? Does a social security system exist in the host country? Does the employer have to register itself in the host country for social security (and/or tax) purposes?
- How to avoid duplication effects. If coverage in the host country exists for certain insurances, is coverage for that insurance in the home country still needed? Is it possible to negotiate/agree additional coverage in the home country only for the home benefits which are not covered in the host system?
- Home company pension in relation to the host state pension. In principle, home company pension schemes are linked to the entitlements under home state pension. However, if the employee falls liable to the host state pension, it is likely that the coverage then does not match the company pension in the home country. Which actions do the MNC want to take in this respect?
- Coverage of family members. The social security position of accompanying family members can also change due to the international career. Which approach does the MNC want to take towards the family members?

Market observers argue that companies focus now more on host rather than home social security. Furthermore, MNCs aim to save money by entering into agreements with private insurance companies rather than joining state schemes.

The effect of new working patterns and social security

While international employees generally work only in one country we have discussed a range of different types of international employment in earlier chapters. This will have major impact on the social security position of the employee.

1 Employees working in different countries with multiple employment contracts, including international hires. A tendency is that international workers start to have a more global role. More and more, international workers are working in several countries, both treaty as well as non-treaty countries. As a result, the social security position of the expatriate can change under each different assignment. The main challenge is to determine where the international worker is socially insured. Changes in the social security position do not only influence the employee him- or herself, they can also have a big impact for the MNC. For instance, registration obligations in the other country or higher costs with respect to social security contributions will have an impact on the organization.

2 Another tendency that can be seen is that more employees are working (partly) from home while employed by a company established in another country. As soon as an international worker changes her or his work location, this can have consequences for the social security position. For instance, a resident of France is working in Spain for a Spanish employer. Since the individual is only working in Spain, s/he is socially insured in Spain. If the employee starts working two days per week at home s/he will become socially insured in France. The employee will be entitled to other benefits, while the employer needs to register itself in France. Next to the obvious administrative costs, non-compliance can result in heavy fines retrospective over years. Companies with international employees should therefore be aware of the consequences when they allow employees to work from home or to have another small job in their home country next to their normal employment.

3 The impact of a Global Employment Organization (GEO). A GEO is a separate corporate entity that exists for the sole purpose of providing employment-related services globally to the organization's international operations or projects. Thus, it means that all 'international assignees' are ideally employed by a GEO using the same or similar employment terms. A GEO is described in more detail in Chapter 11.

If a company implements a GEO structure all employees who are assigned worldwide, are likely to receive an employment contract with the GEO who then assigns the employees. GEOs can provide advantages while structuring the IM of employees.

One advantage of structuring the assignments via a GEO is that social security planning is possible. The GEO can be established in a country in which the social security costs are low. If the requirements are met, the employees can remain covered in the social security scheme of the country in which the GEO is established. However, there is also a range of challenges which we will describe below.

As repeatedly outlined in this section, an important question is where the employee will be socially insured. The following situations are possible:

- The individual continues to have home social security coverage. This is normally only possible when the formal employer is established in the home country.
- The individual is socially insured in the host country. This is often the legally easiest solution.
- The individual is socially insured in the country of establishment of the GEO. One of the main important requirements to remain covered in the home social security system is that an employee is assigned by a company who has substance in the country of assignment. The question that arises is whether a GEO can meet this requirement.

It is generally very important to an international worker, whether or not s/he can remain covered by the home company pension scheme. A lot of company pension schemes require, in order to ensure continuation of the company pension during an assignment, that the employee is still employed by the formal employer. If an employee receives an employment contract with the GEO, this requirement will not be met. An international pension scheme might resolve this issue.

Overall, GEOs do not only provide advantages for companies while assigning employees but can also cause huge challenges in relation to social security. For the majority of the employees who will be assigned via a GEO, no major issues in relation to social security will arise.

However, if a lot of the employees who will be assigned via the GEO are assigned to treaty countries, the issues mentioned above can become an important obstacle, especially the fact that employment contracts are concluded with the GEO. It is therefore advisable to determine whether the assignment contracts can still be concluded with the home country for employees who might have issues with regard to social security. All other employment-related services can then still be arranged through the GEO. Furthermore, it is advisable to verify with the company pension provider whether it is possible to include the participation of international employees in the pension scheme where they have an employment contract with the GEO.

The career impact of the social security context

There are a number of organizational policies and practices in the areas of international selection, development, career management etc. that can either act as incentives or barriers to global careers. A specific example where recruitment patterns impact a range of diversity issues and trigger different social security circumstances is outlined in Box 10.1. Moreover, the perceived kudos of working abroad within the organization will have an impact on the decisions of individuals to pursue a global career. An extensive discussion can be found in Chapters 5, 7 and 8.

Box 10.1 Diversity and social security in the recruitment of a professor for a German university

A German University was seeking to recruit a professor of management (with a specific focus on leadership and organization) to start in April 2010. Given that the university is a state institution, incumbents can be appointed as civil servants, which has a range of advantages with respect to lower social security contributions and favourable pension conditions.

However, candidates were specifically reminded that they were not allowed to be older than 52 years upon start date. Moreover, with equal qualifications, people with handicaps would be selected. Lastly, the university is actively seeking to recruit women so that qualified female academics were strongly encouraged to apply.

This indicates that state and other recruitment activities can encourage the (national and) international careers of younger academics, handicapped persons and females. It also means that if a candidate who is older than 52 is accepted, then s/he will not become a civil servant but simply a normal employee with substantial effects on social security conditions.

Many individual preferences, family considerations, location specifics and career concepts will have an impact on whether and where people want to work abroad (see Chapter 5). Career and development considerations and a mindset of intercultural curiosity and inherent willingness to work abroad will partly determine whether individuals seek or accept expatriation offers.

A further important influence on global careers is the cross-national context that this chapter concentrates on. Companies and individuals react to the regulatory and compensation differences that they encounter in respect to the system of global mobility and to specific moves. This voluntary or negotiated support enables company-supported individuals to have long-term global careers without facing the perilous situation that self-initiated, non-supported global workers encounter. Thus, company-sent individuals are mostly better off in terms of having lesser insecurities, facing lesser actual dangers (or, at least a higher level of protection) and having mostly better remuneration packages and return assurances. Moreover, they tend to have support and better information regarding their eventual reintegration into their home social security system (Doherty et al. 2011). Thus, many company-sponsored individuals, while potentially worried about the differences in social security and other regulations, actually benefit in the long term from the non-alignments and non-standardization across borders as responsible employers might over-compensate them. In the few publicized cases in which high-ranking executives faced criminal charges in countries such as China, Russia or Venezuela the firms were quick to come to the aid and eventual 'rescue' of their employees.

In turn, self-initiated international workers lack both the financial support that company-sent individuals have and also the non-financial support mechanisms such as advice about social security and other regulatory differences between their home (or current adopted) and host countries. Therefore, they need to be more proactive in seeking information and ways to handle arising challenges. Furthermore, their lives can be much more precarious and guided by serendipity (Richardson and Mallon 2005). Government regulations might change abruptly and they might find themselves being subject to deportation or a forced curtailment of their stay. Overall, they have a much higher degree of risk (Doherty et al. 2011) and a need to understand local social security stipulations and state regulations. And yet, the research by Doherty et al. also found that their sample of self-initiated workers stayed, on average, about twice as long as company-sponsored individuals. This indicates a much higher need to pursue 'host-country' career patterns while working abroad.

In locations where there are few social security agreements between a self-initiated worker's country of origin and his or her host country, this can create an interesting, and so far under-researched, conflict. In these situations one would expect that there is a financial and social security pressure on the individual to return relatively quickly to his or her home country. However, if the individual decided to stay, the situation could reverse in that after a few years the return to his or her country of origin might be inhibited by factors such as the 'pension hit' that the individual could incur through leaving the current host country. Overall, differences in social security, taxation etc. can easily turn out to be detrimental for non-supported workers and immigrants and can act as major barriers at the point of decision to work abroad.

Returning to the issue of company-sponsored expatriates, in effect many national 'systems' differences support global careers as they might create extra incentives for individuals if organizations pay into both social security systems in order not to leave their workers worse off. In turn, they prove to be highly expensive for organizations that 'shoulder the administrative and payment burden'.

While other forms of international work are less impacted by extensive regulations, travel and visa restrictions and tax arrangements for highly mobile frequent flyers – often related to the time they spent in a country – will influence their travel and work plans as well as personal taxation. Organizations often have relatively extensive experience and help arrangements for international assignees. In turn, cross-border commuters and frequently flying managers and specialists are relatively neglected.

Summary and learning points

States have a rich and diverse history of social security laws and regulations. Differing social security regulations between countries create a substantial financial and administrative burden for organizations. They also have an impact on the international careers of individuals. This chapter has argued that differing social security approaches influence the global careers of self-initiated expatriates (including migrants) more than company-sponsored individuals who are 'cushioned' through their employers. We have outlined a range of options that companies and other organizations can choose in dealing with diverse social security regimes in states, given the existence or non-existence of international treaties.

Where supra-national regulations or bi-national treaties exist – such as totalization agreements or the EU Regulation 883/2004 – the challenges for organizations and individuals can become less extensive. This chapter gave an overview of important issues and challenges, key regulations and presented real-life scenarios and case studies. Moreover, it depicted the options that organizations have and discussed the impact on the global careers of individuals.

Key learning points include:

- The regulatory context varies substantially between countries. Organizations have to observe compliance pressures while balancing these with cost and motivational considerations.
- Social security regulations are highly complex. The main challenges and how organizations deal with these are outlined.
- A key consideration is where the individual is seen to contribute to the social security system and where s/he pays taxes. Decisions range from home-based and host-based approaches to a combination of these and the integration in a GEO.
- The effects for individuals are their entitlements to benefits in cases such as illness, unemployment, disability or old age pension. Therefore, much is at stake for individual careerists – an unfavourable design of the company's approach can be a barrier to mobility and can have negative motivational effects.
- While company-sponsored international assignees have the benefit of their organizational support mechanisms, including advice and financial support, self-initiated workers have a much more precarious situation. They have to be more proactive and bear higher risks.
- Companies and individuals have to be well informed to avoid some of the traps in social security and taxation regulations. For instance, moving from exclusively working in Spain (while living in France) to working part-time from home, triggers company establishment needs, taxation and other social security implications.
- States are working on creating more clarity with respect to social security and taxation issues. Totalization agreements can help to create more security and orientation for both organizations and individuals.

References

Dickmann, M., Doherty, N., Johnson, A. and Wood, M. (2007) 'Measuring the value of international assignments', Mysis, London: PricewaterhouseCoopers and Cranfield School of Management.

Doherty, N., Dickmann, M. and Mills, T. (2011) 'Exploring the motives of company-backed and self-initiated expatriates', *The International Journal of Human Resource Management*, forthcoming.

Pieters, D. (1993) *Introduction into the Basis Principles of Social Security*, Kluwer: Amsterdam.

Richardson, J. and Mallon, M. (2005) 'Career interrupted? The case of the self-directed expatriate', *Journal of World Business*, 40(4): 409–420.

11 International mobility at work: companies' structural, remuneration and risk considerations

MICHAEL DICKMANN AND CHRIS DEBNER

Objectives

This chapter:

- describes a range of strategic and operational approaches to compensation and risk issues;
- depicts a Global Employment Organization (GEO), a centralized structure that plans and administers IM on behalf of the whole organization – core underlying reasons are to reduce complexity and to achieve high degrees of standardization and integration;
- outlines key criteria and steps to design a global mobility policy;
- investigates the thorny issues related to international compensation – it identifies more than half a dozen different compensation approaches;
- explicates three key compensation approaches in detail: home-based, host-based and better of home or host approaches to international remuneration;
- discusses risk management issues after identifying a variety of diverse risk sources and areas;
- explores two approaches to localization, one in which the incumbent expatriate is being localized and the other where the post is localized, and outlines the different implications;
- distinguishes three approaches to taxation: tax equalization, tax protection and laissez faire;
- identifies the impact of the compensatory context and the organizational and individual reactions to these;
- illuminates the impact on global careers;
- introduces an integrative case study that allows the reader to work with a real-life example.

Michael Dickmann, Cranfield University, School of Management, UK and Chris Debner, Ernst & Young, Human Capital, Switzerland

Introduction

By now, the reader has accompanied us on a long journey through the world of global careers. On the way we have explored diverse strands of career theories and discussed their application to international work experiences. Throughout, we have distinguished between organizational and individual perspectives and have, where appropriate, introduced further viewpoints, e.g. those of national cultures, institutions, societies or national states. We looked at IHRM configurations in the new competitive world of work and explored a range of corporate strategies, structures, policies and practices, including those of a variety of non-traditional forms of international work. Then we explored individual and organizational considerations, before, during and after work abroad and their short- and long-term outcomes, concentrating on global career implications.

Having covered these topics allows us to approach compensation and risk elements of international work with a different mindset. In terms of our overall framework (see Figure 11.1) we will, as started in Chapter 10, cover the base box which influences much of the organizational context in which individual global careers unfold. It was argued in Chapter 9 that multinational firms have a tendency to approach IM predominantly using operational and cost (return on investment) considerations. As such, the design and running of the IM framework is one of the key responsibilities of the HR department.

Beyond discussing some of the above issues in more depth, we have two key objectives in this chapter. First, we will argue that MNCs and other international

Figure 11.1 A framework of global careers: remuneration and risk

organizations would be well advised to incorporate strategic aspects, risk considerations and career effects to a higher degree than is currently often the case. Second, we strive to provide hands-on, practical models and thought processes to enable the reader to reflect and improve on the design and maintenance aspects of IM approaches within organizations.

Structures and processes: considering a GEO

In Chapter 2 we introduced a range of organizational configurations that strive to increase global competitive advantage through worldwide innovation, local responsiveness and global efficiency (Bartlett and Ghoshal 1989; Dickmann et al. 2009). The higher the degree of standardization within HRM, the lower the complexity of administration and the higher the scale and scope effects (Dickmann and Müller-Camen 2006). A GEO is based on this idea, which, according to some industry experts, is becoming more fashionable among large MNCs who have a base of permanently mobile staff. In its most basic sense, a GEO, also referred to as a Global Employment Company, is a separate corporate entity that exists for the sole purpose of providing employment-related services globally to the organization's international operations or projects.

Typically a multinational company's assignee population can create complex home- and host-country combinations with various short-, long-term or permanent cross-border moves happening, making it difficult for the organization to keep track and administer (see Figure 11.2).

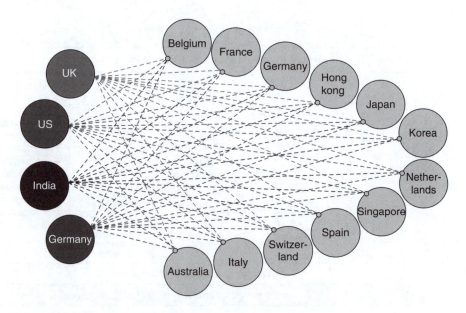

Figure 11.2 Example model without GEO
Source: © Ernst & Young 2009, printed with permission

A GEO can be the solution to some arising challenges such as heavy administrative burden, inequities among expatriates and high cost of the IA programme management. The reasons for this include that the GEO allows a more consistent application of IM policies and practices standardization and, thereby, helps to reduce costs. This standardization will also reduce inequities among IAs. However, depending on the chosen compensation approach, given that these expatriates come from diverse home environments, it might not be perceived as positive by those who originate from high-salary and extensive benefits countries. In addition, a GEO can help to relocate employees in a tax-effective and compliant way as well as providing equitable employment terms and conditions for the expatriates.

As such, a GEO forms a Centre of Excellence for assignment management and can provide employees with incentives that promote global mobility in a consistent manner. Furthermore, a GEO provides a centre for career and succession planning, performance management and salary administration for the internationally experienced global talent pool. This links well to suggestions in the IM literature to keep employees 'on a radar screen' (Harris and Dickmann 2005) and to create an integrated global career system (Lazarova and Caligiuri 2001; Lazarova and Cerdin 2007; Chapter 9).

When establishing a GEO, the new entity becomes the recognized employer of the company's international assignee population, and subsequently seconds or leases these employees to the various international operations or projects of the parent company in return for a management fee (see Figure 11.3). These fees are used to pay the salaries and benefits of the employees in the GEO and a mark-up is kept

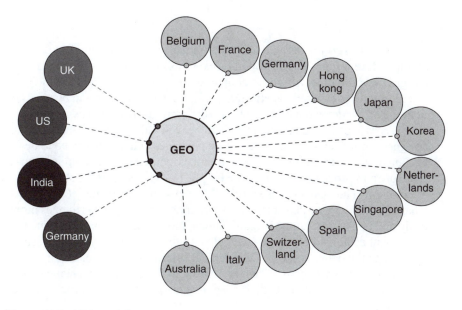

Figure 11.3 GEO model
Source: © Ernst & Young 2009, printed with permission

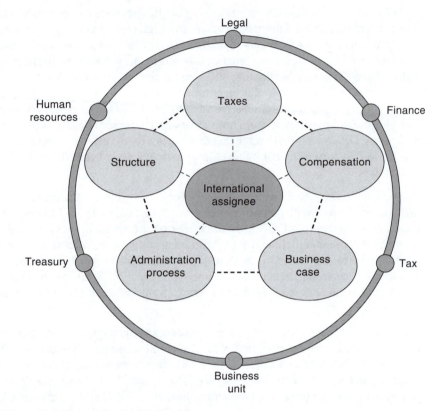

Figure 11.4 Potential organizational issues
Source: © Ernst & Young 2009, printed with permission

for the GEO's services as an employer. Typically, in the set-up of a GEO structure, all the different functions and operational units need to be considered to which the assignees would otherwise have contact with regarding moving around the globe. These functions can include HR, tax, legal, treasury, finance and business units. Sending an assignee out of a GEO is no different from a usual assignment – the business case of the assignment needs to be well validated with the business of the assignee's home country, compensation packages and policies need to be designed, tax and immigration consequences evaluated, while having consistent structure and processes in place (see Figure 11.4) to support the success of the assignment. The business cases for GEOs can vary significantly (compare Chapters 2 and 5), while some companies try to handle their assignees more centrally and consistently, other organizations implement GEOs to mitigate potential permanent establishment risks (see below in the risk section). Other business cases can pursue the better control of the transfer pricing aspects (regulatory legislation surrounding intercompany transfers of money) or corporate substance objectives (entities need to substantiate their corporate tax position by the means of being an employer).

Despite the numerous advantages described above, there are also potential non-financial and financial risks to be considered when setting up a GEO. Employees who are seconded from the GEO are sometimes so-called 'global nomads' with back-to-back assignments and often no ties to their original home countries. This population has often higher expectations towards the company as a return for their flexibility. An example for permanently mobile staff is that of the International Managers in HSBC, a large global bank. Young graduates are being chosen for high-flying banking careers and are sent on a global career path in which they are routinely moved from one country to the next. The approximately 360 International Managers occupy key positions within HSBC but do not expect to work for a substantial time in their home country (Harris and Dickmann 2005).

The organization needs to put significant effort into global career management to enable continuous employment and to identify reasonable assignments to fit the business and assignee needs in order not to lose this valuable talent. For further policy suggestions see Chapters 8 and 9. A GEO makes it easier to enforce corporate policies and to create standardized procedures.

Other concerns when establishing a GEO are whether the company has the infrastructure to deliver global benefits and an international pay scheme, and if the organization can meet the needs of its international employees. Furthermore, there are significant compliance risks around corporate and individual taxation, social security and immigration and employment law, which should be well analysed and managed in order to avoid penalties and reputational risks. Compensation and risk considerations are explicated below.

Global mobility policy development

A global mobility policy (GMP) is a document provided to an employee going on an IA, which outlines the compensation and benefits approach, tax and social security treatment, allowances, terms and conditions, process and assignment support for the employee and his/her family. GMPs are often customized for the type of assignment. Design, implementation and maintenance of these documents are usually the responsibility of HR (or a specialized global mobility team). They contain the regulations and specifications concerning:

- pre-assignment preparation;
- shipment of goods and travel expenses;
- home and host accommodation;
- family, dual careers and training provisions;
- compensation, benefits and assignment allowances;
- tax treatment, social security, pension and insurances;
- repatriation and localization;
- information with regards to assignment termination.

When developing a new IA policy a holistic approach can be most effective. Global mobility strategic objectives, process management, compensation

---

Box 11.1 Key considerations when designing a global mobility policy

When drawing up or reviewing a global mobility policy (GMP), a number of key factors should be taken into account:

- eligibility and scope (e.g. including post-return considerations);
- cost to the company (ongoing, one-off, risks);
- market rates and competitiveness;
- attractiveness to international assignees and their families (general);
- specific attractiveness of career, training, development, general support, security, health, housing, education and dual career approaches;
- tax and social security;
- legality considerations;
- transfer pricing and re-charge agreements;
- corporate tax rules;
- employment law implications.

Source: based on Ernst & Young (2009),
additions by Michael Dickmann

---

approaches, corporate tax, tax and social security compliance, as well as vendor and risk management should be addressed during the developmental phase. The first step is to clarify global mobility strategic considerations and the identification of the objectives of the GMP (see Chapter 2). There needs to be a discussion on the current and future assignee population, the required assignment types and the existing and future country combinations of assignments. It should be identified if new policies for further types of assignments have to be developed. Once these basic conditions have been set, it is recommended to compare these conditions with the existing policy elements and to transfer the results of this analysis into a standard policy framework format in a second step.

A policy framework is a logically structured document, enabling an overview of all the policy benefits as well as terms and conditions the company would like to offer to the assignees. Organizations often attempt to align the framework with the global mobility strategy. Comparing the policy with those of other organizations inside and outside the industry (external benchmarking) can enable an assessment as to whether terms and conditions offered to international assignees are too generous or below market. Of course, direct comparisons are difficult and each IA might vary on a range of dimensions as discussed in earlier chapters in this book.

Table 11.1 Overview of standard policy items

Introduction	Method of payment	Automobiles	Leave and working hours
Pre-location preparation	Income tax	Education	Spouse assistance
Compensation and benefits	Travel	Medical	Termination
Career development	Accommodation	Insurance	Other

Source: Ernst & Young (2009)

The policy framework forms the basis for writing the policy itself. It tracks outstanding decisions, attempting to generate a good overview of the main topics and provides a back-up document that can be referred to in order to see the reasoning behind some benefit decisions and process information. It also enables the viewing of a variety of policies side by side to enable an alignment of their terms and conditions. Additionally the policy framework can be used as a basis for an HR manual that helps HR and the IA team, to design and maintain underlying processes behind some policy items. The reader is reminded that Chapters 7 and 8 outline further policies that increase expatriate success and retention.

Box 11.2 Policy review criteria

There is a range of policy review areas that are useful to consider:

Policy review area	Sample question
Strategic alignment	Is the policy aligned with business/HR strategy and future expansion plans? Is the policy aligned with the career system and talent management process?
Policy alignment	Is the policy aligned with other (group) global mobility policies?
Compliance	Does the policy promote tax, social security and pension compliance?
Cost effectiveness	Are the salaries, benefits and allowances paid in a tax-effective way? Is the company protected against claims and losses?
Completeness Consistency	Are all (important) practice items covered? Is the organization consistent in its market comparisons? Is it consistent across different groups of individuals in terms of procedural and distributive justice? Are all items covered consistently in terms of level of detail?
Attractiveness to international assignee	How attractive is the policy to the assignee? How attractive is the policy to the partner? How attractive is the policy to dependents?
Structure and wording	Is the policy built upon a logical structure (often following assignment process)? Are potential misunderstandings minimized?

Source: Ernst & Young (2009), additions by Michael Dickmann

In the third step, the policy framework will be turned into a live policy document. After the development, the new policy has to be implemented. There are various strategies available to implement a policy, but the most commonly used strategy is to 'grandfather' the existing assignees under the current policies while using the new policies for all new assignees from Day 1 of the implementation. The effort to implement a new policy for existing assignees is considered very burdensome, as basically their terms and conditions are likely to change, which in most cases causes assignees to lose some of their benefits. The phasing in of a new policy takes a high administrative effort, as normally the cases of all assignees need to be looked upon individually, since they differ by country combinations, family size and income. A consistent treatment during a phase-in of a policy is very hard to achieve.

Once a strategy has been chosen the communication to the employees needs to be developed and the policy has to be made available by using different tools and information channels. Often, it is seen as helpful to include a frequently asked questions (FAQs) section. As different mobility policies would run different HR internal processes, the development of an HR manual as an internal handbook for policy handling should be considered. If deemed necessary, the manual can also detail processes that are specific to existing country combinations in the company's GMP.

It is suggested that companies review their GMPs more often than in the past and on an annual basis. One of the results is a subsequent change and refinement. Below, we will discuss the thorny issue of international compensation.

Compensation for international work

There are various compensation approaches available that multinationals have been adopting for their international assignee population. Dowling et al. (2008) argue that organizations strive for consistency in the design of the compensation systems in order to achieve comparability and equity. Moreover, MNCs need to attract and retain staff, facilitate cost-effective transfers of individuals to their host country, put mechanisms in place to guard the lives and health of their staff working abroad (and, of course, working domestically) and need to implement systems that are easy to administer. The complexity of administration, despite the high incidence of the outsourcing of IM activities, is demonstrated by a study that found that the ratio of expatriates to IM specialists is approximately three times as high as the ratio of staff to total HR specialists (Dickmann et al. 2007).

Individuals, in turn, look to gain financial protection and financial advancement from an international compensation system (Dowling et al. 2008). The authors also argue that prospective expatriates would like their employer to help them with housing, education (of their children or partners) and recreation. Dickmann and Mills (2010) suggest that issues of security, health, development and career advancement are also important in the decision to go abroad. These might be specified in an IM policy framework (discussed above).

Briscoe and Schuler (2004) distinguish seven compensation approaches: negotiation/ad hoc, balance sheet, localization, lump sum, cafeteria, regional systems and global. These approaches can sometimes be combined (e.g. global/cafeteria or negotiation/lump sum). However, research from Ernst & Young, a professional services firm, indicates that in recent years companies tend to use the following two approaches: a home-based approach (balance sheet or tax equalization) or a host-based approach (Ernst & Young 2009). Therefore, we will concentrate on the latter approaches, only briefly introducing some of the others.

Negotiation/ad hoc means that each time there is an expatriation or other form of international work, the company will negotiate with prospective international assignees to agree on a mutually acceptable contract. This is likely to be more frequent in firms that are in the early stages of internationalization (Adler and Ghadar 1990; Briscoe and Schuler 2004) and there is a tendency for the company to 'offer whatever it takes' to send their valued employees abroad. In fact, monetary compensation for any perceived hardships or problems is quite common among corporations that lack a good IM framework or a sophisticated understanding of the international aspirations of their staff (Dickmann et al. 2005; Dickmann et al. 2008).

The lump-sum approach is often the result of negotiation and might be a reaction to the mindset of not interfering with the lifestyles of international assignees. This is achieved by refraining from setting certain budgets regarding housing, travel etc. Instead, a lump-sum is agreed that covers all compensation aspects in relation to the assignee's stay in a foreign country, his or her family matters (including education needs), travel, or incentive to work abroad. Sometimes the amount to be paid to the expatriate is split into payments at the outset of the IA, during and after assignment completion. This is often not tax effective for either the employee or the employer, depending on the chosen taxation approach.

Global or regional compensation systems simply refer to the geographic reach of this IM policy and are linked to the IHRM configurations discussed in Chapter 2. They are reminiscent of Heenan and Perlmutter's (1979) distinctions of regiocentric or geocentric organizations with a pragmatic turn. Thus, some firms have developed a regional benefits and compensation system in order to establish a more equitable treatment across national borders in that region. Global approaches reflect a similar concern but are also restricted by local market rates. Thus, in practice it is mostly for the top managerial hierarchies that a global compensation package is developed and applied.

A cafeteria system – akin to the domestic approaches used – enables expatriate workers to choose between a range of benefits including, typically, company cars, insurance, housing provided by the employer, and education allowances for children. The services are priced and the international worker has a 'budget' up to which they can choose to 'buy' the benefits. The issue with a cafeteria system is the different tax treatment of benefits in various jurisdictions. If a company chooses to pick up the host-country taxes, the cost to the employer will depend on the benefit choices of the assignee. The latter is the reason why this approach is only very rarely seen in an international context.

The other compensation approaches outlined by Briscoe and Schuler (2004) are integrated in the wider discussion below. According to the Ernst & Young Expatriate Survey (2009) about 80 per cent of the multinationals use the home-based compensation approach. In general terms, following this approach the assignee compensation is built on the home-country base salary, adjusted to the cost of living in the host country and tax equalized back to the home country. This approach is normally easily accepted by the employees as they neither encounter a loss nor a win compared with had they not taken the assignment. Assignees are kept as long as legally possible in their home-country social security and pension schemes with the aim that there will be no gaps in the benefits level at the time of repatriation. Thus, the home-based approach is applicable to a diverse population of assignees.

Home-based country compensation approach

An example of home-based compensation is the balance sheet approach (see Figure 11.5) which attempts to equalize purchasing power for staff who have comparable level positions without leaving the international assignees worse off than before (Dowling et al. 2008). Its starting point is the assignee's home compensation including salary, benefits and other incentive elements. As outlined in Figure 10.8 then the organization factors in incentives to accept working abroad and elements that take care of the different local cost of living, tax and remuneration situation. This will result in the deal offered to the prospective assignee. Overall, there are two major forces exerting pressures for moves into two different directions. The need to be efficient and to save costs is one driver to reduce the incentive components in the deal. In turn, the need to attract high-calibre candidates exerts pressures to increase the benefits associated with working abroad. This is why many commentators urge companies to focus on non-monetary incentives, most prominently on managerial and personal development as well as on global career paths and prospects (Lazarova and Cerdin 2007).

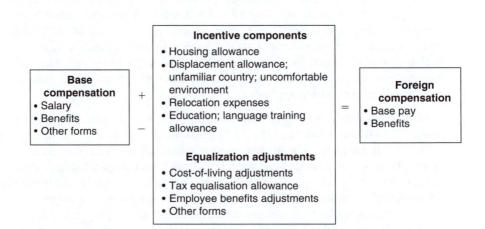

Figure 11.5 A balance sheet approach to international compensation
Source: Briscoe and Schuler (2004: 312)

In terms of possible drawbacks of the home-based approach, administrating the assignment benefits and tax-equalization can result in high costs for the company due to many factors that add to complexity. Depending on the nationality of the assignees and their home country salary levels, there are differences in pay and allowances for the same grade assignees in the host countries (Dowling et al. 2008). As a result, there might be inequities not only among the assignee population but also between assignees and local employees in the host countries. These differences can go both ways. While it is common to assume that the expatriate earns more than a local employee, this could also be the reverse. For example, a manager from Thailand going to the USA is likely to find that domestic managers will have a much higher salary. This has increased the voices that demand less expatriation and more investment in local talent (Hailey and Harry 2008). Overall, despite its disadvantages, the home-based compensation approach remains the most commonly used approach among multinationals. Often the gap between an assignee and a local employee is bridged with a so-called position allowance that raises the income to the level of a local peer.

Host-country compensation approach

The host-country compensation approach – often called the 'going rate approach' or localization – has gained more popularity recently due to its cost savings opportunities for the company. In a study of the pay and general cost associated with 3,450 expatriate assignments in nine companies, Dickmann and his colleagues (2007) found that those two organizations that had host-country compensation approaches had the lowest costs. Interestingly, the level of additional expatriation costs (over and above the cost of non-expatriated peers) had no statistically significant impact on retention or performance.

According to the Ernst & Young Expatriate Policy Survey (2009) this approach is only used by less than 10 per cent of the multinationals. The host-country compensation approach means that the assignee is transferred to the host country's local compensation terms and conditions. Essentially, the organization needs to decide what is the right local benchmark. For instance, a German engineering company such as Siemens operating in the UK would need to decide whether the relevant benchmark would be other UK engineering companies or other German companies operating in the UK or all companies active in Great Britain.

From the company's point of view it is a cost-effective way to assign people, as no or minimal administration is required regarding the assignment benefits. Equality is established among assignees as well as local employees in the host country. It is a suitable approach when localization is foreseen or preferred at the end of the assignment. For the assignee such a compensation approach, however, can result in a potential decrease in salary level and quality of living in the host country. Also, such an approach can result in loss and/or gaps in home-country social security and pension schemes and therefore cause a troublesome repatriation. Moreover, other potential drawbacks of the host-country approach are that they might lead to variations between expatriates of the same nationality in different countries and to differences in compensation between different assignment options for the same employee (Dowling et al. 2008).

Due to these considerations, certain high salary and quality of living 'preferred locations' among international mobile workers might emerge, whereas no acceptance might be gained to meet business and assignment needs in countries with lower salary levels. For these locations, extra incentives might be needed to gain sufficient interest from qualified candidates. Without these incentives, the applicability of a host-based approach depends very much on the markets in which a company operates.

Better of home or host country approach

The third approach is to structure the assignee compensation based on better of home or host approach. This approach is well accepted by the expatriates as they are always subject to better, or at least similar, equalized employment and living conditions as in their home countries. It also leads to equity among assignees and locals in high-cost locations. In other countries, however, expatriates can end up on very different compensation terms and conditions. Better of home and host is the most costly approach as the salary and benefits difference between host and home countries is covered by the company, whereas an assignee is never worse off. In addition, this approach results in a double administrative burden, especially related to the home benefits administration and may again cause 'preferred locations' as assignees can easily calculate in which host country they can gain most. However, this approach is a seldom used one that bears few advantages for organizations.

Overall, Dowling and his colleagues remind us about the complexity, challenges and choices in global pay (Dowling et al. 2008: 175). They distinguish between the internal context, choices regarding the pay context and the external context. Key internal context parameters include industry, size, level of internationalization, life cycle and organizational structure, all of which influence organizational choices with regards to the organizational and sub-unit strategy, HR strategy, organizational culture and employment relationships (cf. Chapter 2). The external context refers to the local market conditions, national and supra-national laws, institutional factors (e.g. trade unions, employer federations, educational systems and standards) and general cultural norms. Both internal and external factors exert influence on the compensation choices that firms will have to take. These choices are about the general pay approach as discussed above, pay levels and the enduring tensions with regards to the global–local dilemma. Moreover, the usual pay considerations, such as remuneration of job vs. skill, performance vs. seniority, individual vs. group, short vs. long term, internal vs. external equity, hierarchical vs. egalitarian, organizational vs. sub-unit performance, the degree of pay at risk etc., apply. However, due to the influence of different national cultures and institutions they become more complex. These challenges relate to the degree of standardization and localization of remuneration approaches which might vary according to the hierarchical level under consideration (Dickmann et al. 2009).

Risk management and taxation considerations in international work

The business world is more interconnected than it has ever been. Multinationals require more efficient ways of managing their global mobility in terms of cost pressures, pressure for better compliance and, at the same time, managing the continuing business need for sending employees around the globe. The risks of operating a globally mobile workforce are multiplying, and so is the likelihood of those risks materializing as tax and immigration authorities around the globe cooperate to investigate any cases of non-compliance. Some of the key risks evolving from IA programmes (as shown in Figure 11.6) are:

- *Cost risk*: non-compliance with local legislation, e.g. expatriate-related tax positions that turn out to be incorrect can mean a cost in interest, and penalties in the local jurisdiction.
- *Regulatory compliance*: failing to comply with local regulations, or getting that compliance wrong, can seriously expose the business to a legal challenge from employees, partners or the authorities. Non-compliance, for example with local immigration laws, does not only mean the withdrawal of visas and potential

Figure 11.6 Risk management for international assignments
Source: © Ernst & Young 2009 from a 2009 internal presentation, printed with permission

deportation for the individuals, but also significant financial penalties in some markets.

- *Risk of prosecution*: immigration and tax laws in many countries have criminal penalties, including imprisonment of individuals for tax evasion.
- *Permanent establishment risk*: depending on the level, function and nature of the activities of the assignees they might create a permanent establishment, meaning a corporate taxable presence for their employer in the host country.
- *Business reputation risk*: in an age of stakeholder activism, activities that can be perceived as doubtful, however flimsy the charges, can contribute to loss of reputation and eventual loss of value. No business wants to be seen (either knowingly or through negligence) as careless of its people or engaged in breaches of local law, or for top executives around the world to be viewed as such.

To manage global mobility risk appropriately requires a holistic approach, involving HR, tax, the legal department, internal audit, support teams (such as payroll) and operating units. Ernst & Young surveys chief financial officers and other international experts regularly. It is surprising that fewer than 50 per cent of the respondents in Ernst & Young's global tax risk survey 'Steady Course, Uncharted Waters' (2008) said that employment tax risk and associated cost was within their remit. Thus, organizations seem to expose themselves to substantial risks.

Taxation of international assignees

The amount of taxes that individuals pay often has an impact on their lifestyles and, therefore, taxes on expatriate incomes are likely to impact on what they can afford and how they live. However, from the point of view of the organization, this is a highly complex challenge as different countries have different tax systems. In order for international assignees not to suffer in terms of taxation in a host country, organizations have adopted the following main taxation approaches: tax equalization, tax protection and the so-called 'laissez-faire' approach. Taxes are repeatedly reported to be the most difficult aspect of global mobility and also to be one of the main cost drivers of IAs. Moreover, most MNCs provide a range of tax-related services cost free to their international assignees, including advice by a tax specialist (Briscoe and Schuler 2004).

Tax equalization (TEQ) is a process that ensures that the tax costs incurred by an assignee on an assignment approximate to what the tax costs would have been had they remained at home. It is the most common taxation approach in the global mobility world (Dowling et al. 2008). The intent of TEQ is that the assignee neither suffers significant financial hardship nor realizes a financial windfall from the tax consequences of the assignment. The employer bears the responsibility for paying the assignee's actual home- and host-country tax costs. In exchange, the assignee 'pays' to the employer a stay-at-home hypothetical tax as determined under the company's tax equalization policy. The advantages of TEQ are that it keeps assignees' tax-neutral and that it promotes equity among the assignees. Also, assignees have no incentive to go to one country rather than another for tax reasons. While the company offsets the higher taxes due to the assignee being taxable in a host country with higher taxes, it can also gain a windfall, achieving lower employment costs when an assignee moves from a high-tax country to a low-tax country. As a consequence, the use of a TEQ approach can result in significant cost savings especially for companies with large outbound populations from high-tax countries. On the other hand hypothetical taxes can potentially create endless arguments and negotiations with the employee in absence of a consistent TEQ policy, especially regarding items such as personal income and stock options, which are often not handled in a consistent manner by companies. Companies should also consider the potential additional administration responsibilities and the cost of running the TEQ programme for their existing global workforce. Many companies tend to outsource hypothetical tax calculations and tax return preparation to external tax providers to ensure consistency and compliance.

Tax protection, a simpler approach to taxation, is a process that reimburses an assignee the excess taxes he or she incurs while on an IA, versus the taxes that would have been paid in the home location. The employee is responsible for the payment of all actual home- and host-country taxes. The annual tax protection calculation then compares the stay-at-home hypothetical tax to the actual worldwide taxes paid by the employee. If the actual worldwide taxes exceed the stay-at-home tax amount the company will reimburse the excess to the employee. If the actual worldwide taxes are less than the stay-at-home tax, the employee can keep the windfall. The main advantage of the approach for the assignees is that they are never worse off in terms of taxes. For the company it means minimal administration effort, if the assignee is not worse off there is no need to get involved in calculations of hypothetical tax. On the other hand the tax protection approach is less transparent for the assignee than TEQ as the potential tax cost reimbursement only takes place at the year end. Depending on policy and country combination it might cause a cash flow issue for the assignee. Another disadvantage of this approach is that the popularity of high-tax destinations will be low among assignees, while low-tax destinations are incentivized by a tax protection policy. As with a TEQ approach, it is necessary to define the income that is protected from higher taxes very precisely in a policy to avoid arguments about tax payments.

The laissez-faire approach means for an employer to do nothing about the taxation of their employees and to basically leave the full responsibility for filing home and host tax returns to the assignee. As the company does not get involved in the taxation matters of the assignee, there is no cost, nor administrative effort for applying the approach. As an advantage for the employees, they can lower their tax bill in countries where taxes are lower than in their home countries. Higher tax costs in some locations would then need to be picked up by the employee and can make these locations less attractive. This approach is, however, not advisable as it might cause high tax and payroll compliance risk for the assignees and company, which in turn can translate into high penalties and interest costs. In many countries the responsibility for paying employment taxes rests with the employer and makes the employer liable for potential non-compliance with local tax laws. It also adds significant administration responsibilities on the assignees' shoulders, while host-country tax laws and regulations can vary significantly from the home taxation system. In addition, employees are likely not to accept assignments to higher tax cost countries.

Most countries tax foreign nationals working in their countries based on their worldwide income with a few exceptions, e.g. some Middle Eastern countries, where there is no individual taxation (e.g. UAE, Saudi Arabia etc.). Many companies are dealing with expatriate tax compliance through outsourcing as professional tax services firms are seen as better equipped with the tax knowledge and tools. These service providers also have access to the frequent changes in international and local tax laws and can monitor these to support compliance. This is akin to the changes in social security associated with payroll and which are one factor in the decision to outsource (Dickmann and Tyson 2005).

Outsourcing is a means of passing a part of the control for tax compliance over to the service provider and its advisors, while assignees remain responsible for providing timely and accurate compensation information from other sources than work-related income. One of the main challenges regarding expatriate taxation administration is obtaining complete and accurate compensation information for compliance purposes. This is especially challenging as taxable benefits during the assignment might be provided in the home and host country. Currently, there are no truly global payroll systems to meet the demands of multinationals, where companies have tax reporting and withholding requirements in multiple countries simultaneously. Payroll systems require the integration with accounts payable or other non-recurring payments with multi-currency delivery and foreign exchange conversion. In addition a global banking partner would be needed. Non-compliance with local legislation, in turn, can lead to financial damage for the assignee and company in terms of interest and penalties cost, as well as reputational risk for the corporate image. Furthermore, additional time and money spent on tax administration means loss of productivity and unhappy employees at the workplace.

Localization of assignees or positions

We have extensively discussed, especially in Chapters 2 and 5, the reasons for using international workers, often expatriates. While there is a mix of advantages and disadvantages, expatriation is often regarded as costly with uncertain benefits. Triggered by increasing cost pressures, MNCs are considering more efficient solutions to pursue their global goals. Besides a fundamental reconsideration of the IHRM strategies and operational implications, two approaches stand out that do not involve extensive changes in the IM approach: assignee localization and position localization.

Assignee localization

Assignee localization takes place when the foreign incumbent of a position changes his or her contract to accept a local employment deal. The reasons for this could be manifold. If the impetus comes from the organization, it might have defined a maximum time in (foreign) post – such as 3 or 5 years – and if the expatriate decides to stay on, a localization process will be triggered. Some of the key motivations for individuals' decisions to stay include finding a local partner, broader life style reasons or the earning and career potential of working in the host country (especially when it is a case of inpatriation or the case of an expatriate from a developing country of origin who works in a developed, high-salary country). While the organization still has a foreign professional in the post – with all the positive and negative implications discussed in Chapters 6 and 7 – the cost and contractual structure is comparable to host-country employees. In many countries – especially the low-cost ones but also higher cost hosts depending on the IM policy – the MNC is likely to save substantial amounts of money. In a conservative estimate, Dickmann and his colleagues (2007) estimated that this would save approximately 50 per cent of total employment costs.

Where localization is primarily driven by the employer, the process becomes complex due to the need to find a balance between cost savings for the organization and the attractiveness to the individual. Essentially, organizations need to factor in the risk of losing experienced staff in a foreign position and compliance risks from changing the status of the employment contract. While a first step often involves identifying persons who could be localized (sometimes by the analysis of assignment lengths or patterns, sometimes through interviews with staff), a determination of the gap between current and future compensation and benefits, including social security issues, tends to follow. Where MNCs have used a host-country approach to compensation, the gaps are likely to be less pronounced than with a home-country approach and, therefore, gaining the buy-in from the expatriate might be easier to achieve.

Ernst & Young (2009b) outline some scenarios where localization seems to be easier, mainly where the expatriate is benefiting from the move. This is the case where the individual incurs lower tax costs in the host country, is a member of a better social security programme, where the person wants to localize due to better career prospects or other personal reasons and where he or she receives a higher salary than in the home country. However, the reverse is true in a context in which the expatriate will not benefit from the localization move. These contexts include where:

- the tax costs for the employee are higher;
- there is a less favourable social security system;
- benefits are to be withdrawn that are judged as attractive by the expatriate (schooling for family, housing, medical insurance etc.);
- there are family issues that create an interest by the individual to return to the home country (e.g. elderly parents); and
- the person earns a lower base salary in the host location.

The list of challenging context factors in localization can be extended to cover further barriers to stay in the country indeterminately. Further elements include working in countries that are highly insecure or are viewed as hardship countries for other reasons, home pension arrangements that rely on payments into the home scheme (e.g. defined benefit plans) or the employee having a very promising career path in the country-of-origin operation. Organizations are also unlikely to insist on localization if they believe that their valuable employee is highly likely to leave the organization if the contractual situation worsens or where the regulatory consequences of working long-term in the host country are highly complex.

Overall, the critical issues that organizations should evaluate in the assignee local-ization decision include salary and bonus, immigration, labour law, housing, schooling, family issues, individual taxation, social security and pension and indi-vidual drivers of expatriates to (continue to) work abroad.

It might be decided to localize the assignee using a phase-out approach where changes happen gradually over time or by using a 'big bang' approach of immedi-ate localization (with or without further compensation through lump sum pay-ments etc.). The advantages for the individual through a phase-out approach are clearly monetary and emotional through a longer adaptation time. The 'big bang' approach that includes no compensation could cause hardship for the employee and might not be possible for all locations or circumstances (e.g. the assignee has recently bought a house and had included the assignment premium in personal affordability calculations). Obviously, a mixture of approaches is possible depend-ing on the circumstances of individual and organization. For instance, organiza-tions might strive to have an immediate change in salary, COLA (cost of living adjustment) and bonus terms, while providing a phase-out in terms of international schooling for family members and a lump sum to compensate for housing arrange-ments.

Position localization

To eliminate current and future assignment costs, MNCs might decide to localize a position so that they will not send a further expatriate to fill it. In essence they have two options – either international assignees are charged with identifying and train-ing a local successor, or the organization seeks local talent to replace the existing incumbent with or without a development period. Filling positions with local man-agers which were traditionally occupied by expatriates sends a number of positive messages to host-country employees. The key ones include, first, the distribution of power might be seen as becoming more equal and host-country employees might find it easier to identify with the local and overall organization (Dickmann and Müller-Camen 2006). Second, where the localization of position includes the top jobs in the local operation unit, high potentials are not confronted with a 'glass ceiling' in terms of careers and might be more motivated to learn and perform well (Hailey and Harry 2008). Naturally, this will place higher demands on local selec-tion, development and career management approaches. Third, the increased career opportunities and the access to jobs with potentially higher levels of responsibility might reduce the labour turnover of top local talents.

But there are also risks and costs with regards to position localization. For instance, local talent simply might not be available or might take too much time to develop. Next, there is an influence on the global leadership approaches for highly international organizations. Their top talents are likely to have less foreign work experience or will have to acquire international insights through different forms of cross-border mobility (see Chapter 4). If organizations distinguish between cul-tural sensitivity and cultural understanding – where the latter takes a much longer time to develop – this raises questions as to the feasibility of large-scale position localization. Lastly, Edström and Galbraith (1977) distinguish a control and coordination reason for expatriation. Restricting the available positions to work abroad will also have consequences with regards to cultural and social coordination (see Chapters 2 and 5).

The career impact of the compensation and risk context

Differences in regulations and compensation structures between countries can be a driver for some individuals to work in a foreign country due to these persons perceiving direct and indirect benefits. For instance, a move to a low-cost country while retaining a high salary, moving to a more secure country or a location with lower administrative burdens is likely to appeal to many individuals. However, the complexity involved in the regulatory and compensation context, a low degree of transparency and information and the resulting insecurity are likely to act as barriers to IM (cf. Chapter 10). This is why inter-country differences are most often seen as a burden rather than a motivation to global careers.

Organizations have reacted to support company-sent individuals in their moves abroad, while they work in the foreign location and when they return home/move to the next location. The pattern of administrative, regulatory and tax support varies between organizations and depends on a range of factors. First, the IHRM configuration (as discussed in Chapter 2) will determine the strategic and operational role of IM and the frequency and duration of international moves.

Second, and interrelated, the underlying principles of IM policies and practices will impact the personal considerations of individuals whether to go on a foreign sojourn. This chapter has outlined that companies have a choice whether to keep expatriates always better off, whether to design policies and practices that give them a similar monetary and non-monetary position as before, whether to integrate international assignees with their local context in terms of remuneration or whether to employ a laissez-faire or negotiated system. As we have discussed in Chapter 5, compensation effects of working abroad are important (but normally not the most important) factors in the decision to expatriate. Where the IM regime is 'generous' the chances are that individuals are more likely to accept foreign work. Moreover, Dickmann et al. (2006) have some case study evidence that the higher the positive salary difference between expatriates' remuneration before and during assignment, the longer the average assignment duration.

Third, self-initiated international workers are most likely to simply fit into the local compensation structure in their organizations. They are unlikely to receive any (or much) financial support for working in their host country and bear much higher risks if things go wrong. For instance, while company-sent expatriates have mostly a guaranteed relocation in their contracts, self-initiated foreign workers might find themselves unemployed or without residency/work permit in their chosen country.

In summary, the above corporate international management approach, the individual's mindset and his or her motivational patterns will have an influence on the length and location(s) of an ensuing global career. However, the dynamics of global and sectoral competition (see Chapter 2) as well as happenstance and serendipity (Richardson and Zikic 2007) will also influence the flow of global careers and shape some of the outcomes.

Summary and learning points

This chapter described a number of strategic and operational approaches in the areas of regulation, compensation, taxation and risk associated with IM. The strategic elements of our considerations related to all of these areas, especially to the discussion of the GEO and the design of a GMP. The operational elements related to a bewildering range of organizational approaches to remunerating and motivating their international personnel, different tax treatments and risk management ideas.

Organizations are faced with an institutional and regulatory environment that limits their freedom of action, sometimes so much that they have no choice but to comply. With respect to diversity considerations, a range of states operate an immigration policy on a points basis that will give or withhold points for (lack of) qualifications, age and health. Generally, people who lack sought after qualifications, who are older and might have fragile health or a known illness, have lower chances to gain residence permits and the right to work in countries (e.g. Australia).

Immigration laws, work permits and tax requirements have to be observed and any non-compliance can result in serious consequences for both organizations and individuals. Beyond these isomorphic relationships that compel firms and other organizations to compliance, organizations have a degree of choice. Of course, the choices can result in idiosyncratic elements of IM policies and practices. However, we have introduced a range of most common policies and practices with a 'sprinkle' of leading-edge activities thrown into our discussion.

The combination of areas of tight regulation and organizational IM strategies, policies and practices has a powerful effect on global careers. In terms of traditional expatriation from the organizational centre, decisions as to the number of international assignees, their length of stay, their key objectives and functions will determine what global careers are feasible. Linked into our discussion earlier in the book (see Chapter 2), the IHRM configuration of an organization has a major impact on the global experience that individuals can gather. This chapter added another vital piece in the jigsaw puzzle: the inducements, incentives and leverage effects that organizations can provide to steer their flows of international careerists. In turn, decisions about localization of posts can create a powerful incentive for local talent to rise to high organizational positions. Where organizations have moved to use host-based compensation approaches it is likely that professionals from lower-cost countries (mostly from developing countries) might see more incentives to work abroad than the 'traditional' expatriate from a developing country home base. This has the power to fundamentally change the nature of global careers and the origin of careerists.

Key learning points include:

- The compensation and risk context varies substantially between countries, creating substantial administrative and cost challenges.
- To reduce complexity and to achieve high degrees of integration some organizations have created a GEO. This centralized structure combines the design of GMPs, and administers the international operational aspects on behalf of the whole organization. Performance management, salary administration, talent development and career as well as succession planning considerations should be reflected in the remit of the GEO. One advantage is that inequities among expatriates are reduced. Another plus is that international assignees stay 'on the radar screen', even if they are permanently global.
- There are many variations of GMPs. In essence, they need to address a number of core criteria, especially the link to the organization's key objectives and international configuration.
- Seven different compensation approaches were outlined with home-based and host-based covered in more depth. Each of these international remuneration types is associated with a range of advantages and disadvantages, the host approach often being the least costly for organizations. However, not just cost considerations but also resourcing, internal and external equity and motivational factors need to be considered when drawing up an international compensation scheme.
- Organizations need to effectively deal with risk. Key areas of risk in IM are regulatory compliance, cost risks, business reputation risks, permanent establishment risks and prosecution risks, especially as related to tax regulations.
- Organizations have the choice between a variety of approaches to taxation. The key ones are TEQ (tax in host country is made to approximate tax at home), tax protection (reimbursement of excess taxes should they have to be paid in the host location) and laissez-faire (full responsibility of tax matters rests with the assignee). Often, the organization will provide tax advice and arrange assistance for their international staff.
- Localization is one means to reduce costs in international work. Assignee localization means that the incumbent expatriate is being localized. Position localization indicates that the post will be filled with a local or an individual on local terms. Localization has an impact on resourcing, talent development, the relationship between the operating unit and corporate centre, local commitment levels and career systems.

Case study 11.1 explores the complex regulatory, compensation, and tax elements further and provides a real-life example.

Case study 11.1 An integrative case study: international remuneration, risks and regulatory considerations in action

An international manufacturing company headquartered in country X would like to send one of their engineers to their subsidiary in country Y in order to support a new project. The assignment will last two years. After a thorough selection process within line management, they identify the employee who is best suited for the job requirements abroad and who is also willing to relocate and to take the challenge of an IA (Richard).

A few months before the start of the assignment Richard and his wife have a meeting with the international human resource department. The company's classical long-term assignment policy and the defined compensation approach are explained to them in detail. The company applies a home-based, cost of living adjusted and tax-equalized compensation approach. Furthermore, their HR expert mentions that country X and country Y have a totalization agreement for social security. This means that it can be arranged for Richard to remain covered under his home-country social security system so he does not have to contribute to the host-country social security scheme. It is also made clear that a re-entry into the home social security system upon repatriation is not expected to pose issues.

The company's policy also states that the housing in the host country will be fully paid by the company and that the employee cannot therefore expect to be reimbursed for any potential costs in connection with their current home housing (e.g. home sale assistance, renovation costs, lease cancellation). If a suitable accommodation cannot be found at the start of the assignment, the employer grants Richard and his wife up to 30 days in temporary accommodation.

Richard's spouse has decided to accompany him, but wishes to continue her own career in the country of assignment and takes advantage of the company's offer to provide some help. The company engages a local specialist who will assist her in understanding the local labour market and recruitment processes and, when a job is identified, also assist in securing a local work permit. The costs for this spousal assistance are covered by the company. If, however, it should not be possible to find a suitable job and to obtain a work permit, the company is willing to pay for education and professional training course fees up to a defined cost limit and to provide a local network of social clubs.

In order to ensure global compliance with tax and social security legislation, the company provides Richard and his spouse with tax advice in the home and host locations. They will conduct a so-called exit interview in the home location where all questions related to exiting the home tax system are addressed, also affecting any potential personal wealth and income that might exist besides the work-related income. In the host location Richard will have a tax entrance interview where the local tax system is explained. It is often important for assignees that the impact that a change of tax systems can have on their private and non work-related income and wealth is also clarified. An external provider thereby ensures the confidentiality of the process, so that the employer does not get an insight into the private income and wealth of their employee. During the course of the assignment the tax provider will also assist Richard with the filing of their tax return. This is a company policy to ensure local compliance for all employees and the organization.

The further preparation of the assignment now comprises a cultural awareness training and a language training, which both Richard and his wife attend in order to prepare for their upcoming life and work in country Y. Approximately two months before the assignment starts, they are sent on a look and see trip to get to know their new host country, to identify suitable housing and to start familiarizing themselves with the location. In former times the company granted these trips before a decision was made by the employee to relocate, but realized that this was often too costly.

However, during the pre-assignment phase two critical discussions take place between the Richard and his company:

1 When Richard realizes that taxes he would have to pay in the host country are lower than those he has currently to bear, he asks his company to be exempted from the TEQ. HR explains to him why this is not possible and why this is being applied to all assignments regardless of whether it results in a windfall for the employee or the employer. The reasoning behind this consistent application is that all assignment locations shall be equally attractive to the assignee. Should exceptions from the TEQ for lower tax countries be granted, the attractiveness of such locations to assignees would increase, since they would be able to augment their savings part of their compensation. In turn, other locations would become less attractive and employee equity among assignees would be lost.

2 Having accepted TEQ on assignment, the employee understands that the cost of living in the host country will be 30 per cent higher than what he currently faces in his home country according to what Richard heard and found in the public domain. Therefore he expects a 30 per cent increase of his salary. It needs to be explained that the increased cost of living will only affect the spendable income and not the savings part which is also an element of his net salary. Any differences in the cost of goods and services (on what the spendable is being used) will be adjusted, but not the remaining part of the net salary which is usually used towards savings. Therefore, a cost of living adjustment is only granted on top of the spendable income and not the whole salary. But since the figure that is being applied as a cost of living adjustment on top of his spendable income is still lower than the 30 per cent expected, it needs to be explained further that the survey he read probably included differences in the cost of housing, taxation and social security costs. Since suitable housing is being paid for at actual costs and the tax difference is being equalized, the survey figure he might have found is not the relevant one. The figure, obtained from a specialized cost of living provider is entirely based on a pre-defined shopping basket of goods and services in the home and host locations and does not include housing or tax differentials. It does, however, include the exchange rate and takes any fluctuations into account on a bi-annual basis.

Still in the preparation phase, there are two detail changes that the employer is setting up for this particular assignment:

1 Because of massive exchange rate fluctuations between the home and host countries the company decides internally to deal with this by applying a so-called split payroll, where a part of the assignee's compensation is paid in the home-country currency in the home country. The other part of the compensation that is expected to be spent in the host country on daily living cost is paid in host currency in the host location. Therefore, the statistical data that defines the spendable part of his net income is the basis for calculation of the part paid out in host currency. By applying such a split payroll approach along the lines of the spendable income and savings part of the net salaries, exchange rate fluctuations do not affect the savings quota, while exchange rate changes for the spendable part are neutralized by the cost of living adjustments that take exchange rates into account. This, in turn, poses a potential tax compliance risk, if the employer does not manage to report the part of the salary paid outside the host country for taxes in the host locations. Since employees are in general taxable on their worldwide income at the place of their defined tax residency, it has to be ensured that there is a proper internal reporting in place to ensure compliance.

2 The second adjustment relates to optimizing the cost of the assignment. The company uses a specific tax planning idea that works in Richard's prospective host country. Instead of paying a housing allowance to Richard to fund his housing, they decide to pay the housing costs directly to the landlord in the host location. While a payment of an allowance would become taxable, with the company bearing the additional tax costs according to policy, tax law in the host country stipulates that housing costs paid directly by employers for assignees can be treated as tax-free. So the company decides to pay the housing cost directly to the landlord.

After two years, the assignment ends as was planned by the company. Six months prior to the official end, the line management in the host and home locations and the responsible IHR representative discuss together with Richard his repatriation and possible job opportunities in the home country. Having found a suitable position Richard and his spouse return and re-adjust to personal and professional life in their home country.

Case questions

1 Why is it important not to allow individual assignees to be exempted from tax equalization?
2 Richard had two misconceptions regarding the cost of living adjustment. What were these misunderstandings?
3 What are the effects of calculating COLA in this way? What might be possible disadvantages for individuals?

References

Adler, N.J. and Ghadar, F. (1990) 'Strategic human resource management: a global perspective', in R. Pieper (ed.) *Human Resource Management: An International Comparison*, New York: de Gruyter.

Bartlett, C. and Ghoshal, S. (1989) *Managing Across Borders*, London: Hutchinson Business Books.

Briscoe, D. and Schuler, R. (2004) *International Human Resource Management*, 2nd edn, London: Routledge.

Dickmann, M. and Mills, T. (2010) 'The importance of intelligent career and location considerations: exploring the decision to go to London', *Personnel Review*, 39(1): 116-134.

Dickmann, M. and Müller-Camen, M. (2006) 'A typology of international human resource management strategies and processes', *International Journal of Human Resource Management*, 17(4): 580–601.

Dickmann, M. and Tyson, S. (2005) 'Outsourcing payroll – beyond transaction cost economics', *Personnel Review*, 34(4): 451–467.

Dickmann, M., Doherty, N. and Mills, T. (2005) *Understanding mobility – influence factors in the decision to accept an international assignment, repatriation issues and long-term career considerations*, Report, Cranfield: Cranfield School of Management.

Dickmann, M., Müller-Camen, M. and Kelliher, C. (2009) 'Striving for transnational human resource management – principles and practice', *Personnel Review*, 38(1): 5–25.

Dickmann, M., Doherty, N., Johnson, A. and Wood, M. (2007) *Measuring the Value of International Assignments*, London: PricewaterhouseCoopers and Cranfield School of Management

Dickmann, M., Doherty, N., Mills, T. and Brewster, C. (2008) 'Why do they go? Individual and corporate perspectives on the factors influencing the decision to accept an international assignment', *International Journal of Human Resource Management*, 19(4): 731–751.

Dowling, P., Festing, M. and Engle, A. (2008) *International Human Resource Management: Managing People in a Multinational Context*, 5th edn, London: Thomson Learning.

Edström, A. and Galbraith, J.R. (1977) 'Transfer of managers as a coordination and control strategy in multinational organizations', *Administrative Science Quarterly*, 22(2): 248–263.

Ernst & Young (2009) *Expatriate Policy Survey*, Zurich: Ernst & Young.

Hailey, J. and Harry, W. (2008) 'Localisation: a strategic response to globalization', in M. Dickmann, C. Brewster and P. Sparrow (eds) *International Human Resource Management – The European Perspective*, London: Routledge.

Harris, H. and Dickmann, M. (2005) *The CIPD Guide on International Management Development*, London: The Chartered Institute of Personnel and Development.

Heenan, D.A. and Perlmutter, H.V. (1979) *Multinational Organizational Development*, Reading, MA: Addison-Wesley.

Lazarova, M. and Caligiuri, P. (2001) 'Retaining repatriates: the role of organizational support practices', *Journal of World Business*, 36(4): 389–401.

Lazarova, M. and Cerdin, J.-L. (2007) 'Revisiting repatriation concerns: organizational support versus career and contextual influences', *Journal of International Business Studies*, 38: 404–429.

Pieters, D. (1993) *Introduction into the Basis Principles of Social Security*, Kluwer: Amsterdam.

Richardson, J. and Zikic, J. (2007) 'The darker side of an international academic career', *Career Development International*, 12(2): 164–186.

12 Global careers: a synthesis with a view to the future

Objectives

This chapter:

- provides a reflective discussion of earlier chapters;
- integrates the presented arguments;
- distinguishes global career strategies from practices;
- identifies trends that are likely to shape the future of global careers;
- discusses possible implications of global careers for the future;
- outlines multiple directions for careers in the future;
- proposes global career lessons and challenges as we move further into the twenty-first century.

Introduction

It has been popular to refer to Hall's seminal work to define careers as 'unfolding sequences of work experiences over time'. Some of the appeal of this definition might lie in that work can be seen as a universal experience in which people engage in all countries of the world. And yet, while the actual experiences of people differ widely – partly due to their occupation, their individual preferences and interpretations and their personal circumstances – their concept of career also diverges substantially. Thomas and Inkson (2007: 462) argue that where a society is characterized by subsistence conditions, low labour mobility, high unemployment and high collectivism, the Western-centric concept of (individual) career has limited value. Concepts that carry less meaning in terms of cumulativeness and continuity, such as work or employment, may be at times more applicable to such situations. Therefore, the national, institutional and cultural context is highly important in the study of global careers.

Nicholson (2007) uses the metaphors of destiny, drama and deliberation to capture some of the career patterns. He argues that destiny has continued relevance as we are subjected to forces that shape opportunities, choices and constraints beyond an individual's control. The institutional context of educational provision and quality or the cultural setting that allows or restricts equal opportunities and openness to certain functions, hierarchies or industries, widely diverge among countries and an individual is largely embedded in this context. The context, therefore, exerts some normative influence that partly shapes the careers of many. Drama results from non-normative life events that have the power to interrupt the 'normal' flow of career decisions, to upset a tendency to automaticity and which might lead to highly unexpected career choices, transitions and behaviours. Deliberation, finally, lies between destiny and drama and refers to the power of the reflective self to either choose between the obvious career choices or to break 'freer' from the constraints embedded in the institutional context. It is a capacity that distinguishes humans from animals and other species, and that allows choice in how we seek those experiences that shape our careers. This book has tended to focus on people who used their deliberation to work with or in work contexts that either span several national jurisdictions and behavioural patterns or that are distinct from their own countries of origin.

Career behaviours and outcomes are influenced fundamentally by structure and agency (Peiperl and Arthur 2000), and writers on global careers do well to acknowledge that the structures vary dramatically in different countries. Moreover, the patterns of agency also have specific trends in different states and among cultural groupings. Agency, therefore, is subject to certain perceived and real boundaries. Although the literature often refers to 'boundaryless careers', it is, of course, clear that boundaries continue to exist. Many boundaries can be overcome by the determined. Others 'melt' slowly rather than disappear overnight. While this book has outlined some of the structural context variables that face individuals in specific settings, it has concentrated on those persons who have crossed boundaries, mostly focusing on the crossing of geographical borders. However, with working in a host country comes a range of challenges with respect to further areas of flexibility such as psychological flexibility (Sullivan and Arthur 2006).

Our framework (Figure 12.1) has reflected a wide range of structure and agency considerations. We have explicated structural determinants on the organizational, cultural and national levels and have, at times, reflected on other contextual influence factors such as industry career patterns. In terms of agency, we have explored a range of individual and organizational drivers, attitudes, behaviours and activities. Within the globalized and highly competitive world of work we delineated interaction effects and individual and organizational outcomes. While we distinguished a large number of different forms of global careers, we tended to focus on the international rather than the cross-country comparative dimension. Exceptions to this are Chapters 10 and 11 where the local context and legal regulations predominate within countries. These were explored to illuminate organizational mobility principles, policies and practices. It is now time to summarize the key insights of the book, explore pertinent trends on global careers and discuss possible lessons, implications and challenges for the future.

Figure 12.1 A framework of global careers: organizational and individual interactions today and in the future

Summary and integration of the book

Chapter 1 set the scene for the book. It discussed globalization and its implications and explored international labour market trends as well as migration patterns. While we presented a brief overview of career theories amid the context of globalization, we endorsed the argument that global careers need to be seen as long-term international phenomena. Shifting the perspective of workplace-based experiences beyond expatriation to long-term career insights allows a fuller discussion of implications and outcomes. These effects have to be seen from a variety of perspectives, including individual, organizational and societal. International streams of workers, including large numbers of migrants, are growing and the diversity at work – even for a domestic worker – is increasing. Cross-cultural communication, work and careers are becoming more common and individuals, organizations and governments would benefit from an in-depth understanding of structural contexts and individual agency in an increasingly boundaryless world.

Chapter 2 concentrated on the new competitive world of work in rapidly globalizing economies. It has traced the historical development of international organizations and outlined the global context with its variety of competitive pressures. It depicted tensions and illustrated these with the global–local dilemma. It explored SIHRM considerations and presented ideas of how to be successful in a globalized world. Illustrating and further developing these ideas, the chapter explored frameworks of SIHRM aimed at worldwide innovation, local responsiveness and global efficiency. Depending on which configuration a multinational organization chooses, there is a range of implications for global careers. One of the learning points was that depending on the IHRM policies and practices within MNCs, there are different sets of individual and organizational capabilities that are most valuable. These have distinct implications for the individual capabilities needed and, therefore, affect global career patterns. Overall, given the increased worldwide operations of MNCs, higher numbers of individuals are working in a country in which they did not grow up. We would expect that in future, successful careers will include more cross-cultural work experiences, will need more fine-tuned international capabilities and wider cross-border networks.

Chapter 3 explored the individual and organizational management of careers in more depth. We outlined pertinent career theories and traced their historical evolution. The so-called 'new career' increasingly moves the locus of responsibility for careers from the organization to the individual in response to competitive pressures and the highly dynamic environment that organizations face. In the world of 'boundaryless careers', employability, the identification of own drivers, the expansion of one's own skills, knowledge, abilities and networks has become more important. Inkson and Arthur (2001) suggest that we all become career capitalists while Hall, and his various associates, suggest that individuals are engaged in protean careers. With respect to boundaryless careers, we have made our reservations regarding this metaphor clear. With respect to much international work the boundaries are still formidable. For instance, immigrants will be confronted with a host of laws and statutes regulating immigration and work permits in different countries. Diverging social security and taxation constitute other barriers to mobility. In future, we see some of these structural context variables becoming less diverse through international treaties and bi-national contracts and, thereby, will increase the frequency of global careers. Much of traditional expatriation will also hinge on how organizations manage their international work flows and how they encourage career diversity worldwide.

Chapter 4 developed a variety of international career moves, moving the analysis beyond expatriation and repatriation moves. We outlined a 'glossary' and analysis of the various types of global career moves, with an underlying distinction between company-sponsored foreign work (including short-term, long-term expatriation, frequent flying) and individual-sponsored work in a host country (including legal and illegal immigration, some forms of globetrotting, self-initiated expatriation). Based on these different forms of international work we drew up an integrative framework. Our framework clarified the meaning of 'real global citizen', and outlined the different dimensions available for an analysis of international work and career patterns.

Working across cultures is highly influenced by the national business systems, national cultures and other elements that give guidance and structure to careers. They have obvious relevance and implications for the organizational and individual management of cross-cultural moves. The practice of HRM has high potential to deal with global moves in a positive way, as well as the potential to lead to disastrous outcomes. In Chapter 4 we also discussed the diversity within local and global teams. In so doing, we employed the Earley and Gibson model for multinational work teams to manifest different facets of global work and we discussed the concept of cultural intelligence and its meaning for global careers. In essence, we see a trend for increased cultural diversity whether individuals work abroad or in their home country. Thus, successful careerists will need to hone their cultural intelligence in order to increase their effectiveness and own satisfaction at work.

The first four chapters have given a broad view of the contexts, logic and limitations of global careers. *Chapters 5–9* focused on strategies, structures and processes of international work. While issues such as immigration, self-sponsored expatriation or diversity continue to be discussed, most attention was given to exploring intra-organizational moves and the associated perspectives of individuals and their employers.

Chapter 5 explored individual and organizational resourcing issues in global careers. It worked from the premise that there exists a dual dependency between individuals and their employers that is especially acute in international sojourns. The chapter has concentrated on the point of making the decision whether to actively seek or to accept international work and has explored associated backgrounds, motivations and drivers.

Key strategic purpose categories for organizations include the improvement of control and coordination mechanisms, the development of global leaders of the future, as well as the creation, transfer and utilization of knowledge across borders. Operational reasons for organizations to use global mobility are related to the staffing of positions where set local persons cannot be found or cannot be developed within a suitable timeframe, the general management of global careers and the launching of new initiatives.

Individuals are driven by many and diverse motives when seeking or accepting international work. Antecedents such as family and social background, early experiences and personality determine their receptivity to international experiences.

Key individual motivations to work abroad include career and development considerations. Other important factors are individual interests and drives, family and partner considerations, organizational factors and inducements as well as national and location-specific factors. The 'dark side' of self-initiated foreign work includes more personal risks and transience and that individuals have a higher propensity than company-sent expatriates to accept a job that they view as being worse than the one they had in their home country. Normally, there is also no repatriation planning or mobility support by the employer.

Understanding and managing the various perspectives in IM and global careers might lead to the formulation of more realistic expectations and career activities by individuals. They would be well advised to evaluate technical ability, cross-cultural suitability, family requirements, country/cultural requirements, organizational requirements and language issues when deciding to work abroad. In the future, their global careers could be supported by the improved design and implementation of more tailored and flexible expatriation and career strategies, policies and processes by organizations.

Chapter 6 has explored the pre-departure preparation of individuals and their families before the actual assignment or new life begins in the destination country.

Obviously, the role of the employer can be substantial and we cover what can be done before the individual(s) leave their home country and after they arrive in their host country.

Tarique and Caligiuri (2004) suggest a five-phase process for global training programmes:

- Phase 1 identifies the type of global assignment.
- Phase 2 determines the training needs in relation to the organizational needs and individual capabilities.
- Phase 3 defines goals and measures.
- Phase 4 develops and delivers the training programme.
- Phase 5 evaluates the training programme.

Overall, cross-border moves are complex, time-consuming, need a period of adjustment and are associated with many ambiguities. Individuals and organizations have to be aware of the different contingencies and various constituencies for the move, including family, colleagues, wider social environment and organizational stakeholders. Administrative support, career planning and mentoring might be some of the levers designed to manage the processes more smoothly and to manage the expectations of the assignee and his or her family. We believe that the ongoing trend for organizations to provide more of the above will continue, so that individuals are likely to gain more support and preparation in future. This would be one, albeit one of many, elements that might enable individuals to pursue global careers with less upset and more success in the years to come.

Chapter 7 has investigated individual and organizational issues during IAs. A wide range of individual characteristics exert an important influence. Expatriate adjustment is a learning process which will be different for diverse individuals. Assignees will experience fluctuations with regards to their emotions, behavioural effectiveness and cognitive confidence. Over time the performance of individuals and their cognitive confidence is seen to steadily improve, while their emotions might have to go through a honeymoon period and a substantial dip before reflecting high levels of adjustment. However, not all international sojourns will lead to high levels of adjustments and cognitive confidence.

There is a large range of organizational activities that can foster successful IAs. Organizations can use sophisticated approaches to selection, training and development, job design, career planning, administrative and logistical support, and influencing the social environment of expatriates. Some firms have designed approaches that link into a variety of career capital areas, strengthen the globalization of the entity and aid the development of more international strategies and policies. The mutual dependency of individuals and their international employers seems to indicate that the traditional discipline of global career planning is still very relevant and will increase in importance in the future.

Chapter 8 has depicted organizational and individual perspectives associated with the immediate time before, during and after returning from an IA. It has developed an overview of some of the pertinent issues and drawn up a recommendation for good organizational policies and practices.

The area of repatriation is perceived to be one of the most difficult to manage for organizations and individuals. Writers have used several perspectives when considering repatriation. These include the organizational management of IM, the proactive management by individuals of their own career paths, the subjective perspective regarding psychological elements of mobility and long-term views of repatriation as the middle of careers rather than the end of assignments.

Individuals want a good management of their return, help during the repatriation phase for resettlement of themselves and their families and, above all, a meaningful job. The existence and extent of the reverse culture shock (RCS) has a substantial impact on performance, career satisfaction, retention and willingness for future expatriation. *Chapter 8* presented a large array of organizational activities on how to manage repatriation successfully.

Most organizations aim at increasing the retention of returnees. They are keen on demonstrating to potential future international assignees that working abroad has positive pay-offs and they strive to have good knowledge management in all aspects associated with their IM approach. Given that global careers are becoming more important in many organizations, we would expect these employers to learn and to develop more sophisticated IM approaches. In future, we foresee longer-term career planning (beyond international sojourns), the use of mentors, sponsors and counsellors as well as increased efforts to manage expatriates' expectations. These should decrease the inherent dangers of company-sponsored IAs and should facilitate global careers.

Chapter 9 has depicted a wide spectrum of outcomes of global careers. Our discussion distinguished individual, organizational and national effects and interactions. A framework that can be helpful in assessing the outcome of global work is proposed. It factors in the international context and dynamic work experienced during international careers.

Organizations and individuals have their own international agendas. These lead to a dynamic interaction in which employers and international assignees adjust to each others' approaches, and develop strategies as well as behaviours to maximize their beneficial outcomes. This chapter has drawn up a list of organizational activities that can be used to improve the outcomes of global work and careers in the future.

Many individuals have identified substantial barriers in applying their acquired career capital from international sojourns and feel unable to use their new skills, knowledge and abilities or their foreign/international networks. Moreover, many returnees experience a career wobble in which they feel undervalued and frustrated. Their interest in seeking alternative employment is often high during this phase.

The diverse flows of international workers lead to a talent flow that is often labelled brain drain. It might, however, also constitute brain gain – especially for the recipients of highly skilled or educated workers from abroad. With increased brain circulation across national borders, we would expect the competition of states, cities and organizations for highly talented persons to intensify in the future. This could lead to the diminishing of barriers to mobility for those individuals who have highly marketable or scarce skills and capabilities.

Chapters 5–9 explored the temporal dimensions of IM and global careers using individual, organizational and national perspectives. Within these, there is often a preoccupation with expatriate assignments and its management. We agree with Thomas and Inkson's (2007) recommendation that this should be extended to a culturally appropriate career management that would understand and address all employees with their different national cultural backgrounds and expectations. With respect to cross-border activities, *Chapters 10 and 11* employed a more comparative perspective and concentrated on social security, remuneration and risk issues as experienced by individuals and organizations.

The regulatory context varies substantially between countries. Organizations have to observe compliance pressures while balancing these with cost and motivational considerations. Social security regulations are highly complex. The main challenges and how organizations deal with these are manifold – they are outlined through praxis cases. These cases show that companies and individuals have to be well informed to avoid some of the pitfalls in social security and taxation regulations.

Organizations often have relatively extensive experience and help arrangements for international assignees. In turn, global managers and specialists who fly frequently are relatively neglected. Given the strong increase in numbers of these employees and some of their particular challenges – such as a severely disrupted social life – we would expect companies to develop more tailored mobility policies with respect to this target group. Moreover, the increase in cross-border working patterns of 'traditional' expatriates and the development of treaties between countries that clarify the social security provisions and obligations will mean more clarity and, ideally, more security for global careerists.

Chapter 11 described a number of strategic and operational approaches in the areas of compensation, taxation and risk associated with IM. Organizations are faced with an institutional and regulatory environment that limits their freedom of action, sometimes so much that they have no choice but to comply. Beyond the regulations that compel firms and other organizations to compliance, organizations have a degree of choice. Of course, the choices can result in idiosyncratic elements of IM policies and practices.

Tight regulation and organizational IM approaches can have a major effect on global careers. Decisions as to the number of international assignees, their length of stay, their key objectives and functions will determine which global careers are feasible within organizational support mechanisms. Moreover, the inducements, incentives and leverage effects that organizations design can guide the flow of international careerists. In turn, decisions about localization of posts can create a powerful incentive for local talent to rise to high organizational hierarchies. We believe that in future localization efforts are going to intensify which could fundamentally change the nature of global careers and the origin of careerists.

Future trends and global careers

This book has explored the phenomenon of global careers from a wide range of perspectives and has drawn together much of the IHRM, careers and IM literature. The brief summaries have already indicated some of the developments we see for the future of global careers. Below, however, we take a step back and use a wider, more integrative perspective, looking at developments that will impact global careers.

We start with a caveat: there is a difference between the rhetoric and reality of globalization in terms of careers. While there is a growing number of global assignments and immigration moves, the largest share of moves still occurs within national boundaries. The most recent example is the case of China, where masses of people move from the west to the industrial areas, mostly to the cities on the east coast.

Whether careers are 'global' depends on the criteria used for evaluation. Take absolute and relative levels of wealth as one criterion. The globalization of careers has made the differences in the meaning of careers between the industrialized societies and the so-called 'Third World' even starker. For the rich and affluent, a wider set of career options has become feasible, involving frequent moves across national borders. In contrast, the majority of the world's population still struggle to survive, and only relatively few people can fulfil a dream of migration or working for MNCs. The former might involve risks, asylum seeking, and illegal immigration options, and the latter means, almost exclusively, working in rank-and-file roles. This means that there is a growing divide between places such as the USA, Europe or Japan, and whole regions that are less developed, such as South America, South-East Asia, and in particular Africa, for people who only possess basic skills.

In contrast, relative levels of education point to other patterns in 'global' careers. Increased access to information, for instance facilitated through the internet, and a wider acceptance of students from developing countries in major universities, can lead to many highly educated individuals from developing countries. While access to computers and a good education is often related to the relative wealth of families and the educational background of parents, the large middle classes in countries such as China, India or other developing countries will bring forth highly educated individuals. A cost-saving focus of organizations, an increased openness of governments to highly skilled talent and a broader search for talent within firms means that careers indeed become rapidly more globalized. In addition, the better information that workers in developing countries have regarding superior opportunities in developed countries has already resulted in large migration movements.

In terms of IM, a recent study looked at the effects of the 'credit-crunch' crisis following the major upheaval of global markets in 2008/9. Aldred and Sparrow (2009) found that the crisis has had major impacts on the planning of MNCs and, therefore, global careers of company-sponsored individuals. The authors suggested four scenarios: First, a reduction in the volume of assignments due to the recession. This was identified especially in automotive manufacturing, IT and financial services. Second, changes in the volume of assignments due to general, not recession-related factors. This scenario, which might be a guide for other industries in the future, was often pronounced in high tech, engineering, retail and logistics firms. The third scenario – no impact so far – was found to happen particularly in food and consumer products as well as cloth manufacturing. Lastly, there were still sectors which experienced an increase in global mobility, regardless of the recession. These were identified particularly in the telecommunications, oil and gas and some professional service companies. Their research shows that different scenarios can coexist and that both industry-competitive trends as well as company-specific rationales and decisions shape GMPs.

Overall, while it would clearly be foolish to claim that all or most careers nowadays are global, we believe that more genuine globalization will exist in the future, for several reasons. Among these are:

• convergence rather than divergence;
• explosion of the use of technology;
• irreversibility of existing changes;
• more equal spread of wealth;
• convergence rather than divergence.

Pugh and Hickson (1996) claimed that two global trends exist – convergence and divergence. On the one hand, nations stick to their national culture and manifest their uniqueness. This is reflected in nationalism, separation for example, of former countries, either peacefully (Czech Republic and Slovakia) or less so (the former Yugoslavia). Nevertheless, from an economics perspective, we witness strong conversion towards a capitalist approach moulded around Western principles. While differences between coordinated market economies (CMEs) and liberal market economies (LMEs) persist, many firms which operate across these borders adjust to some degree to their contexts (Parry et al. 2008). In terms of global careers, however, they are operating in capitalist market economies. Many of the differences between LMEs and CMEs lead only to minor variations and, instead, knowledge networking and coordination goals might encourage IM.

Both the EU and NAFTA (North America Free Trading Agreement) add countries to their membership, and moving across borders has become easier for many of their citizens. The number of firms that work across borders is increasing. Employees with home, host or third-country origin occupy positions on various levels of the organizational hierarchy, often widely distributed geographically. There are large-scale efforts within these firms to create ideas and to make knowledge transparent and accessible. Many universities and students in diverse countries use the same, often English-language, textbooks when studying. In particular, the sciences and management studies have a body of knowledge that is shared worldwide. Thus, the diffusion of knowledge is not limited by geographical boundaries. Even people in places that used to be isolated politically (e.g. China, Albania) or physically (Madagascar, New Zealand) are connected to other places via cheaper and more effective transportation, or virtually, via the internet.

Overall, the convergence that is driven by multinational firms and the integration of leading-edge and relevant knowledge is driving a globalization of career patterns. Western companies tend to use individual, merit-based criteria for hierarchical promotions. However, there are many societies in the world where collectivist norms and criteria built around trust, friendship or family links might have a much stronger weighting in promotion decisions. With the expected rise of MNCs from developing countries where promotion criteria and individual career preferences are often different, it is not clear how these increased global careers will be managed and will unfold. This will be an exciting area to investigate over future decades.

Explosion of the use of technology

Where people have ready access to technology, especially information and communication technology, they have access to a large repository of impressions, dreams and knowledge. Hollywood can indeed be seen as a 'dream factory' that creates insights, impressions and longing for certain occupations, hierarchical positions and geographical locations. The internet allows access not only to international communication but also to a vast array of information and knowledge, as with the case of Wikipedia or free news websites.

As with the access to radios and televisions in the last decades, the access to computers and the internet is spreading fast and the costs are diminishing. It might be argued that the rapid rise of the internet can have similar effects in different cultures and in different countries with respect to career perceptions and choices (Thomas and Inkson 2007). This in itself, as well as better access to valuable information that might be used in a corporate setting, has an impact on the number of people who might be considered by their organization for international moves or who might actively pursue global careers outside their current employer.

Irreversibility of existing changes

People today visit, meet and correspond more globally than ever. The utilization of the internet has shattered old barriers to communication and increased the mutual understanding between members of different groups of people and nations. Even more traditional technology inputs such as faster and more effective and reliable sources of transportation have made the globe smaller than it used to be. These changes are operating in the direction that encourages international communication, information, cross-border knowledge exchange, travel and global moves. It seems unlikely that these changes will be reversed although certain fanatical groups threaten such action.

More equal spread of wealth

When countries have a very low cost of living, and as a result offer a cheap labour force, they attract domestic and foreign direct investment. Examples are off-shore arrangements such as the location of call-centres for Western companies in India. When these are established, indigenous staff start gaining more wealth, and the countries are likely to industrialize more quickly and expand their professional service sector. Consequently, citizens gradually earn more, develop new ventures, and GDP per person increases. When production moves to another country, the knowledge and technology helps people in the host country to develop new competencies, and possibly leads to the development of new products, own design, own marketing etc., as was the case with Japan and South Korea. We believe that in many instances this process will reduce the gap between richer and poorer nations. The cumulative effects over time will lead directly to more global careers of those people who are seen to be good performers/high potentials/possess the right skills from developing countries. Over time, indirect effects include a higher investment in the education of the young generations in these countries which also could lead to more global careers.

Global careers – individual, organizational and national trends

We are now in a position to briefly summarize key current trends that affect global careers and outline some of the likely future developments. Table 12.1 depicts core general trends and global career developments on the individual, organizational and national levels.

This chapter has delineated the trends depicted in Table 12.1 and has traced these to the more in-depth discussions in the various chapters of this book. Therefore, it will suffice to only selectively discuss some of these.

Starting at core HRM research, a clear trend unveiled in recent studies is that of a shift in the way career moves in general, and how IAs in particular, are initiated. One of the core underlying drivers for changes in global careers is the movement from a solely company-driven initiative towards a shared responsibility. Thus, global careers rely increasingly on individual proactivity (Seibert et al. 2001). There is a bewildering array of international careers even outside organizations. However, also within organizations we see a growing number of international experiences initiated by persons who pursue their own global career plans. This self-initiated process places the responsibility for action and outcome on the expatriates themselves (Guzzo et al. 1994), albeit the company sponsorship moderates some of the hardships and risks.

Their pioneering work was followed by a number of studies (see Altman and Baruch 2008) pointing out that indeed more and more expatriates have chosen this path of their own accord. On many occasions, the choice is made with the expectation of career enhancement following the expatriation (e.g. Stahl et al. 2002; Doherty and Dickmann 2009). In search of gaining human capital through expatriate experience employees opt for global assignments, or accept such offers by their employer, in anticipation of an inter-organizational career move that is seen as providing greater career progress than in case of local career moves. Empirical research provides some support for this view (Lazarova and Cerdin 2007; Stahl et al. 2009).

When the actual outcomes fall short of the anticipated career benefits, frustration and disillusion can emerge. In one organizational case, repatriates received fewer intra-organizational promotions than their counterparts (those without expatriate experience), and were not more likely to be contacted by head-hunters for potential inter-organizational career moves (Benson and Pattie 2008). In another case,

Table 12.1 General trends and global career developments on three levels

Level	General trend	Global career trend
Individual	• 'Melting' global career boundaries means more individual international opportunities • Locus of career responsibility and proactivity moves towards the individual • Increased self-sponsored international work mobility	• Active careerists will seek to acquire more international capabilities, networks and insights and will need cultural intelligence • Careerists will seek global career mentors, councillors and sponsors and will plan their own career moves with longer time perspectives, planning two jobs in advance • Many people will be more international in mindset and more willing to accept the risks of international work. They will undertake a variety of global work and experience diverse global career patterns • Global careerists will strive to be able to utilize their international career capital upon return or when moving to the next location
Organisational	• Increased globalization & use of international talent • Increased communication and knowledge networking across borders • Increased cost focus • Increased convergence of international business	• Rise of the MNC from developing countries with diverse forms of company-sponsored global careers • Career 'success' within MNCs will increasingly be based on global careers and cross-cultural capabilities • Organisations will seek to understand their international talent better and will select, manage, repatriate and retain them in a more sophisticated way. Localization of technical positions will increase while managerial positions will be increasingly staffed with 'international talent' (which might originate from the host country) • Global career strategies, structures and planning will be longer term and yet more tailored and flexible • Organizations will provide clearer mobility policies and will reduce some of the regulatory uncertainties – and work on diminishing the extra monetary costs of expatriation they are currently bearing

National and societal

- Increased search for international talent
- Increased migration flows
- Explosion of the use of new technology
- Increasing number of multinational and bi-national treaties
- Larger membership of supranational organisations
- Better education levels of middle classes around the world
- More equal spread of wealth and rapid advancement of some developing countries

- Brain gain and circulation goals will mean increased international experience and immigration of highly qualified individuals. These persons have the power of 'deliberation' and will be encouraged to have a global career within local embedding structures
- International treaties and memberships will moderate some of the insecurities and darker sides of global careers. Lower qualified individuals will also experience more international work but will be subjected to much uncertainty, transience and 'drama'

the proportion of repatriates reporting that they had been demoted and promoted in their employing organizations was similar (Kraimer et al. 2009). These findings might reflect a new state of development, when expatriation experience is more common than in the past, and where it cannot guarantee automatic promotion.

In reshaping the psychological contract of expatriation, there is recognition that both sides – the organization and the prospective expatriate – should share the responsibility and practice. The employee should not expect the organization to present them with a request, certainly not with a demand, but rather the onus is on them to: (1) identify adequate opportunities; and (2) propose themselves in a way that will secure the desired positions.

This change in emphasis creates a new dimension in the organization–individual relationship, and is in line with wider career developments such as the general boundaryless and post-corporate career, and the protean career in particular. It affects the entire phenomenon of expatriation and its process, and repositions expectations.

A smooth repatriation is a challenge for HRM in organizations. Repatriates tend to express dissatisfaction with career prospects within the organization, and this could be another factor leading to a high level of intentions to leave (Bossard and Peterson 2005) or to actually leave within a short period of time following the repatriation (Black and Gregersen 1999; Baruch et al. 2002). Turnover of repatriates might be about double the rate of the rest of the workforce (e.g. see GMAC 2008). Organizations are faced with this challenge and academic scholars are expected to direct further research into this phenomenon. On the organizational side, there is a need to enhance career prospects for returning expatriates and one way is to employ practices such as pre-departure career planning, systematic career revision during the assignment, and the allocation of a formal mentor, coach, counsellor or sponsor based in the parent country (e.g. Bolino 2007; Lazarova and Cerdin 2007; Dickmann and Doherty 2010). Table 12.1 includes these trends and our summary above indicates that there are many more issues that for reasons of space limitations were not included in the table.

Among one of the key themes for global careers are those international work sojourns that are initiated, planned and carried through by individuals themselves which are occasionally sponsored by their families. The desire to gain human capital through expatriate experience might be followed by people opting for global assignments that are external to their employing organization. It might also include going abroad to study or to engage in voluntary activities.

Voluntary and semi-voluntary activities became a major section of the workforce in the industrial societies and is gaining more scholarly attention (Finkelstein et al. 2005) with growing evidence for its pay-offs (Prouteau and Wolff 2006). Globetrotting has become a reality of life for many, but brings with it a number of career and other life issue dilemmas. The erosion in the status and role of the family is one such consideration.

There are many other types of global work. Van Emmerik and Euwema (2009) studied peacemakers and their global experience as a unique type of expatriation.

Bozionelos (2009) focused on mostly self-initiated expatriation of nurses in Saudi-Arabia. Individuals who move globally do not have the organization to rely upon, and thus do not dominate the management literature, but they are growing in numbers. As such, more research needs to follow the wide variety of international moves, either self- or organization-initiated and managed. Another neglected issue is the foreign workers who come under formal arranged deals to other countries – in particular for professions in which locals are less willing to work – be it in patient care, agriculture or construction. Many of the assignments become permanent and are de facto immigration.

Another trend in global work is that of migration leading to human flows in multiple directions. In this book we refer to work and career related immigration. Technology advances have made the physical move more feasible and affordable than ever. The direction of migration is not always singular, from less to more affluent nations. What was once a clear brain drain where the talent flow was one-sided – from the developing to the developed countries – is changing to brain circulation, with mutual sharing of talent and learning.

Immigration might be perceived as an individual act, but nations are highly involved with immigration. Many countries are proactively encouraging people to immigrate and bridge gaps in certain professions. In some cases this can deprive poorer nations of their human capital. Countries try to encourage their former national immigrants to return home, creating a brain circulation initiated and supported by the authorities.

Global careers – lessons, challenges and directions for future research

The highly dynamic context of a globalizing economy, the regulatory and other activities of single or multiple countries, enduring cultural diversity, changing organizational strategies, policies and practices, as well as individual preferences, risk-taking behaviours, career activism and legal or illegal cross-country moves outlined above, represent a highly interesting and fruitful area for further research. At the individual level, there is a wide set of reasons to embark on a global career, and this applies to a growing number of people, and to a larger number of occupations. The impetus can come from organizations, from individuals and from their intra-family and extra-family networks.

Organizations still remain the major factor in global careers, certainly in expatriation and repatriation. We witness conflicting tensions for organizations. Often, organizations are increasing all forms of international work while they also strive to localize for ethical, operational and cost reasons. Current evidence indicates that both trends exist and are expanding.

For individuals – who are possibly encouraged and financially supported by their families – self-initiated global moves might be part of a plan to progress within the firm, but could also be a self-development career episode to build career capital. Many individuals are persuaded that international career capital is beneficial and that this will enable them to look elsewhere for future employment (Dickmann et al. 2006).

Lastly, at the national or society level, new challenges emerge. Not all immigration is welcomed, and when new immigrants are embedded in traditions that are alien to locals, tensions can grow. Certain individuals immigrate in order to become part of the society in their new homeland, whereas others aim to build their own small homeland in the host country. This poses further challenges to these societies.

It is certainly interesting to monitor how nations evolve in how they regulate access to their country. Under what conditions do they allow foreigners to come to the country, to work there – for MNCs, for themselves, for voluntary organizations? Individuals are confronted with work permit regulations as a legal matter – these are drawn up with a national talent and skills strategy in mind. Over time, is there a danger that nations lose their talent to other states in a way that jeopardizes their future progress? If so, what could they do? There is a range of interesting issues open for exploration at the national level.

Other trends are more linked to the interaction of individuals with their employers. The implications for management and organizations of individuals becoming the masters of their own global careers are, on the one hand, that less is expected of them in terms of identifying talent and matching person with position, as many of these activities would be transferred to individuals. Certain responsibility and activity remains with them, however. They need to provide information on emergent opportunities and communicate these effectively to reach a large number of potential candidates. On the other hand, there is likely to be more 'messing' with the hierarchy as both potential assignees *and* internal sponsors bypass and shortcut organizational procedures in order to attain a position (or fill it with their preferred candidate). A growing trend is the reliance on locals where possible, but even then, those local employees need to be incorporated into the firm, its culture and operational ways. The phenomenon is much more complex than it might seem initially, and more managerial attention will be needed in the future to plan and manage global careers.

Summary and learning points

This chapter has explored issues pertaining to structure and agency in global careers. It has depicted a wide range of structural considerations and trends which allow insights that the context of global careers is changing substantially. The existence of supra-national agreements, bi- and multinational treaties and national taxation, social security, immigration and other legislation has a strong impact on global careers. We speculate that increased activities in nations' competition for highly talented or skilled individuals will encourage transnational talent flows and will alleviate some of the darker sides of international careers for this group of people. In contrast, issues of immigration of lesser skilled individuals are high on political agendas and might lead to continued insecurity and transience of permanent and temporary immigrants with less sought-after competencies. Overall, however, the continued process of globalization has an impact on nation states and affects domestic as well as multinational organizations and individuals.

The chapter also outlines the manifold pressures on organizations and the specific influences that impact on their IM and global career strategies, structures, policies and practices. We believe that organizations are becoming more sophisticated in how they design and administer their global careers. In one sense, it extends to the wide array of company-sponsored international work activities, including international project work, short-term assignments, frequent flying, globetrotting or traditional expatriate assignments. In another sense it includes the staffing, management, retention, expectation management, compensation and career management of global careerists. We believe that there will be several 'models' within different companies which have different IHRM configurations and pursue different objectives through their international operations. Overall, however, the challenges of value for investment – including a drive to localization – will often lead to longer-term global career management that is more sensitive and inventive regarding traditionally difficult issues such as culture shock, repatriate retention or the use of acquired capabilities and networks over the longer term. Cost pressures might also lead to novel approaches such as a targeted recruitment strategy of self-initiated foreign expatriates that will identify these individuals, create attractive 'deals' for them and retain them in order to gain access to international talent without the high cost of having to develop the necessary skills.

Individuals, in turn, are coming to realize that even in an area that is fraught with high personal risks and where the dependency of organizations on individuals is relatively high – as is the case for international, company-sponsored work – they are the masters of their own global careers. Therefore, they have to deliberately shape their own destinies and have to increasingly plan their own international career steps and persuade their organizations to give them adequate help. We believe that this will result in more career help through international sponsors, mentors or coaches. Overall, however, it will be the individual careerist who will want to maximize the chances that the 'global career deal' will have positive outcomes.

The field of global careers has many strands. It is important that we realize that self-initiated and self-sponsored global careers are happening often and that these have many different patterns. What is common to most of these, however, is that the risks associated with 'independent' moves to other countries can be substantial and that the original motivations and behaviours are distinct. Doherty et al. (2008) describe the company-sponsored individuals as 'active careerists', while they call the self-initiated foreign workers 'career activists'. Given the broad trends outlined above, we would expect a substantial and increasing number of global career activists in the years to come.

Key learning points include:

- There are many trends that impact on global careers.
- Broad trends include an increased convergence of national business systems, an explosion of modern technologies, a more equal spread of wealth and the irreversibility of existing changes. These trends have a major impact on global careers which are likely to become more widespread and are going to be especially expanded in developing countries.
- Not just company-sponsored work mobility and global careers are likely to increase. Self-initiated global careers – in its many forms – and migration flows are continuing to increase.

- Certain regional associations – such as the EU or NAFTA – enable a high degree of IM when compared to historical standards. They are continuing to enter into treaties that define and clarify immigration, work and social security issues. The increased planning security allows organizations to create mobility frameworks and support that is ultimately encouraging company-sponsored global careers even further.
- Nations are in a contest for talent and highly skilled persons. This will increase the brain circulation or brain drain/gain effects and encourage global careers. Moreover, governments have national strategic considerations in mind when deciding on immigration regulations. Overall outcomes for global careers are less certain and will depend directly on these strategies and their implementation.
- The increased globalization leads to organizations drawing up more sophisticated global resourcing and staffing policies. While cost pressures and ethical considerations encourage localization and the increased use of expatriates from developing countries, the overall effect is likely to be that more people have global careers.
- Individuals are embedded in these structural contexts as they are designed by states and organizations. They have their individual agency and will increasingly seek foreign work experience and longer-term global careers as they strive to acquire international career capital. It is their own capability and willingness to acquire cross-cultural skills, knowledge, abilities, networks and insights and their ability to manage the particular risks of working abroad that continue to be among the biggest challenges to a global career. Linked to this is that it is the continued utilization of their global career capital over the duration of their working lives that is truly important.

References

Aldred, G. and Sparrow, P. (2009) *International Mobility: Impact of the Current Economic Climate: Global Relocation Trends Report*, London: Brookfield Global Relocation Services.

Altman, Y. and Baruch, Y. (2008) 'Global protean careers: a new era in expatriation and repatriation', paper presented at the *European Academy of Management* conference, Ljubljana, May 2008.

Baruch, Y. Steele, D. and Quantrill, J. (2002) 'Management of expatriation and repatriation for novice global player', *International Journal of Manpower*, 23(7): 659–671.

Benson, G.S. and Pattie, M. (2008) 'Is expatriation good for my career? The impact of expatriate assignments on perceived and actual career outcomes', *International Journal of Human Resource Management*, 19(9): 1636–1653.

Black, J.S. and Gregersen, H.B. (1999) 'The right way to manage expats', *Harvard Business Review*, 77(2): 52–63.

Bolino, M.C. (2007) Expatriate assignments and intra-organizational career success: implications for individuals and organizations, *Journal of International Business Studies*, 38: 819–835.

Bossard, A.B. and Peterson, R.B. (2005) 'The repatriate experience as seen by American expatriates', *Journal of World Business*, 40: 9–28.

Bozionelos, N. (2009) 'Expatriation outside the boundaries of the multinational corporation: a study with expatriate nurses in Saudi Arabia', *Human Resource Management*, 48: 111–134.

Dickmann, M. and Doherty, N. (2010) 'Exploring organisational and individual career goals, interactions and outcomes of international assignments', *Thunderbird International Review*, 52(4): 313–324.

Dickmann, M., Doherty, N. and Johnson, A. (2006) *Measuring the Value of International Assignments*, London: PricewaterhouseCoopers and Cranfield School of Management.

Doherty, N. and Dickmann, M. (2009) 'Exploring the symbolic capital of international assignments', *International Journal of Human Resource Management*, 20(2): 301–320.

Doherty, N., Dickmann, M. and Mills, T. (2008) 'Career activists or active careerists? Upsetting the status quo of expatriate career management', paper presented at the *24ᵗʰ EGOS Colloquium*, Amsterdam, July 2008.

Finkelstein, M.A., Penner, L.A. and Brannick, M.T. (2005) Motive, role identity, and prosocial personality as predictors of volunteer activity, *Social Behavior & Personality: An International Journal*, 33(4), 403–418.

GMAC (2008) *Global Relocation Trends Survey*, Oak Brook, IL: GMAC Global Relocation Services.

Guzzo, R.A., Nooman, K.A. and Elron, E. (1994) 'Expatriate managers and the psychological contract', *Journal of Applied Psychology*, 79(4): 617–626.

Inkson, K. and Arthur, M. (2001) 'How to be a successful career capitalist', *Organizational Dynamics*, 30(1): 48–60.

Kraimer, M.L., Shaffer, M.A. and Bolino, M. (2009) 'The influence of expatriate and repatriate experiences on career advancement and repatriate retention', *Human Resource Management*, 48: 27–47.

Lazarova, M.B. and Cerdin, J.-L. (2007) 'Revisiting repatriation concerns: organizational support versus career and contextual influence', *Journal of International Business Studies*, 38: 404–429.

Nicholson, N. (2007) 'Destiny, drama and deliberation: careers in the coevolution of lives and societies', in H. Gunz and M. Peiperl (eds) *Handbook of Career Studies*, Thousand Oaks, CA: Sage.

Parry, E., Dickmann, M. and Morley, M. (2008) 'North American firms and their HR agendas in liberal and coordinated market economies', *International Journal of Human Resource Management*, 19(11): 2024–2040.

Peiperl, M. and Arthur, M. (2000) 'Topics for conversation: career themes old and new', in M. Peiperl, M. Arthur, R. Goffee and T. Morris (eds) *Career Frontiers: New Conceptions of Working Lives*, Oxford: Oxford University Press.

Prouteau, L. and Wolff, F.-C. (2006) 'Does volunteer work pay off in the labor market?', *Journal of Socio-Economics*, 35: 992–1013.

Pugh, D.S. and Hickson, D.J. (1996) *Management Worldwide*, London: Penguin.

Seibert, S.E., Kraimer, M.L. and Crant, J.M. (2001) 'What do proactive people do? A longitudinal model linking proactive personality and career success', *Personnel Psychology*, 54(4): 845–874.

Stahl, G.K., Miller, E. and Tung, R. (2002) 'Toward the boundaryless career: a closer look at the expatriate career concept and the perceived implications of an international assignment', *Journal of World Business*, 37: 216–227.

Stahl, G.K., Chua, C.H., Caligiuri, P., Cerdin, J.-L. and Taniguchi, M. (2009) 'Predictors of turnover intentions in learning-driven and demand-driven international assignments: the role of repatriation concerns, satisfaction with company support, and perceived career advancement opportunities', *Human Resource Management*, 48: 89–109.

Sullivan, S.E. and Arthur, M.B. (2006) 'The evolution of the boundaryless career concept: examining physical and psychological mobility', *Journal of Vocational Behaviour*, 69: 19–29.

Tarique, I. and Caligiuri, P. (2004) 'Training and development of international staff', in A.-W. Harzing and J. van Ruysseveldt (eds) *International Human Resource Management*, 2nd edn, London: Sage.

Thomas, D. and Inkson, K. (2007) 'Careers across cultures', in H. Gunz and M. Peiperl (eds) *Handbook of Career Studies*, Thousand Oaks, CA: Sage.

Van Emmerick, I.J.H. and Euwema, M.C. (2009) 'The international assignments of peacekeepers: what drives them to seek future expatriation?' *Human Resource Management*, 48(1): 135–151.

Index